SELECTIONS FROM THE MINUTES AND OTHER OFFICIAL WRITINGS

OF

THE HONOURABLE
MOUNTSTUART ELPHINSTONE
GOVERNOR OF BOMBAY

SELECTIONS FROM THE MINUTES AND OTHER OFFICIAL WRITINGS

OF

THE HONOURABLE

MOUNTSTUART ELPHINSTONE

GOVERNOR OF BOMBAY.

EDITED BY

GEORGE W. FORREST, B.A.

GYAN

Published by

Gyan Publishing House
5, Ansari Road
Daryaganj, New Delhi-110002
Phone: 011-47034999, 9811692060
E-mail: books@gyanbooks.com

Distribution Network
gyanbooks.com
India, USA, Canada, UK, Australia

ISBN: 978-93-6208-180-3 (PB)
First Published, 1884

2nd Impression 2024

Printed at: Gyan Press, Delhi.

SELECTIONS FROM THE MINUTES AND OTHER OFFICIAL WRITINGS OF THE HONOURABLE MOUNTSTUART ELPHINSTONE GOVERNOR OF BOMBAY

Author: MOUNTSTUART ELPHINSTONE

SELECTIONS FROM THE MINUTES AND OTHER OFFICIAL WRITINGS

OF

THE HONOURABLE

MOUNTSTUART ELPHINSTONE

GOVERNOR OF BOMBAY.

SELECTIONS FROM THE MINUTES AND OTHER OFFICIAL WRITINGS

OF

THE HONOURABLE

MOUNTSTUART ELPHINSTONE

GOVERNOR OF BOMBAY.

WITH AN INTRODUCTORY MEMOIR.

EDITED BY

GEORGE W. FORREST, B.A.,

DECCAN COLLEGE,

FELLOW OF THE UNIVERSITY OF BOMBAY.

1884.

TO

THE MEMBERS

OF THAT SERVICE WHO HAVE FOR MORE THAN A CENTURY, WITH FIRMNESS AND EQUITY, ADMINISTERED OUR BRITISH INDIAN EMPIRE,

I Dedicate the Official Writings

OF ONE OF THE ABLEST OF THE MANY ABLE MEN WHO HAVE BELONGED TO

THE INDIAN CIVIL SERVICE.

PREFACE.

SOME years ago, when I was employed in looking over the valuable records in the Bombay Secretariat, the idea struck me that a compilation of the official writings of Mountstuart Elphinstone would prove of use, not only to those actively engaged in the administration of India, but also to the daily widening circle of men who take an interest in Indian questions. There is hardly an important problem connected with the government of India which has not been discussed by Mountstuart Elphinstone; and to the discussion of Indian problems he brought vast experience and a liberal and highly-cultivated mind.

In order to make the Minutes more intelligible to the reader, I have thought it advisable to prefix to them a short narrative of Mr. Elphinstone's life, and of the principal historical events connected with his career. In this memoir I have drawn largely upon the admirable memoir written by Sir Edward Colebroke many years ago, and published in the *Royal Asiatic Journal.*

My best thanks are due to Lord Elphinstone for the trouble he has taken in sending me a copy of the letters of Mountstuart Elphinstone describing the battles of Assaye and Kirkee, which are now published for the first time. My acknowledgments are also due to Sir Richard Temple for supplying me with the Minute on Education, and also to Mr. Monteath, C.S., for his kind assistance in procuring me records from the Bombay Secretariat.

G. W. Forrest.

Deccan College, Puna.
October 18, 1883.

CONTENTS.

LIFE OF THE HON. MOUNTSTUART ELPHINSTONE.

CHAPTER I.

EARLY LIFE—INDIA—ASSAYE—ARGAUM—NAGPUR.

1779—1803.

MOUNTSTUART ELPHINSTONE was born in the year 1779—the son of the eleventh Lord Elphinstone, and Anna, daughter of Lord Ruthven. His father was a general officer, and Governor of Edinburgh Castle; and for many years sat in the House of Lords as one of the representative peers of Scotland. As a boy, Mountstuart seems to have been first remarked chiefly for high spirits and love of singing revolutionary songs, which he learnt from the French prisoners confined in the castle. At the age of fourteen he was sent to school at Kensington, where he remained for two years. These two years do not seem to have been devoted to industry and the beaten paths of school-life, but he showed a love of reading; and in after years it was remarked that he was fond of quoting Shakespeare. At school it was said he 'was clever enough for anything, but an idle dog.' Mountstuart Elphinstone was but a lad of sixteen years of age when he left school to proceed to India as a writer in the Civil Establishment of Bengal. He embarked in July, 1795, and was accompanied by two young friends—John Adam, who during a brief interregnum was Governor-General of India, and Houston, who rose to be Sir R. Houston, K.C.B. After a long voyage, the vessel reached India in February of the following year; and a short time afterwards, Mr. Elphinstone was appointed assistant to the magistrate at Benares — the Hindoo Rome of India.

When young Elphinstone landed, Sir John Shore was Governor-General. It was the brilliant courage of Clive which first gained for the English any territorial position in India: it was the daring genius of Hastings which first conceived the policy of reducing Native princes to the position of subordinates without independent rights. He was the first to introduce, in his dealings with Oude, the subsidiary system. When a state consented by treaty to accede to this system, it acknowledged the British Government as the paramount power in India; and, in return, it received the guarantee of that Government for its safety and integrity. It agreed not to make war or peace without the sanction of the paramount power, and to maintain a contingent of troops as a subsidiary force to aid the British Government in time of need. But the policy which commended itself to the capacious mind of Hastings, was not regarded with favour by the Directors, who did not care to strengthen the position of the Company as an Asian power, but were only anxious as to the Company's commercial position and its trade. Lord Cornwallis and Sir John Shore, according to the wishes of their masters, introduced a policy different to that of Hastings. Their desire was to treat all Native sovereigns as equals, and to maintain a balance of power amongst the Native States, so as to prevent any of them becoming too powerful. Sir John Shore, however, found it impossible to carry out the principle of non-interference in the affairs of Native States in its integrity. He was compelled to set aside the claims of Vazir Ali to the throne of Oude. In January, 1799, the followers of the deposed Nawab, who was in surveillance at Benares, attacked the British officers at the Residency, and massacred them. Mr. Elphinstone was seated with his friend Houston when the news reached them of the massacre; and they had barely time to mount their horses, when they were pursued by some of the Nawab's horsemen. They saved their lives by riding through a high sugar-cane plantation, which concealed them from their pursuers.

Two years after this event, Mr. Elphinstone was transferred to the Political Department, or Diplomatic Service. Lord Wellesley was now Governor-General. He saw that the idea of his predecessors of a balance of power was impracticable, and that the British authority must be supreme throughout the country. At the time when he assumed office, the very existence of the British Empire in India was threatened with grave danger. Tippu, the Nizam, and Scindia were all under French influence, and had their armies chiefly officered by Frenchmen. A Jacobin club had been organized in Seringapatam. The men were required to swear hatred to tyranny, love of liberty, and destruction to all kings and sovereigns, except the good and faithful ally of the French Republic—*Citizen Sultan Tippu.* The first war, undertaken by Wellesley, was forced on him by the hostile attitude of Tippu. It began in 1779, and ended in the gallant capture of Seringapatam. The fall of Seringapatam made the English supreme in the Deccan. In a few months, the

Madras Presidency grew from a few scattered districts into the great country known by that name, comprising almost the whole of Southern India. The Governor-General further extended the British dominion in India by compelling the Nawab Vazir of Oude to cede the greater part of his dominion. The districts thus acquired compose a greater part of what is now called the North-Western Provinces. That Lord Wellesley's dealings with the Nawab were harsh and arbitrary, no impartial man can deny; but the increasing certainty of a rupture with the Mahrattas compelled the Marquis to resort to them.

In 1801, Mr. Elphinstone was appointed to Puna, as assistant to the British Resident at the Court of the Peshwa, the chief of the Mahratta Confederacy. But few facts can be gleaned from the mass of legendary accounts regarding Maharashtra and its many independent states antecedent to the inroads of the Mussulmans, under Alla-ud-deen, in the year 1294. The Deccan remained subject to the Emperor of Delhi till 1345, when the Mussulman nobles revolted, and established the Bahamani dynasty, so-called from the supposed Brahman descent of its founder. The capital was first at Kalburgah, sixty miles from Sholapur, and was afterwards removed to Bedar, both which places still possess magnificent palaces and mosques in ruin. Towards the close of the fourteenth century, the Bahamani Empire fell to pieces, and five independent kingdoms divided the Deccan amongst them. Only three of these states—the Adhil-Shahi dynasty, with its capital at Bijapur, the Kutub-Shahi dynasty at Golconda, and the Nizam-Shahi dynasty at Ahmednagar—retained their independence until conquered by Aurangzib. This was not accomplished without many campaigns; and the struggles of Golconda and Bijapur with the great Mogul Emperor favoured the ambitious schemes of Sivaji, who now became an important personage upon the scene. The founder of the Mahratta Empire was born at a hill-fort near Puna in 1627. The family from which he sprang had for some generations been settled in the wild valleys of the Western Ghats, and belonged to the ranks of the lesser Mahratta chiefs. When Sivaji was but a lad, the warlike mountaineers of the neighbouring glens began to have faith in him; and uniting himself to a small band, he, through the native force of his character, made himself their leader. The band grew in numbers, and Sivaji quickly welded a few mountain tribes into a great nation, and from being the captain of a handful of horsemen, he became the sovereign of a mighty empire. In 1674, Sivaji caused himself to be enthroned with great splendour, from which time the Mahrattas rank as a Hindu nationality. Six years afterwards his chequered career was terminated by death. His son inherited his father's vast possessions, but none of his father's greatness. Having destroyed the great monarchies of Bijapur and Golconda, Aurangzib determined to crush his old foes the Mahrattas. The son of Sivaji fell a prisoner into his hands, and was put to death with cruel torture. Satara was captured; nearly all the Mahrattas' strongholds were seized; but the Mahrattas were neither crushed nor subdued. Beaten in a pitched battle, the daring Cossacks dispersed once, to collect again and renew their guerilla warfare. The large but cumbersome army of the Emperor, with its numerous guns, long train of elephants, and elaborate camp equipage, was ill suited for coping with irregular horsemen who slept with their horses' bridles in their hands and swords by their sides, and their trusty spears stuck in the ground near them, ready at a moment's notice to fall on an unwary enemy, or beat a retreat into some wild mountain glen. India had also proved to be the Capua of the Mogul nobles. They had grown luxurious and effeminate, and utterly unsuited for 'wild Mahratta battle.'

The Emperor was now stricken in years, and troubles encircled him on all sides. His armies sustained a signal defeat from the Mahrattas, and he himself narrowly escaped from being taken a prisoner. Aurangzib returned to Ahmednagar, baffled and beaten, and, full of sorrows, descended into the tomb (February 21st, 1707). On his death Shahu Rajah, the grandson of Sivaji, was released; but the young man was not fit to wield a sceptre. He allowed his state affairs to be managed by his chief minister, who from the time of Sivaji was called the Peshwa, or Prime Minister. In 1714 Balaji Vishwanath, a Brahmin, was appointed to that office. He, by his intrigues and ability, contrived to concentrate all the real power in his own hands, leaving to the Rajah the title only of sovereignty. He made Puna the seat of power, the centre of all authority; and from this time the Brahmin Peshwas became the real heads of the Mahratta Confederacy, the Rajahs, the descendants of the great Sivaji, being merely nominal rulers living in splendour as state prisoners in Satara. Balaji caused the office to be made hereditary in his family. He was succeeded by Baji Rao, his eldest son, an able man and thorough soldier, who greatly extended the Mahratta power. Baji Rao was succeeded by his son, Balaji Baji Rao, commonly called the third Peshwa. During his reign the Mahrattas suffered their most disastrous defeat. In 1758 Raghunath Rao, the brother of the Peshwa, a brave, rash man, full of ambition, brought the distant province of the Punjab under the Mahratta yoke. This raised the ire of the terrible Afghan Abdali, and he again invaded India to take vengeance on the Mahratta race. On the plains of *Panipat,* where Baber had won his empire, and where the fate of India had frequently been decided, the Mahrattas, devout believers in Vishnu, and the Afghans, followers of the man of Mecca, met to settle once again the fate of India. At early dawn the battle began. The Mahrattas fought with desperate valour, but ere the sun had set their vast splendid army had become a weltering mass of confusion, a mere rabble rout. Thousands of the vanquished fell on the field, and the great Mahratta leaders were numbered among the dead. Into every Mahratta cottage sorrow entered; some mourned the death of a loved one, all mourned the death of their national greatness. Their hope of supremacy in India had perished. The Mahratta chiefs never again united heartily for a common purpose, though they continued still to be the most formidable power in India. They especially dominated over the British settlement of Bombay. The Bombay Government was anxious to establish its influence at the Court of Puna by making its own nominee Peshwa. The attempt took form, in 1775, in the Treaty of Surat, by which Raghunath agreed to cede Salsette and Bassein to the English, in consideration of himself being restored to Puna. The military operations that ensued were known as the first Mahratta War. They were most eminently successful, and the war ended in the Treaty of Salbai, by which the conquests in Gujarat were given up, with the exception of Salsette, and a provision made for Raghunath Rao.

The Mahratta powers were at this time five in number. The recognised head of the Confederacy was the Peshwa, who ruled the hill-country of the Western

Ghats, the cradle of the Mahratta race. The fertile province of Gujarat was governed by the Gaikwar of Baroda. In Central India, two military leaders—Scindia of Gwalior, and Holkar of Indore—alternately held the pre-eminence. Towards the East the Bhonsla Rajah of Nagpur, sprung from the same stock as Sivaji, reigned from the Berar to the coast of Orissa. When Mr. Elphinstone was appointed to Puna, Baji Rao II., the seventh Peshwa, was on the throne. He was a treacherous, worthless creature, endowed with showy accomplishments and a good address. The death of his powerful minister, Nana Farnavis, one of the ablest administrators India has produced, sealed the ruin of the Mahratta Confederacy. Civil war raged throughout the country. Scindia and Holkar were engaged in hostilities, and the Peshwa espoused the cause of the former. Vittojee Holkar, brother of the Mahratta chief, fell into his hands, and he caused him to be executed in his presence by being dragged along the ground, tied to the foot of an elephant. The cruel murder took place in the spring of 1801, and in October of the following year, Holkar defeated at Puna the armies of the Peshwa and Scindia. Driven as a fugitive into British territory, the necessities of the Peshwa induced him to sign the Treaty of Bassein, by which he pledged himself to hold communication with no other power, European or Native, and ceded territory for the maintenance of a subsidiary force. Mr. Elphinstone was residing with the Resident when the decisive engagement between the Peshwa and Holkar was fought almost at the gate of the Residency. He accompanied his chief, Colonel Close, when the treaty was negotiated at Bassein, and again returned to Puna with Sir A. Wellesley when the Peshwa was reinstated in power. The Treaty of Bassein led directly to the second Mahratta War, for neither Scindia nor the Rajah of Nagpur could tolerate the abandonment of the Mahratta independence. The war was begun on the 3rd August, 1803. The first blow was struck by General Wellesley against Ahmednagar, which surrendered on the 12th August; and it was in August that Mr. Elphinstone joined the General as his secretary. He accompanied him on the famous march to meet Scindia, and the next five months were probably the most stirring in Elphinstone's life.

Leaving a small garrison in the fort of Ahmednagar, General Wellesley moved forward, and marching rapidly, as was his wont, crossed the Godavari, and arrived at Aurungabad on the 29th August. Here, he heard that Scindia and the Rajah of Berar had entered the Nizam's territory with an army of horse only, and had passed Colonel Stevenson, who, with a force of 7,000 men, was watching the Ajunta Pass. The next day, General Wellesley marched southwards towards the Godavari, having received intelligence that the enemy intended to march in that direction, to cross the river and proceed to Hyderabad. But the enemy were quite undecided as to their plans of operation. On hearing of the movement of the English force, they countermarched in a northerly direction. They wished to cross the river, and make a dash southward; but it is certain that they did not like General Wellesley's position upon that river, and his readiness to cross with them. They knew that the river, which was then fordable, must rise again, and they did not dare to be cut off from their own countries and all assistance. Colonel Stevenson made several attempts to bring them in action, but in vain. General Wellesley himself had to remain stationary till the convoys of grain which he expected reached him. On the 18th the last of them arrived, and on the 25th he was enabled to move forwards towards the enemy, who had been joined by large reinforcements. On the 21st, General Wellesley and Colonel Stevenson had a conference, at which they concerted a plan to attack the enemy on the morning of the 24th. It was deemed expedient to separate their forces, in order to pass through defiles quickly and with care. On the 23rd September, 1803, the British troops advanced in two columns against the combined armies of Scindia and Berar Rajah; Colonel Stevenson's division marching about eight miles on the left of Wetlington. The Mahratta horsemen were so numerous that it was difficult, if not impossible, to get exact information of the position of the enemy, who was believed to be in front of Colonel Stevenson, at Bokerdun, the point at which, it is probable, Wellesley intended to join forces. On the morning of the 23rd, however, Wellesley, arriving on the bank of the Kaitna, found the enemy drawn up on the southern opposite side of the river, holding the chief passages, and evidently expecting to be attacked directly in front. Wellesley determined to give battle without waiting for Colonel Stevenson. Mr. Elphinstone used to relate how the General, after the engagement, vindicated himself from the charge of rashness. 'Had I not attacked them,' he said, 'I must have been surrounded by the superior cavalry of the enemy, my troops must have been starved, and I should have had nothing left but to hang myself to these tent-poles.' On the morning of the battle, Mr. Elphinstone tells us in his letter that he 'got on horseback for the first time for a month, owing to a liver complaint, and kept close to the General the whole day.'

General Wellesley's division consisted of five native battalions, each 700 strong; of these one entire battalion, together with 100 men from each of the other four regiments, were left in rear with the baggage, while an additional force of 100 men from each of the same regiments formed a rear guard. There were thus left in front line four native battalions, each 500 strong; the 78th Regiment, 600; 74th Regiment, 570. Total, 3,170 infantry, with 150 artillery and 1,200 cavalry. The enemy, at the lowest estimate, were 17,000 strong, besides thousands of horse, and a fine park of artillery. Wellesley, having reconnoitred, noticed two villages, Pimpalgaon and Warur, one on each bank of the river and beyond the left flank of the enemy, which appeared unguarded, and on the assumption that where villages exist on opposite banks of a river there is generally a passage between them, he directed a flank march for the purpose of crossing there and turning the enemy's left flank. The narrow delta between the Kaitna and its northern affluent, the Juah, gave sufficient space for Wellesley to employ his small force (while the nullahs or river-beds on either side secured his flanks), but the space was so confined as to restrict the enemy from bringing his immense superiority of numbers into action, and the decisive struggle was therefore limited to almost equal numbers of the two forces. At the battle of Cannæ, Hannibal crossed the river Aufidus to secure a similar tactical advantage. The attack on the left flank also gave a great advantage; inasmuch as the enemy's lines of retreat lay to his left rear, he would have run much risk of being cut away from it, and in that case might be driven in the direction towards which Colonel Stevenson's force was coming up; or in case of a less decisive success the enemy would at least be taken in flank on his line of retreat, and as he would have to cross the Juah river, an operation in which he might find difficulty in carrying off his guns. The latter case is what actually happened.

The flank movement was carried out with a manœuvring power worthy of a great and skilful commander. Small pickets of infantry were thrown out to hold the enemy, and give time for the main body to form. The British cavalry in rear and the Mahratta and Mysore cavalry supporting them on the right flank, protected the force against Scindia's cavalry, who had been all massed on the right flank of his infantry. Part of the enemy's cavalry crossed the river, but they were deterred from attacking by the bold front of the British cavalry and their supports. Wellesley crossed the river, and as the heads of his columns appeared on the northern bank, the enemy commenced with all practicable speed to create a change of front to their left in order to face their foe. On the left of Scindia's line lay the village of Assaye which he had surrounded with cannon. Just before the British had got fully into position, the officer commanding advanced troops on the right, contrary to the orders of Wellesley, turned and attacked the village of Assaye, and was followed by the 74th Foot. The attack was repulsed. The enemy's cavalry broke the 74th; and Elphinstone justly remarks: 'This was the critical moment of the engagement; if the enemy's horse had pushed the Sepoy they could never have stood what had overpowered the 74th. But at this instant our cavalry appeared on the right, charged the enemy and drove them with great slaughter into a nullah (or river).' Eventually the whole British line advanced, and the enemy gave way in all directions. He was unable to carry off his guns, ninety of which were captured. Then it was that, having to cross the nullah of the Juah, his infantry became huddled together and cramped for room. A short attack was made by the British cavalry. As the General writes, 'After the action there was no pursuit, because our cavalry was not then in a state to pursue.' Had a pursuit been possible, the battle of Assaye, decisive as it was, would have been as deadly and as complete an overthrow of the Mahrattas as the battle of Panipat. The victory was bought at a heavy price in killed and wounded. 'I fear,' writes Elphinstone, 'we have scarce less than 600 Europeans killed and wounded; 50 officers is the least at which the killed and wounded can be reckoned, and 1,500 odd men and officers appear on the returns.'

The most graphic account of the battle of Assaye is given in the letter which is now published for the first time. It details in clear and simple language the different phases of the fight on which hung the fate of the Indian Empire. There are words of hearty praise for the General's bravery, and the clearness with which he gave his orders at the most anxious and important moment; but there is not a single word about self, though the young civilian rode by the side of the General through the thick of that hot fight.

'Camp near the village of Assaye, ten miles from Jafferabad,
25th September, 1803.

'My dear Adam,

'You will have heard that this army has fought a very bloody battle, and gained an important victory.

'Scindia and the Rajah of Berar, after trying what they could do with an army of horse only, and after getting as far south as the Godavari river, changed their place and moved south to near the Ajunta Pass, to meet a detachment of infantry and guns, which Scindia ordered to join them.

'The detachment consisted (it is said) of seventeen battalions, 500 strong, and upwards of 100 guns. General Wellesley, after halting for some time for supplies, followed the enemy, and Colonel Stevenson also moved north, and halted at Badalapur.

'The two divisions met there on the 21st, and it was settled that they were to move separately towards the enemy, and both attack them on the 24th. When this was settled he marched on the 22nd to Pangey, and on the 23rd to Naulnair, from which place he thought the enemy was at some distance (sixteen miles, or near it); but, as he was taking up our ground, news was brought that the enemy was close at hand.

'General Wellesley sent for the cavalry, and pushed on about three miles, and came to the brow of a rising-ground from which he saw the enemy's two camps at the distance of about three miles. The General halted the cavalry and rode back for the infantry. They came up in an hour, and were shown a road to the enemy's camp. In the meantime a large body of the enemy's horse advanced towards the cavalry. The General went thither; the cavalry were drawn up in line, and I really expected to have had the pleasure of a charge; but when the enemy came near they halted, and the General left the cavalry to watch their motion, and joined the infantry. He went to the head of the line, which soon got in sight of the enemy's camp; and they opened a cannonade upon it, with no effect that I knew of except slightly wounding General Wellesley's Brigade-Major, Lieutenant Campbell, in the leg, and carrying off the head of one of the General's orderly troopers. Going on, he passed some ravines and came to a broad nullah (or river). We were lucky enough to find the only place passable for guns, and he crossed and marched on, and began to form in line, with little or no loss, though we were cannonaded all the time. But while the troops were forming the enemy advanced on us; and then shots which were so ineffectual before, now fell like hail, and knocked down men, horses, and bullocks every shot. A gentleman with the General had his horse shot under him, and I and another gentleman had the dust knocked in our faces, at this time.

After we had gone on a good way (near enough to hear the enemy shout) with the infantry, who were terribly harassed, but cheered as they advanced, we rode back to the cavalry, whom the General had sent for, and who were now about the spot where the line had formed. The General ordered them to take care of the right of the infantry, and rode back, intending to join our line. In going and coming the General crossed a tract where there was very heavy fire; one of the gentlemen with him had two horses, and another one, killed under them. The General pushed for the first line he saw, which happened to be the enemy, but when we got pretty near (not within musket-shot) he saw the guns firing towards us, and towards our own line. In coming back we fell in with several of the enemy's guns (a most delightful sight), and soon after got to our line. We moved on under a very heavy fire. The enemy retreated in front, and fell back on a second line in their rear. They outflanked us greatly to the right, and kept up a very heavy cannonade on our line. The right suffered, particularly the 74th Regiment. The corps on the right was dreadfully cannonaded and cut in on by the enemy's cavalry, and, I fear, almost annihilated; out of 19 officers, 11 killed and 6 wounded; and out of

569 men and officers, exactly 400 have been returned killed and wounded.

'The enemy's cavalry broke the 74th Regiment, and this was the critical moment of the engagement. If the enemy's horse had pushed the Sepoy, *they* could never have stood what had overpowered the 74th; 'but at this instant our cavalry appeared on the right, charged the enemy, and drove them with great slaughter into a nullah (or river) in our front. Our cavalry crossed this, and charged among the enemy's infantry, who had been driven by our infantry across it, and made a great slaughter. They afterwards re-crossed the nullah, and made another charge at a body of infantry with less success. While they were making this charge, the General took the 78th and 7th Regiment of Native Cavalry and led them back to drive off a body of the enemy's foot, who had taken some of our guns which we left behind, and turned them back.

While moving to this attack, the General's horse was killed under him; after which he pushed on, the enemy retreated, and this concluded the engagement. We saw enormous bodies of horse on all sides, but they behaved very ill. They came almost within musket-shot, and threatened us often, but never charged but once, when they cut up the 74th. We have taken 95 pieces of cannon, and there are some more not yet brought in. The enemy's loss in men is almost equal to our own in numbers, but very different in value. I fear we have scarce less than 600 Europeans killed and wounded; 50 officers is the least at which the killed and wounded can be reckoned, and 1,500 and odd men and officers appear in the returns.

'This is, all agree, the bloodiest battle ever fought in India. Cuddelore is the only one I have heard compared with it, and there the force of our army was 12,000 men at least, and their loss 1,600 killed and wounded. Our army consisted of five battalions of natives, 700 strong; of these a battalion was left with the baggage, as was the rear-guard of 100 men from each battalion (total 500), and each battalion left its baggage-guard of 100 men (500 more). So that there were four corps of natives, 500 each; the 78th Regiment, 600; the 74th Regiment, 570; the artillery, 150: total infantry, 3,320. The cavalry were 1,200. Total of all descriptions, 4,520. The enemy, at the lowest number that can be reckoned, were 17,000 strong, besides thousands of horse. The enemy have fled to the northward, and are getting down the passes as fast as they can. Colonel Stevenson marched after them this morning, after having reinforced us with one battalion. His force is 7,000 firelocks and 750 cavalry, but they are ill off for artillery.

'I got on horseback early in the morning of the action (the first time for a month, owing to a liver complaint), and kept close to the General the whole day; slept almost supperless (and really breakfastless and dinnerless), on the ground in the open air, without finding the smallest inconvenience.

'The General will doubtless get great credit for this. I am sure he deserves it. It is nothing to say of him that he exposed himself on all occasions, and behaved with perfect indifference in the hottest fire (for I did not see a European do otherwise, nor do I believe people ever do); but in the most anxious and important moments he gave his orders as clearly and coolly as if he had been inspecting a corps or manœuvring at a review.

'I am afraid to say how well I like the General, for, though I have known him some time, I have only been with him six weeks, and I may change my mind; but all that can be said in six weeks' acquaintance I would have said before this action, which has not lowered my opinion of him.'

The following extract gives a graphic and a poetic description of a visit to the battle-field at night:

Extract of a Letter to 'Strachey,' dated 'Camp of Assaye, 3rd October, 1803.'

'I went yesterday evening to the field of battle. It was a dark, cloudy evening. I rode by myself, and saw *plurima mortis imago*. Some of the dead are withered, their features still remaining, but their faces blackened to the colour of coal; others still swollen and blistered. The Persian I mentioned was perfect everywhere, and had his great quilted coat on; but his face had fallen or been eaten off, and his naked skull stared out like the hermits of the wood of Joppa (in the "Castle of Otranto"). Kites and adjutants, larger than the Calcutta ones, were feasting in some places, and in others dogs howling all over the plain. I saw a black dog tearing in a furious way large pieces of flesh from a dead man looking fiercely and not regarding him. I thought the gaze horrible and sublime. At last I began to feel a good deal of horror—awful, but not unpleasant—when, by way of adding to the sublimity, the evening gun fired, and, to my surprise, I heard a shot whistle over my head. This I suppose was some neglect of the artilleryman.'

The day after the battle of Assaye Colonel Stevenson joined General Wellesley, and was immediately despatched in pursuit of Scindia beyond the Tapti.

The capture of the famous fortress of Aseergurh deprived that chief of his last stronghold in Khandesh. The Rajah of Berar turned towards his own dominions, and was followed by both corps of the British army. Scindia, now thoroughly disheartened, sent an envoy for peace, and suspension of hostilities was granted on November 22nd, by General Wellesley, on condition that Scindia's forces should move to the eastward; but the same terms could not be extended to the Rajah of Berar so long as his army was in the field. Scindia did not comply with the terms of his agreement, and Wellesley determined to attack the two chiefs; and, having been joined by Colonel Stevenson, he advanced on November 28th and 29th. At the close of a long march, General Wellesley found himself suddenly upon the army of the confederates. He made direct towards the enemy, followed by Elphinstone. At last he pulled up. 'There will be time to take those guns before night.' Before night closed in, thirty-eight of these guns and all their ammunition had been captured. Wellesley writes:

'If we had had daylight an hour more, not a man would have escaped.

'We should have had that time, if my Native infantry had not been panic struck, and got into confusion when the cannonade commenced. What do you think of nearly three entire battalions, who behaved so admirably in the battle of Assaye, being broke and running off, when the cannonade commenced at Argaum, which was not to be compared to that at Assaye? Luckily, I happened to be at no great distance from them; and I was able to rally them, and re-establish the battle. If I had not been there, I am convinced we should have lost the day. But as it was, so much time elapsed before I could form them again, that we had not daylight enough for everything that we should have certainly performed.'

The capture of the stupendous mountain-fortress of Gavelgurh, followed the victory of Argaum. It was an operation of exceeding labour and skill, patiently and successfully achieved. It was at this siege that the great Duke told Elphinstone that he had mistaken his profession, and ought to have been a soldier. The capture of the fortress crushed the hopes of the Mahratta confederates, and negotiations were now opened in earnest. The treaty with Raghoji Bhousle of Berar, known as the Treaty of Deogaum, was concluded in December. He was obliged to cede the Province of Cuttack, the whole of Berar lying west of the Wurdah river, and to resign all claims on the Nizam. General Wellesley, when the treaty was concluded, appointed Mr. Elphinstone to act as Resident to the Rajah, and shortly afterwards he was confirmed in the responsible post. Elphinstone had not completed his twenty-fifth year, but Sir Arthur Wellesley had complete confidence in his tact, his coolness, and judgment. He wrote of him to his brother in the following eulogistic language:

'Upon the occasion of mentioning Mr. Elphinstone, it is but justice to that gentleman to inform your Excellency that I have received the greatest assistance from him since he has been with me. He is well versed in the languages, has experience and a knowledge of the interests of the Mahratta powers, and their relations with each other, and with the British Government and its allies. He has been present in all the actions which have been fought in this quarter during the war, and at all the sieges; he is acquainted with every transaction that has taken place, and with my sentiments upon all subjects. I therefore take the liberty of recommending him to your Excellency.

'To the Governor-General, Camp at Ellichpur,
'17*th December*, 1803.'

CHAPTER II.

EMBASSY TO CABUL.

1808—1810.

THE merchants of the East India Company could not appreciate Wellesley's imperial policy; they praised 30th July, 1805. him for his 'ardent zeal to promote the well-being of India, and to uphold the interest and honour of the British Empire;' but they recalled him. Lord Cornwallis for the second time became Governor-General, with the avowed intention of reversing as far as possible the policy of his predecessor. A policy of self-repression, of retreat from fancied dangers and real responsibilities, took the place of that bolder and wiser system by which Wellesley had crowned the fabric of our power in India, and by which it must always be maintained.

Lord Cornwallis's second administration continued little more than two months, and it was left to Sir George Barlow, the senior member of Council, to carry out the new policy. During these quiet times literature divided the attention of Mounstuart Elphinstone with his political duties. He always had a genuine love of books; and during the whole of his Indian career he devoted a vast amount of time to classical reading and research. From his private journal we have an account of his studies at Nagpur:

'*April* 2.—Rose at four. Read "Antigone" with Jenkins. Walked on the veranda. Returned to "Antigone," and read till half-past seven. I had not time to finish my breakfast before Yaswant Ráv came. He stayed till twelve. Then read some of Page's "History of the French Revolution," on which I have been employed for these two days. Jenkins tiffed at Close's, where I joined him. I stayed there some time, and read some of Gibbon's "Life," my old inspirer and guide. Read some more of Page. He is republican, and consequently hostile to the royalists, and insensible to their sufferings; but not on the whole furious or partial, as one would expect him to be.

'*April* 3.—Rose at four. Read "Antigone." Rode out. Ran a jackal, but did not kill. Breakfasted. Read thirty-six pages of the "Memorabilia." Ate sandwiches. Rode to Sydenham and Kennaway. Read Grotius. Went out in the buggy.

'*April* 4.—Read 300 lines of the "Antigone." Breakfasted. Put my papers in order. Set off in my palanquin for Hall. On the way finished Mackintosh. He is eloquent and acute, but inexperienced and enthusiastic. Also read some of Page. At the Hall ordered repairs. Read an Idyll of Theocritus, and Jenkins read aloud almost the whole fifth book of Homer. At five rode back, dined. In bed, read Locke on "Liberty and Necessity."

'*April* 5.—Finished "Antigone." I perceive this to be a very affecting play, though reading it in company does not give it a very fair chance. We began to read Sophocles with more ease than we did Euripides.'

Mountstuart Elphinstone spent four years at Nagpur pleasantly and profitably. He studied much, he rode much, he hunted the wild boar, and by the way he conducted his public duties he confirmed the confidence of the Government in his tact and ability. From Nagpur he was transferred, in March, 1808, to the temporary charge of our relations with the Court of Scindia.

In the July of the previous year Lord Minto had taken his seat as Governor-General in the room of Sir Charles Barlow, who had those business qualities which make dulness respectable, but possessed none of those qualities which make a statesman. Lord Minto was no blind adherent to the policy of Lord Wellesley, but he had a keen sense of what the honour and true interest of England demands. He was among those whom Burke loved best and trusted most, and had been one of the managers of the prosecution of the great Proconsul. Indian experience had the same effect on him which it has on all wise men. It greatly altered his preconceived opinions on all Indian matters. Sent out to uphold the policy of peaceful isolation, he soon found that it was impracticable.

The year after Lord Minto landed, a conjuncture arose which seemed to threaten England's power in the East. The peace of Tilsit left her without an ally. The close alliance which was then formed between the victorious Napoleon and Russia boded ill. French intrigues had been active in Persia; and for the Indian Government the advance of hostile influences to a country of so much importance was a compulsion to act with promptitude and vigour. A memorandum was sent to Persia, for the purpose of countermining the progress of France at that Court. But even if France succeeded in gaining a paramount influence in Persia, much would remain to be done before India could be successfully invaded. The States between the British and Persian frontiers, aided by British arms, could check the force of her advance, if they could not entirely stop it. Lord Minto therefore wisely determined to send Embassies to the States lying on and beyond the Indus—Lahore, Cabul, and Sindh—for the purpose of making defensive alliances with their rulers. Mr. Elphinstone was selected to conduct the British Mission to be despatched to the Court of Cabul. The Governor-General was personally unacquainted with him, but he had formed a very high opinion of his character and attainments.

'The countries under the sovereignty of the King of Cabul had,' writes Mr. Elphinstone, 'once extended sixteen degrees in longitude from Sirhind, about 150 miles from Delhi to Meshed, about an equal distance from the Caspian Sea. In breadth, they reached from the Oxus to the Persian Gulf, a space including thirteen degrees of latitude, or 910 miles.' This great empire had suffered a considerable diminution before the days of our Embassy, but it was still a powerful kingdom. The rule of the sovereign extended not only over all the territories which we now reckon in Afghanistan, but over part of the western and all the southern portions of the Punjab, Multan, Cashmere, and Sindh. The power of this monarch was measured by the memory of the days when Ahmed Shah had marched to the gates of Delhi, and defeated the Mahrattas at Paniput. The King of Cabul had, and has always been the resource of all the disaffected in India. To him the Mohammedan sovereigns addressed their complaints against the Mahrattas, and the Mahratta princes addressed their complaints against us. To confront so great a monarch with due dignity, it was determined that the Mission should be in a style of great magnificence, and suitable preparations were made at Delhi for its equipment. The Envoy's suite and staff were chosen with care; and the escort was numerous, consisting of 200 infantry and 100 irregular cavalry.

The Embassy left Delhi on the 13th October, 1808. It proceeded by the route through the desert which lies between Delhi and the Indus, in order to avoid the dominions of the ruler of the Punjab—the Lion Ranjit. One hundred miles from the capital of the Moguls, the Embassy came to 'naked piles of loose sand, rising one after another, like the waves of the sea, and marked on the surface by the wind like drifted snow.' After a weary march over dismal hills and valleys of loose and heavy sand, they reached the walls and towers of Bikaneer, which presented the appearance of a great and magnificent city in the midst of a wilderness. At that time, five hostile armies were encamped around it. The Embassy was well received by the Rajah, and Mr. Elphinstone displayed considerable tact in avoiding any entanglement in the quarrels of the contending parties.

On the 16th November they marched from Bikaneer, and after five weeks' sojourn in the desert, they reached a place where the desert and the cultivated country were separated as if by a line. A long row of trees ran along the edges of the sands, and beyond it were clumps of trees, green fields, and wells of abundant and clear water, with houses and every sign of fertility and cultivation. They had reached the banks of the Hyphasis, and encamped beneath the walls of Bahwulpoor. Elphinstone received much hospitality and kindness from the Khan, who seemed to be a man endowed with a considerable amount of common-sense. He praised the King of Cabul highly, but said he had never seen him, and, please God, he never would; he could live in his desert and hunt his deer, and had no desire to follow Courts. The Mission marched on the 5th December from the right bank of the Hyphasis, and reached Multan, 400 miles from Delhi, on the 11th.

Here they were detained by the necessity of obtaining correct intelligence of the King of Cabul's movements, as well as waiting for an officer from his Majesty to accompany the Mission after it entered the lands of the Afghan tribes. During his stay at Multan, Mountstuart Elphinstone wrote a long letter to the Governor-General, in the course of which he pointed out that it would be impolitic to send an army to Cabul, 'because it would be to meet the French on equal terms, and to wave the advantage of the strong frontier to the westward, presented by the rivers of the Punjab, the Indus, and the desert.' Mr. Elphinstone, however, said that if it were practicable, it would be desirable for us to contribute more directly to prevent that country from falling into the hands of the French, 'for if they were once in possession of it, their invasion of our territories would no longer be a great and desperate enterprise, but an attempt which they might make without risk when they pleased, and repeat whenever the state of our affairs gave a prospect of success.' He then shows the real danger of any foreign power having a paramount influence at the Court of Cabul. What he writes concerning the French is equally applicable to the Russians in the present day.

'If that specious people send an emissary to the King of Cabul, he will probably assure his Majesty's entire safety from the French, offer protection against the designs of the English, and promise, in the course of the operations against India, to reduce this Soubah Bhawul Khan's country and Sindh entirely under the King's authority ; perhaps he may also promise the Punjab, Kutch, Gujarat, or some other country on this side of the Indus ; or he may engage to procure a desirable settlement of the disputes about the Khorassan, getting over all difficulties by promising indemnities in India.

'Amidst all these dazzling prospects, I fear an Eastern monarch might lose sight of the danger to which he exposes his crown, by associating with such a nation of military adventurers, and would not give a very favourable hearing to a person who could only offer to destroy the illusion.'

Mr. Elphinstone asked the Governor-General to instruct him how far to offer pecuniary aid in case he found it necessary to counteract French promises, and what assistance he should give in ordnance stores and officers.

'It is desirable that I should be furnished with these materials to treat on as soon as possible, as some open negotiation will probably be required as a pretence for my remaining at Cabul. The Asiatics know nothing of the character of a resident minister, and so much are the Afghans impressed with the idea of an ambassador being always charged with some important communication, that their etiquette allows him only one audience to deliver his message, receive a reply, and take his leave.'

The King was at Candahar when Mr. Elphinstone reached Multan, and the Mission at first intended to join him there. After preparations were completed, and after many projects for overcoming the difficulties of a journey through the snow, they had the satisfaction of hearing that the King had set out on the road to Cabul. The news of the arrival of the Mission reached the sovereign while on his journey, and its object was at first regarded with strong prejudice and distrust. The Afghan lords were adverse to an alliance which would strengthen the King, to the detriment of the aristocracy; and the King himself, who at that time was much troubled by dissensions at home, thought it very natural that we should profit by the internal dissensions of a neighbouring kingdom, and endeavour to annex it to our empire. The exaggerated reports, however, which he received of the splendour of the Embassy, and of the sumptuous presents by which it was accompanied, determined him to admit the Mission, and to give it an honourable reception.

On leaving Multan the Mission marched up the great Indus, which they crossed on the 7th of January. The people of the country were always very civil. They, however, entertained some strange notions concerning the strangers. They believed they carried 'great guns packed up in trunks; and they had certain boxes so contrived as to explode, and kill half a dozen men each without hurting themselves.' Some thought we could raise the dead, and there was a strong current rumour that we had made an animated wooden ram at Multan; that we had sold him as a ram, and that it was not till the purchaser began to eat him that the material of which he was made was discovered. After crossing the Indus the Mission marched to Dera Ismael Khan, where they waited near a month for an officer from the King. At the end of January they heard that the King was coming to Peshawar, and an officer had been appointed to escort them. On the 7th February they continued their journey, under the guidance of the King's troops, and, after some dreary marches, they encamped at the mouth of the Kurrum. From this they made three marches, across a highly cultivated plain, to the Calla-baugh, or Karra-baugh, where the Indus is compressed by mountains into a deep channel, only 350 yards broad. The road runs along the mountain, and is cut out of solid salt at the foot of the cliffs of that mineral, in some places more than 100 feet high above the river. 'The salt is hard, clear, and almost pure. It would be like crystal, were it not in some places streaked and tinged with red. In some places salt-springs issue from the foot of the rocks, and leave the ground covered with a crust of the most brilliant whiteness.' Shortly afterwards they halted in the fertile plain of Kohat. Here their eyes were delighted by finding English plants, from which they had been long estranged in India. 'The walks were covered with green sod, and there were hedges of wild raspberry and blackberry bushes.' There was also clover, chickweed, dandelions, common dock, and many other English weeds. After leaving the verdant plain of Kohat the Mission proceeded through the valley belonging to the tribe of Kheiber, and saw a great many armed Kheibrees sitting on the hills, looking wistfully at the camels passing. The chief came and asked for a present, but the Afghan nobleman who was deputed to conduct the strangers to Peshawar told them to come to the camp after the baggage was past. 'It gave me a strange notion,' writes Mr. Elphinstone, 'of the system of manners in Cabul, that these armed robbers should come up and ask for a present; and that Moosa Khan, in his rich dress and golden arms, should sit almost unattended in the midst of their matchlocks and refuse them.'

On the morning of the 25th the Mission made their entry into the fine old city of Peshawar. A week, however, lapsed without their being introduced to the King, in consequence of a dispute about the forms of their presentation. Points of etiquette having been overcome on the morning of the 15th March, the Embassy set out in procession for the palace. They found Shah Sujah, the man of many misfortunes and some faults, seated on a throne covered with cloth of gold and pearls. His crown and all his dress were one blaze of jewels. Large emerald bracelets were on his arms, and in one of them shone the Mountain of Light, the romantic Kohinor. The King was a handsome man, almost thirty years of age, of an olive complexion, with a thick black beard. The expression of his countenance was dignified and pleasing, his voice clear, and his address friendly. The English Ambassador found him to be a courteous, well-mannered gentleman, who preserved his dignity while he seemed only anxious to please. On being told that the climate and productions of England greatly resembled those of Cabul, he said the two kingdoms were made by nature to be united.

On subsequent occasions the Envoy was admitted to more private interviews with the King, when business was discussed. The King had definite news, and was ready to make definite engagements. The Envoy had definite views, but no definite engagements to offer. The King had a dangerous revolution to cope with in his own kingdom. Whilst the English wanted him to make an alliance concerning a remote danger, and yet were unwilling to give him any aid against the enemies at his gate. The Afghans were shrewd enough to see that the English wished to make a very one-sided bargain. 'They stated,' wrote Mr. Elphinstone, in a letter to the Governor-General, 'that an alliance for the purpose of repelling one enemy was imperfect, and that true friendship between two States could only be maintained by identifying their interests in all cases; that Shah Mahmoud had no influence over the Douranees, and would be obliged, if he obtained the Crown, to put himself under the protection of the Persians to maintain his authority; that he had before connected himself with that people, and was naturally inclined to them; and that from the moment of his restoration to the government of this country we might consider the French and Persians as already on the Indus. They said the Afghans were a powerful people against a foreign invader, and that when the French and Persians came they might not require our assistance; but that we might regret our tardy aid if, before the threatened attack commenced, the present Government of this country was overthrown, and all the fruit of our alliance with it destroyed. Supposing a weaker case, and that Shah Sujah was only able to make head against the rebels without destroying them, they said that an attack from the French and Persians might then be difficult to withstand, and it would cost us millions to effect what might now be done for thousands. Throughout their whole discussion they seemed to consider the invasion of the French and Persians to be by no means formidable, unless aided by intestine divisions; but they were candid enough to admit that the war with these nations concerned them as much as they did us. In reply to this, I said that my instructions went only to the conclusion of a defensive alliance against the French and Persians, and that I knew your Lordship would never wish to take any part in the domestic quarrels of the Afghans; that your Lordship would of course be anxious that his Majesty's means of repelling invasion should be strengthened by the removal of the disturbances within his dominions, but unless it could be proved to your Lordship's satisfaction that the party in rebellion was connected with the common enemy, it would be entirely out of your plan to interfere in them. I said that we did not profess to act towards this State merely from motives of disinterested friendship. If we did, the King would have cause to suspect us of harbouring designs which we thought it impolitic to avow. I frequently urged them to bring forward any information they possessed respecting Shah Mahmcud's connection with the Persians, but they always acknowledged their belief that he had no transaction with that nation.'

Mr. Elphinstone continued to press upon the Afghan diplomatists the necessity of signing a treaty against the common enemy; and they, on their part, continued to beseech the English Envoy to grant assistance to their sovereign, to enable him to suppress the rebellion of his brother, which every day was growing more formidable. The English Ambassador tried to persuade them 'that the war concerned them more than us,' and that 'the Afghans must fight, or lose their country;' but they were neither convinced nor alarmed. The Afghan Minister replied that his Majesty was resolved not to give a passage to the French and Persians; but if he did, there seemed no reason to apprehend the dangers the English Envoy had described. If ten thousand French were in search of the cities of Herat, Candahar, Cabul, and Peshawar, the word of one Mullah would be sufficient to destroy them without the assistance of a single soldier. The Afghan Minister added a remark, the force and truthfulness of which has been impressed on our mind of late years by painful experience. 'The Afghans,' he said, 'were divided among themselves; but such was their national spirit, that a rebel would rather deliver himself up to the King than accept the assistance of a foreign power.' Mr. Elphinstone stated in conversation that the English depended on their own means of warding off the danger. 'I then gave a short account of our expeditions to Spain and Portugal, and explained the preparations at Bombay as far as I could with propriety; and concluded by saying that we had often been at war with all the world, and had never suffered in the contest; and that if the French by any means get this country into their power, we should still be able to oppose them, as we had been in many more difficult junctures.' The Afghan duly replied that 'he could not allow that it was so easy for us to repel our enemies on our frontier. If the King gave them a passage, he would join in their enterprise; and we should find a war with the Douranees very different from one with the French.' The English Envoy enlarged on the frankness of the English character; but even to this statement the Afghan Minister refused to give a complete assent. He said that he did not believe that we intended to impose upon the King, but he did not think that we were so plain as we pretended to be. He said our reputation was very high for good faith and magnanimous conduct to conquered princes, but he frankly owned that we had the character of being very designing, and that most people thought it necessary to be very vigilant in all transactions with us.

The Afghan Minister proved himself skilled in the art of diplomacy; but after many negotiations, Mr. Elphinstone surmounted the difficulties in his path, and a treaty of friendship with the Shah was signed on the 19th of April. It bound the Governor-General to assist the King of Cabul with money against a confederacy of French and Persians, and the King of Cabul to resist these powers while their confederacy lasted, and to exclude all Frenchmen from his country for ever. The events of the hour materially helped the Envoy in getting the treaty signed. The troubles of the King had so increased, that he would have made any terms with the English, in the hope of gaining their assistance against his internal enemies. Shah Sujah had succeeded to his half-brother, Shah Mahmoud, who was deposed in consequence of a popular insurrection. Shortly after his march to Peshawar, the King heard of the capture of Candahar by Shah Mahmoud. An army was sent to attack the rebels of the west. Four days after the treaty was signed, this army was disastrously beaten in a pitched battle. News came to the King of the advance of his brother, of the capture of Cabul, and also a report of the immediate advance of the enemy towards Peshawar. It was determined to march to Cabul to meet the enemy, and the King quitted Peshawar. On June 14th, after having paid a farewell visit to the sovereign, the Mission quitted the city. On June 17th, the treaty was signed at Calcutta by the Viceroy. Before the month had expired, Shah Sujah had been completely routed, and had fled from his dominions.

On their return home the Embassy marched through the Punjab, and reached Delhi, from which it had started twelve months before. During his stay at Peshawar, Mr. Elphinstone had proposed that the Indian Government should receive the Province of Sindh in return for money paid to Shah Sujah. The State of Sindh had come within the scope of the defensive arrangements proposed by the Governor-General. Mr. Elphinstone was rebuked for the proposal which he made, and on his way back, at Hassan Abdul, in the Punjab, he wrote a letter of explanation. No one had a greater horror of spoliation than Mountstuart Elphinstone.

'The expediency,' he wrote, 'of accepting of the cession of Sindh has clearly been removed by the change which has taken place in the state of affairs, and the consequent alteration of the views of Government; and I have to beg the Right Honourable the Governor-General's excuse for having at any time submitted a plan founded on such imperfect information. I was induced to do so by the consideration that the slowness of the communication between Peshawar and Calcutta rendered it necessary to lose no time in pointing out the disposition of the Court of Cabul with respect to Sindh, and the advantage which might be derived from it. I trust that the following explanation will make it clear that the plan which I proposed did not involve any step at all inconsistent with the strictest principles of political morality.

'When I had the honour to address to the Governor-General my letter No. 12, I had not the same information respecting the state of Europe which I now possess, and I was very far from considering any event that had taken place in that quarter of the globe as fatal to the French invasion of India. I understand that the chiefs of Sindh had given a cordial welcome to an Agent of France and Persia, while they had received the British Envoy with coldness and distrust. I had also received intelligence (which has proved to be erroneous) that Mr. Smith had arrived at Hyderabad, and had been immediately dismissed. I had no doubt that the views of the chiefs of Sindh were entirely repugnant to an alliance or anything like the terms proposed to them, and I conceived the period to be fast approaching, which had been anticipated in the 67th and 68th paragraphs of your despatch, when the submission of the chiefs of Sindh to the King of Persia would render it just and necessary for our Government to assist in reducing them into complete subjection to the King of Cabul. Considering an attack on Sindh to be, in the event of certain probable contingencies, determined, I addressed the Governor-General, chiefly with a view to show that it was more for the benefit of both States that we should take Sindh for ourselves than for the King of Cabul. Though my principal object was to enumerate the advantages we should derive from the possession of Sindh, I was aware that our obtaining them depended on the conduct of the chiefs of Sindh and on the facility with which we could occupy their country if the state of our relations with them rendered it necessary to attack them; but with these subjects I was unacquainted, and was obliged to content myself with alluding to them, and referring them to his Lordship's better information.

'It did not,' he continued, 'fall within the range of this discussion to examine the King of Cabul's right to Sindh; and from what I was in the habit of hearing daily, it did not occur to me to question his title. There seemed little or no difference in point of form between the manner in which the King held Sindh and that in which he holds the countries most subject to his control; nor is there any real difference, except that he cannot remove the Governor, and that more of the revenue is withheld on false pretences (of inundation, etc.) than in other provinces. The King does not appear ever to have renounced his right to the full sovereignty of Sindh. His march in that direction last year was, professedly at least, for the purpose of settling the province; and the reduction of Sindh is as commonly spoken of as that of Cashmere. On the other hand, I understood the chiefs of Sindh to acknowledge the King's sovereignty in the fullest manner, and to pretend no right to the countries they govern, except what they derive from the King's Hukkum. These facts would have rendered it necessary for us to attend to the King of Cabul's claims in any arrangement we might make for Sindh, but it was on the supposed transfer of their allegiance to Persia that I conceived our right of interference to be founded. I have said so much on this subject because I am very anxious to show the Governor-General that I did not intend to recommend a wanton attack on Sindh for the mere purpose of aggrandizement.'

From Delhi the Embassy proceeded to Calcutta, where Mr. Elphinstone stayed throughout the year 1810, writing his Report for the Government. When the task was finished, Mr. Elphinstone was selected to fill the difficult office of Resident at Puna, and at the beginning of 1811 he embarked for Bombay. At the capital of Western India he met the man of promise, Sir James Mackintosh, who formed a very just estimate of his new acquaintances. He wrote of him—'He has a very fine understanding, with the greatest modesty and simplicity of character.' Sir James Mackintosh also urged Mr. Elphinstone to publish the results of his Afghan labours, advice which afterwards bore good fruit.

CHAPTER III.

PUNA.

1810—1817.

In March, 1810, after seven years' absence, Mountstuart Elphinstone found himself once more in the capital of the Peshwas. He took advantage of having again a settled home to renew his old studies, though a less energetic man would have found the laborious duties of his office sufficient to engross his time. He used to rise early, and, like Macaulay at Calcutta, devote the first cool hours of the day to the study of some classic author, ancient or modern. He studied in the garden at the Sungum the 'Hecuba' of Euripides. 'It is, as far as I have read, a noble production, rising at every step in dignity and interest.' Two hours a day were devoted to the study of Greek, and he thinks that 'four months' such study as the present would enable me to read most books in Greek with ease.' His spare times were devoted to the 'Concilio Tridentino,' but he found doctrinal discussions tedious and useless. At this time Mountstuart Elphinstone was employed not only in the study of the writings of others, but in the labours of authorship. He had pondered over the advice given him by Mackintosh to let the public share in the information which he had gathered regarding the countries beyond the Indus. But he, however, could not come to a decision on the point until he knew what Malcolm intended to embrace in his book on Persia, which he was then preparing for the press. 'It is necessary,' he wrote, 'that I should know with some precision what you intend to do, or I shall spoil your work and waste my trouble (and no small trouble it is writing quires of paper, let alone writing for the public), while I might be hunting, hawking, reading, and doing my business with much more profit both to myself and the public, even if I do not take in hand the account of India which you so fully convinced me was required.' Malcolm wrote back that he intended to confine his work to Persia; and, on hearing this, Elphinstone began his account of the kingdom of Cabul. His method of composition was slow and toilsome, his care and corrections as to matter and style endless. He knew well that,

> 'There is no workeman
> That can bothe worken wel and hastilie;
> This must be done at liesure parfaidlie.'

At last the work was finished, sent home, and published. It attracted much attention, and was favourably noticed by the leading reviews. The article in the *Edinburgh* spoke of the style of Mr. Elphinstone as very good. 'It is clear, precise, significant, and manly, often nervous, always perfectly unaffected, severely guarded against every tendency to Oriental inflation (*totum munere hoc tuum est*), quite exempt from that verbosity and expansion which are the sins that most easily beset our ingenious countrymen in the East.' After the lapse of fifty years, Mountstuart Elphinstone's 'Cabul' is the book which contains the best description of the manners and political condition of the remarkable tribes which constitute the Afghan nation.

The time was now fast approaching when Elphinstone was to be occupied, not in writing, but in making history. At the close of 1813, Lord Minto left India, and was succeeded as Governor-General by the Earl of Moira, a man of mature age and experience, who had been in England an opponent of Lord Wellesley's imperial policy. But the new Governor-General had not been many months in India before he became aware of the grave mischief which had been brought by the peace-at-any-price policy of the merchants of Leadenhall Street. The Ghoorkas had made encroachments upon the country lying south of their mountains. Lord Minto had tried to persuade them to retire by negotiations with the Nepaul Court, and had failed. Lord Moira was then driven to try the force of arms; and, in 1814, active hostilities began against the mountaineers. The Ghoorkas fought as valiantly against us as they have subsequently done for us. Rashness and incompetency on the part of our generals brought disaster to our arms. But the hour of need is the opportunity of heroes; and a hero arose at this severe crisis in our Eastern Empire in the person of David Ochterlony. Lord Moira appointed him to the supreme command of the army of operation; and, with 17,000 men, the new chief determined to advance upon the capital of Nepaul. The pass which led to Khatmandoo was found impregnable; but, by a clever strategical movement, the flank of the enemy's position was turned, and they retreated. General Ochterlony advanced to within fifty miles of the capital. The Ghoorkas, seeing that resistance was hopeless, signed a treaty, and peace was established. Lord Moira, for the statesman-like manner in which he had conducted the war, was created Marquis of Hastings, the title by which he is better known in Indian history.

When the Peshwa heard of our early disasters in the Nepaul War, he began to intrigue against those to whom he owed his throne. The English had not only placed Baji Rao on the throne, but they had, by the Treaty of Bassein, bound themselves to defend it against external foes, and to protect it from rebels. From the period of his restoration, the Peshwa had made use of us in endeavouring to establish his authority over his own powerful feudatories; and Mr. Elphinstone found much work in acting as mediator between the Peshwa and his powerful vassals. But Baji Rao not only wished to reduce his own vassals, but he wished to get rid of the instrument by which he conquered them. He was assisted in his design by Trimbakji Dengle, a vicious man of considerable courage and ability, who had gained complete ascendency over his weak and vicious master. The Peshwa, under the advice of his Minister, took advantage of our difficulties in Nepaul to establish secret agencies at the Courts of Scindia, Holkar, and the Rajah of Berar. Mr. Elphinstone was not unaware of the intrigues which were being carried on, and was preparing to act decisively, when matters were brought to a crisis by a foul and horrible murder.

Certain differences had arisen between the Gaikwar and the Peshwa, concerning the forming of the Peshwa's districts in Gujarat. A distinguished Brahmin, by name Gangadhar Shastri, was sent to Puna as the Envoy of the Baroda Government, to endeavour to effect a settlement of the pecuniary questions at issue. The Gaikwar asked and obtained the guarantee of the British Government for the safety of his Ambassador. The unfortunate Shastri was received with every mark of outward respect by the Peshwa; and, to make the friendship apparently more complete, a matrimonial alliance between the Peshwa's sister-in-law and the Shastri's son was arranged. The Shastri, however, feared that the marriage would give offence to his master, and he broke off the engagement. This gave mortal umbrage to the Puna Court. The Shastri now made preparations for returning home; but the Peshwa and his Minister were afraid this might bring them into trouble with the English. They therefore persuaded the unfortunate Brahmin Envoy to delay his departure; and went so far as to invite him to accompany the Peshwa on a pilgrimage to the annual great festival of Pandharpur, on the Bhima. Here, on the night of July 14th, 1816, shortly after he had left the Peshwa, who had been unusually courteous to him, the Shastri was attacked in the streets, and hacked to pieces.

Mr. Elphinstone was at Ellora when the murder took place, but on his return to Puna he received sufficient proofs that the daring Minister had ordered the murder. He immediately addressed an earnest remonstrance to Baji Rao, in which he pointed out the gravity of the crime. 'A foreign ambassador,' he wrote, 'has been murdered in the midst of your Highness's Court. A Brahmin has been massacred almost in the temple, during one of the great solemnities of your religion.' He called upon the sovereign to punish the authors of the crime, and to apprehend and confine the chief culprit—the Prime Minister—till his Highness and the Governor-General could have an opportunity of consulting on the subject. Baji Rao hesitated to surrender his favourite, for he knew that the master was implicated in the guilt of the servant. He thought of opposing the Resident's demand by force, and Mr. Elphinstone was compelled to gather troops to support his authority. Just as hostilities were on the point of commencing Baji Rao yielded, and surrendered to justice his Minister. Trimbakji was confined in the fortress of Tanna. His imprisonment was of short duration. He effected his escape in a romantic manner, on the 12th September, 1816, and retired to the wild hills near Nasik, where he began afresh his intrigues against the English.

Mr. Elphinstone informed the Peshwa of Trimbakji's escape, and asked him to issue stringent orders for his arrest. Baji Rao promised to do so, but took no measure to carry his promise into effect. No exertions were made to seize the captive, although it was a matter of notoriety that he was collecting armed followers within a short distance of the capital. Authentic information reached the Resident that the Peshwa had had several secret interviews with his favourite, and that large supplies of money had been conveyed to him from Puna. Matters rapidly grew worse. Tidings came from all quarters of gatherings of armed men, and the insurgents grew bolder, and began to capture the Mahratta strongholds. Mr. Elphinstone felt the time had come for vigorous measures, and troops were sent to quell the insurrection. He referred to the Governor-General for orders as to the course of proceedings to be adopted towards the Peshwa. Baji Rao continued, in spite of all remonstrance, to carry on his warlike and threatening preparations, and at length the Resident was forced to act decisively on his own responsibility. He ordered the subsidiary force to assemble in the vicinity of Puna, and he sent a written demand for the surrender of Trimbakji within a specified time, and the immediate cession of three forts as pledges for the act. The Peshwa at first absolutely refused compliance, but on May 8, 1816, when he found that troops guarded all the outlets of the city, he agreed to the demand.

The concession came too late. On the 10th May Mr. Elphinstone received instructions from the Marquis of Hastings to require the Peshwa to promise that he would neither maintain any envoys at other Courts, nor receive any at Puna; and that he would renounce all claims to the titular leadership of the Mahratta Empire. He was called upon to surrender valuable territories for the support of the military contingent; and to acknowledge on the face of the treaty his belief in the guilt of his Minister. These were hard terms. They could not have been harder if made at the end of a successful campaign. No statesman could expect an independent prince to adhere to them unless compelled by force of arms. There was one last chance of escape for the Peshwa. Mr. Elphinstone was instructed only to make these demands in the event of no serious efforts having been made to arrest Trimbakji. The Peshwa, however, exhibited his usual vacillating conduct, and took no measures to arrest the Minister. Then, after a few days hesitation, Mr. Elphinstone was forced to ask Baji Rao to sign the new treaty. The Peshwa refused. His military adherents urged him to save honour by an appeal to arms, but Baji Rao was lacking in the courage of his race. Sullenly he ratified the treaty, protesting that he submitted to the conditions solely because he was wanting in the power to resist, and that they had not his acquiescence.

The treaty was signed in May, and at the close of the year the Governor-General determined to make effective preparations for the crushing of the 1816. Pindaries of Central India. These irregular horsemen owed their origin and power to the anarchy produced by Mahratta invasions, and their number had increased with every Mahratta army. They now received secret encouragement from the Mahratta States, who regarded them as useful instruments to aid in the destruction of the English power. Towards the end of 1817 the military preparations of Lord Hastings were completed, and they were made on a scale to meet any open hostilities from the greater Powers. The subsequent conduct of the Peshwa proved that the Governor-General was wise in his caution. After the signature of the treaty Baji Rao went on his annual pilgrimage to Pandharpur, and in that sacred city he had an interview with Sir John Malcolm, whom he pretended to regard as an old friend. He succeeded in convincing Sir John of his peaceful intentions, but Mr. Elphinstone's suspicions were not so easily lulled, and he viewed with serious apprehension the march of the greater part of his troops to their position in the general distribution of the grand army. Only three weak battalions of Bombay infantry, under Colonel Burr; a battalion of the Puna Brigade of the Peshwa's own troops, under Major Ford; and two companies of Bengal Sepoys, forming the Resident's guard, were left to protect Puna. It had, however, been arranged that a regiment of European infantry should be sent up from Bombay.

Baji Rao, finding the Mahratta capital denuded of our force, began to levy more troops, and call in feudatories under the shallow pretence of acting in concert with the British in their operations against the Pindaries; but the insolence of his men showed their master's real intentions. He also began to tamper with the fidelity of our Sepoys. These proceedings were well known to Mr. Elphinstone, but he did not like to take any active steps to counteract them 'for fear of interfering with our negotiations at Gwalior by any appearance of a rupture here.' The Resident knew that Scindia was well acquainted with Baji Rao's vacillating and treacherous nature, and that the sovereign of Gwalior would not commence hostilities against the English until the Peshwa had committed himself. There was grave danger that Baji Rao would strike the first blow before the European regiment could reach Puna. Mr. Elphinstone wrote to the European regiment to come on as fast as possible, without regard to anything except the health of the men. On the 30th October, the British battalion marched into Puna; Mr. Elphinstone now took a bold and decisive step. He ordered the regular troops to leave the cantonments, and to march to Kirkee, a village two miles north of Puna, and near to Dapuri, the station of the Puna Brigade. Others were sent to hasten the arrival of the battalion stationed at Sirur. General Smith, who commanded the Puna Division of the grand army, having heard of the threatening aspect of affairs at Puna, halted his forces at Pultamba, on the Godavari, and promised to march immediately on Puna if communications should be interrupted. The Peshwa now saw that the time had come when he must throw off the mask, and hostilities could no longer be delayed. Accordingly, he sent a bullying message to desire the Resident to remove the cantonment to such place as he should direct, reduce the strength of the Native Brigade, and send away the Europeans. This was, of course, refused. Within an hour the Resident was a fugitive from the Residency, which was set in flames by the Mahrattas. He got safely to the Kirkee troops, and the battle of Kirkee followed. We had 2,800 in all, while the Peshwa had 18,000 horse, 8,000 foot, and 14 guns. This is the history of nearly all our Indian battles. The courage shown in brilliant attack—courage shown in coolness under danger, presence of mind, and fertility of resource in the most terrible emergencies, were the means by which we won our Indian Empire. The most graphic description of the battle is that written by the chief actor, Mountstuart Elphinstone, a few days after the victory was won. It is characteristic of the man that he says so little of himself in the letter. But Mountstuart Elphinstone fought the battle of Kirkee, and won it. He urged the folly of acting on the defensive with an Asiatic foe, ordered an instant attack, and this gained the day.

'To Captain Robert Close. (*Private.*)

'Camp Kirkee, *November* 11, 1807.

'MY DEAR CLOSE,

'I make no doubt you are astonished at my long silence, and perhaps think I am murdered, or that the communication is quite cut off. The truth is, I did not like to trust your dawk with my secrets, for fear of their being intercepted, and so influencing Scindia's resolutions. Now they are no longer secret, so I sit down to write to you.

'The Peshwa, under cover of Malcolm's desire that he should raise troops, got together a large army at Puna—about 25,000 horse, and half as many foot. These he encamped at Ghorparé, pressing on and almost surrounding our brigade; he had long since set to work to corrupt our Sepoys, and pushed on with increasing vigour and publicity. In short, everything tended to a rupture; and it was necessary to watch the moment when it would break out.

'On arrival of the Bombay European regiment, I moved the cantonment to this delightful position, and felt quite relieved when I saw it was established here; but the impression made on the town and diligently encouraged by Gokhle was, that the Firangies had fled before the invincible arms of Srimant, and would soon be clear out of the country.

'These feelings were shown with great insolence. Our cantonments were plundered; a gentleman was wounded and robbed of his horse at Ganesh Khind, and it was unsafe for an officer to ride even between our old camp and our new. Moro Dixit warned Ford of an approaching attack in which all our Sepoys were to leave us, and offered to save his life if he would remain quiet in Dapori.

'The Peshwa treated every application I made to him with contempt, although I had complained of troops coming near in our old ground. We were scarcely out when the Vinchurkar sent 1,500 horses to skirmish and have a sham fight between the Sangam and the Saits Garden.

'Maddu Sing Pindare came out with 700 or 800 horse to the place where the dead are buried, and sat for an hour examining the Sangam at his leisure, while we were at breakfast; and Gokhle pushed on 2,000 men, and threatened to form a camp on the river in front of Ghorpuri.

'All this could not be borne with, without leading to more insult; so I very moderately remonstrated, and ordered on the Light Battalion from Sirur. About the same time General Smith, of his own accord, concentrated on Fort Camba. The Peshwa, who perhaps had been flattered by Gokhle that all his preparation should be made without his getting into a scrape, now saw that he must throw off the mask; accordingly he sent a very bullying message to desire I would move the cantonments to such place as he would direct, reduce the strength of the Native Brigade, and send away the Europeans. If I did not comply, peace could not last. I refused, but said I was most anxious for peace, and should not cross the river towards Puna; but if his army came towards ours, we should attack it.

'Within an hour after, out they came with such readiness that we had only time to leave the Sangam with the clothes on our back, and crossing the river at a ford under Chilando, march off to the bridge with the river between us and the enemy. A little firing, but no real fighting. The Sangam, with all the records, all my books, journal, letters, and manuscripts, was soon in a blaze; but we got safe to the Kirkee Bridge, and soon after joined the line. While the men and followers were fording, we went ourselves to observe the enemy. The sight was magnificent as the tide rolled out of Puna. Grant, who saw it from the heights over the Powder cave, describes it as resembling the Bore at Cambay. Everything was hushed except the trampling and neighing of the horses, and the whole valley was filled with them like a river in flood. I had always told Colonel Burr that when war broke out he must recover our character by a forward movement that should encourage and fire our own troops, while it checked our enemies; and I now by a lucky mistake, instead of merely announcing that the Peshwa was at war, sent an order to Captain Grant to move down at once and attack him. Without this, Colonel Burr has since told me he certainly would not have advanced. However, he did advance; we joined, and after some unavoidable delay the Dapori Battalion joined.

'When opposite to the nullah, where there used to be a plantain-garden, we (injudiciously, I think) halted to cannonade, and at the same moment the enemy began from twelve to fifteen guns. Soon after the whole mass of cavalry came on at speed in the most splendid style; the rush of horses, the sound of earth, the waving of flags, the brandishing of spears were grand beyond description, but perfectly ineffectual. One great body, however, under Gokhle and Moro Dixit and some others, formed on our left and rear; and when the 17th were drawn off by its ardour to attack, Major Pinto, who appeared on our left, and was quite separated from the European regiment, this body charged it with great vigour, broke through between it and the European regiment. At this time the rest of the line were pretty well occupied with shot, matchlock, and above all with rockets; and I own I thought there was a good chance of our losing the battle.

'The 17th, however, though it had expended all its ammunition, survived, and was brought back to the line by Colonel Burr, who showed infinite calmness and courage, and after some more firing and some more advancing together, with detaching a few companies to our right towards the little hill of Ganesh Khind, we found ourselves alone in the field, and the sun long set. I was at first for advancing to the water at the Saits Garden, but was persuaded it was better to return to camp, which it was. If we had not made this move forward, the Peshwa's troops would have been quite bold, ours quite cowed, and we doubtful of their fidelity. We should have been cannonaded and rocketted in our camp, and the horse would have been careering within our pickets. As it is, the Peshwa army has been glad to get safe behind Puna, and have been almost as quiet as if encamped on the Pirti* of Delhi. We did not lose 100 men altogether; and we have quite set our name up again. Our life here is delightful—no plots or cares, but idling, looking through spy-glasses, and expecting another field-day. That the Peshwa should not give us one before General Smith comes in, which he will by the 14th, is incredible; but the Mahrattas are unaccountable.'

The Peshwa did not give them another field-day. On the 12th, General Smith arrived at Puna. The Mahrattas

* Plain.

had taken up a strong position in our old cantonments, and it was expected a great battle would be fought. On the evening of the 16th, the English army crossed the river in two principal divisions; and next morning having united, they advanced on the Peshwa's camp, but found it deserted. Measures were now taken for reducing the city, and for securing it, if practicable, from the fury of our troops. 'This,' Mr. Elphinstone writes, 'had long been an object of great anxiety to General Smith, and the consideration of it had entered into all his plans for the defeat of the army. The plunder and destruction of our Residency and cantonments, the lives of many of the Sepoys, the disgraceful circumstances of the murder of the officers at Fort Mallegaum, the massacre of the wives of the Sepoys that had fallen into the enemy's hands on the 5th, the mutilation of a Sepoy who had been taken prisoner while straggling from General Smith's line of march, and many other acts of impotent rage on the part of the Peshwa's Court, had raised the indignation of the men to the highest pitch, and they did not conceal their eager desire to revenge themselves by sacking and plundering the enemy's capital. Through the exertions of the Resident, Puna was taken possession of without bloodshed. The capture of the capital did not close the war. Baji Rao fled to Purandhar, and the campaign which followed consisted in the pursuit of a beaten foe. On the 9th February Satara, the stronghold of Sivaji, surrendered after a show of resistance, and the flag of the founder of the Mahratta Empire was again hoisted on the citadel. The descendants of Sivaji were, however, released from their dependence on their Mayors of the Palace only to be made dependent on the power of the English.

Baji Rao had destroyed the empire which Sivaji

founded. After the fall of Satara, Mr. Elphinstone, acting under the instructions of the Governor-General, issued a Mahratta proclamation to the people of the Deccan. The document points out that Baji Rao was restored to power by the English; that 'at Baji Rao's restoration the country was laid waste by war and famine, the people were reduced to misery, and the Government derived scarcely any revenue from its lands.' 'Since then, in spite of the farming system and the exactions of Baji Rao's officers, the country has completely recovered, through the protection afforded it by the British Government; and Baji Rao has accumulated those treasures which he is now employing against his benefactors. The British Government not only protected the Peshwa's own possessions, but maintained his rights abroad.' The proclamation then dwells on the murder of the Ambassador; the demand for the punishment of Trimbakji; the Peshwa's refusal 'until the British Government had marched an army to support its demand. Yet it made no claim on the Peshwa for its expenses, and inflicted no punishment for his protection of a murderer. It simply required the surrender of the criminal; and on Baji Rao's compliance, it restored him to the undiminished enjoyment of all the benefits of the alliance. Notwithstanding this generosity, Baji Rao immediately commenced a new system of intrigues, used every exertion to turn all the powers of India against the British Government. At length he gave the signal of disturbance, of fomenting an insurrection in his own dominions, and preparing to support the insurgents by open force. The British Government had then no remedy but to arm in turn. The troops entered Baji Rao's territories at all points, and surrounded him in his capital before any of those with whom he had intrigued could strike. Baji Rao's life was now in the hands of the British Government; but that Government, moved by Baji Rao's professions of gratitude for past favours, and of entire dependence on its moderation, once more resolved to continue him on his throne, after imposing such terms on him as might secure it from his future perfidy. And on this being agreed to, the British Government restored Baji Rao to its friendship, and proceeded to settle the Pindaries, who had so long been the pest of the peaceful inhabitants of India, and of none more than the Peshwa's own subjects. Baji Rao affected to enter with zeal into an enterprise so worthy of a great Government, and assembled a large army on pretence of cordially assisting in the contest. But in the midst of all his professions he spared neither pains nor money to engage the powers of Hindustan to combine against the British; and no sooner had the British troops marched towards the hordes of Pindaries, than he seized an opportunity to commence war without a declaration, and without even an alleged ground of complaint. He attacked and burnt the house of the British Resident, contrary to the laws of nations and the practice of India, plundered and seized on peaceable travellers, and put two British officers to an ignominious death. Baji Rao himself found the last transaction too barbarous to avow; but as the perpetrators are still unpunished, and retain their command in his army, the guilt remains with him. After the commencement of the war, Baji Rao threw off the mask regarding the murder of Gangadhar Shastri, and avowed his participation in the crime by uniting his cause with that of the murderer. By these acts of perfidy and violence, Baji Rao has compelled the British Government to drive him from his Musnad and to conquer his dominions.' The proclamation then put forward the intention of Government of setting apart a portion of the Peshwa's territory for the Rajah of Satara. 'The rest of the country will be held by the Honourable Company. The revenues will be collected for the Government, but all property, real or personal, will be secured. All Wattan and Inam (hereditary lands), annual stipends, and all religious and charitable establishments will be protected, and all religious sects will be tolerated, and their customs maintained, as far as is just and reasonable. The farming system is abolished. Officers shall be forthwith appointed, to collect a regular and moderate revenue on the part of the British Government, to administer justice and to encourage the cultivation of the soil; they will be authorized to allow of remissions, in consideration of the circumstances of the times.'

To carry out the provisions of this proclamation, distinguished for its moderation and good sense, Mr. Elphinstone was appointed sole Commissioner for the settlement, and administrator of the conquered territory, and was invested with full authority over all the civil and military officers in it. No better choice could have been made. As Resident, he had shown much administrative ability, and to his coolness and courage the English owed the decisive victory which won them the Mahratta land. The words spoken by Canning in the House of Commons were not mere words of eulogy. 'Mr. Elphinstone (a name distinguished in the literature as well as the politics of the East) exhibited, on that trying occasion military courage and skill, which, though valuable accessories to diplomatic talents, we are not entitled to require as necessary qualifications for civil employment. On that, and not on that occasion only, but on many others in the course of this singular campaign, Mr. Elphinstone displayed talents and resources, which would have rendered him no mean general in a country where generals are of no mean excellence and reputation.'

CHAPTER IV.

COMMISSIONER OF THE DECCAN.

1818—1819.

In the year 1818 Mountstuart Elphinstone entered upon his new duties as Commissioner of the lands lately ruled over by Baji Rao, the head of the great Mahratta Confederacy. The rapidity and apparent ease with which the British rule was established over a country of wild valleys and precipitous mountains inhabited by a race of warriors is worthy of note. Many causes contributed to the rapid spread of British authority over the Deccan, but the main cause was the energy and the character of the new ruler, and the broad and impartial views which guided his administration. When the war first broke out, every Mahratta thought Baji Rao would drive the foreigner out of his dominions. The defeat at Kirkee did not destroy their hopes, for the Mahrattas suffered no crushing loss, and Baji Rao still possessed an army. The battle of Ashte dispelled all illusions; for in that engagement Gokhle, the only military commander of repute among them, was killed, and Baji Rao, deserted by the Mahrattas, retired from his dominions, and surrendered finally to Sir John Malcolm. The populace now had nothing to gain from the favour, nothing to fear from the resentment of the Peshwa. In every village the new proclamation began to be discussed. Weary of war and an unsettled government, the people hailed with joy the hopes of peace and the promised immunities. Mr. Elphinstone took advantage of this feeling, and, by wise and conciliatory measures, succeeded in reconciling the several classes of Mahratta society to the foreign rule.

Mountstuart Elphinstone's success as an administrator was chiefly due to the fact that he saw that political institutions and social usages which had lasted for centuries could not be entirely devoid of merit. His great endeavour in the civil administration was 'to show the people that they are to expect no change but in the better administration of their former laws.' He felt that not only the privileges, but even the prejudices of the people ought to be respected. He wrote to the Governor-General: 'It is, however, to be remembered that even just government will not be a blessing if at variance with the habits and character of the people.' Mountstuart Elphinstone knew that foreign dominion must ever be a hardship, and the most that conquerors can do is to take care that the yoke presses as lightly as possible, and that it galls at the fewest points. The Marquis of Hastings left him the choice of giving the Raja of Satara a jahagir or a small sovereignty; and he adopted the latter course, for he felt the importance 'of leaving for part of the Peshwa's subjects a government which could afford them service in their own way.' The re-establishment of the Satara Rajah in some measure reconciled the old Mahratta chiefs to the destruction of the more modern authority of the Peshwa. The English were no longer fighting against the House of Sivaji, but against a successful Mayor of the Palace. Many of the old families, let it be recorded to their credit, resolved to share the fortunes of their fallen prince; but the majority, from fear of forfeiting their lands, gave in their allegiance to the conquerors. To preserve the old families from destruction, to maintain their influence, was one of Mr. Elphinstone's first cares. He saw that the nobles of the Deccan were not like the chiefs of a Mohammedan government, foreigners to the people; but they were of the same nation and religion, and the descendants of those who had been their leaders since they rose to independence. He also saw that the Mohammedans in their most powerful days never attained complete success in taking the place of the local princes, and in substituting their own for native law and organization; and he tried to avoid as far as possible, attempting what the Mohammedans failed to do.

The local princes of the Deccan were the jahagirdars, or owners of jahagirs, which, both in nature and history, had a strong resemblance to feudal beneficences. A jahagir was at first granted to some successful warrior during life, for the purpose of maintaining troops to serve the King. A small portion was set aside as a personal possession for the chief. On his death, the grant was renewed on condition of the heir paying a relief. The jahagirs, as in Europe, came in course of time to be regarded in the light of hereditary property. 'The period,' wrote Mr. Elphinstone, 'for which a jahagir had been held, was therefore a very important point to advert to in deciding how long to continue it. I recommend that all granted by the Mogul Emperors, or the Rajahs of Satara, should be hereditary in the fullest sense of the word. The former most generally have been very long in the families which held them, and had survived two changes of dynasty. These do not seem now to be interfered with. The latest of the Satara grants must now be near a century old, and must have survived a change of dynasty, besides our conquest. Surely there is enough to entitle the possessor to feel secure from future disturbance! On this principle, I believe we stipulated with the new Rajah of Satara that he should not resume such grants of his ancestors as lay within his territory, binding ourselves by implication (if the fact be as I have supposed) not to resume those within ours. The Jahagirdars of the Peshwa stood on a different footing: they had arisen under the dynasty which we subverted; none could have been in possession for more than seventy years, and they had been kept in mind by the exactions of service, as well as by occasional resumptions, of the real nature and extent of their tenure. Much consideration was, however, due to them as the actual possessors of power; and they were allowed to retain their private lands for one or more generations, according to their merits or importance. No change has taken place in the condition of this class; and I cannot see how any claim which they possessed at the conquest has been weakened since.'

Mr. Elphinstone had a regard for hereditary rights; and not only were jahagirs given back to their owners, but all other rent-free lands—all established pensions, charitable and religious assignments and endowments were restored. 'The preservation of religious establishments,' he wrote, 'is always necessary in a conquered country; but more particularly so in one where the Brahmins have so long possessed the temporal power. The Peshwa's charities and other religious expenses amounted to nearly Rs.1,500,000, besides those of the wealthy persons in employment under his Government. It would be absurd to imitate this prodigality, but many expenses of this nature are rendered necessary by the proclamation of Satara; and it would be worthy of a Liberal Government to supply the place of the Peshwa's indiscriminate charities by instituting a Hindu College at once in both of the sacred towns of Nasik and Wai.' Mr. Elphinstone, however, found it was no easy task to conciliate the Brahmins. A plot, in which a few of them were the chief conspirators, to murder the Europeans and restore the Peshwa was discovered. The Commissioner ordered the ringleaders to be blown from the cannon's mouth. Sir Edward Nepean, the Governor of Bombay, approved of the vigorous act, but advised Mr. Elphinstone to ask for an indemnity; but he rightly refused. 'If I have done wrong,' he said, 'I ought to be punished; if I have done right, I don't want any act of indemnity.'

The suppression of rebellion was accompanied by a settlement of the land revenue. The system introduced did not essentially differ from the comparatively patriarchal scheme of management of Nana Farnavis, by which the agents of the Government settled directly with the people. The advantage of the Rayatwari system is that it enables us to know the Rayats, and them to become acquainted with us. The abolition of the farming system of Baji Rao, by which districts were rented to contractors, removed many grievances. Mr. Elphinstone felt that many novelties must accompany every revolution, and he tried to limit the number as much as possible. He ordered the collectors to administer the government 'without the restraint of any regulations but those which they found established.' He did all that lay in his power to revive the public spirit which once animated the village communities, ancient institutions which have existed from time immemorial, and which centuries of alternating tyranny and anarchy have never been able entirely to extinguish.

He preserved the influence of the village officers, for he knew what other English administrators have been ignorant of—that the task of really governing India down to the villages and the people is too great for a foreign Government, and can only be done through native agency and communal self-government. In the important matter of the administration of justice, Mr. Elphinstone refrained from any hasty introduction of English machinery and agency, for his knowledge of the people taught him that the state of society and civilization which pervades the many millions of India calls for a simple, cheap, and expeditious administration of justice. Under native rule, the main instrument of dispensing justice was the Panchayat or assembly of village elders. This ancient institution had its defects, but it also possessed many advantages. 'The intimate acquaintance,' wrote the Commissioner, 'of the members with the subject in dispute, and in many cases with the character of the parties, must have made their decisions frequently correct, and it was an advantage of incalculable value in that mode of trial that the judges being drawn from the body of the people could act on no principles that were not generally understood, a circumstance which by preventing uncertainty and obscurity in law, struck at the very root of litigation.' Mr. Elphinstone felt that the object of the conquerors ought not to be to destroy the native system, but to take means to remove its abuses and revive its energy. He proposed that the Patel or head of the village in the country districts, and the heads of trades in the towns, should have the power to summon a Panchayat.

In very large cities native judges were appointed. In all cases appeals were allowed to the collector, with whom all powers of criminal and civil administration remained. One of the main secrets of Mr. Elphinstone's success was the faculty that he had for choosing good men, and the power he confided to them. The tendency of the present day is to make the collector a mere machine for writing and forwarding reports and yards of useless statistics. His time is so occupied in writing reports that he has but scanty leisure for administration. Mr. Elphinstone thought it indispensable 'that the collector should give audience for at least two hours every day to all ranks, receive revenue complaints *vivâ voce*, and grant decisions and orders on Mamlutdars as the cases require. If he confines himself to receiving petitions in writing, it is impossible that he should have time to become acquainted with the state of things in his district.' The modern collector is fast becoming a mere instrument for carrying out orders, and all originality and independence is fast perishing. The administration in which the people have the largest share in their own government is the best; after that comes strong personal rule; but the worst form of government ever invented is government by secretariat. It was the personal rule of the Munros and Malcolms, of the Elphinstones and Metcalfes, which created the Indian Empire, and the rule by resolutions and statistics will go far to destroy it. The effect of government by bureaucratic resolutions is to be read in letters of blood in the history of the Ancien Régime; to do everything for the people, and let them do nothing for themselves—this was the ancien regime. The Council of State settled arbitrarily not only taxes and militia and roads, but anything and everything. There is no new thing under the sun. Like the Indian Government, they tried to teach agriculture by schools and pamphlets and prizes; they sent out plans for every public work. A town could not establish an octroi, levy a rate, or mend the parish steeple without an order from Council. Everywhere was meddling. There were reports on statistics—circumstantial, inaccurate, and useless as Indian statistics. Every centralized bureaucracy has been a failure, and is ever likely to be a failure, because it regards and treats men as things, and not as persons. One of the reasons why the English Raj has not won favour of the people is that there is too much of the powerful machine and too little of humanity in us. We try to be just, but we are often unjust and cruel, because we believe our system of government to be adapted to all races and conditions of life. We have forgotten the principles which Elphinstone enforced in his report.

'The plan I have proposed has many obvious and palpable defects, and many more will no doubt appear when its operations are fully observed. It has this advantage, that it leaves unimpaired the institutions, the opinions, and the feelings that have hitherto kept the community together; and that as its fault is meddling too little, it may be gradually remedied by interfering when urgently required. Any opposite plan, if it fails, fails entirely; it has destroyed everything that could supply its place, and when it sinks, the whole frame of society sinks with it. This plan has another advantage likewise, that if it does not provide complete instruments for the decision of suits, it keeps clear of the causes that produce litigation. It makes no great changes, either real or apparent, in the laws, and it leads to no revolution in the state of property. The established practice also, though it be worse than another proposed in its room, will be less grievous to the people, who have accommodated themselves to present defects, and are scarcely aware of their existence; while every fault in a new system, and perhaps many things that are not faults, would be severely felt for want of this adaptation. I do not, however, mean to say that our interference with the native plan is odious at present. On the contrary, several of the collectors are of opinion that a summary decision by a European judge is more agreeable to the natives than any other mode of trial. This may be the case at first; but if the decisions of Europeans should ever be so popular as to occasion the disuse of the native modes of settlement, there would soon be a run on the Courts, and justice, however pure when obtained, would never be got without years of trouble.'

Mr. Elphinstone had not the opportunity, as Commissioner of the Deccan, of carrying out personally the principles enforced in his great report; for before the document reached Government, Mr. Elphinstone had become Governor of Bombay. But he devoted the weight of his great office to the execution of the plans and principles sketched out in one of the ablest State papers ever written by an Indian statesman.

CHAPTER V.

BOMBAY—RETURN TO ENGLAND—DEATH.

1819—1859.

Mr. Elphinstone had been only a year Commissioner of the Deccan, when the Governorship of Bombay fell vacant by the resignation of Sir Evan Nepean. The great statesman who was then President of the Board of Control named three distinguished Indian administrators—Munro, Malcolm, and Elphinstone—for the post. The East Indian Directors unanimously elected the last; and his rule justified their choice. Mountstuart Elphinstone brought to his new office those qualities which make a man a successful administrator. With a masculine understanding, and a soft but resolute heart, he had unlimited powers of application. His rise, through all the gradations of public service, was due not to birth or favour, but to a thorough knowledge of its constitution, and a perfect practice in all its business. But by being conversant in office his mind had not become narrowed. He was not only a great official—he was a great statesman. Mr. Elphinstone recognised the obligation which lay upon the rulers 'to raise the natives by education and public trust to a level with their present rulers.' His 'Minute on Education,' now published for the first time, combines comprehensive and elevated views with so

5

much circumspection and dignity, that it must ever be shown as a model of what a State paper ought to be. In this document many fallacies regarding Indian education, which appear from time to time, are ruthlessly destroyed. He felt, in order to successfully start education, you must first create a desire for education; and that this desire would naturally be more easily raised in the higher than in the lower orders. 'I will here only remark, that I consider that it is more important to impart a high degree of education to the upper classes, than to diffuse a much lower sort of it among the common people. The latter object also is highly important, but it is not the point in which there is most deficiency at present. It will, besides, be much easier to make the lower orders desirous of learning to read, after a spirit of inquiry and improvement shall have been introduced among their superiors.' Mr. Elphinstone disposes of the common argument against higher education, that it rears a class whose only object is Government employment. He writes: 'The most important branch of education, in my opinion, is that designed to prepare natives for public employment. It is important, not only from its contributing so directly to the general improvement, but also from the stimulus it affords to education among the better class of natives, by connecting it with their interest.' Regarding the advisability of Indian education being entirely secular, he wrote: 'To the mixture of religion, even in the slightest degree, with our plans of education I most strongly object. I cannot agree to clog with any additional difficulty a plan which already has so many obstructions to surmount. I am convinced that the conversion of the natives must infallibly result from the diffusion of knowledge among them. Evidently they are not aware of the connection, or all attacks on their ignorance would be as vigorously resisted as if they were on their religion. The only effect of introducing Christianity into our schools would be to sound the alarm, and to warn the Brahmins of the approaching danger. Even that warning might perhaps be neglected as long as no converts were made ; but it is a sufficient argument against a plan, that it can only be safe as long as it is ineffectual, and in this instance the danger involves not only failure of our plans of education, but the dissolution of our empire.'

These are grave words of warning to any Government who may be tempted to enter upon the dangerous path of proselytism in India. A charge has often been brought against Government high education that it mainly benefits one class—the Brahmins. On this point, Elphinstone has some sensible remarks: 'It is observed that the missionaries found the lowest castes the best pupils ; but we must be careful how we offer any special encouragement to men of that description ; they are not only the most despised, but among the least numerous of the great divisions of society. It is to be feared that if our system of education took root among them, it would never spread farther ; and, in that case, we might find ourselves at the head of a new class, superior to the rest in useful knowledge, but hated and despised by the castes to whom these new attainments would always induce us to prefer them. Such a state of things would be desirable if we were contented to rest our favours on our army, or on the attachment of a part of the population, but inconsistent with every attempt to found it on a more extended basis.' Mr. Elphinstone attached little value to schemes for improving the education of natives, unless *pari passu* steps were taken for extending to them a greater share of the honours and emoluments of office.

With regard to their employment, he wrote: 'It seems desirable gradually to introduce them into offices of higher rank and emoluments, and afterwards of higher trust. I should see no objection to a native member of a board, and I should even wish to see one district committed experimentally to a native judge, and another to a native collector.' Mr. Elphinstone, however, was a statesman, and he appreciated the fact, that in statesmanship prudence is the first of virtues. He qualifies his remark regarding the admittance of natives into offices of trust: 'At the same time, I think very strict supervision requisite, and many Europeans necessary for that purpose. If this be not attended to, the natives will introduce their own corrupt practices into the system at the first outset, and we shall never be able to eradicate them.' It was the same spirit of prudence which caused Mr. Elphinstone to be decidedly against the introduction of a free press in India; but freedom of speech once having been permitted, he objected to any retrograde movement.

After education, the next great question which engaged Mr. Elphinstone's attention was legislative and judicial reforms. He has left a monument of his labour in the 'Code of Regulations' which bears his name. He had no mania for passing a multitude of Acts, but he saw the necessity of simplifying the law in India. His rules were framed to lessen the written pleadings, and to bring matters to a speedy issue. He saw that if justice was to be meted out, the language of the Court must be the language of the district; and that the evidence of the witnesses must be taken in their own vernacular.

No man was more impressed than Mr. Elphinstone with the importance of Indian officers knowing the vernacular of the country. His own administrative success was in a great measure due to his knowledge of the people, gained by a thorough knowledge of their dialects. His thorough knowledge of the native languages added greatly to the value of the two tours which he made through each part of the Presidency. On these journeys he made himself accessible to all classes, and insisted on seeing everything. He was fond of the land in which he laboured, and took an interest in its antiquities, and would go out of his way to visit an ancient river or celebrated temple. He thoroughly enjoyed Bijapur, and thought it well worth the pains of a journey even after Delhi and Agra. He was fond of sport; and the Under-Secretary, who accompanied him during his tour, writes: 'We always had in the camp a Shikaree, whose business it was to inquire for hog; and whenever he brought in intelligence of game, Mr. Elphinstone would proclaim a holiday, and go hunting for one or perhaps two days; and he was fond of the chase at any time. In the midst of many striking excellences, that which placed him far above all the great men I know of, was his forgetfulness of self, and thoughtfulness for others.'

The eight years of Elphinstone's rule passed away without any epoch-marking event, but it was a period of consolidation and improvement. The best testimony of the success of his government is the address presented to him by the native inhabitants of the Presidency on the eve of his departure. The address is headed by the name of the very princes and chiefs whom he helped to conquer a few years previously, and opens as follows:

'We, the native princes, chiefs, gentlemen, and inhabitants of Bombay, its dependencies, and allied territories, cannot contemplate your approaching departure from the country without endeavouring to express, however faintly, the most profound and lasting regret which has been occasioned in our minds by your resignation of the government of this Presidency; for until you became Commissioner in the Deccan and Governor of Bombay, never had we been able to appreciate correctly the invaluable benefit which the British dominion is calculated to diffuse throughout the whole of India. But, having beheld with admiration for so long a period the affable and encouraging manners, the freedom from prejudice, the consideration at all times evinced for the interest and welfare of the people of this country, the regard shown to their ancient customs and laws, the constant endeavours to extend amongst them the inestimable advantages of intellectual and moral improvement, the commanding abilities applied to ensure permanent amelioration in the condition of all classes and to promote their prosperity on the soundest principles, by which your private and public conduct has been so pre-eminently distinguished, has led us to consider the influence of the British Government as the most important and desirable blessing which the Supreme Being could have bestowed on our native lands.'

Besides presenting him with the above address, the native community subscribed the handsome sum of £20,000 for the foundation of professorships for the purpose of teaching the natives the English language and the arts, sciences, and literature of Europe; to be held in the first instance by learned men to be invited from Great Britain, until natives of the country should be found perfectly competent to undertake the office. The European community of Bombay were not less emphatic than their native brethren in expressing their regard for the departing ruler. In this address they dwelt upon the noble qualities by which he had attached the people to his sway, and they concluded it by asking him to allow a marble statue of himself to be erected in Bombay and to accept a service of plate which would be prepared and presented to him in England. The Bombay Literary Society, founded by Mackintosh and fostered by Elphinstone, voted a memorial bust to be placed in the Society's rooms.

On the 14th November, 1827, Mountstuart Elphinstone quitted Bombay, and no statesman ever left the shores of India more beloved by all classes of the community. Having no near ties at home, he made no haste to reach England, but travelled slowly through Egypt, Syria, Palestine, Greece, and Italy. During all his years of hard official life he had read much of the classic lands; and the unhappy gift of 'beauty,' which has attracted men of all ages to the Italian peninsula, exerted a strong influence on his cultivated mind. Poetic and historical associations guided his steps, and the two years spent in wandering must have been years of sunshine to the weary statesman. It was not until the spring of 1829 that he reached England, at the age of fifty, after having spent thirty years in India. His health was shattered, but his abilities were not at all impaired. But a man who returns to England after a thirty years' residence in India will find, be his talents what they may, that he has much to learn. 'When I met them,' said Elphinstone of his intercourse with the literary lions of the day, 'I used to find myself constantly out of my depth.' To remedy the defects caused by a long exile from the world of letters, the great Indian statesman retired to a roadside inn to study the Greek grammar. He also, by close reading, advanced the boundary of his knowledge of European history and historical antiquities. With the same zeal that he had qualified himself to be a great administrator, he laboured to fit himself for the vocation of historian. During his residence in India he had always devoted much attention to the history of the land, and collected much valuable material, and in 1835 he commenced writing his great book. For five years he laboured hard in weaving it into form, and in the spring of 1841 the 'History of India' was published. The book is one of great merit and value, but it must not be measured by the standard of criticism of the present day. Since it was written German erudition has opened up unexplored wilds of Indian history and mythology. Mr. Elphinstone brought to his task a mind familiar with Oriental modes of thought, but he was unfortunately no Sanscrit scholar, and consequently the Hindu period is the most unsatisfactory portion of his book. Whether the Hindu period could ever be written thoroughly by one scholar is doubtful. The historian of ancient India has to form his narration at one time out of the legends of a mythical age not more historical than that of Theseus, at another out of the bewildering records of co-existing dynasties, more numerous and as shifting as those of the Saxon heptarchy. In the Mohammedan period Mr. Elphinstone was treading on firmer historical ground, and one more familiar to him. No part of the history is more worthy of attention than his estimate of Akber, or of the virtues and faults of Baber. The book has been called dull, and it may be to those who regard history as mere canvas for word-painting; but the scholar will always admire the calm and equitable style, free from all inaccuracy of language or statement. Mr. Elphinstone spoke diffidently of his history as a contribution to the great subject he had taken in hand that might aid the work of some future men of genius. The volume published, it must be borne in mind, formed only a part of a greater undertaking, embracing the rise of the British power in India, which failing health compelled him to abandon.

The last fifteen years of Mr. Elphinstone's life were passed in the delicious retirement of Hookwood, in Kent, in alternate communing with books and old friends. He had always loved books, and they were now necessary to him. At times he would throw aside his books, and then to his friends he was delightful company through a flood of subjects and an unaffected cheerfulness and civility. Though he had retired from the world he was not forgotten by the world, and his opinion regarding matters of Indian policy was often sought by the leading statesmen of the day. The letters written by him to his friends from his retirement are charged with wisdom and foresight. To Lord Mayo and the Marquis of Ripon is due the credit of having introduced local self-government into India; but upwards of thirty years ago Elphinstone wrote, 'Leave the inferior presidencies independent on all matters that do not affect the general politics or imperial legislature of India.' Mr. Elphinstone viewed with regret and alarm Lord Dalhousie's policy of stealing other men's lands under the specious pretence that it was for the good of the people. His alarms were justified by the events of 1857, when the taking of Oude and the confiscation of Jhansi was avenged by blood.

When the East India Company, which had reared the stately fabric of our Indian Empire, fell by the mutiny of its soldiers, Mr. Elphinstone took a keen interest in the reconstruction of the Home Government. He did not look kindly on the innovations, and time has proved how shrewd and just his criticisms were. Writing about the Indian Bill he said: 'The great point of course is the Council, and I think that proposal will furnish a body of excellent advisers for an honest, able, and moderate secretary (such as Lord Stanley appears to be), and that it will supply the deficiencies of a lazy or indifferent one much better than the ordinary clerk of a Board of Control would do; but that it will afford very little protection against a rash, fanciful, and self-willed chief, and none at all against one who shall combine with a ministry in a deliberate plan to appropriate the patronage of India, or to make use of that country in any other way favourable to their own power or stability.' Events have proved that Elphinstone's fears were not purely imaginary. He desired that the Council of the Secretary of State for India should retain the special knowledge and exclusive devotion to Indian interests which characterized the old Directors. Above all things, he desired that Indian questions should be removed from the platform of party politics, and that the welfare of our Indian subjects should never be sacrificed to the exigencies of political strife. 'It is more astonishing,' he wrote, 'considering how much our safety depends on the contentment of our Indian dependents, that in all the late discussions there has not been a single speaker of note, except Gladstone, that has laid the least stress on this part of the subject. They probably rely on the Indian Government for looking to public opinion among the natives; but what could the strongest Indian Government do against a clamour for levying a new tax (say an income tax) on India to make up for the deficit occasioned by *its own expenses*, including the Persian and Chinese Wars, and many other charges in which the people of India take quite as little concern.'

Mountstuart Elphinstone did not live long enough to see the working of the new system. On the 29th of November, 1859, in the eightieth year of his age, death came to him suddenly. Before men heard he was ill, news reached them that the great Indian statesman was dead. To the quiet parish church of Limpsfield was borne the coffin of a great man. In war he had shown the abilities and courage of a great commander, and in peace the virtues of a successful ruler of men. He possessed the two great elements of all social virtues—respect for the rights of others, and sympathy for the trials and sufferings of all men. These qualities have caused the descendants of the brave Mahrattas whom he conquered to cherish the memory of Mountstuart Elphinstone.

MINUTE,

BY THE

HON. MOUNTSTUART ELPHINSTONE,

DATED MARCH, 1824,

ON

EDUCATION.

MINUTE,

BY THE

HON. MOUNTSTUART ELPHINSTONE,

DATED MARCH, 1824.

1. I HAVE the honour to lay before the Board a letter from the Secretary to the Education Society, enclosing a report from a Special Committee of that Association.

2. As it is principally at my recommendation that the Society has come to solicit the aid of Government, I am bound to afford every support I can to their application. I have, however, some suggestions to offer in addition to those of the Committee; and the late order of the Court of Directors against the foundation of a Native College at Bombay, obliges me to advert to topics which I did not mean to have connected with the Society, and to give a wider range to the discussion than is required by the letter now before us.

3. I have attended, as far as was in my power since I have been in Bombay, to the means of promoting education among the natives, and from all that I have observed and learned by correspondence, I am perfectly convinced that without great assistance from Government, no progress can be made in that important undertaking. A great deal appears to have been performed by the Education Society in Bengal, and

it may be expected that the same effects should be produced by the same means at this Presidency. But the number of Europeans here is so small and our connection with the natives so recent, that much greater exertions are requisite on this side of India than on the other.

4. The circumstance of our having lately succeeded to a Brahmin Government likewise, by making it dangerous to encourage the labours of the missionaries, deprives the cause of education of the services of a body of men who have more zeal and more time to devote to the object than any other class of Europeans can be expected to possess.

5. If it be admitted that the assistance of Government is necessary, the next question is, How it can best be afforded? and there are two ways which present themselves for consideration. The Government may take the education of the natives entirely on itself, or it may increase the means and stimulate the exertions of the Society already formed for that purpose. The best result will probably be produced by a combination of these two modes of proceeding. Many of the measures necessary for the diffusion of education must depend on the spontaneous zeal of individuals, and could not be effected by any resolutions of the Government. The promotion of those measures, therefore, should be committed to the Society; but there are others which require an organized system, and a greater degree of regularity and permanence than can be expected from any plan the success of which is to depend upon personal character. This last branch, therefore, must be undertaken by the Government.

6. It would, however, be requisite, when so much was entrusted by Government to the Society, that all the material proceedings of that body should be made

known to Government, and that it should be clearly understood that neither religion nor any topic likely to excite discontent among the natives should ever be touched on in its schools or publications.

7. The following are the principal measures required for the diffusion of knowledge among the natives: 1st, to *improve* the mode of teaching at the native schools, and to *increase* the number of schools; 2nd, to supply them with school-books; 3rd, to hold out some encouragement to the lower orders of natives to avail themselves of the means of instruction thus afforded them; 4th, to establish schools for teaching the European sciences and improvements in the higher branches of education; 5th, to provide for the preparation and publication of books of moral and physical science in native languages; 6th, to establish schools for the purpose of teaching English to those disposed to pursue it as a classical language, and as a means of acquiring a knowledge of the European discoveries; 7th, to hold forth encouragement to the natives in the pursuit of these last branches of knowledge.

8. First, the *improvement* of schools must be almost entirely left to the Education Society, with such pecuniary assistance as Government may think it expedient to afford. The constant and minute superintendence which will be requisite over the schools in all parts of the country, is such as can only be expected from a very general spirit of anxiety to promote the object. Any attempt to produce it on the part of Government would require a large and expensive establishment, and, after all, would have very little chance of success.

9. The establishment now recommended by the Committee for teaching schoolmasters may be sanctioned. It will be some time, perhaps, before properly

qualified persons are found, but no slackness should appear on the part of Government in providing the means of securing their employment. It ought at the same time to be communicated to the Committee that Government would be gratified by receiving occasionally accounts of the progress made, and of the number of schoolmasters to whom instruction had been afforded. In the meantime it appears probable that a very beneficial effect would be produced if an attempt were made to disseminate the improved method of teaching by means of the press. For this purpose a very concise treatise * might be prepared in each of the native languages, containing a few rules for the management of schools in the modern way, along with a short exposition of the advantages which would accrue both to masters and scholars from the adoption of these improvements. The same tract might contain a notification of the persons from whom school-books might be procured, and likewise of the manner in which prizes might be obtained by persons properly qualified in this stage of education. The circulation of these tracts, and a few corresponding ones in English, together with the superintendence and assistance which might be voluntarily bestowed by gentlemen throughout the country, and the aid from the vaccinators which will presently be explained, would probably effect much towards the improvement of common schools, and would pave the way for the employment of those schoolmasters who are to be trained under the institution proposed by the Committee.

10. The means by which the direct exertions of Government can be best applied to promote schools is by endeavouring to increase their number, and on this I am of opinion that no pains should be spared.

* Or rather two treatises, as proposed by Mr. Farish.

The country is at present exactly in the state in which an attempt of the sort is likely to be most effectual. The great body of the people are quite illiterate; yet there is a certain class in which men capable of reading, writing, and instructing exist in much greater numbers than are required, or can find employment. This is a state of things which cannot long continue. The present abundance of people of education is owing to the demand there was for such persons under the Mahratha Government. That cause has now ceased, the effect will soon follow, and unless some exertion is made by the Government, the country will certainly be in a worse state under our rule than it was under the Peshwa's. I do not confine this observation to what is called learning, which, in its present form, must unavoidably fall off under us, but to the humbler acts of reading and writing, which, if left to themselves, will decline among the Brahmins without increasing among the other castes.

11. The advantage of the present time is not confined to the facility of finding masters. The funds are more easily obtained at present than they will be hereafter. The Gram Kharch (village expenses), except in the old districts, have not yet undergone regulation, and many Warshasans,* Nemnuks,† allowances to fakirs, etc., might now be turned to this useful purpose, that will soon be lost altogether.

12. Mr. Chaplin formerly suggested an allowance of from three to ten rupees from the Gram Kharch should be offered to any properly educated master who would undertake to teach a village; and if the smallest of

* An annual allowance or stipend given for charitable purposes to priests, pandits, etc.

† Allowance or appointed provision given to Government servants; a salary or pension.

these sums should seem too little for the poorest village, it may be increased by consolidating the funds in all cases where villages are sufficiently near each other. It would not, however, be politic (as Mr. Chaplin has since remarked) that this expense should fall directly on the village; such a measure would too closely connect the ideas of education and taxation, and the Rayats might endeavour to bring about the failure of the school in hopes that they might thus get rid of the impost. The school-money, therefore, should be taken from the gross income of the village before the Government share is separated, and the amount should be made good by reductions in the Gram Kharch. If the saving does not cover the expense, the loss will still be very small either to Government or the Rayats when compared with the advantage gained.

13. The schoolmasters should be allowed to take the usual fees from their boys besides this allowance, and should receive a certain degree of assistance in printed tables and books of the cheapest description.

14. An important addition to the resources applicable to the maintenance of schools might be obtained by diverting towards that purpose other funds derived from the Government Treasury, and not from villages, which are at present employed on objects of no utility, and which are equally lost to the State and to the people. Occasions continually occur in which Haks, Warshasans, Inams, and other lands and allowances are granted unconditionally, from humanity or policy, to persons claiming them on doubtful titles; in all such cases the grantee might be obliged to submit to a small annual payment towards a fund for maintaining schools. There are also many religious allowances which it would be impolitic to resume, but which might by proper management be diverted to this purpose. Lands

and allowances are also often held on condition of performing religious or other services; it would be unpopular to exact a payment in commutation for those services if the benefit went to Government, but it might easily be levied for an object so advantageous to the people themselves. In most cases, however, the purpose for which any deduction is made from an allowance should be kept entirely out of sight, to avoid raising odium against our plans of education. It at first seemed to me to be practicable by giving a small addition in money to the allowances enjoyed by village priests, astrologers, etc., on condition of their teaching a certain number of boys, to induce them to undertake a more useful profession, which might gradually supersede their original one; but many objections presented themselves to the arrangement, of which the most important was that it necessarily rendered the situation of schoolmaster hereditary in all instances where it was adopted.

15. Even if funds were provided for the support of schools, we should still feel the difficulty of securing the useful employment of them. If we could at all depend either on a judicious selection of schoolmasters in the first instance, or on a moderately careful supervision afterwards, there could be no doubt of the entire success of the proposed measure; but the over-employment of the Europeans and the indolence and indifference of the natives make both of most difficult attainment. The object, however, is too important to be given up without an effort. The collector might have the general charge of all schools which derived any aid from Government, and a power to resume the allowance in all cases of gross neglect. At stations where many Europeans reside, some might probably be found to undertake the care of the schools in the

neighbourhood. The Education Society might perhaps induce some to charge themselves with this task, and all officers, of whatever description, who had any share in the management of schools, should be encouraged to correspond with the Society and to promote its improvements.

16. In all subordinate villages a great deal may be probably expected from the vaccinators. If these gentlemen should enter with zeal into the promotion of education, there are none by whom so much assistance could be afforded. They belong to a learned and liberal profession, and are selected for their activity and humanity. Their duties lead them on tours precisely of the nature of those required for the superintendence of schools, and bring them into contact with all classes of the people. Their duties also at each place must soon be transacted, and a good deal of time left applicable to such employments as are now recommended. Some remuneration ought to be given for this additional trouble; perhaps 150 rupees, with the actual expenses of carrying books, might be sufficient. The line of each person's charge should be well marked, to prevent all mistakes which would be likely to damp zeal. The vaccinator should be quite independent in all places of which he took charge, and the collector should be requested to attend to his suggestions on all points connected with his schools. Any person who voluntarily took charge of a school should receive similar support, and should be encouraged to procure a successor to take up his charge when he should be removed from the station. On this subject, however, the Education Society will be best qualified to suggest the most desirable mode of proceeding.

17. Inquiries relating to the possibility of providing salaries for teachers out of the Gram Kharch, or even

by a small addition to that fund, and likewise regarding the possibility of diverting any of the religious or other Mahratha grants, in the manner before alluded to, should immediately be addressed to the collectors (those in the Deccan through the Commissioner), who may also be requested to send a statement, showing the villages in their district, and the number of schools in each, accompanied by such a general report on the state of schools as they may have the means of affording. They might, for instance, give a guess at the number of boys taught at each, the learning they acquire at each, and the particular classes who attend them, whether only those whose trade requires a knowledge of reading and writing, or others also. Their opinion should likewise be solicited as to the persons who could, with most advantage, be employed as schoolmasters, and as to any other expedients that may seem practicable for promoting the object at a small expense. I am aware that a reference of this sort is usually fatal to a proposal for improvement. The time of public officers is so fully occupied by current business, that they have little leisure for general inquiries, and must commonly lay aside the letter in despair of being able to answer it; while we, equally suffering under the pressure of current business, often allow a long period to elapse before we revive a subject which has been disposed of by such a reference. One important question, however, in the present instance—that of the number of schools and scholars—can be ascertained through the Commavisdars and Shekdars with the utmost facility, and on the others a few reports from intelligent collectors is all we can expect. The Secretary will also be able, by making the questions distinct and simple in the first instance, and by occasionally repeating the call in cases of delay, to prevent the usual fatality from attending this highly important and interesting inquiry. It is a very great satisfaction to me that, since the draft of this minute was finished, a plan nearly of the same nature has been proposed by Major Robertson, who has also pointed out funds for supporting it. I consider this voluntary opinion from so experienced a collector to be of the greatest value, and recommend that his proposal should be sanctioned without delay; at the same time, a copy of this minute, if agreed to, may be sent to him.

2nd. School-Books.

18. The expense of printing school-books may, for the present, be undertaken by the Government; the superintendence of the printing and the distribution, except in certain cases, must be managed by the Society.

3rd. Encouragement to Schools.

19. The encouragement to be afforded to native schools is a point of greater difficulty, but is one of the utmost importance, and one which, if properly made use of, would be sufficient to secure very general improvement in the education of the lower order. The first step would be to institute examinations in the principal town or village of each Pargannah, and to distribute prizes to those who showed the most proficiency in each class. A book, such as will be published under the superintendence of Government or of the Society, would be a sufficient prize for ordinary proficiency, while those of the highest order might receive a medal; and those who are well qualified to act as writers, or Kulkarnis, might be given a certificate to that effect. The value of that certificate, however, would depend upon its being cautiously given, so that public officers in want of a person of that description might prefer taking one with a certificate as the surest means of obtaining the requisite qualifications. Prizes should likewise be given to those schoolmasters who produce

the greatest number of well qualified scholars. It will be no easy matter to provide for the due adjudgment of prizes, for few English gentlemen are qualified to proncunce on the acquirements of Indians; the employment of natives would lead to corruption; and many wrong judgments, from whatever motive, would weaken or destroy the effect of the examinations. In the earliest part of education, however, this will be least felt; and if the plan of taking places were ever introduced, there would be little difficulty in allotting the prizes, as the contest for the first class might then be confined to the upper boys at different schools—say the three or four upper boys of each. With regard to the prizes for the higher acquirements to be mentioned in a subsequent part of this despatch, the gentlemen who preside might select a certain number of natives to assist them, guarding against corruption or partiality by making a new choice each day, and giving no warning of the persons on whom it was likely to fall. The judge or a committee, consisting of the collector and the judge, might be able to spare time and attention for an annual examination at the head station, while in the smaller towns the duty might be best conducted by the vaccinators. The vaccinator himself might distribute the prizes to boys; the prizes to schoolmasters he should recommend officially to the collector, who should be instructed to pay immediate attention to his application. These prizes should consist of an honorary dress, or some other present, which would be of a nature acceptable to natives. It might be accompanied either on the part of the collector or the vaccinator with a present of such printed books or tables as are most useful in teaching a school. The vaccinators should be furnished with a considerable number of books of all descriptions to be distributed at their discretion. The present vaccinators should be requested to undertake this charge, and none should be appointed to it without his previous acquiescence. Henceforward the appointment should be inseparable.

20. The following might form a tolerable scale of prizes for each Pargannah; but it can be altered to meet any object of convenience:

CLASS.	NUMBER OF MEDALS.	VALUE OF EACH MEDAL.	NUMBER OF BOOKS.	VALUE OF EACH BOOK.
1st.	1	5 Rs.	1	10 Rs.
2nd.	3	2 „	3	6 „
3rd.	3	2 „	6	6 „
4th.	3	2 „	10	3 „

Prizes to schoolmasters (one in every two Pargannahs), a 'shela' and 'turban,' or other presents worth thirty rupees.

21. In the establishment of schools for teaching the European sciences, we can do no more than lay the foundation, if, indeed, we can do more than sketch an outline of the plan. We may at present establish certain stipends to be granted to any person who can pass a prescribed examination, and to be increased when he shall obtain a certain number of scholars. These stipends should at first be very liberal; without such encouragement we would scarcely expect to procure teachers, when we remember the lucrative employments open in other departments to persons qualified for such offices. A man with such a knowledge of English as we require would easily get 150 or 200 rupees as a clerk to a merchant. The pupils of whom

4th. Schools for European Science.

Mr. Cumin has had the goodness to take charge, and some who might be similarly educated by the naturalist expected from England, would probably be among the first candidates for these offices. Some of the young men educated at the English school at Bombay, which will afterwards be mentioned, might also qualify themselves to aspire to this employment, and the prospect of a handsome stipend would be a powerful incentive to all who had any prospect of success. No preference ought, however, to be given either in the choice of professors, the distribution of prizes, or any other mode of encouragement to persons educated in particular schools. Proficiency alone, however obtained, should constitute a claim. It is obvious that these sciences could not be taught without active European superintendence. As soon, therefore, as a sufficient number of native professors could be procured, it would be necessary to place a European gentleman at the head of them. He might be chosen from any line of the service where the requisite requirements could be found; although the necessity of economy in his allowances would probably confine the choice to the junior ranks of the military and medical lines.

22. When things should have reached to this stage (which must be considered as remote), the college at Puna might be put under the same officer, and the European and native establishments might be united. By this arrangement the means of improvement would be held out to those already in pursuit of knowledge, and as the European branch might in time be expected to swallow up the Hindu one, the whole funds of the Puna College would become applicable to the diffusion of useful science. At present such a union would be fatal to both branches. The jealousy of the Brahmins would repel the approach of foreign doctrines, and the disadvantageous comparison between their own salaries

and those of the new-comers would increase their hostility, and would soon occasion the desertion of the college.

23. There is one science in which great progress may immediately be made. The Commissioner was not at first able to procure a medical professor for the college at Puna, private practice being more lucrative than the salary he had to offer. This deficiency might be easily supplied, as there are few sciences in which the natives have so little to preserve, or in which we have so much to teach, and so much facility in teaching. If the attention of our medical establishment could only be called to this object, we might almost without an effort communicate to the natives a vast store of sound and useful knowledge. A small prize (of the value of 200 or 250 rupees) might be offered to any native who could acquire a certain knowledge of anatomy, medicine, or chemistry, and the warm approbation of Government might be held out to any surgeon who would impart that degree of knowledge. The situation of civil surgeon is generally reckoned desirable, and it requires no peculiar qualifications. It might with great advantage be intimated to the Medical Board, that the first vacancy in these appointments would always be conferred on any assistant-surgeon who should either produce an elementary treatise on one of the sciences connected with the profession in a native language, or bring a native instructed by him to a certain pitch in some one of those sciences. A medical man already a civil surgeon might be promised promotion to the superior situations of Puna, Satara, or Cutch, on the same terms; for the same temper and knowledge of the natives which would enable him to accomplish the condition, would secure his possessing the qualities peculiarly required at those stations. Each surgeon should also be indemnified for all the expense incurred

on account of the native whom he instructed, provided he proved to possess the requisite knowledge. The Medical Board must, however, be required to fix with some precision the nature of the treatise to be produced and the exact amount of proficiency to be required from each native student. When so educated, these native students might be employed as a superior class of native medical assistants, and might furnish one or two professors for the college.

24. It should be an incitement to attempt something in this branch to know that in Bengal there is an institution with a medical gentleman at the head of it who has an allowance of 1,600 rupees a month; and a number of students who receive an exhibition for their maintenance during their studies.

25. It is of comparatively little use that people are taught to read if their studies are to be confined to legends of Hindu gods; and it seems at first sight to be extremely easy at a trifling expense to supplant the few inaccurate and expensive manuscripts which are in the hands of the natives, by an abundance of simple and rational publications through the means of the press. The difficulty, however, has been found to be much greater than was thought. In four years we have only accomplished the publication of two native books, and they also are translations from the Sanscrit, undertaken more with a view to bring printed books into use than on account of any instruction they were themselves calculated to afford. The principal cause of this delay has no doubt been the extreme slowness of printing in India, at least at Bombay; but had the printing not retarded us, we should soon have been brought to a stand for want of translations to publish. The best remedy appears to be that suggested by the Society—to advertise for the best

5. Books.

translations of particular books, or for the best elementary treatises on particular subjects in specified languages. The books recommended by the Committee in No. 1 are most of them well judged; but next to a system of arithmetic, which is already in hand, I should think a treatise on the elements of geometry, with the application of them to practice in mensuration, etc., would be desirable. A system of ethics, as suggested, would certainly be valuable, but it would be of difficult execution. In the meantime, a few tracts, or one tract containing those prudential maxims which are most important to the poor, and which are least known in India, would be of the greatest utility. Those most repugnant to their prejudices, as those which discountenance the marriage of infants, expensive feasts to the caste, etc., might be introduced in the mode most likely to elude or disarm opposition; but the success of such books must depend almost entirely on their execution, and they need only be undertaken by persons who feel a strong desire to inculcate the truths to which they refer.

26. When the labour required for these translations is considered, and likewise the previous knowledge necessary to render them useful, it is obvious both that the reward must be very liberal and that we need be under no apprehension from the number of successful claimants. Each book should, when recommended by the Education Society, be submitted to a committee or one individual appointed by Government, who should pronounce on its fitness for publication. It might be expedient to have at least two rates of reward, one for books absolutely fit for publication, and another for books which could, with moderate attention, be adapted to the press. I should propose that the remuneration should vary from 100 to 300 or 400 rupees for school-books, to 4,000 or 5,000 rupees for superior produc-

tions, the amount being left to the Committee, provided it does not exceed the largest of these sums. In extraordinary cases, where a higher reward seemed due, the Committee might submit the claim to Government.

6. English Schools.

27. If English could be at all diffused among persons who have the least time for reflections, the progress of knowledge by means of it would be accelerated in a tenfold ratio, since every man who made himself acquainted with a science through the English would be able to communicate it in his own language to his countrymen. At present, however, there is but little desire to learn English with any such view. The first step towards creating such a desire would be to establish a school at Bombay, where English might be taught classically, and where instructions might also be given in that language on history, geography, and the popular branches of science. This school might be managed under the Education Society. A master, I understand, could be found at a salary of 50 rupees, to be doubled when he should pass an examination in Mahrathi, and again increased by the amount of his original salary when he should pass in Gujaratti. He might also be allowed to take fees from the scholars that attended him, the amount of which might be fixed by the Committee. To prevent such a mixture of ranks as might prevent the higher order of natives from using the school, no boy should be admitted until he was approved by the Committee, and a preference should be given to the sons of wealthy natives and to boys that should show particular promise of talent. When the school became more extended a separate class should be instituted for the lower castes. There might be two examinations a year by the Committee, with the assistance of one or more gentlemen whom they might themselves select; and on those occasions prizes of books or medals should be distributed.

28. Should we ever be able to extend English schools to the outstations, admittance to them might be made a reward of merit in other studies which might tend to render it an object of ambition, or at least to remove all suspicion of our wishing to force our own opinions on the natives.

29. If it is difficult to provide the means of instruction in the higher branches of science, it is still more so to

7. Encouragement.

hold out a sufficient incitement to the acquisition of them. The natives being shut out from all the higher employments in their own country, neither feel the want of knowledge in their ordinary transactions nor see any prospect of advancement from any perfection of it to which they can attain; nor can this obstacle be removed until, by the very improvements which we are now planning, they shall be rendered at once more capable of undertaking public duties and more trustworthy in the execution of them. In the meantime their progress must be in a certain degree forced and unnatural, and for this reason must require more assistance on the part of the Government than would be necessary in a better state of society.

30. The first step in this stage also would be to give prizes. These must be of more value, and distributed with more care than the prizes formerly recommended. Part of the prizes of the Dakshina have by long custom become fixed annuities to certain persons, who are supposed for a succession of years to have best merited them; but the remainder ought henceforth to be given with a very strict attention to proficiency: and as the annuities fall in, the amount of them should be employed in the same manner. It would certainly give much disgust if any part of this fund were immediately to be applied to the encouragement of European science. A preference has, however, already been given to the

more useful branches of Hindu learning, and this might be gradually increased as well by assigning all new prizes arising from lapsed annuities to that species of attainment as by taking advantage of other opportunities that might arise. In the meantime a certain number of prizes distinct from the Dakshina should be instituted for persons who might stand an examination in particular branches of European knowledge. The exact species of knowledge ought not at first to be too nicely insisted on, but geometry, algebra, the higher branches of arithmetic, geography, and the knowledge of our system of astronomy might be among the number. The principal prizes should be of considerable value; and as they would probably not be claimed for several years, they ought to be allowed to accumulate till the amount became sufficiently dazzling to be of itself an inducement to study the elements of a science. Smaller prizes might in the meantime be granted, that even attempts at improvement might meet with some reward.

31. An obvious means of giving effect to public instruction would be to render a certain examination a necessary preliminary to admission to all offices; but as it is essential that the selection of public functionaries should depend as much as possible on their fitness for their particular duties, it is inexpedient to embarrass the choice of them by any extraneous conditions. There are, however, instances in which stipends are enjoyed without the exaction of any corresponding service, and in these cases it would be by no means unreasonable to oblige the possessor to confer a benefit both on himself and the public by devoting some portion of his life to study. It might, therefore, at some future period be announced that no Warshashan, Nemnuk, or other religious grant or pension would be continued to

the heirs of the actual incumbents, unless they should first pass a prescribed examination. The notification might be so expressed as to avoid giving perpetuity to such allowances as it might be intended to resume, and a power might be reserved to dispense with the examination in cases where there might be peculiar claims. It may be a question whether a condition like the present might not be annexed to the enjoyment even of Inams when they have avowedly been granted for religious purposes, and it certainly might be attached to the succession to such pensions or jahgirs as it may be thought expedient to make hereditary, with the exception of such as are given for the maintenance of the representatives of great families. As many of the claimants to the allowances in question reside at a distance from European stations and even from the principal native towns, it would be necessary that a moderate knowledge of any useful Indian science should be sufficient to entitle a person to the benefits of the grant. Where opportunities of instruction were afforded, some knowledge of European science might be required, or at least a smaller portion of European learning might be made equivalent to much more extensive qualifications in the sciences of the country. All this, however, is for future consideration; at present everything that is likely to render large classes hostile to our views on education should be carefully avoided.

Measures to be immediately adopted.

32. We are now to see what steps are to be taken immediately. I have already recommended a reference to the collectors regarding the number of schools now in existence, and the possibility of increasing it by means of the Gram Kharch and other funds distinct from those of the Government. It will be expedient to wait their report before any decision is passed on those points.

33. The vaccinators (should they accept the office) may, however, be authorized to commence on the granting of allowances to schoolmasters experimentally in villages where their instructions seemed likely to be well received, and where they might be able to see that their duties were not neglected.

34. The attention of the School Society might be called to the preparation of a tract on the best mode of teaching. The whole of this minute, if concurred in, might indeed be communicated to them.

35. The allowance proposed for the native secretary might be sanctioned as well as that for the native instructors of schoolmasters to be entertained as an experiment; and to help to cover the expense, the persons now employed in conducting translations from the Sanscrit might be discharged. A place might perhaps be found in some of the public offices (as the old sadar adalat) where the books of the Society might be safely deposited, and the native secretary might be entrusted with the care and issue of them.

36. The necessary communication should be made to the Medical Board regarding the employment of the vaccinators and the means suggested for diffusing medical science. The vaccinators also should be consulted as to their disposition to undertake the task proposed for them.

37. The printing of the school-books suggested by the Society should immediately be sanctioned, and the Society should be authorized to issue advertisements inviting translations and promising remuneration at the rate already mentioned.

38. The Society might be requested to give directions for the preparation of medals, and the Persian secretary might direct some of the books already printed under his superintendence to be bound—some handsomely

and some plainly—as prizes. The expense of each, however, should not exceed in all the sum laid down in a former paragraph, including the prime cost of the book. Those prizes might then be distributed to the collectors and to the vaccinators if they should enter into the design; and they might be requested to commence the distribution either generally or gradually and experimentally, as they thought most expedient.

39. The Society should likewise have some of the cheaper publications which are printed under its superintendence properly bound at the expense of Government for distribution as prizes, and the expense of prizes to schoolmasters should be authorized.

40. The expense of the English school at Bombay may be immediately authorized, and the School Society requested to take the management of it; the expense being limited to 2,500 rupees a year.

41. The professorships for English sciences cannot be promised without the sanction of the Honourable the Court of Directors, to whom the question should be referred; unless some part of the money allotted to religious purposes should become disposable, when stipends and prizes may be held out as far as the sum recovered will go. The Commissioner at Puna should be requested to avail himself of any such opportunities.

42. There are many details to be filled up on these plans for which I must depend on the kind assistance of the secretary, and as the correspondence is chiefly with the collectors, the execution may be as well committed to the Revenue as any other department. I am led to wish it should be so on this occasion from the attention Mr. Farish has already given to the subject, and still more from the belief that Mr. Henderson is likely to be intercepted before he can make any great progress in organizing the proposed plans.

43. I can conceive no objection that can be urged to these proposals except the greatness of the expense—to which I would oppose the magnitude of the object. It is difficult to imagine an undertaking in which our duty, our interest, and our honour are more immediately concerned. It is now well understood that in all countries the happiness of the poor depends in a great measure on their education. It is by means of it alone that they can acquire those habits of prudence and self-respect from which all other good qualities spring; and if ever there was a country where such habits are required, it is this. We have all often heard of the ills of early marriages and overflowing population; of the savings of a life squandered on some one occasion of festivity; of the helplessness of the Rayats which renders them a prey to money-lenders; of their indifference to good clothes or houses, which has been urged on some occasions as an argument against lowering the public demands on them; and, finally, of the vanity of all laws to protect them when no individual can be found who has spirit enough to take advantage of those enacted in their favour. There is but one remedy for all this, which is education.

44. If there be a wish to contribute to the abolition of the horrors of self-immolation, and of infanticide, and ultimately to the destruction of superstition in India, it is scarcely necessary now to prove that the only means of success lie in the diffusion of knowledge.

45. In the meantime, the dangers to which we are exposed from the sensitive character of the religion of the natives, and the slippery foundation of our Government, owing to the total separation between us and our subjects, require the adoption of some measure to counteract them, and the only one is, to remove their

prejudices and to communicate our own principles and opinions by the diffusion of a rational education.

46. It has been urged against our Indian Government that we have subverted the States of the East and shut up all the sources from which the magnificence of the country was derived, and that we have not ourselves constructed a single work either of utility or splendour. It may be alleged with more justice that we have dried up the fountains of native talent, and that from the nature of our conquest not only all encouragement to the advancement of knowledge is withdrawn, but even the actual learning of the nation is likely to be lost, and the productions of former genius to be forgotten. Something should surely be done to remove this reproach.

47. It is probably some considerations like these that have induced the Legislature to render it imperative on the Indian Government to spend a portion of its Revenue in the promotion of education; but whatever were the motives that led to it, the enactment itself forms a fresh argument for our attention to the subject. It may be urged that this expense, however well applied, ought not to fall on the Government; that those who are to benefit by education ought to pay for it themselves; and that an attempt to introduce it on any other terms will fail, from the indifference of the teachers and from the want of preparation among those for whose benefit it is intended. This would be true of the higher branches of education among a people with whom sound learning was already in request; but in India our first and greatest difficulty is to create that demand for knowledge, on the supposed existence of which the objection I have mentioned is founded.

48. With regard to the education of the poor, *that* must, in all stages of society, be in a great measure the

charge of the Government. Even Adam Smith (the political writer, of all others, who has put the strictest limits to the interference of the Executive Government, especially in education) admits the instruction of the poor to be among the necessary expenses of the sovereign; though he scarcely allows any other expense, except for the defence of the nation and the administration of justice.

49. I trust, therefore, that the expense would be cheerfully incurred, even if it were considerable and permanent; but that of the schools is to be borne by the villages; the prizes and professors by funds already alienated; the press, as the demand for books increases, may be left to pay itself; and when the plans I have proposed shall once have been fully organized, I hope that the whole of the arrangement, so beneficial to the public, will be accomplished without any material expense to the Company.

50. The immediate expense may be considered according to the different branches which I have suggested.

51. The expense of the native secretary and the head schoolmaster is to be met in part by a reduction to the same amount in the allowances to persons now employed in superintending native publications, enough having been done in that way. There will remain about 350 rupees a month to be paid.

52. The allowances to the four vaccinators, if accepted, will be 7,200 rupees a year. The prizes are for the most part books, the charge for which will be accounted for under that head; that for medals will not be considerable, and that of the prizes to schoolmasters may be guessed at 2,000 rupees a year.

53. I do not think we shall be required to incur a greater expense in printing, even for the first year, than we now incur for that purpose; and although the

rewards for translations are considerable, I think the chance of their being often demanded extremely small —perhaps three a year of different value, in all about 4,000 or 5,000 rupees, is the most we can expect—but we have the satisfaction to know that any increase in this branch of expenditure will bear an exact proportion to the extent of the success and utility of that part of the present plan. This expense might also at any time be stopped by advertising that no more rewards would be given after a certain time. Six months' warning should, however, be given to allow people to complete any translations they had begun on.

54. I have already drawn one example from the liberality of the supreme Government. I may now add, as applicable to the whole question, that, in addition to large subscriptions to education societies, the Governor-General in Council has lately allotted the whole of the town duties, amounting to about six lacs of rupees, to local improvements, of which the schools form a most important branch.

55. Annexed is a memorandum which Mr. Farish was so good as to draw up at my request, and which contains much information and many valuable suggestions. I have already availed myself of many of the ideas thrown out in it. The following points, however, still remain to be noticed and recommended:

Remarks on Mr. Farish's Memo.

> The importation of types and sale of them at a cheap rate, with a view to encourage printing;
>
> The allotment of prizes for essays in the vernacular languages of India, and for improvements in science;
>
> The annual report by each collector on the state of the schools;
>
> The obligation on villages to pay for school-

books after the first supply, or (as that might prevent their applying for them) the obligation to pay for such as were lost or destroyed.

56. Some of the other plans suggested seem to me more doubtful. The payment of schoolmasters in proportion to the number of boys taught is in itself highly advisable; but in the present state of our superintendence it would lead to deceptions, while the payment of a very small fixed stipend will keep a schoolmaster to his trade, and his dependence on the contributions of his scholars for the rest of his maintenance will secure his industry.

57. It is observed that the missionaries find the lowest castes the best pupils. But we must be careful how we offer any special encouragement to men of that description. They are not only the most despised, but among the least numerous of the great divisions of society; and it is to be feared that if our system of education first took root among them, it would never spread further, and that we might find ourselves at the head of a new class superior to the rest in useful knowledge, but hated and despised by the castes to whom these new attainments would always induce us to prefer them. Such a state of things would be desirable, if we were contented to rest our power on our army or on the attachment of a part of the population, but is inconsistent with every attempt to found it on a more extended basis.

58. To the mixture of religion even in the slightest degree with our plans of education I must strongly object. I cannot agree to clog with any additional difficulty a plan which has already so many obstructions to surmount. I am convinced that the conversion of the natives must infallibly result from the diffusion of knowledge among them. Fortunately, they are not

aware of the connections, or all attacks on their ignorance would be as vigorously resisted as if they were on their religion. The only effect of introducing Christianity into our schools would be to sound the alarm, and to warn the Brahmins of the approaching danger. Even that warning might perhaps be neglected as long as no converts were made; but it is a sufficient argument against a plan that it can only be safe as long as it is ineffectual, and in this instance the danger involves not only the failure of our plans of education but the dissolution of our empire.

59. I take this opportunity of adverting to the remarks offered by the Honourable the Court of Directors on the institution of the Native College at Puna. Before I enter on the general merits of the question, I beg to notice three particular objections which have occurred to the Honourable Court, and which I trust I may be able to remove.

Native College at Puna.

60. The Honourable Court is pleased to observe in Paragraphs 20 and 21, that we have taken it for granted, without inquiry, that a favourable impression would be made on the minds of the natives by the institution of a college; but that experience has shown in other places that no such effect is produced. It may, however, admit of a doubt, supposing the institutions alluded to—the colleges of Benares and Calcutta, for instance—to excite no visible feeling at the present moment, when they are no longer novelties, and when the spirit of our Government is thoroughly understood, whether they may not yet have produced a most beneficial impression at the time of their first establishment. In the case of the college at Puna, the fact can scarcely be contested. One of the principal objects of the Peshwa's Government was the maintenance of the Brahmins. It is known to the Honourable Court that he annually distributed five lacs of rupees among

that order under the name of the Dakshina; but it must be observed that the Dakshina formed but a small portion of his largesses to Brahmins, and the number of persons devoted to Hindu learning and religion, who were supported by him, exceeded what would readily be supposed. With all the favour that we have shown this class of his dependents, great numbers of them are reduced to distress, and are subsisting on the sale of shawls and other articles, which they received in better times, while others have already reached the extremity of want which follows the consumption of all their former accumulation. Considering the numbers and the influence of this description of people, it surely cannot be reckoned unimportant towards influencing public opinion that such a sum as could be spared should be set aside for their maintenance; and as it is the object of our enemies to inculcate the opinion that we wish to change the religion and manners of the Hindus, it seems equally popular and reasonable to apply part of that sum to the encouragement of their learning.

61. The Honourable Court has on these grounds been pleased to approve of the partial continuance of the Dakshina; but by the approbation expressed of Mr. Prendergast's objections to the college on the score of expense (Paragraph 32), the Honourable Court appears to understand that a new and considerable addition to our charges is to be occasioned by that institution. The fact, however, is that the whole expense of the college has been saved out of the Dakshina, and not one rupee has been expended for the encouragement of learning that was not already required to prevent popular discontent.*

* The accompanying statement shows that when the college is complete, nineteen professors are maintained and stipends allowed to one hundred of the students at an annual expense of 15,320 rupees.

62. I may here observe that I must have expressed myself indistinctly in my report, as the Honourable Court has understood my sentiments to be adverse to an institution like the present. It was my intention in the passage quoted in Paragraph 33 to say that instead of expending two lacs of rupees on religious charges, including two colleges, I intended to allot 50,000 rupees to the Dakshina, giving the prizes as much as possible to proficients in law, mathematics, etc., to support a certain number of professors who might teach those sciences, and to circulate a few well-chosen books. The only deviations from this plan that have taken place are that the professors have been paid out of the funds allotted to the Dakshina, and that some of those appointed are meant to teach Hindu divinity and mythology. It cannot be denied that this is an unprofitable part of the establishment, and it is to these branches of learning that Mr. Chaplin alludes when he says that some are worse than useless; but we must not forget that we are founding (or rather keeping up with modifications) a seminary among a most bigoted people, where knowledge has always been in the hands of the priesthood, and where science itself is considered as a branch of religion. In such circumstances, and supporting the expense from a fund devoted to religious purposes, I do not think we could possibly have excluded the usual theological professorships without showing a hostility to the Hindu faith which it was our object to avoid, and irritating those prejudices of the people which it was the professed design of the institution to soothe or to remove. I trust these arguments may be satisfactory to the Honourable Court; but at all events I may venture to assure it that the measure was not undertaken without very full investigation of its probable effect, and that I am rather afraid that my inquiries while

Commissioner in the Deccan, may have led the Mahrattas to expect some more important measures in favour of the learned of their nation than it has been found expedient to carry into execution.

63. I come now to the question whether, considering the establishment of the college, without reference to the conciliation of the people, it was desirable for its own sake to encourage the learning of the country. It must be clearly understood that the question is not whether we are to encourage Brahmin learning or European learning, but whether we are to encourage Brahmin learning or none at all. The early part of this minute has shown that we do not possess the means of teaching in the native languages the very rudiments of European sciences; and that if we did possess them, we should find few or none among the natives who are disposed or fitted to receive our instructions. The only point to discuss therefore is, whether or not the knowledge now in existence is to be allowed to be extinguished. It may be supposed that as Hindu learning formerly subsisted independent of our aid, it might continue to do so without our incurring the expense of a college; but this conclusion would be entirely erroneous. The Dakshina, which has already been mentioned, was expressly designed to encourage learning: it formerly amounted to eight or ten lacs of rupees, and though Bajee Row reduced the expenses, he still gave a small sum to each of 50,000 Brahmins, besides large prizes to all who distinguished themselves by their learning. Both he and all his sirdars and ministers employed many learned Brahmins in various offices connected with the Hindu ritual; and all, on a religious principle, allowed stipends and grants of land to many others for whose services they had no call. Add to this that learning was a certain title to

the countenance of the great and to the respect of the people, and we may estimate the incentives to the acquisition of it which were destroyed by our conquest. It is true that this encouragement may not have been judiciously directed, but the effects of it on the whole were beneficial, and such as I cannot but think that it is still desirable to preserve. A class of men was maintained whose time was devoted to the cultivation of their understanding; their learning may have been obscure and degenerate, but still it bore some affinity to real science, into which it might in time have been improved. They were not, perhaps, much inferior to those monks among whom the seeds of European learning were long kept alive; and their extinction, if it did not occasion the loss of much present wisdom, would have cut off all hope for the future.

64. These arguments are founded on the supposition that the Puna College was always to remain unaltered, but this was by no means a necessary consequence of the institution; when once the college had become an established place of resort for Brahmins, it would be easy to introduce by degrees improvements into the system of education, and thus render the institution a powerful instrument for the diffusion of civilization. Some such alterations are suggested in the course of this minute, and others must be the fruit of time, and cannot be adopted until we have instruments better fitted to impart instruction as well as auditors better prepared to receive it.

65. At no time, however, could I wish that the purely Hindu part of the course should be totally abandoned. It would surely be a preposterous way of adding to the intellectual treasures of a nation to begin by the destruction of its indigenous literature; and I cannot but think that the future attainments of the

natives will be increased in extent as well as in variety by being, as it were, engrafted on their own previous knowledge, and imbued with their own original and peculiar character.

66. The attention of the Honourable Court has been attracted to the appointment among others of a professor of poetry. That class was admitted without much reflection as one that exists in all Hindu colleges. At first sight it seems of little practical utility, but on a closer examination it will probably appear worthy of being looked on with more favour. The Honourable Court are aware how large a portion of the Hindu literature is formed by Sanscrit poetry. It is this part which seems to have the most intrinsic merit, and which has called forth the enthusiastic admiration of no mean judges among ourselves. It is this part also which it is both most practicable and most desirable to preserve. Even without the example and assistance of a more civilized nation, the science possessed by every people is gradually superseded by their own discoveries as they advance in knowledge, and their early works fall into disuse and into oblivion. But it is otherwise with their poetry; the standard works maintain their reputation undiminished in every age, they form the models of composition and the fountains of classical language; and the writers of the rudest ages are those who contribute the most to the delight and refinement of the most improved of their posterity.

67. The Honourable Court draws anticipations unfavourable to the college at Puna from the ill success of those at Calcutta and Benares; but I am not sure that such a fact, even admitted in its utmost extent, would form an argument against the plan adopted. Every institution is liable to fall in time into neglect and inefficiency; and of all others the

most liable are those which have the maintenance of learning for their object. Other establishments derive strength from their connection with the transactions of common life, but those for the cultivation of letters have no such support, and it is for this reason that the aid of Government is required to enable them to subsist. It would perhaps be giving way too readily to despondency to suppose that because the colleges in Bengal have admitted of some abuses, that they neither have been nor will be of great utility. In the want of leisure for careful superintendence among the Europeans such establishments must be exposed to fluctuations. They will be neglected under one Government. They will be reformed under another; and on the whole they will go on and flourish, a monument of the genius of the great man who planned them in the midst of pressing difficulties and dangers, and of the liberality of the Honourable Court which has supported them, notwithstanding occasional discouragement and temporary ill success.

68. Having been led so far into the consideration of the despatch of the Honourable the Court of Directors, I shall proceed to that part which relates to the college which it was intended to establish at the Residency for the education of young civil servants; and I shall propose such a substitute as occurs to me for the plan which has been forbidden by the Court.

College for young Civil Servants.

69. The great advantages of a college are, that it affords the best opportunities of instruction both from European professors and native munshis, that it supplies books, that it affords some superintendence over the conduct of the young men, so that in the event of idleness or dissipation it can be checked before it has had time to reach any very injurious pitch. The exam-

inations, rewards, and degrees of honour complete the advantages of the college system.

70. Its disadvantages are that it brings young men too much together, that it detains them at the Presidency, and, above all, that by regulating and watching over a young man's studies it takes from him the stimulus which he would derive from the consciousness that his good or ill success was in his own hands.

71. These advantages are so great that they in some measure reconcile me to the loss of the proposed college, as far, at least, as the young civil servants are concerned.

72. We must now endeavour, as well as our means permit, to unite the benefits and avoid the disadvantages of both plans of instruction.

73. With the aid of European professors it is necessary we should dispense, but something might be done to increase the number of native munshies, provided it could be effected without so great an addition as would render their business insufficient to support properly qualified men. If they could not be found here, men with every requisite qualification might easily be procured from Calcutta. On this subject we could not perhaps do better than consult the gentlemen who have hitherto had the goodness to examine the students. The same gentlemen might be requested to state what they conceived to be the best books for young students, and means might be taken to procure sufficient numbers from Calcutta, or to print them here. Superintendence will not be required if we can succeed in preserving the impression that young men themselves at present entertain of the importance of their acquiring a sufficient knowledge to enable them to pass the examination. If a young man knows that such a trial must be submitted to before he can enter on the advantages of his pro-

fession, and that he has nothing to trust to for carrying him through it but his own industry and attention, it is not too much to expect that those qualities will be excited.

74. The examinations, I understand, are at present much easier than those in Calcutta. Something might be added to the difficulty, but it ought not to be so great as either to discourage the student or to detain him too long among the temptations of a Presidency, and at a distance from the active employments of the service.

75. The grammatical part of the languages should be particularly attended to. If that be once completely mastered, the rest must follow from practice.

76. The accompanying note by Captain Ruddell, one of the Examiners to the College of Fort William, will show the plan pursued there.

77. The whole of this plan depending on the examination, it becomes necessary to take care that it shall be effectual. We have hitherto been able to accomplish the object by the voluntary assistance of such gentlemen as have happened to possess the requisite qualifications at the Presidency; but such a casual aid can scarcely be relied on in a matter of so much importance, especially after the regulation Committee shall have been dissolved.

78. The best plan will probably be to appoint a junior member to be also secretary, with such a salary as may secure the occasional services of an eminent linguist. This gentleman, with the Persian secretary, will always make us sure of two efficient members, and we may trust to accident for a third.

79. The Examining Committee may continue to meet as at present, once in three months, and every student should be required, at the first meeting after

his arrival, to declare whether it is his intention to stand the examination at the next meeting. If such should not be his intention, he should immediately be appointed to a station up the country, as has been ordered by the Court of Directors. I think this better than sending every young man up the country at once, according to the letter of the Court's order, because much time is lost and expense incurred in the journey; and if a young man has a disposition to study, it is better that he should at once have done with the Presidency, and enter on the duties of his profession.

80. It has occurred to me to make it obligatory on every student to pass an examination in Marathi, or in Gujarathi, as well as in Hindustani; and experience has shown that, without such a rule, those languages will not be studied. My unwillingness to keep young men at the Presidency, however, induces me to abandon that proposal, and to recommend in its stead the publication of a rule that no young man shall henceforward be promoted to the second step in his line (whether from Assistant-Registrar to Registrar, or from third Assistant-Collector to second) until he has been examined in the language of the district where he has been stationed. This second examination, however, might be conducted by a committee on the spot.

81. All these expedients are designed to secure a bare sufficiency of knowledge to provide for the discharge of ordinary duties. To obtain higher proficiency, other measures must be devised; and, for that purpose, I know no means more likely to be effectual than the system of prizes already in use in Calcutta. I subjoin a copy of the statute on that subject, and I would have it understood that a separate prize will be given for each language; so that if any one obtains the required

proficiency in three languages, he will receive 2,400 rupees instead of 800.

82. It is my anxious wish that the higher degrees of those prizes should be thrown open to military men. It is the encouragement of Oriental learning rather than the transaction of business that they are designed to promote, and it cannot be the object of Government to exclude any labourers from a field the extent of which is so much beyond our power of cultivation.

83. The orders of the Court of Directors to the Supreme Government are, however, so positive against the admission of military men, that I can only propose the address of an earnest representation to the Honourable Court to induce them to permit its adoption.

NARRATIVE

OF

PROCEEDINGS RELATING TO THE MURDER OF GANGADHAR SHASTRI,

THE

GAIKWAR'S MINISTER DEPUTED TO PUNA.

NARRATIVE

OF

PROCEEDINGS RELATING TO THE MURDER OF GANGADHAR SHASTRI,

THE

GAIKWAR'S MINISTER DEPUTED TO PUNA.

Narrative respecting the murder of the Gaikwar's Minister.

Hostilities with the Peshwa.

TRIMBAKJI DENGLE, in whose conduct the late discussions with the Court of Puna have originated, was first appointed to carry on the communications between the Peshwa and the Resident, after the notification of the recall of Gangadhar Shastri to Baroda, and the suspension by the British Government of its arbitration of the disputes between the Peshwa and the Gaikwar. Trimbakji, who had been a menial servant of the Peshwa, and had found some opportunities of rendering his Highness essential service, had always enjoyed a large portion of his master's confidence, and became by this appointment the real and efficient Minister of the State of Puna, although Sadashiv Maenkshwar still retained the rank and designation of First Minister. The effects of the elevation of his Highness's favourite to a situation of such power and importance were soon discovered in an entire change of the internal policy of the Court of Puna, and in repeated infractions of the Treaty of Bassein; all of which were, from time to time, reported to the Governor-General, and on one occasion brought to the notice of the Peshwa's Government in a detailed and forcible remonstrance, addressed by Mr. Elphinstone to his Highness's Ministers. The Resident had, from the unfavourable opinion which he entertained of Trimbakji's character, and the knowledge which he possessed of the motives which led to his appointment to be Minister (as fully explained in the Resident's letter, dated the 27th May, 1815), anticipated the probability of the British Government being soon involved in discussions with the State of Puna. These changes in the internal policy of that Court, together with the apprehensions which Mr. Elphinstone had of the consequences to which they might lead, were submitted to the notice of the Governor-General soon after the nomination of Trimbakji to conduct the communications between the Peshwa's Government and the Residency.* These expectations were soon realized, although in consequence of events entirely unexpected.

It is known that mutual claims have long depended between the Government of the Peshwa and that of the Gaikwar, arising out of the former connection between those States. By the provisions of the treaties concluded between the British Government and the Peshwa and Gaikwar respectively, the British Government is bound to arbitrate these claims. A further subject of discussion arose respecting the farm of Ahmedabad, comprehending the principal portion of the Peshwa's lands in Gujarat, which had been granted to the Gaikwar on a lease of ten years; the term of the lease being nearly expired, and the renewal of it being an object of considerable importance both to the British and the

* 25th March, 1815.

Gaikwar's interests in Gujarat, a negotiation was opened for the purpose of endeavouring to obtain it. With this question were connected others referring to the Peshwa's interest in Katiawar, the whole forming a subject of considerable delicacy and moment, in which the honour and interests of the British Government were directly concerned.

It was very desirable that the Government of Puna and Baroda should endeavour to come to an understanding on all these points by direct negotiation; and that the arbitration of the British Government should not be resorted to, except in the event of a failure of those endeavours. This course was accordingly recommended; and after an effectual attempt to accomplish a satisfactory arrangement through the agency of the Gaikwar's Vakil at Puna, whose measures were counteracted by every species of intrigue, both there and at Baroda, instigated unquestionably by Trimbakji, who had a personal interest in the resumption of the Peshwa's direct authority in Gujarat, it was determined that Gangadhar Shastri, the Gaikwar's principal Minister, should be deputed to Puna to bring matters to a close. He accordingly proceeded to Puna in the character of a public Minister, and under the declared protection and guarantee of the British Government, the renewal of the lease of Ahmedabad was positively rejected by the Peshwa, and the lands delivered over to his Highness's officers. Every possible delay, procrastination, and evasion were thrown in the way of the negotiation of the other depending points; at length, with the concurrence of the Resident, he determined to retire from Puna, leaving the unadjusted questions to be arbitrated by the British Government. A remarkable change in the conduct of the Peshwa and his Minister Trimbakji, and in their demeanour towards the

Shastri, induced him to suspend this intention. His Highness and the Minister now began to show extraordinary marks of favour and kindness to Gangadhar Shastri, and to endeavour by every means in their power to conciliate his regard and confidence; his Highness even went so far as to propose that one of his daughters should be married to the Shastri's son, and the preparations for the marriage were in some progress. Hopes of an early adjustment of all the depending questions, on terms which the Shastri thought it would be for his master's interest to accept, were also held out; deceived by these appearances, the Shastri, with the consent of the Resident, deferred his departure from the Peshwa's Darbar. He accompanied his Highness and the Minister on a pilgrimage to Nasik, whither the Resident accompanied the Court, and he returned with the Peshwa to Puna; and thence proceeded on a visit of devotion to Pandharpur, at the earnest entreaty of the Peshwa and Trimbakji, leaving most of his attendants at Puna, at their desire.

On the night of the 14th July, the Shastri received a message from Trimbakji, entreating him to come to the temple and perform his devotions. Being indisposed, the Shastri declined the invitation, which was three times renewed with increased earnestness. Yielding at length to these entreaties, he repaired to the temple, attended by only four or five persons altogether. Having performed his devotions, and conversed for a few minutes with Trimbakji, he left the temple to return home; and had only got a short distance from it, when he was attacked and killed by five armed men who came from the temple, and immediately ran away towards the same place after perpetrating the murder. The particulars of this affair are detailed in a despatch from the Resident at Puna, dated 5th September; and being supported by evidence, left no room to doubt that Trimbakji was implicated in the guilt of the Shastri's assassination. The anxiety shown by Trimbakji for the Shastri's attendance in the temple on the night of his assassination; his desire that he should be accompanied but by few people; the total absence of all investigation on the part of the Peshwa's Government, after the murder had been perpetrated, notwithstanding the atrocity with which it was marked; and above all, the fact of no measures having been taken for the arrest of Bhagwant Ráw and Bandoji, who were at Pandharpur, and on whom suspicion immediately lighted as being the known personal and political enemies of the deceased—seemed, in the general opinion, to be circumstances which irresistibly fixed the guilt on Trimbakji. The Peshwa himself did not escape the imputation of having instigated or approved the murder.

Mr. Elphinstone, who was at Ellora when he learned the murder of the Shastri, immediately addressed the Peshwa,* acquainting him with his intention of returning to Puna without delay, and calling on his Highness to institute an early and serious investigation of the case, with a view to discover and punish the assassins of the Minister of an ally of the British Government, who had come to his Highness's Court under the express guarantee of the former. Mr. Elphinstone at the same time directed Captain Pottinger, his assistant, whom he had left in charge of the Residency at Puna, to take immediate measures for the security of the persons of the rest of the Baroda Mission; and authorized him, should such a step appear to be necessary for their protection, to invite them to encamp in the neighbourhood of the British Residency. Mr. Elphinstone's representations were enforced in a letter addressed

* 25th July.

by the Governor-General to the Peshwa,* soon after his Lordship became acquainted with the tragical event at Pandharpur. Mr. Elphinstone also received his Lordship's instructions in detail with respect to the course which he was to pursue, in the event of his demand to the Peshwa for the discovery and punishment of the murderers being complied with, resisted, or evaded by his Highness. The refusal or the evasion of our demands would unquestionably place the Court of Puna in a state of enmity with the British Government. Under a supposition that either of these courses might be pursued by the Peshwa, from a belief of Trimbakji being the author of the guilt, Mr. Elphinstone, though he was enjoined not to precipitate hostilities with his Highness, was directed not to relax in the prosecution of our demands, which could not be retracted with dignity or security. His attention was also particularly drawn to the importance of preventing the escape of Trimbakji from Puna, either with or without the knowledge of the Peshwa; and as it was possible that his Highness himself might endeavour to withdraw from his capital, it was also recommended that every opposition should be made to this step should his Highness purpose to adopt it. In order to enable Mr. Elphinstone to follow this line of conduct with effect, he was authorized, in addition to the control which he already possessed over the Puna subsidiary force, to make requisition for military aid to the Governments of Fort St. George and Bombay, and to Colonel Doveton, should the progress of events appear to him to require this procedure.

Notwithstanding the urgent demand made by Mr. Elphinstone for an inquiry into the circumstances of the murder, and the punishment of the criminals when they should be discovered, no steps towards an in-

* 15th August.

vestigation were taken either by the Peshwa or his Minister, during their continuance at Pandharpur. As the general voice pointed at Trimbakji as being the instigator of the crime, and from the tone of Mr. Elphinstone's remonstrance to the Peshwa, it was expected that he would not long delay a declaration of the sentiments which he entertained on the subject, extraordinary precautions were taken by his Highness and Trimbakji for the security of their persons. Before the death of the Shastri, the Peshwa had already adopted strong measures for his own protection, which, after the murder, were redoubled. Now troops were entertained and assembled from a distance, on purpose to guard his Highness; and when he travelled, his person was attended, contrary to his usual practice, by a large body of armed men. The entry of the Peshwa into his capital was marked by every symptom of distrust and anxiety. He arrived in a close palankin without giving notice of his approach, and without being met by any of his chiefs. At night strong guards were posted both at his palace and at the house of Trimbakji. It happened also that his arrival at Puna was on the day of a great festival, on which thousands of Brahmins were accustomed to attend in order to receive charity from his Highness, who had hitherto never failed to be present. On this occasion, however, of its recurrence, he was not present. These extraordinary precautions were adopted, as Mr. Elphinstone subsequently learned, in consequence of the fear which the Peshwa and Trimbakji entertained of being assassinated by some of the soldiers of Gangadhar Shastri, who had remained at Puna with Bapu Mairal. After his Highness's arrival at the city, the levies of new troops, and the assemblage of those already in his service, in the vicinity of Puna, continued as before. These measures, which had been before carried on with secrecy, were more openly adopted after Mr. Elphinstone had publicly demanded the surrender of Trimbakji to the British Government.

On learning that no attention had been paid to his first remonstrance from Ellora, and having become possessed of information which left in his mind no doubt of Trimbakji's guilt. Mr. Elphinstone resolved not to delay publicly charging the Minister with the crime of having instigated the murder of the Shastri, and calling on the Peshwa for his immediate imprisonment. Mr. Elphinstone judged that this demand, the advance of which he regarded to be sooner or later inevitable, could then be made with the greatest effect, and the best prospect of success. The mind of the public, as has been above observed, was fully impressed with the conviction of the Minister's guilt; Trimbakji had not had time to work on the feelings of the Peshwa to subdue the popular clamour which was loud against him, and to silence or remove the most formidable of his enemies; and Mr. Elphinstone, foreseeing that the instructions of the Governor-General, when they arrived, would be to call on the Peshwa for justice, deemed that no period could be more advantageous for making such a demand, as the subsidiary force could at that moment be spared from the frontier, and might return to its cantonments at Sirur without creating suspicion.* The considerations by which Mr. Elphinstone was guided in the line of proceedings which he adopted were submitted in detail to the Governor-General and received the most unqualified approbation of his Lordship, whose views on the whole subject he had correctly anticipated.†

* Mr. Elphinstone's despatch, dated 16th August.
† Mr. Adams's despatch, dated 10th September.

Mr. Elphinstone at first determined to take no other precaution against any attack which Trimbakji might make when his case became desperate, than to place the brigade at Puna and the troops at the Residency upon the alert, and to order one of the battalions at Puna to be relieved, by which means he might command a reinforcement by the detention of the relieved battalion; but after communication with Colonel Smith, he resolved to recall the subsidiary force to Sirur, a measure which, in his judgment, appeared to be indispensably necessary, on account of the very small number of troops then at Puna, and of that detachment being wholly dependent on the city of Puna for its necessary supplies of all descriptions. Mr. Elphinstone communicated the return of the subsidiary force to its usual cantonments to the Peshwa, in the manner which appeared to him to be the least calculated to excite alarm or anxiety on the part of his Highness. In order more securely to enable them to send off the family of the late Shastri to Baroda, Bapu Mairal, and the rest of the Mission, were invited to encamp in the neighbourhood of the British Residency, which they at length effected, though not altogether without difficulty, in consequence of a mutiny, supposed to have been excited by the intrigues of Trimbakji and Bandoji, having broken out among some of their troops, who, making a want of pay the pretext for their disaffection, were readily joined by the other. Mr. Elphinstone happily succeeded in suppressing this mutiny without being compelled to resort to force for the protection of the Baroda Mission, a measure which might, in the state of irritation which then prevailed, have led to immediate hostilities between the British troops and those of the Peshwa.

Soon after the Peshwa's return to Puna, Mr. Elphinstone requested an audience of his Highness, which was on various pretexts put off. The Resident accordingly determined to discontinue his applications for permission to wait on the Peshwa, and to adopt some other mode of apprising his Highness of what he wished to communicate. He at length, after some difficulty, succeeded in causing to be conveyed to his Highness a paper containing a direct charge against Trimbakji, and demanding his immediate imprisonment, as well as that of Bandoji and Bhagwant Ráw. Mr. Elphinstone had originally intended to have presented this writing to his Highness, had he obtained the audience which he sought. It commenced by stating his anxiety to have been permitted to visit the Peshwa, in order to express to his Highness the surprise with which he had learned that no inquiries had been made into the circumstances of the Shastri's assassination, a neglect which Mr. Elphinstone distinctly imputed to the Peshwa's Ministers, who had not allowed the truth to reach him, and had consequently prevented his Highness from pursuing those measures, which it was doubtless his desire to adopt, in order to mark his abhorrence of the crime which had been perpetrated, and preserve unimpaired the reputation of his Government. Mr. Elphinstone then informed him that the general voice of his subjects had from the first fixed the guilt of this transaction on Trimbakji. He recapitulated the principal facts attending the Shastri's murder, and the conduct of the Minister after that event had taken place, the accuracy of which he undertook to prove when Trimbakji should be placed in imprisonment, as his great power and influence would otherwise deter witnesses from coming forward. Mr. Elphinstone argued at length on the full conviction which all these circumstances must bring, of the guilt of the Minister, and concluded by demanding that Trimbakji, Bandoji, and Bhagwant Raw should be apprehended, and placed in safe custody until his Highness should have an opportunity of consulting with the Governor-General on the subject, and by enforcing these topics by an impressive appeal to the Peshwa's feelings, as a man of religion and a prince. The paper terminated by distinctly apprising his Highness that all communication with the British Government must be interrupted until its demand on this point should be satisfied, and assuring him that, after the apprehension of Trimbakji, the choice of his successor would be entirely left to his Highness, in the confidence of his making such a selection as would tend to the improvement and preservation of the alliance.

A day or two after the Peshwa received this paper,* a message was sent to Mr. Elphinstone from Sadashiv Bháu Mankishwar, acquainting him that the Peshwa had perused the writing with the fullest attention, and had in consequence ordered Bhagwant Raw and Bandoji in confinement; but with regard to Trimbakji, a more full explanation would be made by a native agent, whom the Bhau requested might be sent to him. This message appeared to Mr. Elphinstone to be insincere, as the Bháu from whom it came had long lost his master's confidence, and as the guards placed over the houses of the Bhagwant Raw and Bandoji belonged to Trimbakji, with whom, as Mr. Elphinstone was credibly informed, Bandoji had had an interview the preceding night. To this message, however, he returned an answer which he thought best calculated to soothe the Peshwa, and to prevent his entertaining any alarm for himself, or supposing that it was designed to obtain our demands by force, at the same time that

* 17th August.

no direct allusion was made to the possibility of his Highness having imbibed such apprehensions. The agent whom the Bháu wished to see being disqualified by his age and infirmities from undertaking a negotiation, Mr. Elphinstone sent another person, to whom the Bháu delivered a long message on the part of the Peshwa, professing his attachment to the British Government, but denying the guilt of Trimbakji, offering, however, at the same time, to arrest him immediately if his guilt should be proved, and promising even to punish him as convicted of the crime if Mr. Elphinstone could prove the fact of Trimbakji's three invitations to the Shastri to come to the temple with few attendants. Mr. Elphinstone replied to this message only by repeating that he was prepared to make good his charges, and had already furnished his Highness with sufficient proofs. He therefore again called on him to arrest Trimbakji, and warned him against the danger which menaced the alliance from the violence and intrigues of Trimbakji, as long as he should continue in power.

Discussions of this nature continued for some days, during which Mr. Elphinstone had occasion to address his Highness on the subject of the assemblage of troops at Puna; but the Resident's remonstrance produced no other result than that of the rendezvous of the troops being fixed at twenty or twenty-five miles from Puna instead of the city, the recruiting still going on as before.

During the whole of these discussions, the Peshwa chiefly based his resistance to the demands of the British Government, on the ground of the injustice of arresting a person before he was convicted of the crime which was laid to him. He persevered in maintaining the innocence of Trimbakji, still promising at the same time to arrest him, if Mr. Elphinstone could substantiate his charges against him. His Highness chiefly dwelt on the circumstance asserted by the Resident, of Trimbakji's having three times invited Gangadhar Shastri to come to the temple with few attendants. His Highness repeatedly declared, that if these summonses could be proved to have been made, he was ready to consider Trimbakji guilty, and to punish him as such. The Peshwa's arguments were forcibly combated by Mr. Elphinstone, by an appeal to the facts which were within his knowledge, and of which he was prepared to come forward with the proof whenever the removal of Trimbakji from the Peshwa's Councils should do away with the dread which must otherwise prevent witnesses from coming forward to depose what they know against a minister, to the violent consequences of whose power and intrigues they were exposed. During the course of these discussions it appeared evident that the Peshwa had become so infatuated as to resolve to make common cause with his favourite, and to stand or fall with him.

Preparations were at one time made to facilitate the flight of Trimbakji, who was to excite a feigned rebellion, in which he was to receive the concealed support of the Peshwa. At another time, several modes of compromise were offered to Mr. Elphinstone, which being inconsistent with the dignity and security of the British interests at the Court of Puna, were, of course, rejected. When intelligence was received of the commotions at Hyderabad, the Darbar assumed a higher tone; and it was then determined that Trimbakji should remain at Court, and in office, and that the demands should be resisted; the Peshwa even went so far as to cause a message to be conveyed to Mr. Elphinstone, which was couched in terms approaching to menace. This procedure, together with an attempt which was at the same time made to obtain false depositions relative to the circumstances of the Shastri's murder, clearly evinced, on the part of the Court of Puna, a disposition to break the alliance. Mr. Elphinstone opposed to this conduct his usual firmness and caution; the intrigues and attempts at deception practised by the Darbar were resisted firmly. Fearing that the exaggerated accounts which the Peshwa had received of the disturbances at Hyderabad might encourage the Peshwa in his scheme of resistance to the demands of the British Government, and impel him to quit Puna, and at once to throw himself into the situation of an enemy of the Company, Mr. Elphinstone seriously warned his Highness against the course which he might be advised to pursue from the violence and intrigues of his favourite, whose interests would alone be forwarded, while the rupture of the alliance would be rendered inevitable, and with it the ruin of his Highness's reputation and Government. Mr. Elphinstone also ordered the subsidiary force to advance to the vicinity of Puna, communicating this circumstance to the Peshwa, and observing that as the tone of the Darbar appeared to be altered, and troops were assembled from all quarters, it became necessary on his part to adopt corresponding measures of precaution. On the 4th September, Mr. Elphinstone having received instructions of the Governor-General,* communicated to the Peshwa the decision which his Lordship had passed, in the event, which had now occurred, of no inquiry having been made into the circumstances of the Shastri's murder; again warned his Highness of the danger which he was incurring by his blind support of his unprincipled favourite, and assured him that the British Government would not desist from its demands for the surrender of Trimbakji.

* Mr. Adams's despatch, dated 15th August.

After a long consultation with some of his principal followers, the Peshwa sent a message to Mr. Elphinstone, informing him that he had determined to imprison Trimbakji, on condition that the British Government should not demand his capital punishment, or his surrender to its own officers, and that no further inquiry should be made into the circumstances of the transaction; these conditions were, of course, rejected by the Resident, who persisted in his demand for the unqualified surrender of Trimbakji to the British Government; but in order to allay any fears which the Peshwa might entertain for himself, Mr. Elphinstone made an unofficial intimation to the Bháu,* that when once Trimbakji should be in our custody, no further inquiry would be judged necessary. In the meantime Trimbakji, after having had an interview with the Peshwa, and received from his Highness assurance of a nature to soothe his feelings, and promises of protection to his family, was sent off to Wassantghar, a hill-fort near Satara; the judicious and persevering firmness of Mr. Elphinstone, aided by the Peshwa's own reflections on the risk which he was incurring of a rupture with the British Government, prevailed on his Highness to comply with the Resident's demands. After a conference with Major Ford, the officer commanding his brigade of regular troops, with whom he had frequently communicated during the course of these discussions, and some of his principal advisers, the Peshwa at length declared his assent to the surrender of Trimbakji Dengle to the officers of the British Government, Mr. Elphinstone assuring his Highness that no further inquiry would be considered necessary; that Trimbakji's life would be spared, and that he would

* 5th September.

undergo no severities which were not implied in a strict confinement.

Accordingly a party of Major Ford's brigade received charge of Trimbakji * and escorted him from Wassantghar to Puna, where he was delivered over to a detachment of British troops, † and conducted to Bombay together with Bhagwant Raw and Bandoji, who were to be given up to the officers of the Gaikwar Government. Trimbakji was immediately placed in strict confinement in the Fort of Tanna. During the progress of these discussions there appeared, from the reports of the several Residents, to have been frequent communications between the Darbars of Puna, Scindia, Holkar, and the Rajah of Nagpur. The perverse obstinacy of the Peshwa was considerably encouraged by the intrigues of these chieftains, and by the commotions at the time at Hyderabad.

Extract from a Letter from the Honourable Mountstuart Elphinstone, Resident at the Court of the Peshwa, to the Governor-General; dated 16th August, 1815; referred to in the preceding Narrative.

Letter from Mr. Elphinstone, 16th August, 1815.

I intended to have made your Lordship acquainted with the circumstances of the Shastri's murder, by submitting the detailed account drawn up by the Gaikwar's Vakil, and some other papers; but as those documents were confined to the mere circumstances of the assassination, I find myself obliged to trespass on your Lordship's time with a narrative of the event, and the transactions that led to it. Your Excellency is already well acquainted with the hostility evinced towards the Shastri by a party in

* 19th September. † 26th September.

the Peshwa's Darbar, which was headed by Trimbakji, and encouraged by the Peshwa. Their blood intrigues at Baroda, their demand for a change in the Gaikwar's Government, their negotiation with Bandoji, and the reception of Bhagwant Raw, have all been submitted to your Lordship. At that period the Shastri received frequent intelligence of plans to murder him, which I always encouraged him to treat with disregard, and which for a time were attended with no visible result. This state of things terminated in the rupture of the Gaikwar's negotiation, and the demand for the Shastri's dismission; and it was succeeded by secret overtures from Trimbakji to the Shastri, and by a negotiation between those Ministers, without my participation, for the settlement of the Peshwa's claims. This led to a degree of intimacy and cordiality between Trimbakji and the Shastri, such as I have never known between natives in their situation in life. It was during this period of confidence that Trimbakji avowed to the Shastri that he had, before their reconciliation, been engaged in plans for cutting up his party and for making away with him by assassination. It seems impossible that such an avowal should have been made, unless the reconciliation had been sincere; and I am inclined to believe it was to a certain extent. I imagine that all intentions of acting against the Shastri by direct force were laid aside, and that it was now designed to gain as advantageous terms as possible from the Gaikwar, by working on the ambition and vanity of his Minister, and at the same time to ruin the Shastri with the Gaikwar and the English, by leading him into a line of conduct inconsistent with his duty, or even to get him entirely into the Peshwa's power, by engaging him in his Highness's service. To effect this object, which the Peshwa certainly thought essential to the accomplishment of his views on Gujarat, every means were taken to gain over the Shastri. His Highness offered his sister-in-law in marriage to the Shastri's son, and Trimbakji persuaded the Shastri that it was the Peshwa's wish to invest him with the principal conduct of his affairs, an offer with which the Shastri, being a native of this place, was dazzled, though I do not imagine that he had made up his mind to accept it. At this time it was agreed by the Shastri and Trimbakji that the Peshwa should forego his claims on the Gaikwar for a territorial cession worth seven lacs of rupees, and that as soon as the Gaikwar should consent to this arrangement, the marriage already alluded to should take place. I imagine the Peshwa's Government was sincere in wishing for this arrangement, which would have afforded a present profit and a prospect of further advantages consequent to the ruin of the Shastri. If these plans were really entertained, I imagine they were overturned by an accident that took place at Nasik. At that time the Gaikwar's consent to the proposed cession was hourly expected, and as the marriage was to take place as soon as the news arrived, both parties took their families to Nasik, and much expense was incurred for the purpose of celebrating the ceremony with splendour; but when it appeared that the Gaikwar's consent was not likely to arrive while the Court was at Nasik, the Shastri became anxious to avoid a connection which would have had an appearance of neglecting his master's interests to provide for his own; and accordingly he desired that the marriage might be put off for the present. About the same time the Shastri declined engaging in the Peshwa's negotiations with me in consequence of my rejecting his interference, and pointing out in the strongest light the imprudence of his making himself a minister of the

Peshwa. This failure of his designs must have irritated Trimbakji; but, above all, the rejection of the marriage which had been negotiated by Trimbakji, and which could not be broken off or suspended, after the bride had been brought and the preparations had been made, without great disgrace to the Peshwa. Unfortunately the Shastri heightened this feeling by starting other objections to the connection. These affronts, as I understood at the time, made a deep impression on Trimbakji, while his conduct on the occasion was inconsistent and unaccountable. He mentioned the Shastri's conduct to me as an instance of gross breach of faith, and as involving him in the utmost disgrace; but at the same time he professed his entire forgiveness of it, and, in fact, he said little on the subject to the Shastri, but continued to treat him with more apparent kindness and affection than ever. During this journey to Nasik, reports were widely circulated at Puna that the Shastri had been seized by Trimbakji; and as I treated them with entire disregard, I could not but be surprised at the earnestness with which Trimbakji and his agent, Harri Aba, endeavoured to convince me that they were mere popular rumours, and were not founded on any measures or designs of theirs. The journey to Pandharpur soon followed that to Nasik. On this occasion the Shastri peremptorily refused to allow his colleague, Bapu Mairal, to accompany him to Pandharpur, although the latter expressed great fears of his safety. This was naturally attributed to Trimbakji's influence, as that person had all along shown a dread of the wary and circumspect character of Bapu Mairal, and had insisted on his exclusion from the conferences with his colleague. His interposition was more open in prevailing on the Shastri to leave behind the best part of his escort, and in dissuading me from accompanying him in his pilgrimage, and that his Highness wished me not to go on this occasion. On the journey to Pandharpur, Trimbakji was followed by Govind Ráw Bandoji, who had been neglected during the time when the plan was to conciliate the Shastri, but who was still connected with Trimbakji, and who had a person, on his part, stationed with him for his protection. This man came to Pandharpur with great secrecy, but his arrival was discovered by the Shastri immediately before his death. Two days preceding that event, guards were posted and great precautions taken about the temple and the Peshwa's house, and the alarm of the Punnee assassins was once more set on foot. The existence of this conspiracy, of the name of which so much use has been made, has lately been fully disproved by Mr. Russell's inquiries at Hyderabad, and it may therefore be fairly assumed that the Peshwa's alarms on the subject of it are either feigned, or inspired by those about his Highness, to cover any measures the motive of which it is inconvenient to avow. In this case the alarm afforded a pretext for increasing the guards, and a way of accounting for the Shastri's murder. Strict orders were also issued against bringing armed men to the temple. The following account of the occurrences on the day of the Shastri's death is extracted from a narrative which was drawn up by Bapu Mairal, and translated by Captain Pottinger, immediately after the return of the party who had accompanied the Shastri to Pandharpur, and was transmitted to me on my journey from Ellora.

'On the 14th the Shastri went to an entertainment given by Ramchauda Gosai Patankar to the Peshwa, and on his return home complained of fever, and desired that if any person came to request him to go to the temple, they might be told that he was indisposed. In the course of half an hour one Laxuman Pant came, on Trimbakji's behalf, to invite him to join him in his devotions; and he said, "I am unwell, and will not go out to day." Shortly after Trimbakji sent a second messenger to acquaint the Shastri that the Peshwa was to go to the temple next morning, and that he, the Shastri, ought to take advantage of this circumstance and attend prayers, but not to bring many attendants. He returned the former answer. Bapu Chiplonkar, a friend of the Shastri's, and Ráwji Mahratta, a relation, then left the Shastri and walked to the great temple, where they met Trimbakji Dengle, who observed, "I have sent twice to the Shastri to come to prayers; he declines doing so, but I wish you would try him again." Ráwji Mahratta came back to the house occupied by the Shastri, and told him what Dengle had said. He at first observed: "I am unwell;" but on reflection, he became apprehensive of offending Dengle by not complying with his different messages, and therefore he agreed to go. He accordingly set off with two Masháljis,* two personal servants, three Harkárás,† and a Kárkûn‡ of Trimbakji. As he passed among the shops, one of his attendants overheard a man in the crowd ask, "Which is the Shastri?" and another reply, "He who wears the necklace;" but he did not think of observing these people. The Shastri entered the temple, performed his devotions, chatted a few minutes with Trimbakji Dengle, and then proceeded towards his house. He desired three of his people to stay behind with one Cheytun Dass Bava, a kind of preceptor of the Shastri, and a very old man; and he advanced himself, accompanied by Trimbakji

* A link-boy. † A messenger.

‡ Officers under the Zemindars, who keep accounts of the collections.

Dengle's Sepoys, who were in front ten or twelve paces; next came two of the Shastri's own Harkárás, then two Masháljis with lighted torches, and about four paces behind them was the Shastri; one Ramchander Barwe, an inhabitant of Pandharpur and a priest of the temple, had hold of the Shastri's left hand, and Bapu Chiplonkar, the Shastri's friend, was on the opposite side, but a step or two in the rear; these three were followed by the Shastri's two personal servants; and when the party had walked some little way from the temple, three men came running up behind them, as if they were clearing the road for some person by calling out "Pais! Pais!" (Make way! make way!): their left hands were folded up in a cloth, probably intended as a shield, and in each of their right hands there seemed to be a twisted cloth, which is usual for striking people in a crowd, to made them stand aside. One of the assassins struck the Shastri a very violent blow, apparently with the cloth, when it was discovered that he had a sword also in his hand; another seized him by the lock of hair on the crown of his head, to throw him down, and when he was falling the third assassin cut him over the head. Two more men at this juncture rushed from the front of the party, and three of the attendants who attempted to stay by the Shastri were wounded; on which his friends, Masháljis, and followers ran away and left him in the hands of the murderers, who mangled him in the most shocking manner, and one of them exclaimed, "We have now finished him!" This was overheard by one of the wounded men. The assassins then threw down two sword-scabbards and made their escape; and the Shastri's people, who were following with the old man already alluded to, saw five men with naked swords running towards the temple; they also observed the flambeau lying extinguished and smoking on the ground, and became much alarmed; but not knowing what had taken place, two or three of them ran home to the Shastri's house, and learning he was not there, they returned to search for him, and found his corpse in the road almost cut to bits. They took the pieces and carried them home; this was about half-past eight at night. The intelligence was immediately carried to the Peshwa, who ordered additional precautions "about his own person," and shortly one of Trimbakji's people came to inquire what had happened. The police officer also attended to see the corpse, and returned to report to the Peshwa, observing that one of the assassins had been seen near the river, and had thrown down his sword, and had escaped in the crowd; but that the sword had been carried to Trimbakji. The news shortly reached the Gaikwar camp; and some of the principal Sardars came to the town to take measures for burning the Shastri's remains, and obtained permission from Trimbakji to that effect, and likewise an order from his Highness the Peshwa for the Shastri's people to have free ingress and egress to and from the city. The following day some of the Shastri's Kárkûns went to Trimbakji, and told him it behoved him, as the friend of the deceased, and also the Minister of the Peshwa, to make inquiries towards ascertaining the cause of the Shastri's murder; to which Trimbakji answered, "I am doing so; but on whom can I breathe suspicion? I have no clue to guide me." The Kárkûns again observed: "It is due to the Shastri, and also to the honour of your Government, to discover the origin of what has happened." Trimbakji replied in terms of civility, and declared that the Peshwa was greatly grieved by the event that had happened; but that the Shastri was wrong to venture abroad without a number of attendants, fifty or a hundred. The Kárkûns replied: "He considered himself in the house of his friend, and besides, it was not usual to bring many people on such an occasion. You know," added they, "who are the Shastri's enemies; the assassins appeared to be Karnatik men." He replied: "What you say is true; but how could I avert what fate had decreed? There is the Purool Sitaram, and you have placed one of the Gaikwar's Kannoji in the Karnatik, though I cannot take the name of any enemy. You must now look to yourselves, but depend on my friendship. He who protected you all is now no more, and I will do so to the utmost of my power." The Shastri's Kárkûns then left the place, and the following day they obtained, through Trimbakji, the Peshwa's private permission for the Baroda people to return to Puna. It was at the same time intimated to them that they need not attend again at either Trimbakji's quarters or the Peshwa's house.

'The murderers appeared to be dressed in short breeches, such as are worn in the Karnatik, but spoke in the Mahratta language when they exclaimed, as already stated, "We have now finished him!"'

In this narrative it is impossible not to be struck with Trimbakji's solicitude, so disproportionate on the occasion, about the Shastri's coming to the temple, and with the proof that he was expected by the murderers, which, in all the circumstances of the case, was almost impossible to have happened, had they not been acquainted with what was passing between him and Trimbakji. By the question asked in the streets, the murderers appeared to have been posted before he left his house, or they must have been so soon after, for his whole absence up to his death did not exceed three-quarters of an hour. The want of inquiry is also very remarkable; it might have been expected that Trimbakji would have hastened to the spot where the murder was committed, or at all events that he would have sent people to make inquiries from the passengers, to trace out which way the assassins had taken; that he would have summoned the neighbouring shopkeepers and the Shastri's attendants to ascertain the dress and appearance of the murderers; that he would have offered a reward to discover the murderers, and that their detection would have been the principal object of his attention for a considerable time: instead of which he neglected every sort of inquiry, and contented himself with stopping all letters and all news for the first day, after which he arrested several persons for reflecting on him. He allowed the men on whom suspicion would most naturally fall to go unquestioned, and exercised his ingenuity in finding out other persons likely to have committed the murder, and reasons why it should have happened as a matter of course. He then employed himself in writing despatches to his turbulent deputy at Ahmedabad, of which we have yet to hear the effect, and afterwards forbade the Shastri's name to be any longer mentioned. This conduct is the more remarkable from the extraordinary exertions which are made by the police of native Governments, in all cases where the chief has an interest, and the success with which acts of violence are generally kept under in the Peshwa's cities. Bandoji, respecting whom the Peshwa's Minister long affected entire ignorance, is now returned to Puna, where both he and Bhagwant Ráw reside at large; one of the two was, I understand, secretly received on the night before last by Trimbakji, on his way to the temple, from which he this day returned.

'To his Excellency the Earl of Moira, K.G., etc., etc.

'My Lord,

'1. In my last despatch I had the honour to report to your Excellency that Trimbakji Dengle had assembled a body of plunderers about fifty miles from Puna; that a detachment of Gokhles had been sent against them by the Peshwa, and that I expected soon to hear of their dispersion. His Highness's detachment, however, instead of dispersing the rebels has quietly sat down in the midst of the tract throughout which they are dispersed, and the commander has reported that there are no rebels in that part of the country. This language is re-echoed by the Peshwa, who says that he can obtain no intelligence of any assemblage of troops within his territories; and that, anxious as he is to act against them, he must depend on me for finding them out.

Letter from Mr. Elphinstone, 11th March, 1815.

'2. The insurrection thereof has now changed its character, and appears as an attempt of Trimbakji's to recover his power, by carrying on war against the British Government under the protection of his Highness the Peshwa. As these facts can scarcely fail to lead to important consequences, it becomes necessary to show the grounds from which I derive my conviction of them.

'3. It is proper, in the first place, to show my reasons for ascertaining that there are assemblages of troops in the neighbourhood of Mahadeo, which is denied by his Highness. I shall at the same time show that they are headed by Trimbakji. The simple fact of such assemblages, in a very frequented part of the Peshwa's country, and within fifty miles of his own residence, will of itself establish that his Highness is acquainted with the proceeding, and his long connivance and subsequent denial of the existence of it, together with his refusal to act against the troops assembled, will probably be thought a sufficient proof that the design for which they have collected is approved by his Highness.

'4. Early in last January I received intelligence that Trimbakji was at Phultan, in which neighbourhood he appeared to have already passed some time during the months of January and February. I heard from numerous sources that he was in that part of the country, constantly changing his residence between Phultan on the west and Pandharpur on the east, extending his range as far as the forts of Saltore and Mymungar on the south. On the 15th January, the news-writer at Narsingpur announces a rumour that some insurgents are collecting; he confirms this report on the 18th, and specifies that 25 horsemen and 100 foot had assembled between Sirsatwarre and Mahadeo, under a Maratta Sardar, and that another body was at Purandhar, about twenty miles to the east of the last village. On the 20th the same writer mentions another party at Mymungar, and adds a rumour that all are to unite under Trimbakji Dengle. On the 24th he writes that the party at Sirsatwarre has moved to Natepota and Burrud, north of Mahadeo, and that those at Purandhar have encamped between Mahadeo and Mymungar. On the 26th he announces that more troops are collecting, and on the 29th he gives the following account of the disposition of the whole :

'Near Nate Potta and Burrud - - -	500
Near Mahadeo - - - - -	300
Near Mymungar - - - -	600
Near Phultan - - - - -	400
Total,	1,800

Almost the whole of these were foot, and the bulk of them Mánug and Ramoshis (low and lawless castes like

Bhils). At this time I doubted whether the troops assembled were under Trimbakji; or, if they were, for what purpose such a gang could be designed.

'5. From this time till the 18th February, the news-writer continues to report the accession of fresh bodies of infantry to the insurgents, and likewise the commencement of measures for collecting cavalry. He also represents that one of his Harkárás, who was sent for intelligence, had been cut off by the insurgents, and that he himself was in such danger that he had been obliged to take refuge in a fortified house belonging to Sadashiv Mánkeshvar. On the 18th February he writes, that bodies of horse, in parties of from ten to twenty, are moving from all points to join the insurgents at Mahadeo; that the whole country is full of Trimbakji's spies, and that dreadful examples are made of all persons who talk of the preparations of the insurgents. On the 19th he reports the same intelligence, and gives a copy of a paper inviting the services of a particular chief and his troops, and promising a specific rate of pay. Similar papers, he says, are circulated in great numbers. On the 22nd he says, nobody now hesitates to speak of the insurrection, or to say that Trimbakji is at the head of it. He also mentions that the 18th of March is the day fixed for the breaking out of the conspiracy.

'6. Early in February the news-writers and intelligencers at Puna began to communicate intelligence similar to that received from Narsingpur, and by the middle of the month a full confirmation of it was received from two Brahmins, who were sent separately to Mahadeo to collect information. The post-office writer at Jewoor (forty miles from Mahadeo, and about the same distance from Narsingpur) also wrote about the 17th that Trimbakji was at Burrud assembling horse, and that he had got 1,500 into the neighbourhood of Mahadeo. All accounts concurred in representing Trimbakji's vigilance to be very great, and the difficulty of passing through his haunts and those of his adherents to be extreme.

'7. On the 24th a person of some consequence, long connected with the British Government, brought to me a Mahratta chief of a village who had actually enlisted in Trimbakji's service with twenty horse. He said that Trimbakji lived in the jungle apart from his horse, and that he had about 500 Ramoshis at some distance round his person; that he had got from 2,000 to 3,000 horse in different villages near his retreat, under the command of his father-in-law, Rewie Ráw Sindia; that he had many others engaged in his service who were still at their villages, and he particularly mentioned different chiefs of horse in his own neighbourhood, which is on the Nizam's border beyond the River Bhima. He said Trimbakji had given him a small advance of pay, and desired him to remain quiet until after the Holi * (the last day of which was the 7th instant), after which he promised him two months' pay at 40 or 50 rupees a month, according to the goodness of the horse.

'8. On the 25th a private horseman was introduced to me through another channel, who, though in the Peshwa's service, was engaged with Trimbakji. His account agreed in most particulars with that last noticed; but he was a particularly intelligent man, and gave good accounts of the present state and future plans of Trimbakji, which derived credit from his knowledge of Trimbakji's past proceedings. The only part of his information that is at present applicable was that Trimbakji had been near two months in the neigh-

* A Hindu festival.

bourhood of Phultan and Mahadeo; that he had 3,000 horse and 300 foot about him; that he had constant communication with Puna and excellent intelligence; that he had a Vakil from the Pindaris with him, and was in close connection with the Peshwa, who had very extensive intrigues on foot against us in different parts of India; and that Trimbakji was to set up his standard about the 18th March.

'9. On the 1st March, the Narsingpur writer sends accounts of more horse-enlisting for Trimbakji. He specifies as usual the villages where they are quartered, and in many cases the names of the commanders. On the 2nd, he writes that 213,000 rupees have been sent from Pandharpur in the night to Trimbakji. He mentions the names of the persons concerned in sending it, and the spot where a party of horse is stationed for the purpose of furnishing an escort. On the 3rd, one of the Brahmins sent to Mahadeo confirms the accounts of Trimbakji's collecting troops, and adds that a confidential agent of Appa Desái's had had an interview with him; he likewise states that the detachment sent by the Peshwa against the rebels had settled quietly at Natepota, and appeared to be on a friendly footing with the insurgents; the people of the country believed they were sent out at Trimbakji's request. On the same day the post-office writer at Jewoor mentions different places where troops of Trimbakji are posted, and states that much activity prevails in recruiting for him, even about Jewoor; and that considerable quantities of treasure have been sent to him from Pandharpur.

'10. On the 5th I received an overture from a person formerly of some consequence, but whose Jahagir has been sequestrated of late, to say that he had been invited by Trimbakji to raise a large body of horse for him, and offering to give me intelligence, and even to concur in apprehending Trimbakji.

'11. About the beginning of this month a villager came to Colonel Leighton and acquainted him that a body of troops was quartered in his village, on the Nira, and that Trimbakji had many parties in the villages around. I sent out Harkárás with this man, whom he carried in the night to this village, and showed them the horse. He also showed them a smaller party picketed in the wood at some distance from the village; while they were looking out for these a party of horse passed them, travelling with secrecy and by night. They heard everywhere of the intended insurrection, and of parties going by night to join it, and understood everywhere that it was to break out on the 18th March.

'12. On the 6th the post-office writer at Meriteh writes that troops are raising at different places in his neighbourhood, which he specifies are for Trimbakji, and that others are collecting for him to the south of the Krishna. The post-office writers at Sangli on the Krishna, and Puse Sávali, near Satara, also reports the assembly of troops under Dengle, in the hills of Mahadeo.

'13. On the 7th a person came to a broker employed by me to collect intelligence, and wished him to exchange some gold money. By well-managed inquiries the broker discovered that the gold had been issued by Trimbakji to a Pathan chief who had enlisted with him, and whose servant the person who offered the money was. He gave much the same account of the state of Trimbakji's preparations with those already noticed. It is to be observed that numerous accounts represent all Trimbakji's money to be in gold, and constant efforts to be made in all the country from Phultan to the Bhima, to procure silver in exchange for it. I have out many accounts brought by Harkárás, all tending to prove the existence of the preparations I have described, and the notice they have attracted throughout the country; I shall only add that for the last fortnight at least Trimbakji's preparations for an insurrection have been the common topic of conversation in Puna, and that every Kârkûn (clerk) who comes to the Residency, if spoken to on the subject, treats it as one of public notoriety.

'14. It is under these circumstances that his Highness the Peshwa asserts that his local officers have allowed preparations, such as I have described, to go on for two months without noticing them; that his ministers have shut their ears to the common talk of the country and of the capital; that even when his Highness's attention was drawn to the subject, his messengers could learn nothing of these notorious facts; and finally, that a detachment of his troops, under an officer selected for the occasion, could sit down in the centre of Trimbakji's army, and know nothing of its existence. After all this, it is scarcely necessary to bring any further proof of his Highness's knowledge of the insurrection, the existence of which he so strongly denies; but his confidential adviser and intelligencer, Prabhakar Pandit, mentioned it to me long ago, and could scarcely have concealed it from the Peshwa had it really been unknown to his Highness till then; and his Minister, Sadashiva Mánkeshvar, who is not in the secret of the Peshwa's intentions, casually mentioned to Kirshan Ráw early in February that he had heard the insurgents in the Mahadeo Hills intended to attack his fortified house at Temburni; that he had therefore increased the garrison, and had applied to his Highness the Peshwa, who promised him assistance, and who afterwards made a merit with him of sending out Gokhale's detachment, as if it had been done in attention to his wishes.

'15. From all these circumstances I think there remains no doubt that the Peshwa is privy to Trimbakji's conspiracy, and has favoured the progress of it; I say nothing of the constant intelligence I have received of his Highness having continual communication with Trimbakji, of his having sent him considerable sums of money in gold, and of his having had more than one secret interview with Trimbakji himself. These statements, although strongly asserted by many different persons, and though highly probable in themselves, are not sufficiently well established to build upon; but it is certain that troops have been raised for Trimbakji in Puna, that treasure has been sent to him from this; in one very recent instance, an Arab Jamadar, who was reported to have joined the rebels, returned to Puna and told a Mohammedan friend that he had been employed to carry a casket of jewels to Phultan to an adherent of Trimbakji's; that Trimbakji's family and dependents are still in his Highness's favour; that most of them make excursions into the country which, if made without design, are unaccountably indiscreet, and which are constantly reported to be for the purpose of consulting with Trimbakji; that Bhasker Pant, one of Trimbakji's principal officers, who commanded one of the divisions of his force attached to Colonel Smith in 1815, has made repeated journeys of this kind from his Highness's Court at Phulsheher; that he finally left that place shortly before his Highness's return to Puna, and is stated on very good authority to be now with the rebels: his Highness has been unable to answer my repeated demands to be informed what has become of him. His Highness's employment in maturing his plan also accounts for several deviations from his fixed habits, which before excited a good deal of surprise. The first is his journey to Junar, when Trimbakji was supposed to be in that part of the country, soon after Colonel Kingscote's attempt to seize him at Nadgaum; his excuse was, a vow of an annual pilgrimage made when he was in prison, which he had forgotten for the last twenty years to perform; another is, his long residence at Phulsheher, out of the way of observation, and the plans he took to explain his motives to me, frequently complaining that he was detained against his will by his arm, though the distance is only sixteen miles, and his arm was but little bruised. The last is his giving up his annual journeys to Goagur and Kopargaum for the first time, I believe, ever since his restoration, although the excuse of his arm has for some time been removed.

'16. It remains to examine the extent and design of the conspiracy. Long before Trimbakji's release, it was the common opinion in the Mahratta country that the Peshwa would endeavour to revenge the disgrace which he conceived himself to have suffered, by raising up wars and insurrections against the British in which he should not appear himself. It was stated on better authority, and in a less vague form, that his Highness would try all means for Trimbakji's release and restoration; that if he did not succeed by entreaties and temptation, he would try intimidation; and if that failed he would secretly foment insurrections, in the hope of wearying us into a compliance with his wishes. All the plans presented, as precursors to the insurrections, have already been tried, and it is remarkable that the language held by his Highness's avowed agents should closely resemble that made use of by Trimbakji's emissaries—the same entreaties and promises at first, followed by the same absurd attempts at intimidation, and the same anxiety to obtain a categorical answer immediately before the time when the insurrection began to be talked of.

'17. It will be in your Excellency's recollection that on the 3rd of last November the Peshwa sent me a secret message, saying that as he was going to quit Puna for a time, he was desirous to leave his country secure; that Trimbakji would probably create disturbances if not conciliated, and he therefore wished to offer him terms on the part of the British Government, and offered to answer for his faithful observance of them. Considering this message as a threat, or at least an attempt to discover the effect which would be produced on the British Government by Trimbakji's raising an insurrection, I returned such an answer, and sent such messages, public and private, as I conceived most likely to impress on his Highness the impossibility of any insurrection on Trimbakji's part for which his Highness would not have to answer, and the total ruin it would bring on his State if such a proof were to appear of his hostility to the British Government, and infidelity to the alliance. As his Highness entered on the present conspiracy in the face of this remonstrance, and it should seem immediately on receiving it, it must be inferred that he will not easily be deterred from the prosecution of a plan so deliberately formed. The same conclusion may be drawn from the apparent extent of his intrigues. It appears from the intelligence already noticed, that troops are assembling for Trimbakji in the centre and southern parts of his Highness's dominions. Mr. Jenkins' information in November and December last showed that similar levies were made at that time in Berar, under the immediate direction of his Highness's officers at Malghaut, and there are reports strongly corroborated by circumstances that troops are also rising in Khandesh. It is now many months since I heard that his Highness had made some communications to Yashavant Ráw Jiváji, who was once a great freebooter in the Mahratta country. I paid no attention to the report at the time, believing that Yashavant Ráw had been long dead; but not very long after I was surprised to hear that Yashavant Ráw was at the head of a body of freebooters in Khandesh. Contrary to the practice of such gangs, this body has remained quiet ever since, and has not been heard of till this time, but it is now reported in Puna that his Highness has a body of men in Khandesh ready to join Trimbakji, and the last khabar from Khandesh revives the mention of Yashavant Ráw Jiváji, and says he is getting ready to move; all which circumstances agree so well as to make it very probable that the whole proceedings of Yashavant Ráw Jiváji have been directed by his Highness. His Highness's repair of his forts have never entirely been discontinued, and they are now carried on with unusual activity. His Highness's overtures to the Gaikwar, and his intrigues at the Courts of Scindia and Holkar, have been often brought to your Excellency's notice. The orders lately issued to the Vakils afford no proof at all that these intrigues are discontinued, but are quite as likely to have been agreed to on purpose to blind the British Government at a moment when his Highness was contemplating a secret operation against it. It is to this motive I attribute the usual profusion of attentions and compliances which his Highness has displayed since the time when he now appears to have entered vigorously into his plots with Trimbakji; his orders to the Vakils are easily rendered negatory by his intrigues through unavowed channels. Of this character is Balaji Kunjar, whose agent, Ballaji Dhondev, manages most of his Highness's communications with the other Mahratta powers, and who himself, as well as his son, are pointed out by several reports as engaged in constant communication with Trimbakji. There is a circumstance which appears to be connected with his Highness's intrigues in Hindustan, though it may possibly only relate to the levies of troops in Khandesh. It is that large sums of money have been remitted from this place to Choli Maheshwar, or Ujjain, which are said to be remitted on his Highness's part, and which really appear to be sent by his directions. Though I have long heard rumours of this nature, I was first led to inquire into them by the seizure of a large sum of money (about 30,000 rupees) by one of our detachments in the Ghauts. This money was passing off to Malwa in a secret manner; care was taken to elude our parties, and various subterfuges were resorted to to account for appearances after it had been seized. No application was made to me to release it, although the banker to whom it avowedly belonged is a frequent attendant at the Residency; and when he was at length called on for an explanation, he gave no satisfactory reason for his long silence. While this subject was under inquiry, I received intimation that the money was his Highness the Peshwa's. I afterwards received information on which I think I can rely, that his Highness has remitted several lacs of rupees to Hindustan in the name of five different Márwári bankers, the principal of whom is Amar Chand. It appears from the state of the market that these remittances are not made for mere commercial purposes; and several convoys which have been seized by the Peshwa's officers in consequence of a standing prohibition against exporting the current coin have always been released by his Highness's own orders. It is to be observed that the greater part of the treasure intercepted by our detachment consists of the prohibited coin (Halli sicca).

'18. I now proceed to report the communications I have had to his Highness, and the answers I have received since the date of my last despatch. Up to the 24th February I treated the insurrection as equally offensive to the Peshwa and to the British Government, and expressed my confidence in his exertions to put it down; at the same time pointing out the bad consequences of any remissness on his part. On the 24th, the Peshwa's Ministers sent me a letter from the commandant of Gokhle's detachment, that had gone against the insurgents, dated from Phultan, denying that there was any insurrection, and enclosing a letter from the revenue officer at Natepota to the same effect. The Ministers triumphantly referred me to those papers for a complete refutation of all that I had said about Trimbakji and his proceedings; they also pointed out in polite language the propriety of deliberation and inquiry previous to bringing forward charges of so much importance. I replied by stating the disagreeable impression made on me by their denying all knowledge of a rebellion that everybody else knew of, and saying that I had done my part, and that the responsibilty now rested with them. This only producing fresh denials, I sent a message on the 2nd March, requesting an explanation of his Highness's conduct and intentions, and saying that I should consider his mere denial of a fact so generally known, as a proof that he was determined to avoid all open and friendly discussions with the British Government. His Highness merely replying by general professions, it was apparent that if the insurrection continued, it would require to be put down by British troops, and that the presence of Gokhle's party would only lead to mistakes favourable to the rebels. I therefore took measures to form a detachment, and sent to beg that his Highness would recall his troops, as their remaining inactive so near the insurgents only led the people of the country to suppose that there was a concert between Trimbakji's and his Highness's Government. I also desired to be informed whether any troops which his Highness said were not rebels were his, or whether he had any troops in the tract round Mahadeo; I also begged to know what precautions had been taken to check the intrigues of Trimbakji's family and adherents, and what was become of Bhaskar Pandit? His Highness now said that there must be an insurrection, as I had such a positive account of it; but asked what he could do? He did not know where Trimbakji was, and he could not obtain intelligence about his followers; and that however anxious he was to show his sincere friendship for the British Government, it was totally out of his power to do anything which might convince it of his cordiality. I replied on the 4th, that his Highness might give them over as hostages to the British Government; that he might also give such orders to his troops and officers as would soon change the face of affairs. Signs of his cordiality would then appear of themselves, intelligence would pour in, both on him and us; he would offer his troops to act with our officers, and those who acted by themselves would attack and disperse the rebels wherever they were assembled. On the other hand, if appearances continued as formerly, I begged his Highness to consider the suspicions they would lead to. His Highness continuing his present professions, offering more troops, and ordering out Major Ford's brigade, but without taking any of the steps that were in his power, or even ceasing to deny the existence of an insurrection, I addressed, on the 7th, a long and serious message to him, pointing out the impossibility of his continuing his present course without being involved with the British Government; the impossibility, in that event, of his ever being trusted more, and the fatal character which the dispute would therefore assume. I endeavoured to show the uselessness of assisting Trimbakji, who surely was not expected to conquer us, and with whom he could never make terms; the impossibility of any arrangements that should even secure the life of that fugitive, until he was lodged in a British prison; the difficulty his Highness would have in satisfying your Lordship of his good intentions, even if this insurrection were to die away, and the wisdom of adopting such a course as should show that his Highness was sincere in his professions, the result of which I said could not fail to be the speedy capture of Trimbakji. To this his Highness sent the usual answer, that his troops were at my disposal, that they should move wherever I should point out the rebels, and that he would seize any person whom I should declare to be adherents of Trimbakji. I replied, on the 9th, that my object was less to crush the insurgents, which could not be done by a very small body of British troops, than to obtain proofs of his Highness's good disposition which might be counted on in future times and in all circumstances; that if his Highness were disposed he would find no difficulty in discovering the rebels, and in ascertaining who were Trimbakji's adherents. If, then, he were cordial and sincere, he would act on my former suggestions; if not, he would come back and desire me to point out individuals. His Highness now promised to seize Trimbakji's adherents, requesting me to point out any that he might omit. He also ordered Major

Ford to march against the rebels, and promised him a part of the best horse in his service; but this movement of troops I declined as quite unnecessary, the insurrection being formidable from the appearance of secret encouragement alone, and not from its own strength. I had also received intelligence which I thought might be relied on, that the troops at Mahadeo and the neighbourhood had broken up and dispersed; I have not yet heard what has been done about Trimbakji's adherents.

'19. The above communications were mostly made through Major Ford and Moro Dixit; I sent similar messages by Prabhakar Pandit, but in general still received more unsatisfactory answers. Yesterday, however, Prabhakar Pandit brought me a long message from his Highness, the purport of which was to vindicate himself from the accusations I had brought against him, to persuade me that he was not so mad as to meditate war against the British, or to prefer Trimbakji's friendship to ours; but a considerable part of the message was taken up by very sharp remonstrances against the tone of the messages which I had sent to his Highness by Major Ford, and which his Highness declared were full of unbecoming imputations against him, and expressed with unwarrantable freedom of language. His Highness showed particular resentment at one passage, which he was convinced meant to threaten him with the fate of Tippu Sultan; but as there was not the most distant allusions of the kind in any of my messages, this was easily explained away. His Highness assigned as a reason for not agreeing to some applications that I had made for a personal interview, that in the present state of things such a meeting would be liable to lead to altercation, and to expressions which his Highness might afterwards wish to recall. His Highness also gave some reason for not sending any man of rank and consequence to discuss the subjects now in hand on his Highness's part; I understood him to mean Gokhle, who perhaps has impressed his Highness with high notions of the manner in which he would support his Highness's dignity if he were to conduct a conference on his part. My answer to his Highness's professions was in the same spirit as those which I sent through Major Ford, that his Highness's denial of the insurrection obliged me to give way to very unfavourable surmises; that his Highness's conduct on this occasion, at the time when your Excellency was impressed with a particular conviction of his Highness's friendship and good intentions, was calculated to shake your confidence in him for ever; that it could not be expected that aggressions could be passed over as if they did not exist merely because they were not avowed; that his Highness was therefore in a situation of danger, and that the only wise course for him to pursue was to deliver up Trimbakji, which I said would be the best course even for Trimbakji himself. I took pains to efface the bad impression made by my messages, observing that it is my duty to be explicit with his Highness, and that even if I were his own minister I should still think I served him better by laying open the true state of his affairs to him, however it might offend him, than by encouraging him in pernicious courses by dissembling or assentation; that with respect to the terms in which my sentiments were conveyed, his Highness would recollect that neither I nor Major Ford could be expected to avoid improprieties in an Indian language; but that he might be assured I had every wish to render my communications as acceptable as was consistent with the principle I had just avowed. I then begged Prabhakar Pandit to remind his Highness of the timely caution I had given him on Trimbakji's escape, of the pains I took to warn him in November last of the dangers of harbouring Trimbakji, and of the very cordial and friendly terms in which I at first addressed him on this very occasion, until his Highness by shutting his eyes to the proceedings of the insurgents, compelled me to call his attention by louder complaints. I said that I had now so many interviews with his Highness that he was unable to judge whether anything I should offer, if he admitted me to an audience, were likely to give him offence ; and that with respect to sending Gokhle, his Highness would act entirely according to his own pleasure.

'20. During the above discussions I received two different messages from Gokhle, couched in his usual strain of respect and attachment for the British Government, but complaining of my having applied for the recall of his troops, reminding me of his former services, protesting that there was no insurrection, and assuring me that if the insurgents could only be found out, I should soon have cause to applaud his exertions. I replied that I had imputed no blame to Gokhle, who no doubt acted up to the orders he had received ; that it was my knowledge of his vigour on former occasions that led me to inquire into the causes of his present inaction ; that with respect to the existence of the insurrection, it was with the Government I had to deal, and that unless Gokhle insisted on coming forward for himself, I had no dispute with him on that head. As far as I can learn, Gokhle has been his Highness's great adviser through the whole of the present business, assisted perhaps by Waman Ráw Apte, and some others of his Highness's dependents. The plan I conceive to originate with his Highness and Trimbakji. It suits Gokhle's views to fall into any opinions that his

Highness may entertain ; and as there is no way to win his Highness's favour like standing between him and danger, I should not be surprised if Gokhle should not have talked of his own military powers, and offered to take all consequences on himself. Considering the craft and treachery of his confederate, it is not unlikely that this may cost Gokhle dearer than he intends ; but I cannot suppose that he had any deliberate intention of incurring the resentment of the British Government, or of embarking in a cause the success of which depends on the constancy of his Highness the Peshwa.

'21. Moro Dixit and his party appear really to be, as they profess, mere instruments of the Peshwa's, without any great share in his confidence, or any influence over his conduct. It is even impossible that they may not be admitted into the secret of his Highness's interior policy ; all his intelligence and some of his Vakils of foreign courts are under the management of Waman Ráw Apte ; Moro Dixit has no share whatever in those departments. A Kárkûn of Gokhle's, named Govind Keshav Joshi, is stated from several quarters to have been lately despatched to Scindia's camp ; I shall apprize Captain Close of his mission to enable him to find out the object of it.

'22. I have omitted to mention in a former part of this letter that the Peshwa has occasional private meetings with the Vakils of Appa Desái, which gives some colour to the alleged connection between that chief and Trimbakji. His late severity to Appa Desai is no argument against the fact, for it is quite in the spirit of his Highness's policy to turn against us the enmity which has been provoked by our exertions in support of his own authority.

'23. I shall now wait a few days to see what course the Peshwa determines on, and if he does not take effectual measures against the insurgents, I shall immediately act against them with a British detachment. For this purpose I have requested Colonel Smith to order the 4th and 8th Regiments of light cavalry to move into the neighbourhood of Parenda, and the light battalion into that of Ahmednagar; I have also suggested to the Resident at Hyderabad to direct Major McDowall to move his detachment to the neighbourhood of Tuljapur; thus I shall be able to assemble a considerable light force in the neighbourhood of the insurgents within three or four days, and at the same time I hope the scattered positions and apparently unconnected movements of the detachments will prevent the insurgents from quitting the part of the country throughout which they are now quartered.

'I have, etc.,

'(Signed) M. Elphinstone,

'Resident at Puna.'

Notes of Mr. Ephinstone's Messages to the Peshwa.

February 12th.

His Highness must long have been aware of the assemblage of Ramoshis near the Mahadeo Pagoda. I have heard of it for a long time, and I have also heard reports that Trimbakji is at the head of the band. This agrees well with what I have long heard, of Trimbakji's being at Phultan, or in that neighbourhood; but I conclude that if he were there, it would be known to his Highness, without whose knowledge it would be impossible for him to assemble Ramoshis. Trimbakji's family and all his adherents are also in his Highness's hands, which is a security that he cannot have entered on so desperate a

Hostilities.

Mr. Elphinstone's Notes.

course. I therefore conclude they are common insurgents, and recommend to his Highness to disperse them immediately. The report that they are headed by Trimbakji will render great promptitude requisite; and I therefore hope his Highness will show as much as in the affair of the last insurgents to the southward. If Trimbakji is really among these rebels, it is evident that, notwithstanding all his Highness's exertions in his favour, he is determined to disturb his country, and, as far as depends on him, to embroil him with us. The only natural conduct for his Highness, in such circumstances, and what everyone will expect of him, will be to act vigorously against him, to seize his family and adherents, and to set a price on his head. This is what will be expected of his Highness.

February 24th.

Inquire the news of the insurgents near Mahadeo. Repeat the inquiry regarding the Killedar and Mymanghar. Inquire what the Ministers have heard of the affair within the last two months, especially the last fortnight, since it has become the talk of the bazar, and since bodies of horse have been openly flocking to join the insurgents. Inquire who is the Mamlatdar of Natepota, and what he and the Killedar of Mymanghar have said to such an assemblage of troops within their districts. Say that I have heard strong and repeated accounts of Trimbakji's being at the head of the rebels. I am unwilling to believe it, because it cannot be without his Highness's knowledge; and I cannot believe his Highness is countenancing anyone in taking up arms against his allies. I must, however, in candour mention the bad appearance of the thing, that his Highness may take measures to counteract it. It is but friendly to tell him beforehand, that if Trimbakji excites a rebellion, his Highness must be held responsible for it; that he had the means of preventing it, and ought to have exerted them; and that it is, therefore, of the last importance to his own prosperity to quash the rebellion even now, if Trimbakji really is there. From the friendly terms we are now on, his Highness will believe that this is meant as real friendly advice; it would be far from friendship to conceal such importaut truths.

February 25*th*.

I am very sorry to learn that the Peshwa's Ministers have not heard of an insurrection that everyone else has heard of. The circumstances cannot but give rise to disagreeable impressions in my mind. Having apprised them of the existence and character of the insurrection, I have done my part; they must now be answerable for the rest. If hereafter there is an insurrection, what am I to think of their present denial of the fact? Gokhle's paper goes for nothing. I never said there were insurgents at Phultan. The Natepota man is of no weight; had he been free of the insurgents, he would have reported their proceedings long ago.

March 2*nd*.

I have no doubt remaining in my mind that Trimbakji Dengle is, or was lately, in the neighbourhood, of Mahadeo, and that he is raising troops. This indeed, is universally known in Puna and the country; yet his Highness the Peshwa denies the existence of the fact. It is impossible to draw any conclusion from this but such as is most favourable to his Highness; I am, therefore, bound to call on his Highness to explain his conduct and intentions. Are the troops assembling in the neighbourhood of Mahadeo raised by his Highness's authority, or are they rebels? If they are rebels, why are they suffered to assemble unmolested, and why are not their agents, who raise men in all parts of the country, including Puna, apprehended? If they are not rebels, I hope his Highness will explain his motives for authorizing or permitting this assemblage? It would be an insult to his Highness's understanding to suppose that he will endeavour to evade an answer by denying a fact so universally known as the existence of an insurrection within twenty-five kosses of his capital, unless he is determined to avoid all open and friendly discussion with the British Government.

March 3rd.

Request explicit answers to the important questions I put yesterday.

What are his Highness's intentions?

Are the troops in the neighbourhood of Mahadeo his Highness's? or rather, as he denies that there are any troops there, has his Highness no troops in that neighbourhood except the detachment of Gokhle's lately sent out there? If he says he has not, then whose are those assembled? If he admit there are rebels there, why are they not extirpated?

His Highness has made himself answerable for the conduct of Trimbakji's family and adherents; what means has he taken to prevent their assisting him in insurrection?

Where is Bhaskar Pandit, who formerly commanded the troops with Colonel Smith?

I beg his Highness to recall the detachment of Gokhle's that was lately sent out; it is of no use, as it does not act against the rebels. It rather does harm, as it shows to the people of the country that the Peshwa's troops do not act against the rebels, and thus leads them to infer a concert between those rebels and the Peshwa.

March 4th.

Where is Bhaskar Pandit, who formerly commanded the body of Trimbakji's Horse with Colonel Smith, and who left Phulsheher shortly before his Highness came in? He is in his Highness's service, and his motions must be known to his Highness.

Has Gokhle's detachment been withdrawn? Its remaining there will only afford to Trimbakji the appearance of concert with his Highness. If they offer to send more troops, say, no troops sent in such a spirit are of the least use. If the Ministers say at Puna that there is no rebellion, the commandant of the detachment will only repeat the assertion when sent out to the spot. The same argument applies to sending Major Ford's brigade. Unless the Peshwa is on our side, Major Ford will never be able to find Trimbakji, who will move from Mahadeo when he moves from Dapori. If his Highness wishes to show that he is on our side, he ought to place guards over Trimbakji's adherents, and especially over his family. If Trimbakji proceeds after that, let his Highness make over those persons as hostages to the British Government. Let him then proceed with cordiality and vigour in the dispersion of Trimbakji's gang and in the apprehension of his person. We shall believe that his Highness is really averse to the rebellion.

If his Highness adopts the course I recommend, the effects will soon be apparent. Instead of his Highness's subjects flocking to Trimbakji, they will flock to tell where he is concealed. Instead of his Highness denying that there is an insurrection two months after it is notorious, his Highness will send me the earliest intelligence of the motions of the insurgents. Instead of his Highness's troops halting in the neighbourhood of the rebels, and declaring that they cannot find any rebels, we shall hear of their dashing at the insurgents—killing some, taking others, and dispersing the rest.

If his Highness's troops fail to do this, he will place large bodies of them under British officers, and thus command our confidence.

When these sort of signs appear, we may conclude that his Highness is disposed to put down the insurrection, and to support his character as a good ally, and a prince who regards his word. If the other course should continue, I need not say what we must infer.

7th March, 1817.

The notoriety of the insurrection is now a great deal too well established to admit of the knowledge of it being dissembled; I can therefore only interpret his Highness's assertion, that he has not heard of it. Having really a sincere desire that his Highness's Government should prosper, I cannot but lament this line of conduct. I do entreat his Highness to consider where it will end. To screen Trimbakji and his gang, is to attack us; and can his Highness suppose that he will pass over an attack without resenting it? His Highness must therefore either embark on the side of the insurgents or on ours; and independent of his friendship and his good faith, his interest strongly recommends his siding with the British Government. What is it to be gained on the other side? Is Trimbakji to conquer the British—what Scindia, Holkar, Tippu, the French and all the world united, could never do? or are we expected to submit without being conquered, and to consent to Trimbakji's restoration when he appears as an enemy, after refusing it to him when a prisoner? When did the British Government ever make such a submission? All wars might be avoided by giving up the point in dispute, but we uniformly prefer a war to an improper concession, and to this we owe our prosperity. If Trimbakji does not conquer us, and we do not submit, what is to secure his Highness? The confidence between him and us was interrupted for some time, and has at length been fully restored. Perhaps at no time were the Governments more cordial than before the breaking out of this insurrection. If in such circumstances his Highness connives at a blow aimed at our welfare, how can we possibly trust him again? This dispute therefore, if it is again renewed, must be fatal to the independence of one of the parties. Why then provoke it? I do assure his Highness that I do not, after reviewing the whole politics of India, see the smallest prospect of any injury to the British Government; yet I do most earnestly deprecate a disturbance, the effects of which would be so fatal. His Highness may perhaps suppose that he will keep clear of the affair by merely denying it, or by affecting to act against the rebels without really doing so; but it is easy for any person to tell when another is in earnest, from his actions, and it is to them that the British Government will attend. His Highness may say that Trimbakji is out of his control; but if that were the case, we should see his Highness acting vigorously against everything that was within his reach. Trimbakji's adherents would immediately be sent to the Hill Forts; a guard would be placed over his family and those of all who had joined him, such as Bhaskar Pant; his Highness's Mamlatdars would strip and dismount every horseman who was going to join him; his Highness's own troops would cut off some of the rebels, and his

Highness, who possesses the whole intelligence of the country, would give information that would enable our troops to cut up others; his Highness's officers would also concur in pursuing Trimbakji, who would soon be taken prisoner if the Government of the country were against him. How is the matter at present? Trimbakji's adherents live at large at Puna, and every soldier in the country, in consequence, thinks he is pleasing the Peshwa by going to join the rebels; all intelligence that reaches the Government is suppressed; and his Highness himself says he knows of no rebellion. The result will be that Trimbakji will break out, and his fate will be sealed. I have always refused to listen to any proposal about him that did not tend to replace him in a British prison. My language may be rendered still more discouraging by disturbances, but never can be softened; if, therefore, his Highness has any regard to Trimbakji's safety, he will manage to have him placed once more in our hands, as the only hope he has. Do not let his Highness suppose that I shall receive the stopping of the rebellion at present as a proof of his Highness's good intention; if it be stopped without his Highness's giving proofs of his determination to crush it, the British Government must conceive that it is only suspended till another opportunity, and must act accordingly. There is therefore only one way for his Highness to get well out of the present affair, and that is by acting sincerely against the rebels. If this be his Highness's wish, it will require no argument to convince me of it; I shall perceive at once the altered spirit of his Government, and shall have the greatest pleasure in reporting it to your Excellency the Governor-General, as I have now great pain in relating his present proceedings.

The only way to remove all troubles, jealousies, and heart-burnings is to make over Trimbakji.

9th March.

I hear that his Highness still denies there is an insurrection, and calls on me to point it out.

I reply that if his Highness were sincerely anxious to put it down, he would soon discover it—that it would be of no use my pointing it out. If the only object was to put down the rebellion, I could do it without troubling his Highness; but the object is to get him to show that he is a faithful ally, and that we can depend on his not exciting troubles hereafter. As to the putting down of the insurrection, I would strongly advise his Highness against such a measure; it would be better for him to let it break out, as its stopping in consequence of my remonstrance to his Highness would show that his Highness had it in his hands. His only true way of proceeding, therefore, is to act cordially and sincerely against the rebels; when he does that, it will be no longer necessary for him to ask all these questions. I do not name Trimbakji's adherents, nor point out where the rebels are, because I am making one more appeal to his Highness's candour; but I call on him to act sincerely on the suggestions I have already offered. If he does not, I cannot misunderstand him.

EXTRACT SECRET LETTER TO BENGAL, DATED 5TH JANUARY, 1818.

'2. By your political despatch of the 12th December, 1816, we were informed of the escape of Trimbakji Dengle from the fortress in which he had been confined, and of the ambitious conduct of the Peshwa, who appeared at least to retain a strong attachment to his late Minister, if indeed his Highness were not secretly concerned in his escape.

Secret Letter to Bengal, 5th Jan., 1818.

'3. The reports, however, from Mr. Elphinstone to the Governor-General (copies of which were from time to time transmitted to us by the Government of Bombay), and particularly that which described the Peshwa's manner of receiving the communications of your Lordship's intentions concerning the Pindaries, gave us reason to hope that notwithstanding the suspicious earnestness manifested by the Peshwa in soliciting the pardon of Trimbakji, and the intrigues in which his Highness appeared to have been engaged at the other Mahratta Courts, for purposes inconsistent with his alliance with the British Government, his Highness was duly sensible of the advantages which he derived from that connection, and consequently desirous to preserve it. The language held by Mr. Elphinstone, in obedience to the Governor-General's instructions of the 17th January, 1817, was judiciously calculated to assure the Peshwa of your Lordship's disposition to act cordially with his Highness, notwithstanding the just grounds of complaint which had been furnished by his recent conduct.

'4. But your secret letter of the 12th April last, reporting the flagrant acts of insurrection committed by Trimbakji within the territories of the Puna State, and the repeated refusal of the Peshwa to interfere effectually for the suppression of them, satisfied us that to ensure the adherence of the Court of Puna to the principles of the alliance, and to dispel the dangers incident to the increasing strength and boldness of the insurgents, it might be necessary to evince to the Peshwa a decided resolution to resort even to the extremity of war, if other measures should be found insufficient for the maintenance of that security which under his evasive promises, and in effect hostile conduct, was daily menaced and endangered.

'5. We have learnt, through the Government of Bombay, the series of discussions at Puna which led to the treaty concluded with the Peshwa on the 13th June, 1817; and we have recently received, through the same channel, a copy of the treaty.*

'6. It would have been most satisfactory to us if the Peshwa had, by a frank and friendly conduct before any demonstration of force was employed towards him, rendered it possible to bury all that had passed in oblivion, and to leave things on the footing on which they had stood previously to those discussions.

'7. We feel all the objections which lie against measures tending to reduce or humiliate those Native States, which from the extent of their dominions and from their military habits were formerly ranked as substantive and protecting powers. It is not now necessary to review the circumstances under which the Puna State was first brought down from this character. We sincerely and anxiously wish that the Peshwa had not furnished occasion for a further change in his political situation.

'8. But after all that has passed on former occasions, when our interference has been solicited by the Peshwa himself for the purpose of recalling his own feudatories to their allegiance, and after his passiveness on the occasion of the recent insurrection, whether proceeding from inability or from unwillingness to act effectually against it, we cannot but acknowledge, however reluctantly, the existence of a necessity for giving new efficiency and solidity to our connection with the Puna State, by assuming a more direct control both over the Peshwa's military force and over his political conduct.

'14. The course of these transactions sufficiently proves the almost irrepressible tendency of our Indian power to enlarge its bounds and to augment its preponderance, in spite of the most peremptory injunctions of forbearance from home, and of the most scrupulous

* See the Collection of Treaties.

obedience to them in the Government abroad. But although it may not be in our power permanently to assure the peace of India by any moderation of our own, so long as, whether from motives of natural feeling or from habits of restless and perfidious policy, the States of India are continually finding or seeking opportunities of intriguing or combining against us, the difficulty of maintaining a system of peace and moderation does not absolve us from the obligation of pursuing it with the most sincerity and perseverance. A pacific and unambitious policy is that which the interests of the Company, as well as its duty, and the general sentiments of the nation as well as the positive enactments of Parliament, prescribe to the Government of India.

'15. While we are expressing our approbation, therefore, of those measures, political and military, to which you have been compelled to have recourse by the circumstances of the case referred to in this despatch, we think it particularly important to declare that we consider any such case as forming an unwelcome though justifiable exception of the general rule of our policy. The occurrence of such exceptions has been unfortunately much too frequent; but however numerous the instances in which we may be driven from an adherence to our rule, nothing in our opinion could warrant a systematic departure from it.'

Secret Letter from Bengal, dated 9th June, 1817.

Bengal Secret Letter, 9th June, 1817.

'The despatch of the ship *Boyne* affords a favourable opportunity, of which we are desirous of availing ourselves, for submitting to your Honourable Committee a continuation of the summary of proceedings and transactions of Puna, which was communicated to you in our address of the 12th April, forwarded by his Majesty's ship *Lyra*.

'That address was accompanied by copies of our instructions to the Resident, under date the 7th April. Previously to his receipt of those instructions, however, the perseverance of the Peshwa in the infatuated course of proceedings he had adopted has led to a situation of affairs which compelled the Resident to act on a private communication, conveying to him, in general terms, the outlines of the resolutions we had adopted and transmitted in that form, with a view to save the time necessarily occupied in the preparation of detailed instructions, involving so many points for deliberation and reflection.

'It was fortunate that this precaution was adopted, since, in consequence of the disturbances in Cuttack, which will form the subject of a future communication, the posts by the ordinary route were interrupted for several days, occasioning a further delay in the receipt by the Resident of his official instructions, which did not reach him till the 10th May; although every endeavour was made to secure his early receipt of them as soon as the interruption of the post was known, by despatching copies by various routes, and by establishing a communication by sea with the coast of the Northern Circars.

'The receipt of a general intimation of our views, and the judgment and resolution of Mr. Elphinstone, have prevented the public interests from sustaining any injury in consequence of the untoward circumstances just mentioned; his proceedings having, both in the outline and the detail, been in entire conformity with the spirit of our instructions.

'It is not necessary on the present occasion to submit to your Honourable Committee a detailed review of the proceedings of the Peshwa, and of the incessant endeavours of Mr. Elphinstone to recall him to a just sense of his duty and interests. The Peshwa continued to deny the existence of the insurrection, and to call on Mr. Elphinstone, if he believed it did exist, to take his own measures for putting it down, while he proceeded with the greatest vigour to raise troops, and to place his forts in a state of preparation. At last he went so far as to send his treasure, and even his wardrobe, to different places of security—in a word, to manifest a determination of resisting the earnestly repeated advice and remonstrances of the Resident, so as to rest the decision of the question on the issue of the word. It was Mr. Elphinstone's object, until he should receive our instructions, to keep the question open for any decision we might make, omitting, in the meanwhile, no effort to induce the Peshwa to adopt a better course of proceeding, and to await the result of Mr. Elphinstone's communications to the Governor-General in Council. Your honourable Committee will accordingly find that all his communications to the Darbar, written or verbal, tended to this purpose, and that he met the evasions, equivocations, and delusive promises of the Peshwa by a steady and unalterable adherence to the principle of action. As the preparations of the Peshwa and of the avowed partizans of Trimbakji advanced, Mr. Elphinstone continued to urge on the Peshwa's attention the danger of his measures, and the certainty that a perseverance in them must involve them in ruin. He now thought it expedient to authorize Colonel Smith to adopt active measures against the insurgents, with a view to break their strength and disperse them before they should have time to make head and become formidable, in the event of a rupture with the Government itself; the public professions of the Peshwa still affording the colour that our troops were employed to suppress risings against his Highness's authority.

Among the Peshwa's proposals, that of sending troops to co-operate with our detachments was constantly brought forward, but declined by Mr. Elphinstone, on the ground that their services in that manner would not merely be useless, but would embarrass the operations of our troops; and he invariably declared that it was not the aid of his Highness's troops, but a distinct expression of his sentiments against the proceedings of Trimbakji that was required of his Highness. We shall advert generally to the operations of the troops in the sequel of this despatch. We now beg to draw the attention of your honourable Committee to the demands which Mr. Elphinstone deemed indispensable to be made on the Peshwa, and the measures he judged it necessary to adopt in consequence of his Highness's continued evasions of his promises. Finding that every assurance given by his Highness was either secretly evaded or openly violated, and that the Peshwa evidently either hoped Mr. Elphinstone would recede in his demands, or that his Highness actually entertained the design of proceeding to a rupture, Mr. Elphinstone determined to bring the matter to an issue; he therefore, on the 1st of April, sent a written message to his Highness, in which, after recapitulating what had passed, and noticing the breach of his Highness's promises to discontinue his preparations, disband his new levies, and replace his forts in the situation in which they were before the late measures were taken regarding them, Mr. Elphinstone signified his intention of placing the British troops at Puna in a state of preparation. He further communicated the obligation under which he should hold himself, of taking still more active measures if his Highness continued his array; adding, that if his Highness suspended his preparations, Mr. Elphinstone would forbear from any ulterior steps until he received the orders of his own Government; declaring, at the same time, that he should consider his Highness's quitting Puna to be a clear indication of a design to go to war. Mr. Elphinstone, after transmitting this message, gave the necessary instructions to the officer commanding the troops of Puna, according to the intimation conveyed to his Highness. This procedure seemed at first to have made a suitable impression on the Peshwa, who deliberated with his Ministers, and communicated through them with Mr. Elphinstone on the mode of complying with.

REPORT

FROM

LIEUTENANT-COLONEL BURR OF THE BOMBAY ESTABLISHMENT,

AND

DESPATCHES

FROM THE HONOURABLE M. ELPHINSTONE TO THE GOVERNOR-GENERAL.

REPORT

FROM LIEUTENANT-COLONEL BURR OF THE BOMBAY ESTABLISHMENT,

AND

DESPATCHES

FROM THE HONOURABLE M. ELPHINSTONE TO THE GOVERNOR-GENERAL.

'To the Deputy Adjutant-general of the Fourth Division of the Army of the Deccan.

'Sir,

'My letter of yesterday's date will have informed you of my having removed the whole of the stores, treasure, and provisions from our late cantonments to the village of Kirkee, and of their being lodged in security therein; and of the brigade being in a state of preparation to move as circumstances may require.

Lieut.-Col. Burr's Report.

'I have now the honour to report, for the information of the general officer commanding this force, that soon after I had despatched it I received an intimation from the Resident of the probability of an immediate rupture with the Peshwa, followed by a requisition to move out and attack the Mahratta force, which was then visible and advancing to the attack of our camp.

'I in consequence formed the brigade, and leaving the headquarters of the second battalion of the 6th Regiment, who were previously weakened by several strong detachments, in charge of the post of Kirkee, together with the drill, sick, unfits, and two iron twelve-pounders, under the command of Major Roome, advanced to meet the enemy, a party of whose horse hovered near the column and preceded our march.

'Having chosen a situation in advance of our position, at the distance of about one mile, we formed line, waiting the junction of the Dapori* battalion, under the command of Major Ford, with three field-pieces. At this period I was joined by the Resident, who most gallantly exerted himself throughout the day, in setting a distinguished example of zeal and animation to the troops, encouraging the men wherever it became necessary, and, by his suggestions and information, aiding by judgment in the execution of the measures it became necessary to adopt.

'On the approach of Major Ford's division, and being reinforced by the Resident's escort and troops which had been stationed at the Sangam,† under the command of Major Cleiland, who had handsomely offered his services to me. I order the line to advance, which we continued doing for half a mile.

'The Mahratta army, which was drawn up with its left resting on the height of the front of Ganesh-Khind, where a large body of the Vinchur Rajah's horse were posted, extended its right to the Mutah river, in which direction the principal masses of their cavalry were formed, the total amount of which is supposed to have been 15,000 ; the intermediate undulating plain being occupied by a long line of infantry and guns, supported by successive lines of horse, as far as the eye could see, who, seeing us advance, moved forward from

* Part of a brigade raised by the Peshwa, but officered and disciplined by Europeans.

† The Residency.

their position, and at the very moment we were unlimbering for action, commenced a brisk cannonade from their centre, while the masses of cavalry on both their flanks endeavoured to turn ours, and succeeded in getting in our rear.

'The action now became very interesting. A body of Gokhle's regular infantry made an attack, in solid column, on the first battalion of the 7th Regiment of Native Infantry, which was on the left of the line, and who had scarcely succeeded in repelling it and a number of horse, when a select body of the enemy's cavalry seeing their infantry repulsed and pressed by the battalion, who could with difficulty be restrained from pursuing them, made a determined charge on the corps, some of the men wheeling round the flanks, repeating their attacks in their rear. The bravery of the men, however, compensated for the disorder into which they had been thrown by the previous attacks, and enabled them under circumstances of great difficulty, and with the powerful co-operation they derived from the left brigade of guns, and a part of the Bombay Regiment, to beat off the assailants, who left many men and horses on the ground, withdrawing to a distance, and never after hazarding a repetition of their attack.

'By this time, Major Ford, with his battalion and his field-pieces from Dapori, joined us, and formed line on our right, when we again immediately advanced near half a mile, the left of the line being thrown back to check any attack of the enemy's horse, who were in great force between them and the river; while the light companies of the first battalion of the 7th Regiment, which had at first preceded the line, were sent to the rear, to keep in check a large body of horse who had been watching Major Ford's movement, to our support, and who now came down in rear of our right flank.

'Soon after the enemy withdrew the greater part of his force to a distance, retiring and drawing off his guns towards the city; and as we advanced, the greater part of his infantry also, computed at 8,000 (part of whom had been posted in advance of his guns and centre in the bed of a nullah,* and in walled gardens, extending along the front of our position), now sent out their skirmishers, which, with others on the right of the line, and rockets from both front and rear, continued to occasion us a few casualties. The light infantry of the line, however, under the command of Captain Preston, easily drove them off and occupied their ground; and it being nearly dark, I submitted to the Resident, as the enemy were evidently in full retreat, the expediency of withdrawing the troops to camp as soon as it was dark, having fortunately succeeded in our principal object, meeting and driving the enemy from the position they had originally taken up. This was accordingly done, and the whole returned to camp soon after eight o'clock.

'I am happy to say, the casualties during the action have been less than could have been expected. The greater part have fallen on the first battalion of the 7th Regiment; only one European officer, however, Lieutenant Falconer, of the second battalion of the 1st Regiment, is amongst the wounded. Accompanying, I have the honour to forward a return of the number.

'I have not yet heard a correct statement of the loss the enemy suffered; I should imagine that it could not be less than 300 or 400 killed and wounded. Native reports make it treble that number. Amongst the latter are said to be the Minister and some officers of distinction.

* A rivulet.

'A more pleasing duty now arrests my attention, the rendering that tribute of grateful acknowledgment due to the exertions of the gallant force I had the honour to command, and of those individuals to whose official rank and situation I feel so much indebted, for their cheerful support and devotion to promote the success of the action.

'The Bombay and Dapori Artillery, under the command of Captain Thew and Lieutenant Lawrie, rendered the most important services; and the spirited manner in which the guns were served greatly contributed to the rapid success of the day.

'The detachment of his Majesty's 65th Regiment and Bombay European Regiment, commanded by Major Wilson and Lieutenant Coleman, honourably maintained by their cool and steady conduct the long-established reputation of these valuable corps and the zealous officer who commanded; while Captains Mitford Donnelly and Whitehill, at the head of their respective battalions, were anxious to afford to their deserving corps an honourable example, which was nobly emulated by the Resident's escort, commanded by Major Cleiland.

'To my Brigade Major Captain Halifax, to my Quartermaster of Brigade Lieutenant Inverarity, and Lieutenant Ellis (the Bazaar Master), and the other Staff officers attached to the brigade, I felt extremely obliged for their exertions during the whole of the action. Lieutenant Grant, of the Grenadier Battalion attached to the Residency, most handsomely volunteered his services to communicate my orders, and particularly distinguished himself throughout the action. Captain Gordon and Lieutenant Dunsterville were also cheerful assistants on the occasion; the latter does not belong to this division of the force.

'To Major Ford, and the officers and men of his fine

brigade, I feel the greatest obligations for the cheerfulness and anxiety they evinced to contribute to the general success of the day; while it afforded me much pleasure to witness the anxious and humane attention of Dr. Meek and the medical gentlemen to the important duties devolving on them at this interesting moment.

'On my return to camp, finding Lieutenant-Colonel Osborne had arrived, I delivered over charge of the brigade under my command to him, having solicited his permission to express my acknowledgments, in orders, to the gallant force which I had had the distinguished honour of commanding on an occasion of such particular interest.

'I have, etc.,
'(Signed) C. B. Burr,
'Lieutenant-Colonel.

'Camp at Kirkee,
'*6th November*, 1817.'

'Return of the killed and wounded of the Puna Brigade, under the command of Lieutenant-Colonel C. B. Burr, in the action near Puna, 5th November, 1817:

'Artillery: Two Lascars wounded.

'Honourable Company's Bombay European Regiment: One private killed; one private wounded.

'Second Battalion 1st European Regiment: One private killed; one lieutenant, one Havildar, one Naik, one Bhisti, five privates, wounded.

'Second Battalion 6th Native Regiment: Four privates killed; ten privates wounded.

'First Battalion 7th Regiment: One Havildar, one Naik, one drummer, nine privates, killed; one Havildar, three Naiks, thirty-four privates, wounded.

'Major Ford's Battalion: One private killed; one Jamadar, one Havildar, five privates, wounded.

'Total: One Havildar, one Naick, one drummer, sixteen privates, killed; one lieutenant, one Jamadar, three Havildars, four Naiks, two Lascars, one Bhisti, fifty-five privates, wounded.

'Name of the officer wounded: Lieutenant Falconer, severely in the shoulder.

'(Signed) C. B. BURR,
'Lieutenant-Colonel.

'P.S.—I am sorry to say there is very little hopes of Lieutenant Falconer's surviving, and several of the wounded will either die or require amputation.'

EXTRACT LETTER FROM THE HONOURABLE MR. ELPHINSTONE TO THE GOVERNOR-GENERAL, DATED CAMP, RAJWARRA, 23RD NOVEMBER, 1817.

Letter from Mr. Elphinstone.

'On our obtaining possession of Puna, correct accounts were obtained of some particulars which were before imperfectly known. It appeared that the attack on our troops on the 5th was chiefly brought about by the persuasion of Gokhle; that the Peshwa took the alarm after he had given the order, and even sent to Gokhle, when on the eve of the action, to desire that he might not fire the first gun; but that the message was too late, or rather that Gokhle, hearing his approach, anticipated it by beginning to cannonade. Moro Dixit had been entrusted with the Jari Patka (the standard of the Mahratta Empire), and had 5,000 horse attached to him besides his own 2,000; he is, however, represented as having been very averse to the war, and as being accused by Gokhle of intrigues with us. Raste was one of those attached to Moro Dixit's party; being strongly suspected of disaffection, he was compelled to charge first, but acquitted himself with courage and fidelity. Gokhle avowed to Apaji Laxuman, Appa Desai Vakil, immediately before the action, that his confidence of success and impatience to engage were founded on the certainty that our Sepoys would come over by companies or battalions on the field.

'After the affair of the 5th, the Peshwa's army was dismayed. His Highness sent for Hareshwar, the banker, lamented the breaking out of hostilities, and with his usual insincerity professed his wish to have remained at peace, and threw the whole blame of the war, both plan and execution, on his Sirdars. On this occasion he disavowed the burning of the Residency, and said he would be very glad to build a new one; but his whole discourse appears to me to be merely a specimen of his accustomed double-dealing, and of his wish, even in the worst of times, to keep open some separate channel of intrigue for his own use.

'Some days after the action, the Peshwa's officers picked up some spirit, and set about circulating the most absurd reports of their successes and of the defection of our allies. They were joined by Dharmaji Pratab Raw (the freebooter), and it is said by the son of Raw Rambha; Chintaman Ráv also joined before their flight from Puna. Gokhle set up a white flag as an asylum for all who should desert us before a certain time; after that no pardon was to be given to any man who had served us. All the servants of English gentlemen who happened to live at Puna were hunted out by Gokhle, and many treated with great severity; the houses of most of them were given up to plunder, but none of them were put to death.

'Some time before the breaking out of the war the Peshwa had concerted with all the Bhils and

Ramoshis, and other predatory tribes in his country, to shut up the roads and plunder effects belonging to us. They have readily obeyed an order so much suited to their inclination, and have not confined their depredations to British property. They have, however, shut up the roads; that to Bombay is further obstructed by the garrison of Logus, and by a detachment which has taken possession of and stockaded the Bore Ghat; no dawks have been received from Bombay since the 5th, General Smith, however, has sent a strong detachment to open the road, and one of less strength to keep open the communication with Ahmednagar. No more convoys have been cut off since the first few days after the war; but I am greatly concerned to state that Lieutenant Ennis, of the Bombay Engineers, has been cut off near Sakur Mandava, where he was employed on survey. He had been recalled, but from an over-confidence in the strength of his guard he did not fall back on any station. He was attacked in the night by the inhabitants of Sakur Mandava, and next morning was surrounded by the Bhils and other adherents of Trimbakji, who is still in that neighbourhood. Lieutenant Ennis was shot while engaged with the enemy, and his detachment of a Jamadar and twenty-five men fought their way to a more friendly part of the country. Some koss on this side of Anna Bootch they were received and fed, and sent off in disguise by the Patel of a village, whom I shall not fail to discover and reward. Cornets Hunter and Morrison were in Gokhle's custody; they were at first in charge of Major Pinto, who is said to have treated them well, and resisted Gokhle's orders to use them with severity; but before the Peshwa's flight they were put in chains, and sent to Gokhle's fort of Kongori, in the Konkan.

'In consequence of the execution of Captain and

Mr. Vaughan, I have addressed letters of remonstrance both to the Peshwa and to Gokhle. To the former I only threatened retaliation, in general terms, for any repetition of such atrocities; but to Gokhle I declared explicitly that any individual, however exalted in his rank, who should order the death of a British prisoner, should answer for the crime in his own person.

'I omitted to state that on the 18th General Smith sent out a detachment to take some guns, which, with a body of infantry, had got off to the neighbourhood of the fort of Sinhaghur. Fifteen guns were taken without any loss; besides these, forty-six were taken in Puna, and one in the Peshwa's camp; large quantities of ammunition have likewise been taken.

'The army is now in full march after the Peshwa, who, it is rumoured, intends to return to Puna, or holds that language to encourage his troops. Trimbakji has not yet joined him, whether from distrust on his own part, or policy on the Peshwa's, is not known.'

SUBSTANCE OF A PRIVATE LETTER FROM MR. ELPHINSTONE, DATED 22ND DECEMBER, 1817.

Private Letter from Mr. Elphinstone.

The Peshwa having passed the range of Ghats, north of Juner, which is not practicable for guns at any point west of Ahmednagar, we are moving to the Narbada Ghat; in the meantime, it is not altogether impossible that the Peshwa may descend into the northern Konkan, or may send a detachment to disturb that part of the country. This is the more probable, as all the horse who generally annoy us have disappeared to-day. It is also probable because the approach of General Pritzler from the south, and the probable appearance of a light division to the west of Ahmednagar, will render his escape uncertain while he continues above the Ghats; on the other hand, he may be afraid to risk himself or his troops below the Ghats, from whence retreat must always be difficult. It might, however, be prudent to advert to this chance in considering any plan that would withdraw troops from the northern Konkan, or scatter them in it; and likewise it may be very important in considering whether or not to keep that force at Baroda, or recall it if it should have marched—but of this I cannot judge. Should the Peshwa or his troops descend into the Konkan, Colonel Burr, the moment he hears of it, will detach at least a complete battalion down to the Bore Ghat; and . . . . . I will follow, either by . . . . . more probably by . . . . . none of the intermediate ones being practicable for guns. If the Peshwa should descend immediately, General Smith could not well be in the Konkan by either Ghat in less than ten days, as we should probably be at Ahmednagar before we had certain accounts of his descents, and that would be at least two marches by either route. I have no accounts to lead me to apprehend this movement; but I think it right to mention it, as much mischief might be prevented by a proper distribution of the troops, and above all, by detaining the Brodera force, if there is the least doubt there.

EXTRACT FROM A DESPATCH FROM THE HONOURABLE MOUNTSTUART ELPHINSTONE, RESIDENT AT THE COURT OF THE PESHWA, TO THE GOVERNOR-GENERAL, DATED CAMP AT KOREGAUM, JANUARY 4TH, 1818.

Hostilities with the Pindaries and Mahrattas.

'About the time of General Smith's arrival at Sirur, on the 17th December, the Peshwa reached Wattur, near Junar; from this place he moved up to the Lag Ghat to Bamanwarra, about ten miles, and from thence to Lingdes, about nine miles; between these three places he spent the time from the 17th to the 27th. The more eastern Ghats being difficult for guns, General Smith moved up the Nimba Dewra Ghat. He left Sirur on the 22nd, and on the 25th reached Hanwantgav, nearly on the direct road from Ahmednagar to Kopergaum. From Hanwantgav he made a long march to Sangamner, and on the 27th he marched farther west to Tugav.

Letter from Mr. Elphinstone.

'The Peshwa appears to have calculated on the General's proceeding towards Kopergaum, for he sent his tents to Wasseer, a pass, on the 27th, as if he intended to cross the valley of the Paira, near Akolah, and proceeded by the great road to Nasik; but on hearing of General Smith's approach to Sangamner, he changed his route, and moved to Kotul on the more western side through Rajori. On General Smith's reaching Tugav, he seems to have thought he could not pass to the northward without the risk of being entangled in the hills, and overtaken by our troops, in consequence of which he retraced his steps on the 28th, and arrived on the same day at Wattur, a distance of near twenty miles, through Ghats, from whence he proceeded to Chankan, about forty miles, in two marches.

'At Chankan there is a strong little fort, from which he drove out a party of Peons belonging to Captain Robertson, Superintendent of Police at Puna, and leaving 100 Arabs for a garrison, proceeded to Phulsheher, two miles from this place. Next day he was surprised by the appearance of the small detachment under Captain Staunton, and he spent the first in repeated attacks on it with his whole force, his Highness himself looking on from a distant hill. The detachment, though distressed both in provisions and water, maintained its post against such unequal numbers till the 2nd, when the Peshwa heard of General Smith's approach, and continued his flight to the southward; he ascended the little Bore Ghat on the same day, and was followed by his whole army in the course of the night.

'The details of the gallant defence of Captain Staunton's detachment shall be forwarded as soon as received.

'On the Peshwa's return to the south, General Smith set out in pursuit of him, and ascended the Wassira Ghat, after which he left three battalions with bis heavy guns and stores under the command of Lieutenant-Colonel Boles, and proceeded over the Malsiras and Lag Ghats to this place, where he arrived yesterday, and halted to-day, the first time for a fortnight, during which he had marched upwards of 200 miles.'

'To the Most Noble the Marquis of Hastings, K.G., etc., etc., etc.

'My Lord,

'General Smith's reports will have informed your Excellency with the operations of this force since its march from Puna. The Peshwa kept at a considerable distance, and made moderate marches, merely sufficient to prevent our gaining on him. The troops with him amount to about 10,000 horse, of which the greater part belong to southern Jahagirdars, who refuse to quit his person, and the rest are the remains of his own horse, after the best have been selected by Gokhle. He has likewise 2,000 or 3,000 infantry. He was lately joined by 3,000 horse under Naro Pant Apte, who had been detached to bring the Rajah

Letter from Mr. Elphinstone.

of Satara to Wassota, when General Smith was in that neighbourhood, and who arrived with him in the Peshwa's camp five days ago. The Peshwa has his tents as usual, and is accompanied by his wife. Gokhle remains in the rear with a light force of about 7,000 horse, who have neither tents nor baggage of any description, but sleep by their horses, which are always saddled, and generally shift their ground once or twice in the course of every night. This force consists of parts of Gokhle's own troops, and those of the Vinchurkar and Purandhar. Their object is to hang on the rear of this army, to plunder the baggage, to cut off supplies, to intercept communications, and generally to cramp General Smith's operations. In the first mode of annoyance they have been totally unsuccessful; and though they prevent supplies coming in, unless under strong escorts, yet as they have the grain in the villages, no great inconvenience is occasioned by the prevention. They are more successful in stopping communications; but the effect of them is chiefly felt in their obliging the light and heavy parts of the army to move in one body, and in the delay occasioned by the necessity of guarding against their possible enterprises. Notwithstanding those obstructions, General Smith has marched, on an average, fifteen miles a day ever since he left Puna; and as he is about to leave his battering train at this place, he will henceforth be able to press the Peshwa much closer, and with much less exertion to his army. The Peshwa's course was first direct to the south; but from Puse Savli he turned east, and marched in that direction to Pandharpur, from whence he moved first north and then north-west, towards Puna. He passed within twenty miles of that capital, and is now near Junar, fifty miles north-west of this cantonment. He is said to have lately been joined by Trimbakji, with a body of Bhils and Ramoshis, and some Arabs, and it is believed that he intends to retire into the hills north of Junar, which are impassable for guns, and there to endeavour to defend himself. Both the Peshwa's force and Gokhle's are represented to be harassed and disheartened, of which the best proof is afforded by the reduction of their numbers.

'Brigadier-General Pritzler was at Bijapur on the 12th instant, on his march towards Pandharpur, from whence I have recommended his advancing towards Pedgaum, on the Bhimá.

'I had formerly the honour to report my having addressed letters to the Peshwa and to Gokhle, threatening retaliation if any other British prisoners should be put to death. After some time I received answers, both of which disavowed the murder of Captain Vaughan and Mr. Vaughan. Gokhle promised an inquiry regarding the murderers, and the Peshwa professed a strong desire to be at peace with the Company, under whose protection he had lived so happily.

'Two days after two Harkárás of Gokhle's brought letters from Messrs. Morrison and Hunter, stating that though rather roughly treated at first, they had since their arrival at Puna been well treated, and were in charge of Major Pinto. The letter, however, though not delivered till the 3rd of December, was dated the 9th of November, only two days after their capture, and before they were sent to Kungoree. Their treatment there is represented to be harsh. These letters were delivered without any message from Gokhle; but the delivery of them after so long a period had of itself the appearance of a wish to conciliate; and agrees with popular reports at the time, that the Peshwa wished to treat. This intention, if it was ever entertained, was probably altered by the intelligence of the war with the

Rajah of Nagpur. Yesterday a Brahmin, calling himself Balkrishna Shastri, and professing to be an agent of the Peshwa's, arrived at camp in disguise. He represented himself to have been sent to Puna by the Peshwa from Parali, where his Highness was about the last week in November, but ordered to remain quiet till further orders. These orders arrived about a fortnight ago, when Balkrishna waited on Lieutenant Robertson, who has remained in charge of Puna. He opened his mission to that officer, and the object of it appeared to be to persuade us that the Peshwa was himself our friend, but was not a free agent, being borne away by the violence of Gokhle and Ballaba; to prevail on me to apply for an armistice, and, finally, to ascertain whether we were likely to direct our attention to the person of the Peshwa, or to that of the Rajah of Satara. Captain Robertson very judiciously ridiculed the idea of our asking an armistice, recommended the Peshwa to come forward openly and throw himself on our mercy as the only means of keeping his musnud, and pointed out the ease with which we might set up a new Peshwa. Balkrishna held nearly the same language to me that he had to Captain Robertson, except that he did not mention the armistice, and spoke of the Peshwa's coming alone into the camp if he received encouragement. He did not specify what encouragement was expected; but as he spoke of our behaving as formerly, and not as for the last year, I conceive that he has no thoughts of unconditional submission. My answer was that I did not know that he was sent by the Peshwa, but that what I had to say was no secret, and I would therefore communicate it. It was that I had received no orders, and did not know whether your Excellency would treat with the Peshwa even now; that I was sure you would not if he pushed things to extremities; that he must be sensible how much we lost by not setting up a new government, to which the Sardars who disapproved of his Highness's measures might repair, and that he had better endeavour to obtain terms before it was too late. Balkrishna Shastri was desirous of remaining a day, first to allow me time for consideration, and afterwards for his own convenience; but I thought it best to send him immediately out of camp. If these overtures come from the Peshwa they are probably insincere. It seems his plan to throw the odium of the war on his Sardars, and to endeavour to maintain a sort of neutrality for himself; but his reception of Trimbakji, if true, is a proof that he has no immediate thoughts of peace, or he would not throw so great an obstacle in the way of an accommodation.

'Some time ago I received a letter from Madhav Rao Dadaji, the son of Parsharám Bháw, explaining that he had been obliged to send his nephew, Rao Sahib, to join the Peshwa, but that he was still ours at heart. As nothing better can be expected from the Jahagirdars, while we can neither secure them by setting up a new government, nor alarm them by overrunning their Jahagirs, I thought it best to say that I was sensible that Rao Sahib's joining was the effect of necessity, and that I should wait for any demonstration of his attachment until your Excellency should determine on some plan for settling the government. I used this language in the belief that it would have an equally good effect on the Peshwa and the Jahagirdars to be reminded of the possibility of our effecting a revolution. The chiefs of Miraj, Kurandwar, and Sirwal sent verbal answers; no reply has been received from the other Jahagirdars.

'While General Smith was marching to the southward, I received a Vakil from the Rajah of Kolhapur, professing his attachment, reminding me of his claims to Chikori and Manowba, and offering his services in collecting grain and providing depôts if they should be required. He said any of his forts, including Kolhapur, was at our service.

'General Smith marches to-morrow in pursuit of the Peshwa, whom he will probably now be able to press with more effect than ever. The presence of the Rajah of Satara in the Peshwa's camp is a proof of his want of confidence in his forts, and it will be an additional encumbrance to his flight in the plain.

'I have, etc.,

'(Signed) M. Elphinstone,

'Resident at Puna.

'Camp near Sirur,
'*25th December*, 1817.'

'To the Most Noble the Marquis of Hastings, K.G., etc., etc., etc.

'My Lord,

'When I had last the honour to address your Excellency, on the 4th instant, the Peshwa had ascended the Bore Ghat, twenty miles east of Puna, on his way to the southward.

'When General Smith set out in pursuit of the Peshwa to the northward, on the 22nd of December, General Pritzler was advancing to join this division, with the intention of forming the new distribution so often alluded to in my letters. He was requested to take up a position calculated for intercepting the Peshwa, should he return towards the south to throw his stores and heavy baggage into Sirur, and to take up the pursuit of the Peshwa as soon as he should come into his neighbourhood. To enable him to do so with effect, General Smith sent the second battalion

Letter from Mr. Elphinstone.

of the 15th Madras Native Infantry to join him at Pedgaum. General Pritzler was, however, compelled to return several marches from Pandharpur, to favour the junction of a convoy from the south, and had scarcely set out again from Pandharpur towards Pedgaum, when he received information of the Peshwa's having returned towards the south. On this he judiciously struck off to the westward, although he was still encumbered by his supplies, amounting to sixteen thousand bullock loads, and had not received the intended reinforcement. He fell into the Peshwa's track on the sixth, and immediately turned south, ascended the Salpe Ghat, and on the 8th came up with a body of horse about ten miles from Satara, whom he charged with his cavalry and dispersed, killing thirty, and taking six prisoners and thirty horses. The Peshwa, who was at no great distance during this affair, renewed his flight, and was pursued by General Pritzler past Miraj and across the Krishna, by the ford of Erroor. He seems at this time to have entertained thoughts of standing an action, as he sent for the guns he had left near Satara on his former flight; but it ended in his sending them, with most of his infantry, to Nipani, while he pursued his flight to Gokak, on the Ghatprabha. He left that neighbourhood on the 13th instant, when, finding himself pressed by General Pritzler, and probably aware of the force under General Munro, he turned to the eastward, and re-crossed the Krishna at Galgalla, from whence he moved in a westerly direction along the left bank of the river towards Athni (or Hathni). He had adopted the same plan with General Pritzler that he formerly adopted with General Smith, of keeping a light division in his rear to impede the General's pursuit; but this body, probably intimidated by the cavalry, gave him but little disturbance. On the 17th, however, they appeared in force, and General Pritzler sent out his cavalry against them; Major Doveton, who commanded, charged three successive bodies, amounting in all to 10,000, with three squadrons only, and put them all to flight, killing and taking about forty men. From this time General Pritzler pursued the Peshwa's track to Galgalla, without seeing any more of his horse. General Smith marched from Sirur on the 8th instant with his light division, and proceeded in a southerly direction by Pedgaum on the Bhima, and a pass east of the temple of Mahadeo, towards Athni (or Hathni). His intention was to intercept the Peshwa should he return towards the north, or to support General Pritzler if necessary. When within a march of Athni on the 21st instant, he received intelligence of the arrival of the Peshwa at that place, moving west, on which he marched in the direction of Miraj, to prevent the Peshwa's escaping to the west of him, and then moved down, thirty miles in all, to Ugara, a place on the Krishna where the Peshwa had been encamped the night before. The Peshwa now crossed the Krishna and made a feint of moving on his guns and infantry at Nipani; but suddenly turning north, he marched along the right bank of the Krishna towards Satara, where he arrived on the 27th. General Smith, on receiving intimation of this movement, renewed his march to the northward, but kept the left bank of the Krishna, to prevent the Peshwa's escaping to the westward, as has since proved to be his real design. Near Tasgàv, on the 23rd, General Smith was overtaken by the whole of the Peshwa's light army, which had been reinforced since we last saw it, and amounted to not less than 15,000 men at the lowest computation. This body was commanded by Gokhle, Appa Desai, Trimbakji, the Vinchurkar, and several of the Patwardhans. After leaving General Pritzler they had heard that the Peshwa with his heavy division was pressed by General Smith, and had come by forced marches to his assistance. This appearance was so sudden that they were enabled to cut off a few Sepoys and upwards of 200 men of General Smith's Bazar, in a village where they had gone to procure grain. These men were afterwards released by orders from the Peshwa, and given half a rupee each to pay their expenses to camp. The horse pressed on the rear all the march, rocketing and sniping, and wounded an officer, two Europeans, and seven Sepoys. They continued this sort of attack, but with less boldness, until the 29th, when we approached the Salpe Ghat. On that day the Peshwa, finding General Smith near him on the east with his light division, and his reserve under Colonel Boles approaching from the northward, began to fear being enclosed among the branches of the western Ghats; he therefore left Satara, and by a forced march crossed in front of General Smith, descended the Salpe Ghat, and moved off to the eastward. His light division, after an unsuccessful attempt to pass General Smith and join the Peshwa, made another push at a place where the valley leading to the Ghat is about six miles wide. General Smith moved out with the cavalry and horse artillery, supported by infantry to intercept them, and forced them to separate and fly in great confusion along the face of the hills. Some of their Bazar fell into our hands, but the greater part of the horse got through, and the rest returned towards Satara. All have now joined the Peshwa, who was last heard of at Natepota. On the 30th General Smith descended the Ghat and joined his reserve, having marched for forty days with only three halts, in which time he has gone through 570 miles. The whole pursuit of the Peshwa amounts already to 850 miles. We are now waiting for General Pritzler, who followed the Peshwa to Galgalla, and is now on his return by the route pursued by this division. His cattle are much exhausted during his pursuit of the Peshwa: he moved twenty-three days without a halt, and marched a distance of 300 miles in eighteen days, notwithstanding his heavy convoy and his numerous sick.

'I shall do myself the honour to submit to your Excellency my correspondence with General Pritzler up to this time. General Smith's report of his operations shall be forwarded to your Excellency as soon as it is received. The interruptions of our communications prevent my hearing often from General Munro; my last letter is dated the 21st. General Munro had taken the field (though I am not informed with what force), had reached and taken Dumwal and Gadag, and had reduced all the Peshwa's and Gokhle's country south of the Ghatprabha. The people of the country had cordially assisted him in expelling the Mahrattas. General Munro had also, in a great measure, succeeded in drawing off the Desai of Kittur, and some other local chiefs, from the Peshwa's cause. He had dispersed a body of Pindaries returning from Chittledurg, probably part of the body that passed Malkapur on the 8th of December, and the report of the country states that he had likewise cut up a part of Gokhle's troops under Kashi Rav Kokrah. I shall transmit copies of my correspondence with General Munro to Mr. Adam, from which your Excellency will be informed of my proceedings regarding the southern Jahagirdars.

'Your Excellency will have heard from Bombay that the troops belonging to the northern Konkan, under

Lieutenant-Colonel Prother, have taken the strong fort of Karnalla, and that the fort of Maddangar, in the southern Konkan, has also been reduced. These successes will have considerable effect even above the Ghats, and they will give confidence to our Sepoys, whose families in the southern Konkan are still persecuted by the Peshwa.

'The city of Puna continues quiet and abundantly supplied, but the surrounding country is disturbed by the Peshwa's troops from Sinhaghar, Chakan, and Lohagar. A variety of reports have been circulated of an intended attack on the capital by Arabs and other troops, from those garrisons and from different parts of the country. These accounts induced Colonel Burr to request Colonel Boles to remain for some time at Puna with the reserve; but it is uncertain whether they have their origin in fact, or are purposely circulated by the enemy. A conspiracy had been discovered in Puna to corrupt our troops; one of the criminals had been executed, and several others are in custody. There seems no reason to suspect the bulk of the inhabitants of any designs, or even wishes, against us.

'The country round Ahmednagar has suffered disturbance similar to that experienced about Puna. Small parties of horse move about the country, interrupting our collections of the revenue and collecting for themselves. A party of 2,000 or 3,000 horse, under Dharmaji Pratab Rav, lately appeared near Ahmednagar, on their way to join the Peshwa, probably from the Nizam's frontier. Intelligence of their arrival having reached Captain Gibbon, who is in charge of that district, he set out at midnight with one company of Sepoys and seventy of his own Peons, and succeeded in beating up the party and putting it to flight. It has, however, continued its course, and probably joined the Peshwa. Another party, consisting of 3,000 horse and Arabs, who had fled from Nagpur under Ganpat Rav, lately passed to the south of Jalana on their way to join the Peshwa by the route of Mungi Paithan. Colonel Deacon was in pursuit of them on the 23rd; but I have not heard with what success. Godaji Dengle is said also to be coming to the southward with a party of Arabs raised in Khandesh. These reinforcements must be very welcome to the Peshwa, who seems disposed before long to try the fortune of another battle. His moving out guns at Nipani and other places appears to me to be indicative of such a resolution. Some effort of the kind may be required to prevent the Jahagirdars deserting him, and the state of his cavalry probably renders him averse to place all his hopes in flight. Many of the horse with his army are said to be greatly exhausted, and General Pritzler found many abandoned in the villages through which he had passed. The best horse are with the Peshwa, whose whole personal division does not in all probability exceed from 5,000 to 7,000; the rest are in the light force, which must be 15,000 strong. All the chiefs except Chintaman Rav are with it.

'I continue to receive indirect overtures from the Peshwa, to which I pay no attention.

'I have, etc.,

'(Signed) M. Elphinstone,

'Resident at Puna.

'Camp, Lonad,
'31*st January*, 1818.'

'To Francis Warden, Esq., etc., etc., etc.

'Sir,

'I have the honour to enclose, for the information of the Right Honourable the Governor, a copy of a letter which I have this day addressed to Mr. Adam, reporting the fall of the fort of Satara, and the communications which were made to his Highness's connections and titular officers upon hoisting the flag of the Rajah of Satara.

Letter from Mr. Elphinstone.

'I have, etc.,

'(Signed) M. ELPHINSTONE.

'Camp, Satara,
'12*th February*, 1818.'

'To John Adam, Esq., etc., etc., etc.

'SIR,

'I have the honour to acquaint you with the surrender of the fort of Satara to the force under the command of Brigadier-General Smith.

'The Rajah's flag was hoisted yesterday under a royal salute. I this day assembled such of his Highness's connections and titular officers as are to be found about this place, together with some of the principal inhabitants of the Petta, and acquainted them with the intention of the British Government to deliver the Rajah from confinement, and to place him at the head of a sovereignty sufficient for his comfort and dignity, and that of the other members of his house. I prefaced this declaration by an exposition of the causes of the deposition of Baji Rav, the abject state from which he was raised by the Treaty of Bassein, his subsequent prosperity and professions of gratitude, his protection of the murderer of the Shastri, the magnanimity of the British Government on that occasion, the Peshwa's subsequent intrigues and the insurrection he set on foot, the moderation of the British Government in still maintaining him on his throne, his professions of gratitude and of zeal in co-operation against the Pindaries, his exertions at the same moment for the

Letter from Mr. Elphinstone.

subversion of our power, his treacherous attack on our lines, his violations of the law of nations and usages of civilized states, and his final avowal of his participation in the murder of the Shastri, by his public recall of the perpetrator of that atrocity.

'The promises of the British Government in favour of the Rajah were received with every appearance of gratitude and satisfaction, and I have no doubt will be attended with the most important consequences.

'I have, etc.,

'(Signed) M. ELPHINSTONE,

'Resident.

'Camp, Satara,
12*th February*, 1818.'

'To F. Warden, Esq., Chief Secretary to the Government of Bombay.

'SIR,

Letter from Mr. Elphinstone.

'I have sincere satisfaction in forwarding a copy of the accompanying despatch from Brigadier-General Smith, for the information of the Right Honourable the Governor in Council.

'I have, etc.,

'(Signed) M. ELPHINSTONE,

'Resident.

'Camp, before Sinhaghur,
'26*th February*, 1818.'

'To F. Warden, Esq., Chief Secretary to the Government of Bombay.

'SIR,

Letter from Mr. Elphinstone.

'I have the honour to enclose, for the information of the Right Honourable the Governor, a copy of a letter, dated the 12th instant, which I have received from Brigadier-General Smith, relating his operations against the Peshwa, since the 11th ultimo.

'I have, etc.,

'(Signed) M. ELPHINSTONE.

'Camp, Nira Bridge,
'16*th February*, 1818.'

'To Francis Warden, etc., etc., etc.

'SIR,

'I have the honour to enclose, for the information of the Right Honourable the Governor, a copy of a letter which I addressed to the Chief Secretary to the Government of Fort St. George, under date the 16th instant. Letter from Mr. Elphinstone.

'I have, etc.,

'(Signed) M. ELPHINSTONE.

'Camp, Sirola,
'18*th February*, 1818.'

'To George Strachey, Esq., etc., etc., etc.

'SIR,

'When I had last the honour to address you, suggesting the addition of a battalion to Brigadier-General Munro's force, I wrote under the impression that the Brigadier-General was already at the head of a considerable detachment, placed at his disposal by the Right Honourable the Governor. I am now informed that this is not the case, and I therefore trust I may be excused in pointing out the great necessity there is for the presence of a force to the south of the Krishna. Should it appear in the same light to the Right Honourable the Governor, his own anxiety to promote every branch of the public service will probably induce him to employ such a detachment Letter from Mr. Elphinstone.

as he can spare in that part of the country. The presence of General Munro, the dislike of the inhabitants to the Mahrattas, and their knowledge of the benefits of our Government from their vicinity to the provinces, would enable a small force to gain greater advantages to the south of the Krishna, than a much stronger one in any other part of the Peshwa's dominions. If there were only troops enough to reduce a few strong forts that overawe the country, there can be little doubt that the whole of the inhabitants would come forward to assist us. If it be desirable to undertake this settlement from the facility with which it may be accomplished, it is still more so from the importance of the consequences to which it would tend. The lands of almost all the great Jahagirdars are situated in that direction, and their being occupied or threatened would soon draw off those chiefs from the Peshwa. The direct effect of such a secession on the Peshwa's power would be great, and the effect on public opinion would be much greater. The seizure of this country would also cut off much of Baji Rav's own resources; it would narrow the ground of his operations and it would facilitate ours, by enabling us to form depôts where they are now much wanted, and to derive all the advantages of carrying on war on the borders of a friendly country.

'It would enable General Munro to advance in this direction, so as to meet the progress of this division, and thus to reduce the whole of the country south of Puna before the monsoon. It would likewise shut up the only direct entrance for the Peshwa and his banditti into the Company's territories, and would compel them, if they ventured on such an invasion, to penetrate in the first instance through the dominions of the Nizam, and to traverse a great extent of country before they approached our frontier. But the great argument in favour of the proposed arrangement is its tendency to bring the present war to a conclusion. I therefore submit it to the Right Honourable the Governor, in the confidence that it will meet with his approbation, unless its execution should materially interfere with the general policy of his Government.

'I have, etc.,

'(Signed) M. ELPHINSTONE.

'Camp, Nira Bridge,
'*16th February*, 1818.'

'To Francis Warden, Esq., etc., etc., etc.

'SIR,

'I have the honour to forward, for the information of the Right Honourable the Governor, a copy of a letter dated 16th instant, which I have addressed to Brigadier-General Smith for his future guidance in pursuit of the Peshwa. Letter from Mr. Elphinstone.

'I have, etc.,

'(Signed) M. ELPHINSTONE.

'Camp at Sinhaghur,
'*20th February*, 1818.'

'To his Excellency the Marquis of Hastings, K.G., etc., etc., etc.

'MY LORD,

'1. I had the honour to receive your Excellency's letter, dated April 6th, on the morning of the 25th; the light division was then within a march of Puna, and it occurred to me, as promising great advantages, to request Colonel Smith to arrange so as completely to surround the city on his arrival at his ground, and then to demand that the Peshwa should give hostages for the surrender of Letter from Mr. Elphinstone.

Trimbakji within a fixed time, to give his Highness a certain time to consider of this proposal, and in the event of his not complying, to endeavour to force his palace and seize his person. This proceeding would have been justified by my declarations to his Highness, which bound neither party longer than till the receipt of your Excellency's orders, and which had besides been daily violated by his Highness. It would have been very important if successful, by preventing the Peshwa's escaping to his numerous forts, and thus finishing the war at a blow; but some considerations induced me to give up the plan, and finally to determine not to attack the Peshwa in Puna at all, if it were possible to avoid doing so.

'2. The first of these considerations was that notwithstanding my declarations, the mere circumstance of our keeping up our intercourse with him would lead the Peshwa to expect some formal notice before we proceed to hostilities; and that from the manner in which we obtained our footing in the heart of his country, his Highness was entitled to more delicacy than a prince going to war in other circumstances.

'3. Another equally powerful consideration was the probable fate of the city of Puna. The inhabitants have been so much accustomed to look upon us as friends, that the approach of our troops and all other preparations had excited no alarm; I believe, indeed, the people in the city have more confidence in us than in the Peshwa. His Highness has not less than 7,000 Arabs and other infantry in Puna, besides the cavalry, and he possesses a fortified palace in the centre of the city. It is not, therefore, to be supposed that he could be seized without a struggle; and in the event of resistance, it would scarcely be expected of any troops that they should distinguish between the part of the inhabitants that were hostile and that which was neutral. The city, therefore, would be exposed to the usual calamities of a place taken by assault, and they would be the more felt as none of the people have removed their families or property. In addition to other more powerful motives for avoiding those evils, was the unpopularity it would bring on any government we might have to set up, and on our own measures, which at present, I imagine, are rather looked on with approbation.

'4. For all these reasons it appeared best to allow the light division to occupy its old ground at Kirkee, about four miles to the north of the city, to wait for full instructions from your Excellency, to proceed gradually with the Peshwa, giving him full time to correct his mistakes, if so disposed; and when it became necessary to attack the town, to begin by giving notice to the defenceless inhabitants to quit it, taking proper precautions to prevent the departure of the Peshwa and of his troops, if they should have continued in the city till that period. This plan was settled in communications with Colonel Smith, who came in a day before the light division, for the purpose of concerting the arrangements to be adopted.

'5. After the arrival of the light division things went on as usual the first two or three days. I received information during this time of the increase of the insurrection in Khandesh, and the junction of a body of troops from Hindustan to one division of the insurgents at Bareindir; another division appeared to be forming to the north of Nasik. These two divisions were represented, in the native khabars that came to me, and to Captain Sydenham, as amounting in all to 10,000 men; but this must be greatly exaggerated. The party from Hindustan is under Gangaji Rokelah, and is said to be on the part of Scindia; but it appears to be a part of the Barra Bhái, a famous body of free troops, who were formerly attached to that prince, but I believe have now quitted him; the insurgents to the south were said to have disappeared from the country about Jut and Manu (where, indeed, the presence of Major Macdowell's detachment rendered it impossible for them to remain), and were represented to be in smaller numbers than before in the south of the Konkan, and in the neighbouring parts of the Western Ghauts.

'6. On the 1st of May I received information of the capture of the Peshwa's fort of Prasit Gar by the insurgents, which was also confirmed by the Durbar. On the 2nd Ragho Pant came to me and said that the progress of the rebels had now reached an alarming height, and that it became absolutely necessary for the Peshwa to take vigorous measures against them. The first object was to recover the fort they had taken, for which purpose a force composed of that under Naro Pant Apte, and detachments belonging to Gokhle and Waman Rav Apte should assemble near Ranaur, and some guns should be sent to them from Puna; that as the Mahrattas might be inclined to the rebels, Gokhle had been ordered to entertain as many natives of other countries as he could; that to prevent the capture of any more forts his Highness intended to send military stores and other necessaries to all those belonging to his government, and to increase the garrisons; and that as the fort of Wassota was of particular importance and had no guns mounted on it, his Highness intended to send some to it. Considering all that had passed on the subject of the Peshwa's forts and preparations, I could not but look upon this as a very undisguised attempt to obtain my acquiescence in his open prosecution of the measures on which I had so often remonstrated. I had long supposed that the rebels would be allowed to take possession of some of the Peshwa's forts, and the improbable account given by Ragho Pant of the capture strengthened my belief in the collusion of the Peshwa's officers in the occupation of Prasit Gar; the rebels were represented to have introduced themselves into the fort as countrymen carrying bundles of grass, in which they had concealed arms. This sort of stratagem is often practised in towns where many country people are allowed to carry their goods unsuspected to the market, but it does not at all seem suited to a hill-fort, where there is probably only a small garrison, where there can be no market, and in all likelihood no great consumption of grass, as they are in general difficult of access to animals. Even if Prasit Gar had been taken by some independent insurgents, and not made over to Trimbakji, the same measures that were successful on a similar occasion a year ago, were the most likely to have been adopted on this, without general exertions and new levies on foreign troops, and without sending guns to Wassota, which, as it has been many months preparing for a siege, can scarcely be liable to be surprised by a rabble. I pointed out these suspicions and the grounds of them to Ragho Pant, and said that the Peshwa's proceedings could not be misunderstood; that this was indeed no more than an open communication of the preparations which had been so long carried on unavowed; that his Highness was at liberty to adopt any measures he thought proper; that the British Government was equally at liberty; and that whatever might happen after this, his Highness could not complain of being taken unprepared.

'7. On the 3rd I received intimation of the stopping of the post by the insurgents in Cuttack, which rendered it entirely uncertain when I might receive the instructions for which I had so long been looking, and obliged me to come to the resolution of acting without waiting for them. I understood by a private letter from Mr. Adams, dated the 7th, that the surrender of Trimbakji was likely to be made the preliminary to all negotiations; and it was the universal opinion here, justified by all appearances, that the Peshwa would stand a contest rather than give him up. In the event of war, there was little doubt that his Highness would fly to Rayagar, in the Konkan, where it would be impossible to carry on operations after the commencement of the monsoon. That season seldom commences in this part of India after the first week in June, so that there was only one month left for this important operation; and considering the difficulty of transporting a battering-train down the Western Ghats, few of which are practicable for guns, and the still greater difficulty of bringing it up after the rains began, there appeared to be considerable hazard in undertaking the siege, however early, and a certainty of ill success if it were any longer deferred. On the other hand, if the Peshwa were secure in Rayagar, and had carried his brother with him, as he certainly would do, we should be unable to act at all in the Konkan during the rains, and equally unable to adopt any settled plan for establishing a new government in the Deccan. From this last circumstance, and from the peculiar situation of the Peshwa as nominal head of the Mahratta Empire, it was probable that a lengthened contest would draw in the greater part of the Mahratta powers, if not of the majority of the Mahratta nation. After fully discussing these subjects with Colonel Smith, it appeared to me highly imprudent to delay longer than the 6th, which would give time for my instructions to arrive, supposing a duplicate to have been sent by Nagpur, or supposing the postmaster at Calcutta to have taken measures for forwarding them by sea to the undisturbed ports of the northern Circars. I therefore took the first opportunity of a visit from Ragho Pant, to point out the critical situation at which things had arrived, supposing the Peshwa had determined not to apprehend Trimbakji; and on the 5th I sent a message to the Bháû, to say that I had a proposal of the utmost importance to make to him, that I should give it to him in writing at daybreak on the 6th, and that if he chose to send a person in his confidence, I would accompany it with full verbal explanations. My proposal, I said, was of such a nature as must determine the question of peace or war in one day. In the evening Ragho Pant returned with a request from the Peshwa that I would attend him next evening; I agreed to this request, and afterwards determined to delay the delivery of my proposals, and to ascertain the Peshwa's sentiments on the simple question of surrendering Trimbakji, by discussing it accompanied with the limitation as to time, with the demand for securities, and the prospect for further demands. I enclose the original notes of my conversation with the Peshwa, the result of which was that his Highness, even when warned that his refusal would lead to open war in one day, refused to enter into any engagement to deliver up Trimbakji.

'8. The whole of the Peshwa's behaviour at this meeting displayed a degree of firmness very unusual to him; and his language, at the same time that it was perfectly conciliatory, evinced considerable ability and perfect self-possession. His Highness's coolness during the whole of the present discussions has formed a contrast to his consternation during those after the death of the Shastri; at that time he shut himself up from the sight of everyone; his measures were irresolute and bewildered, and his appearance betrayed the height of confusion and terror; but of late he has held regular Darbars, has entered into partaking of entertainments at the houses of his chiefs, and discussing his preparations along with them, and conciliating them by compliments and professions of his reliance on their courage and fidelity. He showed a temporary alarm for a day or two, after the measures taken to increase the efficiency of the Puna Brigade; and likewise a few days ago, when he sent for Mr. Jefferys, the surgeon of the Residency, on pretence of consulting him about his arm, he showed evident signs of alarm, and told Mr. Jefferys that he saw the dangers of his situation, and was willing to purchase a renewal of our friendship by any sacrifice except that of Trimbakji. His Highness's confidence appears to have been partly founded on the prospect held out to him of success in the old Mahratta warfare of hostilities and flying armies of plundering horse, and partly on a rooted conviction that we would not proceed to extremities. These hopes will perhaps account for his conduct, especially when combined with the favourite Mahratta maxim of holding out in every negotiation till the very last moment, without caring for the disgrace of ultimate submission.

'9. Early in the morning of the 7th I sent in the enclosed paper to the Minister, demanding that the Peshwa should engage, before the expiration of twenty-four hours, to surrender Trimbakji within a month from that day; and should give up the forts of Singhur, Purandhar, and Rayagar, as pledges for fulfilling his engagement. It was necessary, for the reasons already stated, to give a short period for consideration, and a long one could not be required at the end of a discussion of three months' duration. I thought it advisable to allow a liberal time for the apprehension of Trimbakji, and it was absolutely necessary to take some security to prevent a repetition of the same illusory proceedings which I had already so often experienced. I accompanied the first memorandum with a note to the Bhâû, in which I adverted to the nature of your Lordship's probable demands, but assured him that if the Peshwa acceded to the preliminaries now proposed, those demands should not go to deprive him of his musnud.

'10. The Minister received this paper with so much diffidence, and put off delivering it to the Peshwa until after dinner for reasons so very frivolous, that his message would have appeared contemptuous but for the Mahratta practice above alluded to, of putting on a bold face to the last. The whole day passed without a message from the Peshwa, and with an appearance of security which seemed to be intended to conceal a design of his Highness's leaving the city during the night. This suspicion was confirmed by the preparations which were made immediately after sunset. All the horse in the city got under arms, and repaired to the neighbourhood of the Peshwa's palace; powder and ball were delivered out to them, and they were desired to be prepared to move at a moment's warning. One party of 1,000 horse belonging to Gokhle was led out by the chief in person to a place on the southern side of the city, where it remained during the night. The general impression in the city was that the Peshwa intended to retreat; and so strong was my conviction of this intention, that I was on the point of writing to Colonel Smith, to beg that he would put the cavalry in motion for the purpose of frustrating it. I, however, thought it best to run the risk of his Highness effecting his escape, rather than that of driving him to extremities while professing to offer him terms.

'11. At this time I received a visit from Prabhakar

Ballal and Bapu Kourikar, who came applying for a delay of four days, which I decidedly refused. I enclose a detailed account of this conference, because an attempt has been made to misrepresent it. About one a.m. on the 6th, Krishna Ráv came to request a delay of five days, and to beg that I would give up my demand for Rayagar, and be contented with Sinhagar and Purandhar. This of course was refused, and Krishna Ráv was desired to acquaint the Bháû that though our other measures should proceed, the city should not be attacked until the unresisting inhabitants had been allowed time to withdraw. About daybreak Prabhakar Pandit returned with a similar request, to which I gave a similar answer. Part of this short conversation was important in one point of view, but need not be detailed in this place. By this time the troops had passed the Residency, and I was on the point of setting out to join them, when Jayawant Ráv (the principal person under the Bháû) arrived with Krishna Rav. The same attempts to obtain an alteration in the terms, or delay in the execution, were now made once more; and on these failing, Jayawant Ráv consented to give up the forts; after which a discussion took place about the time at which they were to surrender, and the means of removing the property. The time was at length made to depend on the arrival of our detachments alone, and no property was to be removed after possession was taken except the private property of the garrisons. Jayawant Ráv then requested that the troops marching to the towns might be stopped, or removed if they had arrived; but this was declined until the terms should have been carried into execution. It was indeed impossible to have stopped them, for although I lost no time after Jayawant Ráv's departure, I did not reach the head of the line until Colonel Smith's operations were completed.

'12. Colonel Smith had taken opportunities of making himself fully acquainted with all the outlets of the city, and had likewise been furnished with a very detailed plan of the place, drawn up for the occasion by Mr. Coats, vaccinating surgeon, as well as with an excellent map of its environs. He had made his arrangements on the preceding evening, and marched at daybreak from his camp, four miles north of the city. The brigade under Lieutenant-Colonel Leighton moved at the same time, and the city, which is at least five miles in circumference, was completely surrounded within three hours after daybreak. The troops were so disposed that it was impossible for any person to quit the city without a contest; and the whole operation was conducted by Colonel Smith with so much order, arrangement, and temper, that there was not a shot fired, notwithstanding several embarrassing and irritating circumstances.

'13. About ten in the forenoon, the Karkuns who were to deliver over Sinhagar and Purandhar made their appearance, and soon after the detachments moved off. I then voluntarily offered to withdraw the troops posted round the city, which I had before said should not be done till the places were given up; this was done within three hours after they took up their positions. The reserve, which had reached Wuroli, within eighteen miles of Puna, and was advancing, was countermanded at the earnest request of the Peshwa's Ministers. The fort Sinhagar was surrounded last night, and Purandhar this morning; no treasure was found in the former, and I have received no details regarding the latter; more delay was made about Rayagar, the great depository of the Peshwa's treasures. The Karkun did not arrive till three in the afternoon. When he did come he misled the detachment, and he was so mounted as greatly to delay its progress. After furnishing him with a palankin and guides of our own, the detachment set off again, and ought to reach Rayagar by to-morrow evening. About five in the afternoon Colonel Smith moved off with the light division to a position about four miles south of the city, where he still remains.

'14. The people of the city observed the first operations of the troops with the greatest appearance of security; but when they saw the preparations kept up on both sides, they began to apprehend a contest in the streets, and showed considerable agitation and alarm. This ceased when the troops were removed, and, except where their own safety was endangered, the whole of the people appeared to view the contest with the most perfect indifference. Gokhle and Chintaman Ráv are said to have been indignant at the Peshwa's submission, and to have stayed away from his palace, though he sent them messages of explanation and apology.

'I have, etc.,

'(Signed) M. Elphinstone,

'Resident at Puna.

'Poona,

'*9th May*, 1817.'

Notes of a Conference with His Highness the Peshwa, May 6th, 1817.

The Bháû began a long speech on the advantages of the alliance, the Peshwa's desire to preserve it, and the propriety of removing any obstruction that had arisen in it.

Mr. Elphinstone's conference with the Peshwa.

The Peshwa then took up the discourse, and enlarged on the dependence of his family for two generations on the English, the opposition he had met with in all stages of his reign from all the members of the Mahratta Empire, and the report he had received from the British Government. He pointed out in great detail that his ruin was certain if this support was withdrawn, and protested his determination to adhere to the alliance as long as he lived; he said he had many enemies who might misrepresent his conduct, but that these were the real sentiments of his heart. This was replied to by Mr. Elphinstone's saying that his Highness, it appeared, was anxious to maintain the alliance; that the British Government was at last equally so, but that differences had arisen which were now to be removed; that the British had never listened to his enemies, but that he had given his ear to those who were enemies both to the British Government and to his Highness, and that this had brought things to the present pass. The Peshwa protested that he had always considered the enemies of the one state as the enemies of the other. Mr. Elphinstone stated the conduct of the British Government about Trimbakji, and the warnings he had given his Highness till after the march to Natepota, and that it was very gradually, and by great neglect of Mr. Elphinstone's representations, that things had been allowed to gain the length they had. The Peshwa endeavoured to exculpate himself from a connivance at the insurrection, and said that he had sent out Gokhle's horse at a very early stage of it; and if they had failed to obtain information of it, it was not his fault. Mr. Elphinstone enlarged on the notoriety of the insurrection, and expressed surprise that the Peshwa had never heard of it, when Mr. Elphinstone under so many disadvantages had been able to apprize his Highness of the various stages of its progress. Mr. Elphinstone adverted to the general belief that the Peshwa protected the insurgents, and the great advantage the insurgents derived from that opinion. The Peshwa expressed his wonder that people should entertain such an opinion, and said that his state was full of his enemies. Mr. Elphinstone explained the reasons why the people entertained that opinion—that his Highness denied the existence of the insurrection when everybody else knew of it ; that he always treated the insurgents as the enemies of the English exclusively, while his officers offered them no opposition ; and to conclude, that he prepared his forts and armies as if he was determined to support the insurgents, or to resist any demand of the British Government to act against them.

His Highness entered into the usual explanations of his conduct in these respects, and added that he was ready to punish any of the people who had known of the insurrection, and who had not told him of it. Mr. Elphinstone asked why none of them had been punished hitherto, when his Highness was satisfied that there was a rebellion which had not been reported to him. He answered that Gokhle was powerful, but that now Mr. Elphinstone and the Bháû should have an inquiry, and that the delinquent should be punished. Mr. Elphinstone said that it was not Gokhle's officer, but all the officers in the country who ought to have reported ; and their not having done so could only be attributed to a secret influence in favour of the rebels. Mr. Elphinstone added that Trimbakji was still at large, and still exciting an insurrection, and that nothing was done against him. His Highness said that Trimbakji had a number of friends and relations, and much money ; but that if Mr. Elphinstone would show anybody who had assisted him, he should be punished. Mr. Elphinstone replied that it belonged to the Government of the country to make those discoveries ; that Trimbakji had left Tanna without any money, that all his houses were in the Peshwa's country, and all his friends and adherents at Puna, and that he could not have collected his money from all parts of the country, and have assembled troops, without the place of his residence becoming known to the Government. Mr. Elphinstone now came to the point of the demands he had to make on the part of the Governor-General; he had explained that he had received a letter from Calcutta; that it merely contained part of the Governor-General's instructions, which he would communicate on the following day in an official form; that it was his wish to have waited, so as to be enabled to communicate the whole substance of his Excellency's demands at once; that he had now heard that an insurrection in Cuttack had cut off the communication by dawk, and that he was therefore compelled to come forward without an accurate knowledge of any of his Excellency's terms, except a preliminary demand for the unconditional surrender of Trimbakji; that by the time that was done, he would be able to state what further demands would be made.

The Peshwa replied to this by saying that he was ready to meet the wishes of the Governor-General in every particular; that he would do all in his power to seize Trimbakji; but that if he failed, he hoped it would not be concluded that he was insincere; that he would do all that human exertions could effect; that he would pledge himself in the most sacred manner, by placing his hand on Mr. Elphinstone's to make those exertions; and that he would leave no means untried to effect his purpose. Mr. Elphinstone said that he was not disposed personally to doubt his Highness's professions, but that among states some more solid proof of sincerity was usual; and he begged his Highness would consider of some pledge by which the Governor-General might be led to expect more to be done than had been effected during the last eight months by his Highness, in endeavouring to seize the person of Trimbakji.

His Highness replied that his exertions now should be unremitting; that he would issue orders, with his own seal affixed to them, and deliver them to Mr. Elphinstone, directing all his officers to aid in securing Trimbakji's person; that, for himself, he had never seen Trimbakji from the moment he had left Puna to go to Wassandar; that to this fact he was ready to swear by the water of the Ganges; and that the reason of his having made no effort to ascertain where Trimbakji was hitherto, was the knowledge his Highness had of his numerous enemies, who, if he made those exertions, and Trimbakji had escaped out of his dominions, would have represented his flight as connived at by his Highness. Mr. Elphinstone reminded his Highness of his having made a similar declaration about not searching for Trimbakji seven months ago, and of his having afterwards promised, on Mr. Elphinstone's remonstrating, to make the most diligent search for that fugitive; that it appeared his Highness had made no such search; that the same assurances which would have been quite sufficient in the commencement of the discussions were by no means so now; and that his Highness must promise to seize Trimbakji within a certain time, and give some security for performance, otherwise his Highness might put off a settlement for a whole month, and then say that he had endeavoured to find out Trimbakji, but had failed in obtaining the object of his search.

The Peshwa rejoined by saying that he was ready to give this promise under his own hand for the satisfaction of the Governor-General.

Mr. Elphinstone then reminded the Peshwa of the

principles on which an adjustment was brought about when Trimbakji was formerly demanded; that things had by no means come to such a pitch as at present, and yet amity had only been restored by his Highness delivering up Trimbakji and agreeing to abide by any further demands which the Governor-General might dictate, provided they were not of such a nature as to overturn the alliance; that on the present occasion matters had become far more serious, and that the two States were now on the eve of a rupture; that Mr. Elphinstone could not answer for the present state of things lasting an hour, or a day (certainly not two days); and the Peshwa could not expect that the only reparation he was to make was to be a mere promise to exert himself to discover and to seize Trimbakji.

The Peshwa replied to this by mere professions of sincerity.

Mr. Elphinstone observed that in a case like the present no proof of sincerity could be admitted except performance; that unless Trimbakji were seized and given up there could be no security against future disturbances of the same or a more dangerous nature, the moment our army was employed at a distance.

The Peshwa said that his army should, in a case of that nature, be placed in the van to bear the brunt of the battle; that we should see how they exerted themselves; and that, if they were destroyed in the attack, it would be then time for the English troops to act, and not till then. Mr. Elphinstone said that what was wanted was a proof that his Highness's own designs were friendly, and that his declaring his inability to act effectually against an enemy of the British Government within his own territories gave very little reason to rely on his goodwill. Mr. Elphinstone then turned to the Bháû, and asked him if he had received the message sent to him through Krishna Rav regarding a paper which it was his intention to send to his Highness; to which the Bhâû assented. Mr. Elphinstone then recapitulated the state to which things had been brought, said that he begged his Highness to reflect that the demand he now made for Trimbakji was not on his own part, that he was announcing the resolutions of the Governor-General, from which he could not recede if he were inclined; that he would send the paper alluded to to-morrow morning, which specified the security required from his Highness for the fulfilment of this preliminary; and he entreated that his Highness would seriously weigh the matter, for that he had only a day for consideration; and he trusted that he would, by acceding to the proposal, preserve the alliance.

During the latter part of the conversation the Peshwa constantly asked Mr. Elphinstone to point out in what way he should act to seize Trimbakji. Mr. Elphinstone said that it was impossible for him to point out in detail the measures that were to be adopted by his Highness's Government, but that if his Highness would show a serious wish to apprehend Trimbakji, Mr. Elphinstone would answer for his success; that the very question (so unusual with his Highness) how he was to manage an interior affair of his own government, evinced a disinclination to act cordially on the part of his Highness; that Mr. Elphinstone would, however, mention a few of the steps which his Highness might take, though he would not say that there might not be more and better ways that would occur to a person familiar with the country, and with the means possessed by the Government; his Highness might seize all Trimbakji's adherents, some of whom were in Puna, and many in the countries in which Trimbakji had raised his men; such as Mahadáji Pant, the

Mamlutdar* of Natepota, and Bapu Gaikwar, the Patel† of Shetfal; that Mr. Elphinstone could mention a hundred others, and did not mean to say that he required the seizure of those particular persons, nor would he consider it the slightest satisfaction, but he merely pointed out one among many modes of effecting the object in view; that he might also interrogate the Mamlutdars of the countries in which Trimbakji was known to have resided, and might thus trace him from place to place until he was found; that the people who sent treasure to him and those who had returned from his camp might be interrogated, and that many other plans might be suggested, even if his Highness had no information of his own. His Highness declared that the persons in question should not only be seized, but their lands and property confiscated; he begged that Mr. Elphinstone would allow one of his assistants to concert measures with the Bháû for the operation of his intention, and requested that that gentleman should be allowed to act as an assessor to the Bháû in his inquiries, and to point out any method of investigation conformable to the practice of Europe, and not that of the Mahratta country. He denied, however, that it could be proved that Trimbakji had ever been with the insurgents, or in his Highness's country at all; that he might be alive or he might be dead, he might be here or he might be in Mount Himalaya, but nobody had either seen him or could say that he had any share in raising this insurrection, the existence of which, his Highness said, could no longer be denied. Mr. Elphinstone said that many persons had seen Trimbakji, and reminded his Highness that his two nephews, Godaji Dengle and Mahipa Ráv Dengle, were now at the head of insurrections in Khandesh.

* Farmer of revenue. † Head-man of a village.

The Peshwa replied by saying that there were many persons of the Dengle family. Mr. Elphinstone said these were Trimbakji's near relations; to this the Peshwa replied by saying he had, of course, many relations. His Highness then said that the supposed Trimbakji might be an impostor assuming his name, as had happened in the case of the famous Bháû who fell at Paniput. Mr. Elphinstone said there could be no object in the insurgent's taking Trimbakji's name, that he was a person of low origin, and that he only acquired consequence by his Highness's countenance; that generally speaking he was detested throughout his Highness's dominions, and that it was idle to talk of anyone assuming so popular a name as the means of raising an insurrection.

Mr. Elphinstone, in conclusion, conjured his Highness, as he valued the friendship of the British Government and the welfare of his own state, to think seriously of what had been said, and to be prepared with such a resolution as might avert a rupture.

The Peshwa replied by the most cordial professions of his devotion to the British Government, and said that so seriously did he reflect on the present state of affairs, that he loathed his meals, and could not sleep from extreme anxiety. The Bháû asked how the answer to Mr. Elphinstone's demands was to be transmitted. Mr. Elphinstone replied that it did not signify. If it was in acquiescence a common jasûds might bring it; and if not, no messenger could effect a change. While the preparations for the ceremony of taking leave were making, his Highness paid numerous personal compliments in his manner to Mr. Elphinstone, making the warmest professions towards him, and declaring that he knew him to be his best and most valuable friend, and looked to him alone for advice in these times of difficulty.

(Signed) M. Elphinstone.

Notes addressed to his Highness the Peshwa, dated 7th May.

Mr. Elphinstone's Note to the Peshwa.

'I need not repeat what has so often been said on the subject of the pretended insurrection so long connived at by his Highness, or of the preparations made by his Highness, apparently to support that rebellion. The proceedings amounted to a commencement of war on the part of the Peshwa, but I proposed a truce on certain terms, all of which had been broken by his Highness; I proposed to his Highness upwards of a month ago to discontinue his hostile proceedings and wait the answer of the Governor-General to my report of his Highness's transactions. At that time his Highness agreed to forbear from any further preparations, and even promised of his own accord to reduce those which had been already made. His Highness, however, not only failed in the last promise, but systematically departed from other articles of my demand. He continued to recruit his troops, and to prepare his forts, until it became necessary to fulfil the declaration contained in my first note, by similar proceedings on the part of the British Government; since which his Highness has continued his secret preparations, the insurgents have taken the fort of Prasit Gar, and his Highness has formally announced to me his intention of strengthening the garrisons of all his forts, and in particular of sending ordnance to the fort of Wassota, which it is well known has been diligently provided for a siege for many months. Thus it appears that his Highness, instead of waiting the answer of the Governor-General, has carried on all his operations without the least restraint, so that every day improves his situation, while it renders worse that of the British Government, by bringing nearer the setting-in of the rainy season. These considerations render it impossible for me, consistently with prudence, to wait any longer; and in order to prevent the necessity of a rupture, I must insist on the immediate surrender of Trimbakji Dengle within the period of one month. A month is allowed to give time to send orders for seizing Trimbakji and bring him to Puna, but it is impossible for me to allow the season to pass away without some solid proof of the Peshwa's sincerity. I must therefore insist on being put in possession of three of his Highness's principal forts as security for his fulfilling the agreement. These forts are Sinhagar, Purandhar, and Rayagar; of which I expect Sinhagar to be delivered up in the course of to-morrow, Purandhar in the course of the next day, and the other fort immediately on the arrival of the troops before it. If any delay whatever takes place in making over these forts, hostilities shall commence without delay. In the event of his Highness making over the forts in question, he shall be at liberty to put his seal on any treasure or valuables that may be deposited in them, and the whole shall be restored to him in the same state in which it is given over, without hesitation or demur, immediately on the fulfilment of the preliminary article above mentioned. This done, we shall proceed to negotiate respecting the satisfaction to be afforded to the Governor-General for the Peshwa's recent breach of treaty, as well as the security to be given for his future good conduct. It was my wish to have waited for the Governor-General's instructions, and to have made his Highness acquainted with the full extent of his Excellency's demands at first; but as his Highness would not suspend his proceedings, it was impossible for me to suspend mine.

'I must request that his Highness will give me a definite answer to the demand made in this paper before daylight to-morrow morning, until which time no measures of hostility will be adopted by me, unless, indeed, any hostile intentions are displayed by his Highness, or his Highness should attempt to quit the city.

'(Signed) M. ELPHINSTONE,
'Resident.'

NOTE SENT TO THE MINISTER ON THE MORNING OF MAY 8TH, ENCLOSING THE NOTE OF MAY 7TH.

Mr. Elphinstone's Note to the Minister.

'I have now the honour to forward the paper I yesterday alluded to. It was drawn up on the day before yesterday, but nothing has happened to require any alteration in it. I again beg the Peshwa to consider and to prevent the necessity of a rupture, which, if it once takes place, will be difficult to accommodate; the present demands are, with the exception of the security now required, the same as those agreed to by the Peshwa on the last discussions to surrender Trimbakji, and to acquiesce in the Governor-General's further demands. I cannot promise that those demands shall now be as lenient as before, but I will undertake that they shall not affect his Highness's continuance to enjoy the Musnud.

'(Signed) M. ELPHINSTONE,
'Resident at Puna.'

NOTE OF A CONVERSATION BETWEEN MR. ELPHINSTONE, PRABHAKAR PANDIT, AND BAPU KONRIKAR, ON THE NIGHT OF THE 7TH MAY, 1817.

Mr. Elphinstone's Note of a Conversation.

'Prabhakar Pandit came at night and said that Bapu Konrikar was with him; but on Mr. Elphinstone's proposing to call that person in, he said he wished first to discuss the subject he was sent on himself. He then begged four days' delay on the Peshwa's part, saying that he would give up the forts at the end of that time, but that he required the interval to consult his own people. Mr. Elphinstone said there was no need of consideration on a subject that had so often been discussed; that he could not accuse himself of omitting to warn the Peshwa, step by step, of the consequences of his conduct; that he only asked the Peshwa to give security for performing what he had often promised; and that if his Highness meant to comply he could do it then as well as four days hence, whereas if he meant not to do so, the gain of time was an object. Prabhakar Pandit continued to urge his request, and saying that four days were nothing in addition to so many days that were past, Mr. Elphinstone said that he had made up his mind after full deliberation, and that no reason had been brought forward why he should alter it; he added that he was unwilling to speak ill of the Peshwa at all times, and especially on an occasion that might be the last on which he would communicate with his Highness, but he could not but remind Prabhakar Ballal of the repeated promises made by the Peshwa, through him, and of the uniform breach of every one of them by his Highness. After so many disappointments Mr. Elphinstone said he could not trust to his Highness's promises again. There were several pauses in the conversation, after one of them Mr. Elphinstone said that he heard the Peshwa was on the point of flying; that his doing so would bring on hostility, even before the appointed hour; that Mr. Elphinstone could not but be reluctant to destroy an alliance of so many years' standing, but still it was his duty to refuse the delay solicited.

'Towards the end of the conversation Prabhakar Pandit altered his language, which had from the first been ambiguous. He formerly let it be understood that the forts would be given up at the end of four days, and now said that an answer should be returned after that period.

Bapu Konrikar was afterwards called, and the same observations were repeated to him that had been made to Prabhakar Ballal; in addition to what passed before, one of the Brahmins said that the Peshwa requested this delay of Mr. Elphinstone as a mark of his private friendship. Mr. Elphinstone said he was at a loss what to answer to such a request, as the thing was impossible. When the party had risen to break up Bapu Konrikar repeated several of the arguments for delay, and Mr. Elphinstone repeated his answer, and took a solemn leave of them, saying the time for negotiation was now fast expiring, and that he trusted his Highness would yet consider and preserve the alliance.

'(Signed) M. ELPHINSTONE,
'Resident.'

'To the Most Noble the Marquis of Hastings, K.G., etc., etc., etc.

'MY LORD,

'I have not addressed your Excellency since the 9th instant, because I had no change to report in the Peshwa's conduct or measures. I am happy to have it in my power at length to state that he appears to be sincerely desirous to apprehend Trimbakji, and to recover the favour of the British Government. Up to the middle of the month his Highness continued to use every exertion to put things in train for a flight from Puna. He issued three months' pay to the troops in his service, and continued to add to their numbers. His forces out of Puna continued to assemble near Satara, in conse-

Letter from Mr. Elphinstone.

quence of the orders they had formerly received. His principal adherents sent their families away from Puna, and their example was followed by most people in the town whose circumstances admitted of it. His Highness also brought about an entire reconciliation with his brother, with whom he is said to have interchanged the most solemn oaths. His Highness's plan at that time was thought to be to retire with his brother to Satara, and after arranging for the security of the Rajah, to proceed with the force under Naro Pant Apte (10,000 horse and foot) either to Wassota or Dharwar. On the night of the 13th it was the universal belief that his Highness was on the point of quitting Poona, in company with Gokhle: all his horse was ready, and by every account I have received he was nearer setting out than at any other period, excepting, perhaps, the night of the 8th. He was, however, prevailed on to stay, and although he has shown several signs of adhering to his former system, since then I think he has been becoming gradually less inclined to any desperate course. One proof of the continuance of his indiscreet conduct was his issuing four or six lacs of rupees to his principal Sardars for their troops, so late as the 17th instant.

'During all this time the Peshwa sent frequent messages to me through Sadashiv Mankeshwar, requiring a prolongation of the period assigned for the apprehension of Trimbakji, and requesting my consent to his going away from Puna, on account of an eclipse; he first mentioned Nasik as the place he was going to, and afterwards Phulsheher. His Highness also attempted, through the same channel, to draw from me a disclosure of the terms which were to be imposed on him if Trimbakji were seized. I declined complying with any of these applications, observing that his Highness's beginning by soliciting a prolongation of the truce before he had made any exertions to fulfil your Excellency's demands, looked as if he anticipated and intended a failure; that his quitting Puna at such a time was altogether unadvisable, and that my orders were on no account to negotiate until Trimbakji was given up. At these interviews with the Peshwa's Ministers I took constant occasion to impress on his Highness the value of the time he was allowing to elapse, and the impossibility of his persuading the British Government to accept of his exertions as satisfactory if they happened to be successful, when his own procrastination had so obviously contributed to their ill success. I likewise took pains during this period to guard against mistakes and misrepresentations by reminding the Ministers of the serious demands that were yet to come, even if Trimbakji were surrendered, and by making as public as I could the real footing on which things stood between the British Government and the Peshwa.

'I had the honour on the 10th instant to receive your Lordship's instructions, conveyed in Mr. Adams's despatch of the 7th April, but considering the state of agitation in which the Peshwa then was, I thought the immediate communication of your Excellency's sentiments might have too violent an effect on him. On the 4th, when Colonel Smith had returned to his old ground north of the town, and when the Peshwa's mind had become more tranquil, I presented a note, of which the enclosed is a translation, and accompanied it by repeated and earnest recommendations to his Highness to delay no longer the adoption of measures which were necessary for the preservation of his Government. After this the Peshwa's personal alarm appears to have been removed; but he began to see more distinctly than ever the dangers with which his state was surrounded. He began to express great anxiety about the conduct of the British Government at the expiration of the month and respecting the terms to be imposed if Trimbakji were surrendered. He wavered for some days between the different courses that were before him, sometimes consulting Sadashiv Mankeshwar, and sometimes his rival Moro Dixit, on the best means of obtaining good terms from the British Government, but oftener concerting with his old advisers the measures to be adopted in case of hostilities.

'At length, about the 20th instant, he appears to have determined on yielding to the counsels of Moro Dixit. He then issued proclamations offering a reward of two lacs of rupees and a village worth 1,000 rupees a year to anyone who would bring in Trimbakji, dead or alive, promising rewards for every information regarding him, and for the apprehension of his adherents, and granting a pardon to all his followers who should desert him, except twelve ringleaders, against whom, as well as those who should refuse to come in on this proclamation, the severest penalties were announced. Many hundred copies of this proclamation have been issued by his Highness, one hundred were sent to me, and have been distributed through our numerous detachments, and sent to all our news-writers and other agents, as well as to the Government of Bombay and Madras, and to all the Residencies.

'Besides issuing this proclamation, his Highness threw all Trimbakji's adherents who were confined in Puna into chains, and sent them to different hill-forts. He also sent orders to seize the families and destroy the houses of the twelve excepted from the amnesty, and apprehended some others, of whose offences I am not informed, and gave the most public indications of a desire to proceed with vigour against Trimbakji. His Highness had before gone through the ceremony of issuing orders to his officers to seize Trimbakji, and had desired Sadashiv Mankeshwar to employ a number of Harkárás in searching for him; but those steps made no impression upon anyone, especially as the undertaking was committed to the Bháû, whom his Highness is known to regard with distrust and dislike. His present activity is a contrast to his former indifference. He personally takes a great share in all the proceedings of his Ministers; and although he suffers the punishment of his habitual insincerity, in the distrust with which all his professions are received, yet most people are now convinced that he is sincerely desirous of recovering the ground he has lost, and of purchasing the security of his own person and Government by the sacrifice of the favourite for whom he has exposed himself to so many risks.

'It is not certainly known where Trimbakji is at present, but it is thought he is in the hills to the south of the river Perana. He was reported to be expected at Alandi on the 12th, with strong circumstance of probability. I sent a detachment of cavalry and infantry to apprehend him, which failed from various causes. On the next night Colonel Fitzsimon, who commands the reserve at Koregaum, received similar intelligence, and sent a strong detachment to Alandi; this also failed, and though there are some strong circumstances in favour of Trimbakji's having narrowly escaped both times, it is still doubtful whether he ever was at Alandi.

'The insurgents in Khandesh are reported to have assembled near Durab, to the estimated number of 8,000. Colonel Doveton has detached Colonel Walker with a light force against this body. Colonel Doveton himself remains at Borenair with the main body of the Hyderabad subsidiary force.

'Colonel Thompson's detachment is now near Pandharpur; its presence has effectually checked all attempts at insurrection in that part of the country, which Colonel Smith justly considered as the most disposed to rise. Colonel Milne's detachment is at Ahmednagar. The Vinchur Jahagirdar has again had an action with a party of insurgents near Sangamner, and has killed several. The Patwardhans, except Chintaman Ráv, remain at Lassore, where they were posted by Colonel Smith. Chintaman Ráv is at Puna; 1,000 of his horse have joined Naro Pant Apte. Appa Desái has taken no part in these disturbances.

'The Rani of Sawant Wari has succeeded in reconciling her chiefs, and has shown every intention of carrying into effect the plan alluded to in the letter intercepted by Mr. Hall; but it is to be hoped the change in his Highness the Peshwa's conduct will have a great effect on hers.

'Ballaji Koonjar died at Pandharpur on the 17th instant.

'I have, etc.,
'(Signed) M. Elphinstone,
'Resident at Puna.'

Translation of a Memorandum sent to his Highness the Peshwa, on the 14th May, 1817.

Memorandum.

'I formerly explained to your Highness that the dawk from Calcutta was stopped, and that therefore a delay had arisen in the receipt of the Governor-General's answer to my letters; but I was already aware that no discussions would take place with your Highness's Government until the surrender of Trimbakji Dengle. I have since received his Excellency's instructions, and shall communicate all that I am authorized to do to your Highness. His Lordship observes: "I have been made fully acquainted with the late proceedings of his Highness the Peshwa, and I am satisfied that his Highness has entered into a plot to injure the interests of the British Government, and that he is still engaged in it.

'" It became necessary for the British Government to insist on the punishment of Trimbakji for the crime he had committed. But, in consideration of the surrender of that person, it is hardly necessary to remind his Highness of the great moderation and forbearance evinced by me, both towards that person, and also in my communications with his Highness's Government.

'" At the very moment when his Highness was in the full enjoyment of the confidence and protection of the British Government, and was in the habit of expressing his cordial reliance on and friendship for that Government; at a time, too, when no unpleasant discussions had arisen on my part at his Court, and his Highness had not the slightest cause for apprehension or alarm—at such a time his Highness entered into a plot to injure the interests of the British Government, which has lost him the confidence of that state, and it therefore becomes necessary to adopt measures for the security of the British interests and those of their allies." No negotiation, however, can be opened on this subject till the delivery of Trimbakji. Therefore, if Trimbakji is not surrendered within the date of one month from the time he was demanded, war will be declared with his Highness's Government, and the British troops will be directed to attack his Highness's forces in all quarters, and to reduce his territories. Such are the commands of his Lordship. After the delivery of Trimbakji to an English detachment, I shall be prepared to communicate his Lordship's demands, which if not complied with, will prevent the continuation of peace. In the meantime, if his Highness should quit Puna during the present discussion, or if his Highness's troops should move from their present position, it will be considered as a declaration of war, and the British troops will immediately act. I have been directed by his Lordship to communicate this for your Highness's consideration, and I have therefore written the above memorandum.'

'To Sir Evan Nepean, etc., etc., etc.

'Camp at Kirkee,
'*6th November*, 1817.'

'Sir,

'The increase of the Peshwa's preparations having led me to call in the light battalion, and the reports from Puna having induced General Smith to concentrate his force at Pultamba, the Peshwa resolved to take the opportunity of attacking us before our reinforcements arrived. Accordingly, he sent me a message, requiring me to send away the European regiment and to make various other arrangements, as the price of his friendship. On my refusing, he withdrew to a hill on the south of the town, and sent out his troops against our force. The party from the Residency was withdrawn into camp, and the line moved out to meet the enemy at four yesterday afternoon. Their very numerous cavalry did little or no mischief; they had not many guns, and their infantry were not engaged. After a feeble stand they drew off their guns, and, it being now dark, our line returned to camp. The Peshwa is still at the hill of Parbatti, and the Gokhle, with his Highness's troops,

Letter from Mr. Elphinstone.

is in the rear of their yesterday's ground, where they will perhaps stand an action. Their loss is considerable in the affair of yesterday; ours I thought yesterday not above 30 killed and wounded, but I am afraid it will prove 100. The light battalion, and 1,000 auxiliary horse, joined us this morning. I beg you will excuse this scrawl, but all my writing implements, with everything I have, except the clothes on my back, form part of the blaze of the Residency, which is now smoking in sight.

'I am, etc.,

'(Signed) M. ELPHINSTONE.'

'To his Excellency the Marquis of Hastings, etc., etc.

'MY LORD,

'The pressure of business for these several days, and the uncertainty of the result, have prevented my hitherto reporting to your Excellency; but as we are now in a state of open war with the Peshwa, it is necessary to acquaint you with the manner in which the rupture was brought on, leaving all details for a subsequent despatch.

Letter from Mr. Elphinstone.

'The great military preparations of his Highness the Peshwa, his distinct refusal to send any part of the force he had collected away from Puna, the threatening position he had occupied in the neighbourhood of our camp, and above all, his unremitting endeavours to corrupt the fidelity of our native troops, rendered it absolutely necessary, in my judgment, to remove the brigade from the very bad position it occupied at the town, to that selected for it by General Smith.

'This circumstance, and that of our cantonment being on the alert on the 29th ultimo, the night before the arrival of the European regiment, removed the appear-

16

ance of confidence which had been in some measure kept up between us and the Peshwa. This appearance had afforded no advantage, except that of protracting an open rupture, for his Highness proceeded in all respects as if he were at open war; and all his subjects spoke of his declaring against us as an event in which nothing was uncertain but the time.

'The effect of our withdrawing was to encourage the Peshwa's people, who plundered our cantonments without any obstruction from their own Government, and also talked openly of the impending destruction of our detachment. An officer on his road to Bombay was also attacked, wounded, and plundered in open day, about two miles from Puna, and as far from the Residency; and the language of the Peshwa's Minister was that of perfect estrangement and disregard. His Highness also continued to push his troops up towards ours, as if in defiance; it was announced that he intended to form a camp between our old cantonment and our new position, and 1,000 or 1,500 horse moved down for the purpose. On this I sent a message, begging that the motives of our movements might not be misconstrued, but that the Peshwa might forbid these aggressions; at the same time announcing that if any troops attempted to press on us, as in our old position, we should be obliged to treat them as enemies. The Peshwa replied by a promise to restrain his troops.

'On hearing the first intelligence of the preparations on our cantonments, and of our intended removal to Kirkee, General Smith, who had been prepared for a rupture on the Peshwa's part, concentrated his force on Pultamba, recalling his detachments from the Ghats; he likewise ordered the light battalion, which was on its route to join him, to return to Sirur. These proceedings having attracted the Peshwa's notice, and being likely to bring on a crisis, which indeed was rapidly approaching of itself, I wrote on the day before yesterday to order the light battalion and 1,000 of the auxiliary horse that were at Sirur to march to Puna. They had made one ordinary march of fifteen miles, when the intelligence of their approach reached the Peshwa; his troops immediately got under arms, and all preparations were made in the city. This sort of agitation was by no means uncommon for the last ten days, and I therefore merely sent a message to inquire the cause, without making any corresponding preparations. The answer brought by the Peshwa's Vakil at the Residency was that our line at Kirkee had been under arms from daybreak till sunrise (which I found had been the case), and that his Highness was making corresponding preparations. I sent to say that from the distance of Kirkee I was not acquainted with the circumstance; that the Vakil saw that there were no preparations even for defence at the Residency; and that he might assure his Highness there should be none in camp. The Vakil then assured me that the Peshwa would immediately discontinue all his preparations. He went into the city to deliver my message, and we remained quiet, although a battalion of Gokhla's took up ground between the Residency and the cantonment, at the distance of half a mile from each place.

'At length the Vakil returned with Vittoji Naik Gaikwar, an immediate servant of the Peshwa's, who said that his Highness had heard of the approach of General Smith, and the near arrival of the battalion from Sirur; that this was the third time that we had assembled troops at Puna, and the last time we had surrounded the city. His Highness was therefore determined to bring things to an early settlement. His Highness desired that the European regiment should be sent away, and the native brigade reduced to its usual strength; that our cantonments should be removed to a place to be pointed out by his Highness; that the Residency might remain; and on these terms his Highness would maintain his friendship with the British Government. Otherwise, that his Highness was actually mounted, and would repair to some distance from Puna, to which place he would never return until his terms were complied with. I replied that I believed General Smith was still at Pultamba, that the battalion was certainly coming in, and that the great assembly of troops by his Highness, and the positions they occupied, were sufficient reasons for my wishing to strengthen the brigade; but that I could assure his Highness that it was brought on by no design of attacking him, and he must do me the justice to own that none of the former proceedings against his Highness, of which he had complained, were undertaken without full notice to his Highness; that it was out of my power to withdraw the troops; and that his Highness was not entitled by any engagement to demand it; that, on the contrary, he had promised to send his troops to the frontier, and that he ought to fulfil his promise, which would remove every ground of disagreement. Vittoji Naik then began to talk in a style of complaint and menace, adverted to the former disputes, in which he said the Peshwa had given way merely from friendship for the Company; and asked me if I imagined that his Highness was not a match for us on the day when Puna was surrounded. He then repeated his message, and desired a categorical answer. I replied as before, and asked him if I was to understand that when his Highness quitted Puna I was to consider him at war. Vittoji Naik said he had no message on that head, but that his Highness would square his actions by ours. He was afterwards a great deal more distinct, for he repeated his demand, declaring if I did not comply with it, the friendship would not last; and warning me of the bad effects of a rupture. I then renewed my assurances of our wish for peace, and said that if his Highness moved to his army, I should withdraw to camp; that if he remained quiet, or receded, we should still consider him as a friend, and should be careful not to cross the river that separates our camp from the town; but that if his troops advanced towards ours, we should be obliged to attack them. Immediately after Vittoji Naik quitted me the Peshwa left the town, and withdrew to Parbatti; and within less than an hour large bodies of troops began to move in the direction of our camp, and in such a manner as to cut off the Residency. On the receipt of Vittoji Naik's message, I had withdrawn a company that had been left in the old cantonments; and as soon as it reached the Residency, the detachment there marched off to camp, keeping a river between them and the Peshwa's troops, who were moving in the same direction. The Residency was immediately plundered and burned. As the Peshwa's troops advanced, Lieutenant-Colonel Burr fell in, and very judiciously moved out to meet them. He was joined by the battalion formerly in the Peshwa's service, from Dapori. As he advanced a cannonade was opened from the Peshwa's guns, which did little execution, and soon after the line was surrounded by vast bodies of cavalry coming on at speed. The 1st, 7th Native Infantry, which was drawn off from the left of the line, by the eagerness of the men to attack a battalion of Gokhles, was charged while separated, but completely beat off the attack, and the derangement was promptly repaired by Colonel Burr, who immediately joined the corps, and by his coolness and promptitude speedily extricated it from its perilous situation. The horse continued to move round in large masses until the end of the affair, but were deterred by Colonel Burr's skilful arrangements from any more attempts to charge. After firing some rounds from the field-pieces, the line moved forward, the Peshwa's guns were drawn off, and soon after the whole field was cleared of his troops, on which Colonel Burr returned to this camp, it being now dark. The loss of our brigade in this affair amounts to about 90 men; that of the Peshwa's troops is said to be about 500. I am sorry to learn that Moro Dixit is among the killed. The Peshwa is now on the hill of Parbatti, immediately to the south of Puna; and his troops are on the side of the town opposite to this place, much disheartened. There are so many objections to attacking the town, and so little could now be done by pursuing the Peshwa's troops without attacking it, that Lieutenant-Colonel Osborne, who arrived yesterday evening and took the command of the brigade, has determined to remain in his present position until the arrival of General Smith, who may be expected in a week or ten days. Unfortunate as a quarrel with the Peshwa may be at this moment, I have no doubt your Lordship will think it was inevitable. It was evidently meditated at the time of the Peshwa's promises of cordial aid, and had lately been advanced too far to leave his Highness any hope of averting it by professions or explanations. It is, therefore, a happy circumstance that his Highness should have thrown off the mask before he had made any progress in his intrigues with our native army. Nothing could exceed the zeal of the Sepoys in the affair of yesterday. I shall have the honour of transmitting Lieutenant-Colonel Burr's report as soon as I receive it. I beg leave to point out to your Excellency the great zeal and exertions of that officer, in removing the ammunition, stores, and provisions to the new ground, and in all the preparations requisite for opposing the Peshwa's army. Your Excellency will judge from his own report of his conduct in the action that followed, and will, I have no doubt, be of opinion that it was owing to his great coolness and judgment that he was enabled to give so serious a check to the Peshwa, and so great a change to public opinion in this part of India, with so little loss to our own troops.

'I have, etc.,

'(Signed) M. ELPHINSTONE,

'Resident at Puna.

'Camp at Kirkee,
6th October, 1817.'

EXTRACT LETTER FROM THE HONOURABLE MR. ELPHINSTONE TO THE GOVERNOR-GENERAL, DATED CAMP, KIRKEE, 11TH NOVEMBER, 1817.

Letter from Mr. Elphinstone.

'Since the brigade has been in this position we have experienced the good effects of the forward movement made by Colonel Burr on the 5th, and of the impression he then struck, in the timidity and inertness of the enemy, and the tranquillity which we have in consequence enjoyed.

'The Peshwa's army appears to have been in great confusion. On the 6th Moro Dixit* was certainly killed, as was Sardar Khan, a Pathan chief, who had been discharged from the Nizam's reformed horse, and whom the Peshwa ordered to raise 2,000 men for his service; Balwant Ráv Raste Nana Kukare, a relation of Gokhle's† and Narayan Dixit, the brother of Moro

* One of the Peshwas Ministers who generally transacted business with the British Residents.

† One of the Peshwa's officers who has obtained an ascendency in his councils.

Dixit, were wounded, and Abba Purandhare had a horse killed under him. The Vinchurkar was suspected of treachery. The Peshwa himself set off for Purandhar, and was with great difficulty persuaded to remain in camp by Gokhle, who declared that his flight would be followed by the dispersion of his army. In the course of the succeeding days the Mahratta army was concentrated on the side of Puna most removed from our camp, and his Highness encouraged the Sardars,* paid for the horses that had been killed in action, and bestowed presents and distinctions on such men as had been wounded. Yesterday evening the whole army moved out from behind the town and encamped to the east of our old cantonment, in open view of this camp, at the distance of about four miles.

'The only signs of activity which the enemy has displayed have appeared in his attempts to cut off supplies and to shut the roads; in this he has in some manner succeeded, as some officers and some convoys were advancing, on the faith of our alliance, with little or no escorts. Cornets Hunter and Morrison, escorted by a Havildar† and twelve Sepoys, had arrived at Wuroli, within twenty miles of Puna, when they were surrounded by some hundred horse and some Arabs, and, after a fruitless resistance, were compelled to lay down their arms. The Sepoys were not detained, and one of them has arrived in camp; but the officers were made prisoners, and are stated by one report to have been murdered in cold blood; but more authentic accounts represent them to have been carried into Puna. Captain Vaughan and his brother were seized at Tallegám, on their way to Bombay, and although they offered no resistance, they are stated by a negro servant, who brought an account of their capture, to have been

* Military chiefs.

† A native sergeant.

put to death in the most ignominious manner. The negro is so distinct in his relation of their execution that there is no reason to doubt the fact, except what arises from the atrocity of the action.

'The Peshwa's conduct has in some instances borne more of the character of civilized war. A conductor and a Naik's* party belonging to the Peshwa's battalion, that were in charge of some stores in a suburb near the Residency, were induced by assurances of safety to quit a defensible house which they occupied, and the promises made to them were faithfully observed. Mahomed Hariff, the Munshi of the Residency, had also defended his house with Arabs, was invited to quit it, and sent out of the city unmolested. He had an interview with Gokhle before he came, which was interesting in many respects, especially from Gokhle's producing a paper under the Peshwa's seal, investing him with all the powers of the Government, and from the avowal of Vittoji Naik that the Residency and cantonments were burned by the Peshwa's own orders. I had before supposed this wanton outrage to be the work of some of the rabble that compose his Highness's army. On the other hand, Gokhle had shown the utmost activity in seizing and plundering all persons who are themselves or who have relations in our service.'

* A corporal.

REPORT

ON THE

TERRITORIES CONQUERED FROM THE PESHWA,

SUBMITTED TO THE SUPREME GOVERNMENT OF BRITISH INDIA,

BY THE

HON. MOUNTSTUART ELPHINSTONE,

COMMISSIONER.

REPORT

ON THE

TERRITORIES CONQUERED FROM THE PESHWA.

DESCRIPTION OF THE COUNTRY.

THE whole extent of the country under the Commissioner may be very roughly estimated at 50,000 square miles, and the population may be guessed at 4,000,000; but this does not include any of the detached territories beyond the Nizam's frontier.

The grand geographical feature of this tract is the chain of Ghats, which run along the western boundary for its whole length. Between this range and the sea lies the Konkan, now under Bombay. It extends from 40 to 50 miles in breadth, includes many fertile places producing abundance of rice, but, in general, is very rough, and much crossed by steep and rocky hills. Towards the Ghats, the country is in most places extremely strong, divided by hills intersected by ravines, and covered with thick forest. The range itself is from 2,000 to 4,000 feet high, extremely abrupt, and inaccessible on the west. The passes are numerous, but steep, and very seldom passable for carriages. The table-land on the east is nearly as high as many parts of the ridge of the Ghats, but in general the hills rise above it to the height of from 1,000 to 1,500 feet. The table-land is for a considerable distance rendered very strong, by numerous spurs issuing from the range, among which are deep winding rugged valleys often filled with thick jungle. Farther east the branches from the Ghats become less frequent, and the country becomes more level, till the neighbourhood of the Nizam's frontier, where it is an open plain.

The northern part of the chain of Ghats, and the country and its base, especially to the west, is inhabited by Bhils. The kolies, who somewhat resemble the Bhils, but are less predatory and more civilized, inhabit the part of the range to the south of Baughhaud and the country at its base on the west as far south as Bassein. They are also numerous in Gujarat. The Bhils possess the eastern part of the range, and all the branches that run out from it towards the west, as far south as Puna; they even spread over the plains to the east, especially on the north of the Godavari, and are found as far off as the neighbourhood of the Warda. On the north, they extend beyond the Tapty and Narbada, and are numerous in the jungles that divide Gujarat from Malwa, as well as in all the eastern parts of Gujarat. They are a wild and predatory tribe; and though they live quietly in the open country, they resume their character whenever they are settled in a part that is strong, either from hills or jungles. The Bhils differ from the other inhabitants in language, manners, and appearance; they are small and black, wear little clothes, and always carry bows and arrows. In appearance, they much resemble the mountaineers of Baughalpur. The Bhils and kolies, when in the hills or strong places, live under Naiks or Chiefs of their own, who have some influence over those in the neigh-

Kolies.

Bhils.

bouring plains. These Chiefs have in general been little interfered with by the Mahratta Government more than was necessary to prevent the depredations of their followers. South of Puna, the Bhils are succeeded by the Ramoshis, a more civilized and subdued tribe. They do not inhabit the main range of Ghats, but the branches stretching out to the eastward. They have the same thievish habits as the Bhils, but have no language of their own; are more mixed with the people, and in dress and manners are more like Mahrattas. They are of more consequence than elsewhere, in the hills joining the Ghats southward of Satara, where they lately acted so prominent a part in taking forts, and plundering the country, under the false Chittur Sing. They do not extend farther south than Kolapur, or farther east than the line of Bijapur.

Hill-tribes like those mentioned have generally proved quiet when the Government was vigorous, and while they were managed through their Native Chiefs. We perhaps lose some hold on them by the destruction of so many of the hill-forts, which were situated in the midst of their mountains, and served to watch and curb their disposition to plunder.

The districts belonging to the Peshwa in Nemar, being under charge of Sir J. Malcolm, I have no opportunity of inquiring regarding them. Their importance is small, yielding only 25,000 rupees; and, if it is not found necessary for securing the peace of Nemar that we should have some territory there, they might be well disposed of in exchanges.

Nemaur.

Our most northern district would then be Khandesh. This province is bounded on the north by the Satpura or Vindyâdri range of mountains; and on

Khandesh.

the south by the range in which are the fort of Chandore and the Ghat of Ajanta: on the south-west it is bounded by the range of Sahyádri, commonly called the Ghats, at the termination of which south of the Tapti is the hilly tract of Bagalán. The plain of Khandesh descends towards the Tapti from the hills on the north and south (especially from the south): on the east it is bounded by Scindia's and the Nizam's territories on the plain of Berar; on the west, the plain along the Tapti extends, without interruption, from the hills to the sea; but it is divided from the rich country about Surat by a thick and extensive jungle. Though interspersed with low ranges of unproductive hills, the bulk of the province is exceedingly fertile, and it is watered by innumerable streams, on many of which expensive embankments have formerly been erected for purposes of irrigation. Some parts of the province are still in a high state of cultivation, and others, more recently abandoned, convey a high notion of their former richness and prosperity; but the greater part of Khandesh is covered with thick jungle, full of tigers and other wild beasts, but scattered with the ruins of former villages. The districts north of the Tapti in particular, which were formerly very populous, and yielded a large revenue, are now almost an uninhabited forest. The decline of this province, from the flourishing condition which it had long since attained under its Mohammedan masters, is to be dated from the year 1802, when it was ravaged by Holkar's army. This blow was followed by the famine in 1803, and its ruin was consummated by the misgovernment of the Peshwa's officers. The Bhils, who had before lived mixed with the other inhabitants, and had, as village watchmen, been the great instruments of police throughout Khandesh, withdrew to the surrounding mountains, whence they made incursions, and carried off cattle and prisoners from the heart of the province. The Pindaries annually ravaged the open country: various insurgents plundered at the head of bodies of horse; and parties of Arabs established themselves in some of the numerous fortresses and ghuries with which Khandesh abounds, and laid all the neighbourhood under contribution.

The expulsion of the Arabs was a natural consequence of the war, and no parties of plundering horse were able to keep the field; but the settlement of the Bhils was a work of more time and difficulty. Those in the Satpura mountains were the most formidable, as that range, though not perhaps above 1,500 feet high, is deep and strong, and so unhealthy that no stranger can long remain in it. The plan adopted by Captain Briggs, and zealously executed by Lieutenant-Colonel Jardine, was to stop the supplies of the Bhils, which are all drawn from the plain; to cut off any parties that attempted to issue to plunder, and to make vigorous attacks on the points in the hills to which the principal Bhil Chiefs had retired. These measures soon reduced the Bhils to accept the very favourable terms held out to them; which were to forbear their depredations, the Chiefs receiving pensions, and allowances for a certain number of men, and binding themselves to restrain the excesses of their people.

The same plan was carried through, with less exertion, with the Bhils of the Chandore range, and with the Bhils and Kolies in Bagalan. The terms have occasionally been broken by some Chiefs, but on the whole, they have succeeded beyond my most sanguine expectations, and have effectually delivered the province from this species of invasion. The only attacks of the Bhils are now made in parties of three or four, who rob passengers. These outrages have been resisted by the

17

police, and are stated by Captain Briggs to be greatly on the decline. I have little doubt that a continuance of this vigilance, together with the liberal provision authorized by Government for the Bhil watchmen, will soon completely extinguish the remains of these disorders.

The effectual protection of the people is the first and most important step towards restoring the prosperity of Khandesh; but, from the havoc that has been made among the population, a long period must elapse before it can show any great signs of improvement. A very light assessment, and the favourable terms on which waste land is granted to speculators, will, it is hoped, accelerate this crisis, and not only draw back the natives of Khandesh who have retired to Guzarat and other countries, but even attract new settlers from places where the population is over-abundant.

Captain Briggs has applied himself with great zeal to the improvement of the district, and has adopted and suggested various plans for that purpose: among these, a principal one is the repair of the embankments, and the fear of their falling into irretrievable ruin is a strong motive for commencing on this undertaking early. But at present the great want of Khandesh is in population; and where waste land is abundant, people are more likely to be attracted by the easy terms on which that is granted, than by the richness of lands irrigated by means of dams; where, from the necessity of repaying Government for the expenses of erecting and maintaining them, the condition of the cultivator has generally been observed to be worse than on land which has not the advantage of these costly improvements.

Captain Briggs describes the people of Khandesh as peaceable and inoffensive, but timid, helpless, unenterprising, and sunk under the oppression and the multiplied calamities to which they have so long been exposed; but this of course only applies to the trading and agricultural classes: the soldiery (of whom part were till lately the predatory body called Barra Bye, in Holkar's service, and the rest must have often joined insurgents, and even Pindaries,) are, doubtless, bold and restless enough.

Mahratta country, including the districts of Ahmednagar, Puna, and Sattara.

Khandesh is low and hot. Gangatari, which joins it on the south, is from 1,500 to 2,000 feet above the level of the Tapti, and the rest of the conquered territory (except the Konkan) is on the same table-land. From this to the Kristna, or rather the Warna and Kristna, is comprehended in the districts of Ahmednagar and Puna, and the Rajah of Satara's territory. The western half of all this tract is hilly; the valleys rich and highly cultivated, and the country diversified and beautiful. Farther east are plains, but not all in the same condition. The east of Gangatari, though open and fertile, is almost entirely uninhabited since the famine in 1803; the country between that and Ahmednagar is better, and the plains south of Ahmednagar are for many marches in all directions one sheet of the richest cultivation. I do not know the state of the south-east of that district towards Sholapur, but I imagine it is equally prosperous. The country beyond the Nira is in a very different state, thinly peopled and badly cultivated. It is in this tract that most of the horses in the Mahratta country are bred, and that most of the Silledars, or military adventurers, reside. The principal towns in the Peshwa's late dominions are between Khandesh and the Kristna, but none of them are considerable. Puna may be reckoned to contain about 110,000 inhabitants, having lost from a tenth to a fifth since the removal of Baji Rāv with his Court and army. Nasik does not contain more than a fourth of this number. Pandharpur is still smaller than Nasik, and the rest all much smaller than Pandharpur. Ahmednagar, however, must be excepted, which is reckoned to contain 20,000 souls, and is increasing rapidly.

This tract is the oldest possession of the Mahratta Government, and is by far the most decidedly Mahratta in the composition of the inhabitants. The character of that people is fully depicted in the answers to the queries which I sent to the collectors, especially in Captain Grant's.

The Brahmins, who have long conducted all the business of the country, are correctly described by Mr. Chaplin as an 'intriguing, lying, corrupt, licentious, and unprincipled race of people!' to which Captain Grant adds with equal truth, 'that when in power they are coolly unfeeling, and systematically oppressive,' and now 'generally discontented, and only restrained by fear from being treasonable and treacherous.' They are superstitious, and narrow in their attachment to their caste, to a degree that has no example elsewhere; but they are mild, patient, intelligent on many subjects, even liberal and enlightened; and, though regardless of sufferings which they may indirectly produce, they are naturally very averse to cruelty and bloodshed: there are among them many instances of decent and respectable lives, and although they are generally subtle and insincere, I have met with some on whom I could depend for sound and candid opinions.

The Mahratta Chiefs, while in power, and especially while with armies, are generally coarse, ignorant, rapacious and oppressive.

Those settled in their own country, and unconnected with courts and armies, bear a much better character, being sober, industrious, and encouragers of agriculture. It must indeed be remembered, both of this class and the Brahmins, that we see the very worst of the whole, and that it is among those at a distance from the seat of Government that we are to look for any virtue that may exist in the nation.

The soldiery so much resemble the Chiefs, that individuals of the two classes might change places without any striking impropriety. The Chiefs of course are more vicious, and probably more intelligent. The Mahratta soldiery love war, as affording opportunities for rapine in an enemy's country, and marauding in a friend's. In battle, they seem always to have been the same dastardly race; but they are active, hardy, vigilant, patient of fatigue and privations; and, though timid in action, they show great boldness and enterprise in their incursions into distant countries; and on all occasions they appear to have the greatest confidence in their horses, though little or none in their swords. Their plan in a campaign is to avoid general engagements, to ravage their enemy's country, and to cut up convoys and detachments; in an action it is to disperse when attacked, and to return to the charge, when the enemy has broken, to plunder: by these means they are enabled to prevail against better troops than themselves.

The Mahratta peasantry have some pride in the triumphs of their nation, and some ambition to partake in its military exploits; but, although circumstances might turn them into soldiers or robbers, at present their habits are decidedly peaceful. They are sober, frugal, industrious; mild and inoffensive to everybody; and among themselves neither dishonest nor insincere. The faults of their Government have, however, created the corresponding vices in them; its oppression and extortion have taught them dissimulation, mendacity, and fraud; and the insecurity of property has rendered them so careless of the future, as to lavish on a marriage or other ceremony the savings of years of parsimony. The first class of these vices, though prevalent throughout the whole in their dealings with Government, is more conspicuous among the Patels, and others who are most brought into contact with their rulers; and the effects of the second are felt in the debts and embarrassments in which the whole of the agricultural population is plunged.

It may be observed, in conclusion, that the military Brahmins combine part of the character of Mahratta soldiers with that of their own caste; and that the character of the Mahratta soldiery, in like manner, runs into that of the cultivators. Taking the whole as a nation, they will be found to be inferior to their Mohammedan neighbours in knowledge and civilization, in spirit, in generosity, and perhaps in courage; but less tainted with pride, insolence, tyranny, effeminacy, and debauchery; less violent, less bigoted, and (except while in armies on foreign service) more peaceable, mild, and humane.

MAHRATTA KARNATIK.—The country south of the Krishna, or, as the Mahrattas call it, the Karnatik, has few hills and few places incapable of cultivation. Except in the immediate neighbourhood of the Ghats, it consists of extensive plains of black or cotton ground; a large portion of it is, however, uncultivated, especially of the parts which have been under the Government of Gokhle and Appa Desái. The high cultivation of the Patwardhans' lands has often been mentioned. It is no doubt owing in a great measure to their good management; but in a great measure likewise to the oppression of their neighbours, which drove every man who could easily move into their lands. There are no large towns in this part of the country. Hubli is, I believe, the largest, and I have heard it estimated at 15,000 souls. The towns of Belgaum and Shahpur, which, though nearly contiguous, belong, one to Government, and one to Chintaman Ráv, may amount together to 13,000 or 14,000 inhabitants. I have not heard of any other town in this district that contains more than 5,000 inhabitants.

Both this division and Bijapur are inhabited by Kanarese, who retain their own language and manners. The Mahrattas are reckoned by Mr. Chaplin to constitute no more than an eighth or a tenth of the inhabitants: what there is of them seems to consist of soldiers and Brahmins, with a full share of the vice of those classes. The Kanarese Mr. Chaplin describes as resembling their countrymen in the ceded districts; but as being more honest, manly and courageous, though less mild, hospitable and humane: both are equally industrious and frugal.

The Karnatik was at no distant period overrun with independent Desáis or Polligars, but these have all been gradually swallowed up by the Mahrattas, and the Desái of Kittur is the only one who still retains his possessions. The people have always been considered by the Mahrattas to be turbulent and disaffected, which they showed in several rebellions, and particularly in readily joining General Munro to expel their rulers. They seem now to be perfectly quiet, and well affected.

The general use of Shet Sanadis, or landed Militia, which is so common in Mysore, is only found in this part of the conquered territory.

SKETCH OF THE MAHRATTA HISTORY.

The whole of the territory above described does not belong to the British Government; and what does belong to it is not all under our immediate administration. The other possessors of independent territory are the Rajah of Satara, the Rajah of Kolapur; and, on a smaller scale, the Nizam, Scindia, Holkar, the Rajah of Berar and the Gaikwar. The lands held by dependent Chiefs belong to Angria, the Pant Sachiv, the Pritti Nidhi, the Patwardhans, and other Jahagirdars. To give an idea of the situation of all these Chiefs, and indeed of the general state of the country, it is necessary to take a hasty view of the history of the Mahrattas.

The Mahratta language and nation extended from the Vindyadri or Satpura mountains, nearly to the Krishna; and from the sea on the west to a waving frontier on the east, which may be tolerably indicated by a line drawn from Goa to the Warda near Chanda; and thence along that river to the Satpura mountains. The whole of the territory was probably under a Mahratta King, who resided at Deoghari, now Dowlatabad; but this empire was subverted in the beginning of the fourth century, by the Mohammedans, and remained under various dynasties of that religion until the end of the seventeenth century, when the greater part was delivered by Sivaji and his successors. The eastern part still remains under the Moguls.

The grandfather of Sivaji was of very humble origin; but his father had attained a considerable rank under the kingdom of Bijapur; had been entrusted with a Government; and profiting by the weakness of the King's power, had rendered himself nearly independent in the southern part of the Bijapur dominions. The same weakness encouraged 1646. Sivaji to rebel, and plunder the country; and he was enabled, by the increasing confusions in the Deccan, to found a sort of Government, which the desultory operations of Aurungzebe, distracted by his numerous and simultaneous foreign wars, allowed him time to consolidate. His rebellion began about 1646; he declared himself independent in 1674; 1682. and at his death, about 1682, he was possessed of great part of the Konkan; the rest being in the hands of the Moguls of Surat, and in those of the Portuguese, or held for the Bijapur Government by the Siddies or Abyssinians of Janjira. He seems also to have possessed the greater part of the line of Ghats, and to have shared with the Mohammedans the tract immediately to the east of those mountains, as far north as Puna, and as far south as Kolapur.

Most of these possessions were wrested from his son, who was reduced to the hills, and part of the Konkan, when Aurungzebe was drawn off to the sub- 1685-87. version of the monarchies of Golkonda and Bijapur. The convulsions occasioned by the extinction of those states completely unsettled the country, and threw a large portion of the armies, which had hitherto maintained tranquillity, into the scale of the Mahrattas, to whom the Jamidars throughout the Deccan also appear to have been inclined. The consequence was, that although on the execution of Sambaji, the son of Sivaji, in 1689, his son 1689. and heir Shahuji fell into the hands of the Moguls, and his younger brother Rajah Ram, who succeeded him, was shut up in the Fort Till 1701. of Gingee, south of Arcot so that for several years the Mahrattas had no efficient head, yet they

were able, under different leaders, to withstand, and at length to deride the efforts of the Moguls, which were enfeebled by the faction of the Generals, and the de-
1707. clining age of the Emperor, till the year 1707, when the death of Aurungzebe, and the contests among his successors, set them free from all danger on the part of the Moguls. The Chiefs left in charge of the Deccan first faintly opposed, and then conciliated the Mahrattas: a truce was concluded about 1710, by which they yielded the Chouth; and this, on the confirmation of the agreement, together with a formal grant of their territorial possessions by the
1719. Emperor in 1719, may be considered as the final establishment of the Mahratta Government, after a struggle of at least sixty years.

During the period between the death of Aurungzebe and the confirmation of the Chouth, etc., a great revolution had taken place among the Mahrattas. Shàhû Rajah, the son of Sambaji, was released in 1708; but on his return to the Deccan he found himself opposed by his cousin Sivaji, son of Rajah Ram. This Prince had succeeded on the death of his father in 1700; but being either very weak, or entirely deranged in his intellect, his affairs were conducted by his mother, Tara Bái. Shàhû Rajah was enabled, chiefly by the good conduct of his Minister Ballaji Vishwanath, to gain over Kanoji Angre, the chief support of his rival's cause, and to seat himself on the Mahratta Musnud. He immediately appointed Ballaji to the office of Peshwa, which had before belonged to the family of Pingle, but was forfeited by its possessor's adherence to the cause of Tara Bái. Shàhû Rajah being incapacitated by his mental imbecility from exercising the authority with which he was invested, the entire administration devolved on Ballaji Vishwanath.

At the time of the confirmation of the Chouth, although the Mahrattas had numerous claims over several of the provinces possessed by the Moguls, their actual territory does not appear to have extended beyond the narrow limits to which it had reached under Sivaji. The Mogul's grant confirming their possessions enumerates the districts, by which it appears that they extended in the Konkan from the Goa territory to a point considerably to the south of Daman; while above the Ghats they only reached from the Ghatprabha to the river Kukri, 40 miles north of Puna. The greatest length (on the sea coast) is 280 miles, the greatest breadth (from Harni and Pandharpur to the sea) 140; but this breadth is only found to the south of Puna; north of that city the breadth does not exceed 70 miles.

1719.

It was long before the Mahrattas obtained possession of the country in the immediate neighbourhood of their first conquest: the Forts of Junar and Ahmednagar, the first within 40, and the other within 80 miles of Puna, were not reduced until within the last sixty years; long after the Mahrattas had made themselves masters of Malwa and Gujarat, and had plundered up to the gates of Agra. Khandesh was not subdued until within these sixty years, nor the Karnatik until a still later period. The cause of this inconsistency was the close connection between the Mahrattas and Nizam Ul Mulk, who was glad to encourage them as the means of weakening the power of the Court of Delhi; while they, with their usual policy, were pleased to disunite their enemies, and attack them one by one. To this connection also it is to be ascribed that a third of the Mahratta nation should have been left to this day under the dominion of the Moguls.

Ballaji Vishwanath dying in 1720, was succeeded

by his son Baji Ráv Balall. This Chief, who appears to have been a man of activity and abilities, took full advantage of the weakness, the distractions, and the mutual jealousy and treachery of the Moguls. He overran all Malwa, and had entirely reduced it some time about
1735. the year 1735; while the troops of the Senapatti, another great General of Shàhû Rajah, had made similar progress in Gujarat. The rivalry of these Generals renewed the domestic distractions of the Mahrattas; but Baji Ráv finally overcame the Senapatti; as Nana Sahib subsequently did his powerful servant, the Gaikwar, in 1750, when he compelled the latter to submit implicitly to his authority, and to make
1741. over half of Gujarat to his officers. Baji Ráv died in 1741, and was succeeded by his son Ballaji Baji Ráv, commonly called Nana Sahib.

This Prince was the first of the Peshwas who openly exercised the sovereign authority on the Rajah's behalf. His two predecessors had always affected to act under the orders of that Prince; but Rajah Shàhû dying in
1749. 1749, it was alleged by the Peshwa that he had formerly invested him with the sovereignty of his dominions, on condition of his keeping up the name of the Rajah's descendants. I may here remark, that it appears more than doubtful whether the Rajahs of Satara ever pretended to possess absolute sovereignty, or to hold their territories otherwise than as vassals, either of Bijapur or of Delhi. Nana Sahib was an inactive Prince, and entrusted his internal government to his cousin Sadashiv Ráv Bhàû, and the command of his armies to his brother Raghunath Ráv,
1761. the father of the late Peshwa. A temporary exchange of these functions occasioned the defeat and fall of the Bhàû at Paniput, and the death of Balaji, who never recovered the shock.

The Government then fell into the hands of Raghûnath Ráv, who detained Madhav Ráv, the son of Nana Sahib, in a state of tutelage and dependence; but who was not long able to resist the talents and energy which that Prince early displayed. Madhav Ráv then took the reins into his own hands, imprisoned Raghunath, and reigned for eleven years. Though at least equal to his predecessors as a General, Madhav Ráv's chief praise arises from his Civil Government. He was the first who introduced order into the internal administration, and who showed a sincere desire to protect his subjects from military violence, and to establish something like a regular dispensation of justice.

His death, which happened in 1772, was soon followed by the murder of his brother Narayan Ráv; the usurpation of Raghunath Ráv; and a long struggle, in which the English were unsuccessful supporters of the claims of that usurper. During this disturbed period, and the thirteen years of comparative tranquillity which followed, Nana Fadnavis acted as Regent in the name of the infant son of the murdered Narayan Ráv. The territories in the Deccan were quiet, and were governed in a spirit of 1772. peace and moderation, which aided the former measures of Madhav Ráv in softening the predatory habits of the Mahrattas; but at the same time, the great Chiefs of Hindustan began to appear rather as allies than as servants; and, although the connection of the Mahrattas as a confederacy was probably at its greatest height at this period, yet the seeds of dissolution, which were inherent in the nature of it, began evidently to display themselves. A short view of the members of this confederacy will show the loose ties by which the whole was held.

The State of Tanjore was scarcely ever even in alliance with Satara; that founded by Malhar Ráv Ghorapare, in the north of Mysore, was in nearly the same situation; and that of Kolapur never joined it in any war. The confederates must therefore be the Rajah of Berar, the Gaikwar, Scindia, Holkar, the Powars, and the Chiefs of Jhansi and Sagar. The first of these powers was closely united in interest with Puna, and had no points of disagreement; yet it was frequently at war with the Puna State, and seemed to have been almost as much connected with the Nizam as with it. The Gaikwar was oppressed and subdued, a vassal rather than a confederate. He joined the first power that appeared against the Mahrattas in this part of India, and has adhered to his alliance to the last. The other Chiefs were subjects and servants of the Peshwa, and were themselves born and bred in the heart of the Mahratta country, as were the whole of their national troops; not one of whom to this day, perhaps, was born in their foreign conquests. Besides the ties of kindred, language and country, which in most nations keep up a connection for ages, the Mahrattas had a strong interest in opposing their common enemies; yet there is perhaps no instance in which they were all engaged on one side in a war; and it is surprising that states so circumstanced should be unable to keep up a closer alliance for a period little exceeding the natural life of man. These facts do not, however, show that there is not at this moment a confederacy cemented by common country, common interests, and common enmity to their conquerors, but that there is nothing particularly durable in the connection to prevent its dissolving at no distant period.

1796. At the death of Madhoo Ráv Narayen in 1796, the whole of the great Mahratta Chiefs, the Rajah of Berar, Scindia, Holkar, and the Jahagirdars of the Deccan, appeared at Puna, for the last time, as vassals of the empire. The power and weight of the Minister was insufficient to control this tumultuous assembly, and a scene of factions, violence and intrigue ensued, at the conclusion of which Baji Ráv, the rightful heir, but the representative of the unpopular and proscribed house of Raghunath Ráv, was elevated to the Musnud by the military power of Scindia. He, however, was for some time little more than a pageant in the hands of that Prince; and it seemed probable that Scindia would soon imitate the example of the Peshwa's ancestors, and reduce his nominal master to the condition of the Rajah of Satara. It was perhaps the dread or the interference of the British which prevented this change of dynasty; and at the end of a few years the 1801. increasing disorders in Scindia's own possessions obliged him to quit his hold on the Peshwa, and to withdraw to Hindustan. Baji Ráv, now left alone, had neither ability nor inclination to put himself at the head of his turbulent Chiefs and mutinous army. He remained quiet in Puna, while every Jahagirdar assumed independence; and the country was overrun by banditti, formed from the soldiery that were no longer employed in the armies, to within a few miles of the capital. At length his Highness was expelled by Holkar. He returned, supported by a British force; and from that time began a new order of things, which existed at the time of our conquest.

Instead of the extensive but loose confederacy of which the Peshwa was head, which was in a constant state of foreign war and internal disorder, and which could only be held together by constant vigilance and activity, as well as concession and management, the

Peshwa was now to possess in peace a small compact territory; and as this had formerly partaken of the loose government of the general mass, it became the Peshwa's object to consolidate his power, and establish it on such a footing as would allow of his governing with as much ease as other Eastern Princes.

Some progress had been made towards this state of things during the government of Madhav Ráv and Nana Fadnavis; and Baji Ráv himself, from temper as much as from policy, had already adopted the course most suited to his situation. The head of an unpopular party, and educated in a prison, he had little sympathy with the bulk of his nation, and little desire for any enterprise in which he might require their assistance. His only wish was to gratify his love of power and of revenge, without endangering his safety or disturbing his ease. He had therefore begun his administration by plundering all the Ministers connected with his enemy. Nana Fadnavis had seized on the Jahagirs of his principal opponents. When the treaty
1803. of Bassein relieved him from all apprehension of resistance, he gave a loose to his desire for depressing the great and degrading his enemies.

Almost all those who had been connected with the government of his predecessors were discarded; the great Sardars who held lands were either dispossessed or kept at a distance, and obliged to yield implicit obedience to his will. No attempt was made to restore the old army; the Chiefs who had commanded it were left in want. The Court was almost entirely composed of new men; and the few troops that were retained were commanded by upstarts, and paid from the treasury.

A severe famine that followed Baji Ráv's restoration, prevented the natural effect of his reduction of the military force: many men perished, and more horses, and the vacancies occasioned by the deaths of the owners of land, afforded a provision for many who had till then maintained themselves by the profession of arms. Many more went to the camp of Scindia, who was then exchanging his Mussulman retainers for Mahrattas: others found employment with Holkar and the Rajah of Berar.: and many probably joined the hordes of Pindaries, which begun about this time to be conspicuous.

The discontents of the Chiefs were kept under by the presence of a British force, and great progress had thus been made in reducing the country to the state desired by Baji Ráv, when other events occurred to induce him to change his system. The progress that has been made has, however, been favourable to us. The number of Jahagirdars, though still very great, has been lessened; the pride of the nation has been humbled, and its military strength reduced. The war and previous years of intrigue and opposition, however, unsettled men's minds; the reduction of the armies of Scindia, the Bhosale and the Pindaries have increased the numbers of the soldiery; the destruction of the smaller Jahagirdars in Hindustan has thrown them and their retainers back on their old country, and our having raised our irregular horse and formed our civil establishments before Baji Ráv's adherents were sufficiently depressed to come over to us, has left most of them out of employ. So that there are now two irregular armies—the Mahratta one and our own; and three civil establishments—Nana Fadnavi's, Baji Ráv's, and ours—within this one territory.

REVENUE.

The principle I adopted for the civil administration being to preserve unimpaired the practice which I found established, this part of my report ought to consist entirely of an account of the Mahratta system; and although more changes have been introduced than were intended, that will in fact occupy a very considerable portion of the statement which is to follow.

My information is derived, in a great measure, from the Jamabandi reports of the local officers, on revenue subjects; and on judicial ones, from the answers of the same gentlemen to a series of queries which I circulated about the end of last year. These answers are forwarded, and I beg to recommend them to attention. That of Mr. Chaplin is of particular value. Captain Grant's contains much information, both on the points immediately in question, and on the general character of the people; and those of Mr. Thackeray, Sub-Collector of Rane Benore, have likewise considerable merit. Besides this view of the former practice, I shall point out the changes that have occurred; and as local opinions are always of use, I shall add such suggestions as occur to me on the course to be pursued hereafter; though the want of general knowledge, as well as of experience in the departments to which they refer, may often make them crude or erroneous.

Village government.

In whatever point of view we examine the native government in the Deccan, the first and most important feature is, the division into villages or townships. These communities contain in miniature all the materials of a state within themselves, and are almost sufficient to protect their members, if all other governments were withdrawn. Though probably not compatible with a very good form of government, they are an excellent remedy for the imperfections of a bad one; they prevent the bad effects of its negligence and weakness; and even present some barrier against its tyranny and rapacity.

Each village has a portion of ground attached to it, which is committed to the management of the inhabitants. The boundaries are carefully marked, and jealously guarded. They are divided into fields, the limits of which are exactly known; each field has a name and is kept distinct, even when the cultivation of it has long been abandoned. The villagers are almost entirely cultivators of the ground, with the addition of the few traders and artisans that are required to supply their wants. The head of each village is the Patil, who has under him an assistant, called a Chaugulla, and a clerk called a Kulkarni. There are, besides, twelve village officers, well known by the name of the Bara Baloti. These are the astrologer, the priest, the carpenter, barber, etc., but the only ones who are concerned in the administration of the government are the Sonar, or Potadar, who is silver-smith and assayer of money, and the Mhar, who, in addition to various other important duties, acts as watchman to the village. Each of these classes consists of one or more individuals, according as their original families have branched out. The Mhars are seldom fewer than four or five, and there are besides, where those tribes are numerous, very frequently several Bhils or Ramoshis, employed also as watchmen, but performing none of the other duties of the Mhar.

For a full account of the constitution of a village, see Captain Robertson's letter of March 9th, 1819.

The Patils are the most important functionaries in the villages, and perhaps the most important class in the country. They hold their office by a grant

Patil.

from the Government (generally from that of the Moguls), are entitled by virtue of it to lands and fees, and have various little privileges and distinctions, of which they are as tenacious as of their land. Their office and emoluments are hereditary, and saleable with the consent of the Government, but are seldom sold, except in cases of extreme necessity, though a partner is sometimes admitted, with a careful reservation of the superiority of the old possessor. The Patil is head of the police, and of the administration of justice in his village, but he need only be mentioned here as an officer of revenue. In that capacity he performs on a small scale what a Mamlatdar or a collector does on a large; he allots the lands to such cultivators as have no landed property of their own, and fixes the rent which each has to pay: he collects the revenue for Government from all the rayats; conducts all its arrangements with them, and exerts himself to promote the cultivation and the prosperity of the village. Though originally the agent of the Government, he is now regarded as equally the representative of the rayats, and is not less useful in executing the orders of the Government than in asserting the rights, or at least in making known the wrongs, of the people.

The functions and privileges of a Patil are well shown in the enclosed translation of a deed of sale, transferring a share of the office, which was forwarded by Captain Robertson, in his letter of March 9th, 1818, No. 6.

The Kulkarni keeps the numerous records and accounts of the village. The most important are: 1st, the general measurement and description of all the village lands; 2nd, the list of fields, with the name, size, and quality of each, the terms by which it is held, the name of the tenant, the rent for which he has agreed, and the highest rent ever produced by the field; 3rd, the list of all the in-

Kulkarnis.

Vide Captain Grant's report, Aug. 17.

habitants, whether cultivators or otherwise, with a statement of the dues from each to Government, and the receipt and balance in the account of each; 4th, the general statement of the instalments of revenue which have been realized; and, 5th, the detailed account where each branch of revenue is shown under a different head, with the receipts and balance on each. Besides the public records, he generally keeps the accounts of all the cultivators with each other, and with their creditors; acts as a notary public in drawing up all their agreements; and even conducts any private correspondence they may have to carry on. He has lands, but oftener fees allotted to him by Government, from which he hold his appointment.

Chaugulla.

The Chaugulla acts under the orders of the Patil, and assists him in his duties; he also has the care of the Kulkarnis' records.

Watchman.

The most important revenue duty of the Mhar is to watch over the boundaries, both of the village lands and of each individual's field; to see that they are not encroached on, to give evidence in cases where they are disputed; he watches over crops, whether cut or growing, as long as they are in the fields. He is also the public messenger and guide, and will be mentioned again as a most important actor in the police.

Potadar.

The Potadar, besides being the village silver-smith, assays all money paid, either to Government or to individuals.

With the few exceptions already mentioned, all the villagers are cultivators; and these, as there are few labourers, are distinguished by their tenures into two classes, that of Mirasis or landed proprietors, and that of Upris, or farmers.

As I was particularly directed to attend to the

tenures of land, I have called on the collectors to furnish the requisite information; only two answers have been received, but the enclosed Extracts, No. 7, from letters written on other subjects, sufficiently elucidate this question. They are, perhaps, the more to be depended on, because all of them, except Captain Grant's and Captain Briggs's second letter, were written before any question had been put, that could influence the writers; and that they are not produced by any speculations, but forced on the collectors, by the course of their ordinary business. The deeds of sale enclosed in Captain Robertson's letter of March 9th, throw a clear light on the manner in which the Mirasi tenure was regarded by the people and by the Government. The result of those reports, and of my own inquiries is, that a large portion of the Rayats are the proprietors of their estates, subject to the payment of a fixed land-tax to Government; that their property is hereditary and saleable, and they are never dispossessed while they pay their tax, and even then, they have for a long period (at least thirty years) the right of reclaiming their estate, on paying the dues of Government. Their land-tax is fixed; but the late Mahratta Government loaded it with other impositions, which reduced that advantage to a mere name; yet so far, however, was this from destroying the value of their estates, that, although the Government took advantage of their attachment to make them pay considerably more than an Upri, and though all the Mirasdars were, in ordinary cases, obliged to make up for failures in the payment of each of their body, yet their lands were saleable, and generally at ten years' purchase. This fact might lead us to suppose, that even with all the ex-

Mirasis, or landed proprietors, No. 7 A. Captain Robertson, dated Mar. 9, 1818, B. Captain Briggs dated Dec. 2, 1818 C. Captain Pottinger, dated Jan. 15, 1819, D. Captain Briggs, dated June 22, 1819, and Captain Grant, dated Aug. 1817, 1819, E.

I also enclose report on the same subject drawn up by Captain Macleod, from the most intelligent informants he could procure in the Daftars, or in Poona. No. 9.

actions of the late Mahratta Government, the share of the Rayat must have amounted to more than half the produce of the land; but experience shows that men will keep their estates, even after becoming a losing concern, until they are obliged to part with them from absolute want, or until oppression has lasted so long, that the advantages of proprietorship in better times have been forgotten. The Mirasdars are, perhaps, more numerous than the Upris all over the Mahratta country. In the Karnatik, I am informed by Mr. Chaplin that they do not exist at all. Besides Mirasdar, they are called Thalkari about Puna.

An opinion prevails throughout the Mahratta country, that under the old Hindu Government all the land was held by Mirasis; and that the Upris were introduced as the old proprietors sank under the tyranny of the Mohammedans. This opinion is supported by the fact that the greater part of the fields, now cultivated by Upris, are recorded in the village books as belonging to absent proprietors; and affords, when combined with circumstances observed in other parts of the peninsula, and with the light land-tax authorized by Manu, a strong presumption that the revenue system under the Hindus (if they had a uniform system) was founded on private property in the soil.

All the land which does not belong to the Mirasis belongs to the Government, or those to whom Government has assigned it. The property of the Zamindars in the soil has not been introduced, or even heard of, in the Mahratta country.

The cultivated land belonging to Government, except some parts which it keeps in its own hands, to be managed by the Mamlatdars, was always let out to Upris, who had a lease, with the expiration of which their claim and duties expired.

Upris or farmers.

These are all the tenures on which land was held, as far as regards the property of the soil. The assignments by Government of its own revenue, or share of the produce, will be mentioned hereafter. It need only be observed, that in making these grants it could not transfer the share of a Mirasdar. Even Baji Ráv, when he had occasion for Mirasi land, paid the price of it.

Village expenses.

Such are the component parts of a village: its transactions with Government will be explained hereafter, but there are some of its internal affairs still to be mentioned. The maintenance of the village temple; its fixed and authorized pensions, and annual charities; its ceremonies and religious festivals; its alms to beggars and entertainments to guests, especially to Brahmins and Fakirs; its occasional amusements, tumblers, dancers, etc.; its nazars to superiors; its offerings to the Patil and other village officers on occasions of condolence or congratulation; the expenses of the Patil on the public affairs, and the fees of peons stationed in the village, entail a number of expenses on the community, which, unless allowed for from the Government revenue (which is very rare), are defrayed by a tax on the village. This tax falls on the cultivators, especially on the Mirasdar, and is a great source of profit to the Patils and Kulkarnis. In general these expenses were in the proportion of one-tenth, or from that to one-fifth, to the public revenue. The three first charges were called Salabad, or permanent, and were provided for by permanent assessments; and the rest Saudir Warrid, or contingent, which were paid by extra assessments called Saudir Warrid Patti; these last were always liable to a scrutiny by the Mamlatdars, who probably perceived that all expensive charges against the Rayats would in time fall on the

Government. In addition to these, were occasional expenses, such as repairs of the village walls, the necessity of entertaining Sibandies for defence, or of paying an enemy or an insurgent for forbearance, which it was beyond the means of the village to defray at once. In this case the village contracted a public debt, which was gradually paid by an annual assessment included in the Saudir Warrid Patti, and sometimes provided for by mortgages, or grants of land on the part of the villagers. These grants were called Gaum Nishut Inams; if they were so small as to be admitted, or be likely to be admitted by the Government, no rent was charged on them; but if they were too large to be agreed to, or to escape observation, the revenue was paid by all the other Rayats, the creditor still enjoying them rent free; small grants were also made for temples, or to Brahmins, which were always acquiesced in by the Government, but the villagers have never pretended to any property in the soil, beyond the estates of the Mirasdars.

Village debts.

Village grants of land.

The next division is a Taraf, composed of an indefinite number of villages, with perhaps an addition of uninhabited mountain and forest land (there being no other land not included in some village). A Taraf is under no particular officers; several of them make a Pargana, which is under a Deshmukhi or Zamindar, who performs the same functions towards the Pargana as a Patil towards the village. He is assisted by a Despande, who answers to the Kulkarni, and a Deschaugulla. The Deshmukh and Deschaugulla, like the Patil and Chaugulla, are Mahrattas. The Despande and Kulkarni are Brahmins: above these officers there appear to have formerly been Sar Deshmukhis and Sar Despandes; but this order of things is not remembered,

Deshmukhi, Despandes and other Zamindars, or district officers.

though there is still one family of the ancient Sar Deshmukhis extant, beside the Rajah of Satara, who extorted the office of Sar Deshmukhi from the Mogul, as a pretext for some exaction from the country. The only Sar Despandes I have heard of are in the Konkan. There is also an officer called Sar Kanungo in Khandesh, whose office probably corresponds with that of Sar Despande. There are other officers still in existence in some places, such as the Sar Patil, the Nargund, etc., whose present functions are too unimportant to promise any advantage from an investigation of their ancient condition. It is universally believed in the Mahratta country, that the Deshmukhis, Despandes, etc., were all officers appointed by some former Government; and it seems probable that they were the revenue officers of the Hindu Government; that these officers, being hereditary, like most others under the Hindus, they were in possession of too much knowledge and influence to be dispossessed by the Mohammedans, who, though they appointed district officers, availed themselves of the experience of the Zamindars, and allowed them to settle with the Patils, explaining their proceedings to the more immediate officer of Government. They even often farmed out the whole Pargana to the Deshmukhis, who by this means acquired so much authority in some parts of the country as to be able, on the decline of the Mohammedan kingdoms in the Deccan, to maintain themselves, for a time, in independence. The Mahratta, or rather the Brahmin Government, was led by this conduct, and by their embezzlements of the public revenue, almost to set aside the employment of the Zamindars, transacting all business directly with the Patils, by means of its own officers. This change, though probably produced by the policy and avarice of the Brahmins, is considered to have been attended with beneficial effects, as delivering the people from the oppressions and exactions of the Zamindars.

Long after the Zamindars ceased to be the principal agents, they were still made use of as a check on the Mamlatdars, and no accounts were passed, unless corroborated by corresponding accounts from them; but even this practice has been disused since the farming system, except in the distant provinces of Gujarat and the Karnatik.

These officers still hold the lands and fees that were originally assigned them as wages, and are still considered as servants of the Government; but the only duty they perform is to produce their old records when required, to settle disputes about land by a reference to those records, and to keep a register of all new grants and transfers of property either by the Government or by individuals. This register must, however, be very incomplete, as no man is obliged to record his deed unless he chooses. The Deshmukhi's profits are very great; generally, I am told, above five per cent., not only on the revenue but on the land. Five acres in each hundred, for example, will belong to the Deshmukhi, and a twentieth of the collections besides; he has also various claims in kind, as a pair of shoes every year from each shoemaker, a portion of ghee from those who make that preparation, etc., etc.

The Deshmukhi of Falton has even twenty-five per cent., but having been for centuries Jahagirdar of his own Pargana, he has probably transferred a great deal from the Government account to his own. The allowances of the Despande are about half those of the Deshmukhi. The allowances of the Patil and Kulkarni are exactly of the same nature, but much smaller. All these fees are levied by the owners, distinct from the Government revenue. Deshmukhis and Despandes, as well as Patils and Kulkarnis, sell their own land and fees (or Wattan, as both are called), but neither pretends to any property in the rest of the lands. It seems to be thought that they cannot even sell their offices (though Patils and Kulkarnis can), and it is even doubtful if they can sell their fees, though they may pawn them. Their land they can certainly sell.

Mahratta system of revenue.

A number of Parganas formerly composed a Sircar, but this division is now completely disused; and that into Parganas and Tarafs, though still kept up in records, is not always the real revenue division. To explain this completely would lead me into the complicated system of the Mahrattas, which is the less necessary, as that system is now, as far as possible, laid aside. An idea of the divisions to which it leads, and which vary in different places, may be derived from the following account of one of the simplest cases.

Sar Deshmukhi.

Chouth.

Baabti.

Sahotra.

Mokassa.

The first pretension of Sivaji was to levy from the Rayats, as Sar Deshmukhi, ten rupees for every hundred levied by the Government. This was afterwards followed by a demand of a fourth of the Government collections, which at length was yielded by the Moguls. The fourth thus acquired, is called by the Mahrattas the Chouth; it was immediately divided by the Prince with his Ministers and Sardars. A fourth of it was at first reserved for the Rajah, and collected by the Prati Nidhi, the Peshwa, and the Pant Sachiv, under the name of Baabti. Six per cent. on the whole Chouth, before the deduction of the Baabti, was given under the name of Sahotra to the Pant Sachiv. The remainder of the Chouth, under the name of Mokassa, was partitioned among the Sardars, on condition of maintaining troops, of bearing certain expenses, and of paying a certain portion of money to the treasury. The Sar Deshmukhi shared the same fate, and from these funds some Inams were also granted, and some charities defrayed.

Subsequently to the acquisition of the Chouth, the remaining three-fourths of the country (which is called Jahagir, in contradistinction to the Chouth) fell also into the hands of the Mahrattas. The division then stood as follows:

Supposing the Government share -	400	
Sar Deshmukhi - - - -		40
Government Revenue - - -		400
Viz. Chouth, or fourth - - -	100	
Jahagir - - - - -	300	
Total with Sar Deshmukhi -		440

Subdivisions of Chouth.

Baabti - - - - - - -	25
Mokassa - - - - - -	75
Total Chouth -	100

Subdivisions of Mokassa.

Sahotra, 6 per cent. on the whole Chouth -	6
Āyin Mokassa - - - - - -	69
Total Mokassa -	75

This gives but an imperfect idea of the numerous subdivisions which have been made in most parts of the country. Some were assigned to Jahagirdars, and their separation from the bulk of the revenue was thus necessarily perpetuated; but even where they all fell into the hands of the Government, it still kept them up in name, and sometimes even in practice. Thus one man would sometimes collect the Sar Deshmukhi, another the Jahagir dues, a third the Mokassa, a fourth the Baabti, and a fifth the Sahotra, on the same village. In this case the holder of the Jahagir would settle the sum to be paid by the village, the Mokassadar would send and collect his share from the Rayats; but the other claimants would allow the holder of the Jahagir to collect the rest, and pay to each his share, the amount of which each would ascertain from the village accounts. But when there was a defalcation each endeavoured to collect his own and throw the loss on his neighbour, and a general struggle ensued, in which the Rayats were sure to suffer from the violence of the combatants. In addition to this distribution of the revenue, various causes broke up the Parganas, and made the Mahratta revenue divisions exceedingly scattered and intermixed.

Their gradations of authority departed as far from the uniformity of the Mohammedans, as their divisions of the territory. In general each revenue division was under an officer, who in a large district was called Mamlatdar, and in a small one Kamavisdar; under these Tarafdars or Karkuns, who had charge of a considerable number of villages, and under them Shekdars, who had four or five. The nomination of the Mamlatdars rested with Government; that of the inferior agents with the Mamlatdar. There were, however, in every division permanent officers called Darakdars, appointed by Government, and generally hereditary, whose signature was necessary to all papers, and who were bound to give information of all malpractices of the Mamlatdars. These officers were the Divan, who was the deputy to the Mamlatdar, the Fadnavis, or keeper of registers, the Potanavis, or cash accountant, etc.

Mahratta officers of revenue.

In some provinces, especially in remote ones, such

as Khandesh, Gujarat and the Karnat k, there was an officer between the Mamlatdars and the Government, who was called Sar Subhedar; his powers and duties varied. In the Karnatik he was answerable for the revenue, and appointed his own Mamlatdars, but in Khandesh he had only a general superintendence, every Mamlatdar giving in his own accounts, and making his payments direct to Government. The allowances of these officers were not very clearly fixed; before the introduction of the farming system, a considerable Mamlatdar had 5,000 or 6,000 rupees a year, generally about one per cent on the revenue, besides an undefined allowance for his expenses. He also made large unauthorized profits, often with the connivance of Government. He was reckoned reasonable if his whole profits did not exceed five per cent. on the net revenue.

Mahratta manner of collecting the Revenue.

Every Mamlatdar on his appointment, or at the commencement of the year, received from Government an estimate of the revenue of his district, with a list of all the authorized charges, including Sibandis, pensions, religious expenses, salaries, etc., etc. It was his duty to send in the balance to Government, and a proportion of it, generally half, was paid immediately; the rest was paid by instalments, but always in advance. The Mamlatdar then proceeded to his district, and moved about to superintend his offices, and to redress grievances; he kept a Vakil at Puna to receive all orders, and answer all complaints. Complaints are said to have been readily heard; but as all was done by the Prince or his Prime Minister, that must have depended on their leisure and patience. At the end of the year the Mamlatdar presented his accounts of the collections, confirmed by the accounts signed by the Zamindars, and the receipts and ex-

Note — Captain McLeod's paper, and in Captain Grant's letter of August 17th.

penditure in his own office, drawn up by the Fadnavis, and signed by the other Darakdars. These were carefully revised, and, as from the mode of payment in advance there was generally a balance in favour of the Mamlatdar, all unauthorized charges were struck out of it, and often reductions were made on account of supposed embezzlements, without much proof or investigation. The admitted balance was carried on in account from year to year, was sometimes compromised by partial payments, by grants of annuities, etc., but was seldom fully paid. On the other hand, all balances due to the Government were exacted, though the Mamlatdar was not bound to pay the sum inserted in his estimate, if the receipts fell short of it. If the defalcation was owing to corruption on his part, he was obliged to refund; and if to his negligence, he was removed from his office. Though, in this adjustment of accounts, all advantages appear to be on the side of the Government, yet the Mamlatdars do not appear to have complained, or to have suffered much in reality. They had probably many ways of making money, which eluded the utmost researches of the Government, especially as they could generally find means to engage the Zamindars and Darakdars on their side. The sources of their profit were concealment of receipts (especially fees, fines, and other undefined collections), false charges for remissions, false musters, non-payment of pensions, and other frauds in expenditure.

The grand source of their profit was an extra assessment above the revenue, which was called Saudir Warrid Patti. It was levied to pay expenses of the district not provided for by Government, and naturally afforded a great field for peculation; one of the chief of these expenses was called Darbar Kharch, or Antasth. This was originally applied secretly to bribe the

Ministers and auditors. By degrees their bribes became established fees, and the account was audited like the rest; but as bribes were still required, another increase of collection took place for this purpose, and as the auditors and accountants did not search minutely into these delicate transactions, the Mamlatdar generally collected much more for himself than he did for his patrons. It was said that it was chiefly the Government that suffered by these frauds, and that the imposts did not fall heavy on the Rayats. If this were so, it was probably owing to the interest the Mamlatdars had in the prosperity of their districts, from the long periods for which they were allowed to hold them. Many men held the same district for as long as fifty years.

Land revenue.

The following was the manner in which the Mamlatdar raised the revenue from his district. At the beginning of the rains he sent for the Patil, and gave him a general assurance that he should take no more than was usual; the Patil giving a written engagement, specifying the quantity of cultivated land, the quantity of waste, and that granted at a just rent to new settlers, and promising to realize the revenue. He then went to his village, encouraged the Rayats to cultivate, procured them loans, or forbearance from former creditors, promised to get them Takavi (or advances from the Mamlatdar), and prevailed on them to undertake the ploughing of new lands. Takavi was given by the Mamlatdar, not by the Government; it was payable in two or three years with interest, and security was given by the Patil, or several of the Rayats.

About the end of one year, when the principal harvest was nearly ready to be cut, the Mamlatdar moved out into his district, and was attended by the Patils of villages, with their Kulkarnis, who laid before him the papers already enumerated. The whole country has been surveyed, and each field classed and assessed according to its circumstances and quality. The northern districts were surveyed by Mallik Umbar, and the southern by the Adil Shahi Kings, besides partial and imperfect attempts at surveys by the Mahrattas. The assessment fixed by those monarchs is called the Tankha. The whole amount thus assessed was never actually realized in some villages, while in others a greater revenue may have been collected. This gave rise to another rate, being the highest ever paid, which is called the Kamil or Hemaul, and which is considered more applicable to practical purposes than the Tankha; that of the last year, or of any recent year, is called the Wasul or Akar. All these rates are contained in the Kulkarni's papers, with the other particulars mentioned before, which ought to give a full view of the state of the inhabitants and cultivation. The Mamlatdar was enabled, by the intimate knowledge of the village possessed by his Shekdars, to judge of the accuracy of these statements, and he proceeded to settle the revenue of the ensuing season, on a consideration of the amount paid in former years, combined with a regard to the actual state of things. The Patil represented any ground there was for relaxation, in the terms in which he expected the support of the Deshmukhi and Despande; all hereditary officers being considered as connected with the Rayats. The Patil was likewise accompanied by some of the principal Rayats, especially of the Mirasdars, who were witnesses to his proceedings, and who also assisted him with their opinions. These discussions generally ended in a second more particular agreement, on which the Patil interchanged with the Mamlatdar an engagement fixing the revenue; that of the Mamlatdar was called the Jamabandi Pati, and that of the Patil, Kabul Katba. The

Patils had generally settled with the Rayats the share which each was to bear before he came to make the settlements, and if anything unexpected was proposed, so as to derange the distribution agreed on, he returned to his village to consult the Rayats anew. When the Patil continued obstinately to reject the terms offered by the Mamlatdar, a special officer was sent to the spot to examine the fields, and if no other means succeeded in effecting an adjustment, the Mamlatdar would offer what seems to have been the original principle in all settlements, namely, for Government to take half, and leave half to the cultivator. This plan was termed Bhattye. It is generally adopted in the Konkan, but seldom resorted to above the Ghats, until the final settlement was made; the crops in many parts of the country were kept in charge of Havildars on behalf of Government, who allowed them to be carried off as soon as the settlement was completed. In the country immediately round Puna, however, and in that now under Satara, this custom was not observed.

When the time for paying arrived, a Sibandi was sent by the Shekdar to assist the Patil. The Mhar summoned the Rayats, who paid their rent to the Patil in the presence of the Potadar, who assayed and stamped the money, and of the Kulkarni, who granted a receipt. When all was collected the Patil sent it by the Mhar, with a letter to the Deshmukhi, and another to the Kamavisdar, under charge of the Chaugulla, and received a receipt from the Mamlatdar. If a Rayat refused, or was unable to pay his revenue, the Sibandi pressed him for it, confined him in the village chouki, exposed him to the sun, put a heavy stone on his head, and prevented his eating and drinking until he paid. If this did not succeed, he was carried to the Mamlatdar, his cattle were sold, and himself thrown into prison, or into irons. This rigorous treatment was seldom necessary for the regular revenue; it was more employed in exacting extraordinary taxes, and under the farming system the practice of it was frequent and severe. If a whole village resisted, these severities fell on the Patil; but previous to that extremity a horseman was billeted on the village, or a fine levied to induce it to submit. The payments were by three instalments, corresponding with the seasons of the Rabi, Tusar, and Kharif crops; there was frequently another at the end of the year, to recover all outstanding balances.

The above relates to the regular rent or tax on the land, for it may be considered as rent with regard to the Upris, and as a tax with regard to the Mirasdars (it is called by the natives, Ayin Jama, or proper collections). Another regular source of revenue, levied partly on the Rayats and partly on the other inhabitants, is that termed by the Mahrattas, Savai Jama (or extra collections); these taxes vary considerably in different districts, and even in different villages. The following list, though not complete, gives an idea of their nature. The first fall chiefly or entirely on the cultivators, Dakab Pati: a tax of one year's revenue in ten, on the lands of the Deshmukhi and Despande; Hak Chouthai, a fourth of the fees, levied every year; Mhar Mharki, a particular tax, on the Inams of the Mhars; Miras Pati, an additional tax, once in three years, on Mirasdars: Inam Fijavi, a payment of Inamdars, of a third of the Government share of their lands yearly; Inam Pati, an occasional tax, imposed in times of exigency on Inamdars; Pandi Gunna, an additional levy, equal to twelve per cent. on the Tankha, once in twelve years; Vir Hunda, an extra tax on

Extra revenue.

lands watered from wells. Other taxes were on traders alone. These were Mohterfa, a tax on shop-keepers, varying with their means: in fact, an income-tax; Baloti, a tax on the twelve village servants. These, too, are sometimes included in the Ayin Jama, and in some places the Mohterfa forms a distinct head by itself; Bazar Baithak, a tax on stalls at fairs; Kumbhar Kam, on the earth dug up by the potters. The following might fall indiscriminately on both classes; Ghar Pati, or Amber Sari, a house-tax levied from all but Brahmins and village officers. Batchappani, a fee on the annual examination of weights and measures; Tag, a similar fee on examining the scales used for bulky articles; Dekka, or the right to beat a drum on particular religious and other occasions; Kheridi Jins (or purveyance), the right to purchase articles at a certain rate; this was generally commuted for a money payment: Lagna Tikka, a tax on marriages: Paut Dauma, a particular tax on the marriage of widows: Mahis Pati, a tax on buffaloes: Bakre Pati, a tax on sheep. There were also occasional contributions in kind, called Fur Furmanesh, such as bullocks' hides, charcoal, hemp, rope, ghee, etc., which were often commuted for fixed money payments; many other sums were paid in commutation for service. All these collections were made by the Patil in small villages, though in towns there was a separate officer to levy those most connected with the land. Government had other sources of revenue included in the Savai Jama in each village, besides those enumerated. The principal were as follows: Khamawis, Gunehgari, or Kund Furshi, as fines and forfeitures; Baitul Mal (Escheats) amount (profit from deposits and temporary sequestrations); Wancharai, paid by cattle grazing on Government lands; Ghas Kattani, or grass cut on Government lands; Devasthan Dubhi, derived from offerings to idols; Kharbuzwarri, on melon-gardens on the beds of rivers. Besides all this, and besides the Gaum Kharch, or village expenses, there were taxes to defray the Mehel Saudir Warrid, district expenses not already provided for by Government, in which were included many personal expenses of the Mamlatdars, and a large fund for embezzlement and corruption for himself and the courtiers who befriended him.

Extraordinary and occasional impositions.

In addition to all these exactions, there were occasional impositions on extraordinary emergencies, which were called Jasti Pati, and Yeksali Pati. If these happened to be continued for several years they ceased to be considered as occasional impositions, and fell into the regular Savai Jama; but until the introduction of the farming system, they are said to have been as rare as the occasions which furnished the pretext for them.

The farming system.

The changes introduced by that system may be described without much difficulty. They were in fact rather aggravations of the evils of the ancient system, than any complete innovations. The office of Mamlatdar, instead of being conferred as a favour on a person of experience and probity, who could be punished by removal if his conduct did not give satisfaction, was put up to auction among the Peshwa's attendants, who were encouraged to bid high, and sometimes disgraced if they showed a reluctance to enter on this sort of speculation. Next year the same operation was renewed, and the district was generally transferred to a higher bidder. The Mamlatdar, thus constituted, had no time for inquiry, and no motive for forbearance; he let his district out at an enhanced rate to under-farmers, who repeated the operation until it reached the Patils. If one of these officers farmed his own village, he became absolute master of everyone in it. No complaints were listened to, and the Mamlatdar, who was formerly a check on the Patil, as the Government was on the Mamlatdar, now afforded him an excuse for tyranny of bearing the blame of his exactions. If the Patil refused to farm the village at the rate proposed, the case was perhaps worse, as the Mamlatdar's own officers undertook to levy the sum determined on, with less knowledge and less mercy than the Patil; in either case, the actual state of the cultivation was in essentials entirely disregarded. A man's means of payment, not the land he occupied, were the scale on which he was assessed. No moderation was shown in levying the sum fixed, and every pretext for fine and forfeiture, every means of rigour and confiscation, were employed to squeeze the utmost out of the people before the arrival of the day when the Mamlatdar was to give up his charge: amidst all this violence a regular account was prepared, as if the settlement had been made in the most deliberate manner. This account was of course fictitious, and the collections were always underrated, as it enabled the Patil to impose on the next Mamlatdar, and the Mamlatdar to deceive the Government and his fellows. The next Mamlatdar pretended to be deceived; he agreed to the most moderate terms, and gave every encouragement except Takkavi (advances) to increase the cultivation; but when the crops were on the ground, or when the end of his period drew near, he threw off the mask, and plundered like his predecessor. In consequence of this plan, the assessment of the land, being proposed early in the season, would be made with some reference to former practice, and Saudir Warrid and other Patis would accumulate, until the time when the Mamlatdar came to make up his accounts. It was then that his exactions were most severely felt; for he had a fixed sum to complete, and if the collections fell short of it, he portioned out the balance among the exhausted villages, imposed a Jasti (Zedati) Pati, or extra assessment, to pay it, and left the Patils to extort it on whatever pretence and by whatever means they thought proper. We are now suffering from this system, for as we have no true accounts, and are afraid to over-assess, we are obliged to be content with whatever the people agree to. Captain Briggs's collections in Khandesh, though willingly acceded to by the Rayats, are yet much heavier than any that appear in the accounts during the ten years of oppression that have depopulated Khandesh. Some places, no doubt, escaped the oppressions of the farming system. Where a village belonged to a man of influence, or a favourite of such a man, the assessment fell light on him, and he gained by the emigration of Rayats, occasioned by the misfortunes of his neighbours.

The above sources of revenue were collected by the village establishment; the following were in the hands of distinct officers directly under the Government:

Customs.

Zakat, or Customs.—This was a transit duty levied by the bullock load; but the rate varied in proportion to the value of the article; the highest was eight rupees. It was levied separately in every district, so that property was frequently liable to be stopped and searched. To remedy this inconvenience, there was a class called Hundekaris in towns, who undertook for a single payment to pass articles through the whole country. These men arranged with the farmers of the customs, and were answerable to them for the sums due. In addition to the transit duty, there was a tax of 12 per cent. on the sale of animals included in the Zakat.

2. The Government lands were another source of revenue not included in the villages; they were divided into Shairi (cultivated fields); Kurans (grass lands); Bag (gardens); and Ambrai (orchards).

Government lands.

3. The Sheep-pastures.—This was a tax paid by the Khillarries, or wandering shepherds, for the right to feed their flocks on all waste lands, from the Tapti to the Tungbhadra.

Sheep-pastures.

4. Ranwa.—A fee paid for leave to cut wood in the forests belonging to Government.

Forests.

5. Kotvali.—This may be called town duties; it comprised, besides the taxes included in Savai Jama, a variety of other imposts, among which the most considerable was a tax of 17 per cent. on the sale of houses.

Town duties.

6. Tanksal.—The mint.

Mint.

7. Watan Zabti.—Produce of lands belonging to Zamindars, sequestrated by Government.

Sequestration.

Nazar.—Fines, or fees paid on succession to property. If a son succeeded his father he was not liable to this payment, unless he were a Jahagirdar, or other servant of Government. But in cases of adoption (that is, in almost all cases except where a son succeeded) it was exacted from all persons.

Fines and fees.

The first six articles were always, or almost always, farmed; the rest were not. The Zakat, before the cession of Puna, produced about five lacs of rupees, the sheep-pastures about 25,000 rupees, the mint at Puna yielded 10,000 rupees; the others were confounded with the general receipts of the districts where they were situated. The Watan Zabti yielded 50,000 rupees. The amount of the Nazars was too fluctuating to be guessed at.

The Kotwalset in Nana Fadnavi's time yielded

50,000 rupees, of which a great part was produced by money extorted from persons guilty or suspected of adultery. Baji Ráv, much to his honour, abolished this pretext for extortion, but his lenity was far from being approved by the better part of his subjects. The other articles were trifling. Abkarri, which is so important with us, did not yield above 10,000 rupees. The use of spirituous liquors was forbidden at Puna, and discouraged everywhere else; the effect of this system on the sobriety of the people is very conspicuous.

The outline of the revenue system adopted since our acquisition of the country is contained in my letter dated July 10th, conveying instructions to the collectors, and in that dated July 14th, enclosing instructions for Mamlatdars. The leading principles are to abolish farming, but otherwise to maintain the native system; to levy the revenue according to the actual cultivation; to make the assessments light; to impose no new taxes, and to do none away unless obvious and unjust; and, above all, to make no innovations. Many innovations were, however, the result of the introduction of foreign rulers and foreign maxims of government; but in the revenue department most of them were beneficial. The country, which had been under many Mamlatdars, with very unequal extent of territory and power, was placed under five principal officers (I include Satara), with much superior weight and respectability. The chief authority now resided in the district, and devoted his whole time to its affairs, and all subordinate agents were obliged to follow his example. The straggling revenue divisions of the Mahrattas were formed into compact districts, each yielding from 50 to 70,000 rupees a year, and placed under a Mamlatdar. The numerous partitions of revenue (Chouth, Babti, etc.), being thrown into the hands of one agent, were

Present Revenue System.

virtually abolished. The assessments were much lighter than formerly, and much more uniform and clearly defined. The powers of the Mamlatdars were limited, and the system of fixed pay and no perquisites was decidedly introduced in principle, though of course it may be still secretly departed from in practice. The improvements in the administration of the revenue department are greater than in the rulers. Faith is kept with the Rayat, more liberal assistance is given him in advance, he is not harassed by false accusations as pretexts to extort money, and his complaints find a readier hearing and redress. Some of our alterations are less agreeable to all, or to particular classes. We have more forms and more strictness than our predecessors; the power of the Patil is weakened by the greater interference of our Mamlatdars. His emoluments are injured by our reductions of the Saudir Warrid; and even the Rayats, who were taxed for his profit, are made to feel the want of some of their charities and amusements, while they confound the consequent reductions of their payments with the general diminution in the assessment. The character of our Mamlatdars is not entirely what we could wish; as the country was occupied before the Peshwa's cause was desperate, few of his adherents would venture to join us, and we were obliged to employ such persons as we could procure, without much regard to their merit. In Puna and Satara the Mamlatdars are, nevertheless, respectable servants of the old Government; I have more doubts regarding those in Khandesh, being chiefly either from the Nizam's country (which is notorious for bad government) or from Hindustan. I have strongly recommended to all the collectors to take every opportunity to introduce servants of the former Government, but much time must elapse before this can be entirely accomplished. An important change is made by the introduction of some men from the Madras provinces; though very anxious to employ the revenue officers of the Mahratta Government in general, I thought it desirable to have a very few of our oldest subjects, as well from general policy in a new conquest, as to introduce some models of system and regularity. As each collector was to have two principal officers to check each other, I thought it would contribute to that object and answer other ends to have one of them from the Madras provinces. General Munro was also obliged to bring a very great proportion of persons of this description into the country under his charge. They are more active, more obedient to orders, more exact and methodical than the Mahrattas, but they introduce forms of respect for their immediate superiors quite unknown here, while they show much less consideration for the great men of the country, and are more rough, harsh, and insolent in their general demeanour. It might be worth while to consider how much of these characteristics they owe to us, and how much to the Mussulmans.

A detailed explanation of the operations of the collectors will be found in Mr. Chaplin's instructions to his sub-collectors, enclosed in his letter; Captain Brigg's letter, dated June 23rd, 1819; Captain Grant's letter, dated Aug. 17th, 1819; Captain Robertson's letter of Aug. 28th; and Captain Pottinger's instructions to Mr. Wilkins in his letter of August 30th.

The duties of the Mamlatdars are to superintend the collection of the revenue, to manage the police, to receive civil and criminal complaints, referring the former to Panchayats, and sending up the latter to the collector. They have a Sirashtedar, who keeps their records, an accountant, and some other assistants. The pay of a Mamlatdar is from 70 to 150 rupees a month, and that of a Sirashtedar from 35 to 50. The systems adopted by all the collectors were founded on the Mahratta practice, though varying from it and from each other in some particulars. The foundation for the assessment in all this was the amount paid by each village in times when the people considered themselves to have been well governed. Deductions were made from this in proportion to the diminution of the cultivation, and afterwards further allowances were made on any specific grounds alleged by the Rayats. The amount to be paid was partitioned among the Rayats by the village officers, and if all were satisfied, Patas were given, and the settlement was ended.

All the collectors abolished Jasti Patis (or arbitrary taxes having no reference to the land or trade), and all regulated the Saudir Warrid, doing away all exactions on that account, more than were necessary for the village expenses. Captain Briggs even abolished the Saudir Warrid Pati altogether, and defrayed the village expenses from the Government revenue, limiting the amount to 4 per cent. on the gross Jama. The expediency of this arrangement is, however, doubtful, both as to the close restriction of the expense and the laying it on Government; all paid great attention to the circumstances of the Rayats, and made their assessment studiously light. There were, however, some points of difference in their proceedings. Mr. Chaplin and Captain Grant contented themselves with ascertaining the extent of the land under cultivation, by the information of neighbours, and of rival village officers, aided by the observation of their own servants. Captain Pottinger and Captain Robertson had the lands of some villages measured, but only in cases where they suspected frauds; and Captain Briggs began by a measurement of the whole cultivation either of Gangtari alone, or of both that and Khandesh. All the collectors kept up the principle of the Rayatwari settlement, and some carried it to a greater extent than had been usual with the Mahrattas. Mr. Chaplin and Captain Pottinger, after settling with the Patil for the whole village, settled with each Rayat, and gave him a Pata for his field. Captain Grant and Captain Robertson settled with the Patil and gave him a Pata, but first ascertained the amount assessed on each Rayat, and inquired if he was satisfied with it; and Captain Briggs, though he settled for each field, did it all with the Patil, taking an engagement from him to explain at the end of the year how much he had levied on each Rayat.

This refers to the settlement with the villages. The customs have been farmed on account of the difficulty of preparing a tariff, and of superintending the introduction of a new system, while the collectors were so fully occupied in other matters. No complaints are made, from which it may be inferred that the present system, if not profitable to Government, is not oppressive to the people. The exemptions of our camp dealers have been done away, the original motive of them (to prevent disputes between our people and the Peshwa's) being no longer in force. The exemption made no difference in the price of articles to the troops, though it afforded a pretence for great frauds in the customs. The only good effect it had was to attach dealers to the camp bazaars; but the exemption from taxes while in cantonments, and from the customs also when on service, may be expected to be sufficient to retain them.

The sheep-pastures are still a distinct farm, but the arrangement is so inconvenient, from the want of authority in the hands of collectors over shepherds entering their districts, that I propose to alter it.

None of the taxes called Kotwali are now levied, they having either been done away or suspended by Baji Ráv. If they should prove only to be suspended, the unexceptionable ones ought, if possible, to be restored.

The Abkari I would recommend keeping in its present low state, by prohibitions or by very heavy taxes.

The mint is still farmed, but this should be changed as soon as a system regarding the coinage has been resolved on.

The other taxes require no particular remark. The tax on adoptions ought to be kept up as one that is little felt, and is attended with advantages in recording successions.

POLICE AND CRIMINAL JUSTICE.

The Mahratta system of police is that common in the Deccan, which has already been too fully described to require a minute account.

Mahratta system of police.

The Patil is responsible for the police of his village. He is aided by his Kulkarni and Chaugulla, and when the occasion requires it, by all the inhabitants. His great and responsible assistant in matters of police is the village watchman, who is called the Talarri in the Karnatik, the Mhar in the Mahratta country, and the Jagla in Khandesh; in the first-named district he is by caste a Beder, in the second a Dher, and in the third a Bhil. Though there is only an allowance for one watchman in a village, the family has generally branched out into several numbers, who relieve and aid each other in their duties. The duties are to keep watch at night, to find out all arrivals and departures, observe all strangers, and report all suspicious persons to the Patil. The watchman is likewise bound to know the character of each man in the village, and in the event of a theft committed within the village bounds, it is his business to detect the thief. He is enabled to do this by his

Village police.

early habits of inquisitiveness and observation, as well as by the nature of his allowance, which being partly a small share of the grain and similar property belonging to each house, he is kept always on the watch to ascertain his fees, and always in motion to collect them. When a theft or robbery happens, the watchman commences his inquiries and researches: it is very common for him to track a thief by his footsteps; and if he does this to another village, so as to satisfy the watchman there, or if he otherwise traces the property to an adjoining village, his responsibility ends, and it is the duty of the watchman of the new village to take up the pursuit. The last village to which the thief has been clearly traced becomes answerable for the property stolen, which would otherwise fall on the village where the robbery was committed. The watchman is obliged to make up this amount as far as his means go, and the remainder is levied on the whole village. The exaction of this indemnity is evidently unjust, since the village might neither be able to prevent the theft nor to make up the loss; and it was only in particular cases that it was insisted on to its full extent, but some fine was generally levied; and neglect or connivance was punished by transferring the Inam of the Patil, or watchman, to his nearest relation, by fine, by imprisonment in irons, or by severe corporeal punishment. This responsibility was necessary; as, besides the usual temptation to neglect, the watchman is often himself a thief, and the Patil disposed to harbour thieves with a view to share their profits. This peculiar temptation in case of theft has made that offence to be most noticed. In other crimes, the village has less interest in connivance, and probably is sufficiently active; but gross negligence in these cases also would have been punished by the Government. I have mentioned that besides the regular village watchmen others were often entertained from the plundering tribes in the neighbourhood. Their business was to assist in repelling open force, and to aid in the apprehension of all offenders, but chiefly to prevent depredations by their own tribes, and to find out the perpetrators when any did occur.

The Patil was under the same authority as a police officer that he was as a revenue one—the Mamlatdar, who employed the same agents in this department as in the other. The Mamlatdar saw that all villagers acted in concert, and with proper activity; and when there was a Sarsubhedar, he kept the same superintendence over the Mamlatdars. These officers had also considerable establishments to maintain the tranquillity of their districts. These were the Sebandis or irregular infantry, and the small parties of horse which were kept in every district; they were, however, employed to oppose violence, and to support the village police, not to discover offenders. With the Mamlatdar also rested all general arrangements with the chiefs of Bhils or other predatory tribes, either for forbearing from plunder themselves, or for assisting to check it in others. The Mamlatdar had great discretionary powers, and even a Patil would not hesitate to secure a suspected person, or to take any measure that seemed necessary to maintain the police of his village, for which he was answerable.

District Police.

This was the plan of the police up to the time of Baji Ráv, during the reign of Madhav Ráv I., and likewise during the administration of Nana Fadnavis; it is said to have succeeded in preserving great security and order.

The confusions in the commencement of Baji Ráv's

reign, the weakness of his own government, the want of employment for adventurers of all kinds, and the effects of the famine, greatly deranged the system of police; and to remedy the disorders into which it fell, an office was instituted, under the name of Tapasnavis, the special duty of which was to discover and seize offenders. The Tapasnavises had districts of different extent, not corresponding with the usual revenue divisions, and only comprehending those portions of the country where the services of such officers were thought to be most required. They had a jurisdiction entirely independent of the Mamlatdars, and had a body of horse and foot which was the principal instrument of their administration. They had also Ramoshis and spies, whom they employed to give information; and on receiving it, they went with a body of horse to the village where the theft happened, and proceeded to seize the Patil and the watchmen, and to demand the thief, or the amount of the property stolen, or the fine which they thought proper to impose, if the offence were any other than theft. The detection of the offender they seem to have left in general to the ordinary village police. It may be supposed that such a violent proceeding, and one so foreign to the ordinary system, could not fail to clash with the former institutions; and accordingly there were constant and loud complaints by the Mamlatdars and villagers, that the Tapasnavises were only active in extorting money under false accusations, and that robbers rather flourished under their protection. The Tapasnavises, on the other hand, complained of indifference, connivance, and counteraction on the part of the villagers and revenue officers.

Alterations under Baji Ráv.

Tapasnavis.

Great abuses, it must be mentioned, are stated to

have at all times existed, even under the regular system. Criminals found refuge in one district when chased out of another; some Jahagirdars and Zamindars made a trade of harbouring robbers; and any offender, it is said, could purchase his release, if he had money enough to pay for it. False accusations were likewise made a cloak to exaction from the innocent; and villagers were obliged to pay the amount of plundered property, in the loss of which they had no share, and for which the losers received no compensation. There cannot be a stronger proof of the enormous abuses to which the former police was liable than is furnished by an occurrence in the city of Puna, under the eye of Government, in the days of Nana Fadnavis. There was at that time a Kotwall, called Ghasi Ram, a native of Hindustan, who was much trusted, and rose to great eminence. This man was convicted of having for many years employed the powers of the police in murders and oppressions, which the natives illustrate by stories far beyond belief; his guilt was at length detected, and excited such indignation, that though a Brahmin, it was decided to punish him capitally; he was therefore led through the city on a camel, and then abandoned to the fury of the populace whom this exposure had assembled, and by them stoned to death.

Abuses.

In Baji Ráv's time 9,000 rupees a month was allowed to the officer who had charge of the police at Puna: from this he had to maintain a very large establishment of peons, some horse patrols, and a considerable number of Ramoshis; besides being answerable for the amount of property plundered, whenever the Peshwa thought proper to call on him. Still his appointment was reckoned lucrative, as the pay of his establishment was very

Police of Puna.

low, and both he and they derived much profit from unavowed exactions. The police, however, was good; on the whole, murders or robberies, attended with violence and alarm, were very rare; and I have never heard any complaints of the insecurity of property.

Next to the prevention of crimes and the apprehension of criminals, comes the manner in which offences, etc., are tried and punished: in this are involved the authorities competent to try, the forms of trial, and the law by which guilt is defined, and punishment awarded.

Criminal justice under the Mahrattas.

The power of administering criminal justice, under the Mahratta Government, was vested in the revenue officers, and varied with their rank, from the Patil, who could only put a man for a few days in the village choki, to the Sarsubhedar, who in latter days had the power of life and death. Formerly this power was confined to persons invested with the full powers of Government by being entrusted with the Mutalliki seal, and to great military chiefs in their own armies, or their own Jahagirs.

By whom administered.

The right of inflicting punishment was, however, extremely undefined, and was exercised by each man, more according to his power and influence than to his office. One Patil would flog and fine, and put in the stocks for many weeks; and another would not even venture to imprison. Most Mamlutdars would hang a Ramosi, Bhil, or Mang robber, without a reference; and those at a distance would exercise their power without scruple, while the highest civil officers, if at Puna, would pay the Peshwa the attention of applying for his sanction in a capital case. A Chief was thought to have authority over his own troops and servants, wherever he was. Scindia, while he affected to act under the Peshwa, put many of his Chiefs and Ministers (even Brahmins), who had been accused of plots, to death. At Puna, Appa Desái, in 1813, while completely in the Peshwa's power, blew away one of his Sardars from a gun, for conspiracy against him, and was never questioned, though the execution took place within a mile of Puna.

There was no prescribed form of trial. A principal rebel, or a head of banditti, would be executed at once, on the ground of notoriety; any Bhil, caught in a part of the country where the Bhils were plundering the road, would be hanged immediately. In doubtful cases the chief authority would order some of the people about him to inquire into the affair. The prisoner was examined, and if suspicions were strong he was flogged to make him confess. Witnesses were examined, and a summary of their evidence and of the statement of the accused were always taken down in writing. They were sometimes confronted with the accused, in the hope of shaming or perplexing the party whose statement was false; but this was by no means necessary to the regularity of the proceedings. The chief authority would generally consult his officers, and perhaps employ a committee of them to conduct an inquiry; but I should doubt whether Panchayats were ever generally employed in criminal trials, though mentioned by Captain Grant to have been so in the Satara country.

Trial.

In crimes against the State, the Prince made such inquiries, or directed his Ministers to make such, as seemed requisite for his own safety, and gave such orders regarding the accused as their case seemed to require. Torture was employed to compel confession and disclosure of accomplices.

Trials of this sort were naturally considered in a

despotic Government as above all law; but even in common criminal trials, no law seems ever to be referred to, except in cases connected with religion, where Shastris were sometimes consulted. The only rule seems to have been the custom of the country, and the magistrate's notice of expediency. The Hindu law was quite disused, probably owing to its absurdity; and although every man is tolerably acquainted with its rules in civil cases, I do not believe anyone but the very learned has the least notion of its criminal enactments.

Criminal law.

The following were the customary punishments. Murder, unless attended with peculiar atrocity, appears never to have been capital, and was usually punished by fine. Highway robbery was generally punished with death, because it was generally committed by low people, for a greater distinction was made in the punishment on account of the caste of the criminal than the nature of the crime. A man of tolerable caste was seldom put to death, except for offences against the State. In such cases birth seems to have been no protection. Vitoji, the full brother to Yeshwant Ráv Holkar, was trampled to death by an elephant for rebellion, or rather for heading a gang of predatory horse. Sayaji Atole, a dispossessed Jahagirdar, was blown away from a gun for the same offence, yet it is well observed by Mr. Chaplin that treason and rebellion were thought less of than with us. This originated in a want of steadiness, not of severity, in the Government. When it suited a temporary convenience an accommodation was made with a rebel, who was immediately restored, not only to safety, but to favour. Balkrishn Gangadhar received a Jahagir for the same insurrection for which Vitoji Holkar was put to death. Viswas Ráv Ghatge, who headed a

Punishments.

large body of plundering horse and was cut up by the Duke of Wellington at Mankaisur, was treated with much favour by the Peshwa; but Abdulla Khan, a relative of the Nabob of Savanore, who committed the same offence at a subsequent period, was blown away from a gun. The other punishments were hanging, beheading, cutting to pieces with swords, and crushing the head with a mallet. Punishments, though public, were always executed with little ceremony or form. Brahmin prisoners, who could not be executed, were poisoned, or made away with by deleterious food; bread made of equal parts of flour and salt was one of these. Women were never put to death; long confinement, and the cutting off the nose, ears, and breast, were the severest punishments inflicted on them. Mutilation was very common, and the person who had his hand, foot, ears or nose cut off, was turned loose as soon as the sentence was executed and left to his fate. Imprisonment in hill forts and in dungeons was common; and the prisoners, unless they were people of consideration, were always neglected, and sometimes allowed to starve. Prisoners for theft were often whipped at intervals to make them discover where the stolen property was hidden. Hard labour, in building fortifications especially, was not unknown; but, like most ignominious punishments, was confined to the lower orders. Branding with a hot iron was directed by the Hindu law, but I do not know that it was practised. Flogging with a martingale was very common in trifling offences, such as petty thefts, etc. But the commonest of all punishments was fine and confiscation of goods, to which the Mamlutdar was so much prompted by his avarice, that it is often difficult to say whether it was inflicted as the regular punishment, or merely made use of as a pretence for gaining wealth. On the one hand, it seems to have been the Mahratta practice to punish murder, especially if committed by a man of good caste, by fine; but on the other, the Mamlutdars would frequently release Bhil robbers contrary to the established custom, and even allow them to renew their depredations, on the payment of a sum of money. No other punishment, it may be averred, was ever inflicted on a man who could afford to pay a fine; and on the whole, the criminal system of the Mahrattas was in the last state of disorder and corruption.

Prevailing crimes.

Judging from the impunity with which crimes might be committed under a system of criminal justice and police such as has been described, we should be led to fancy the Mahratta country a complete scene of anarchy and violence. No picture, however, could be further from the truth. The reports of the collectors do not represent crimes as particularly numerous. Mr. Chaplin, who has the best opportunity of drawing a comparison with our old provinces, thinks them rather rarer here and there. Murder for revenge, generally arising either from jealousy or disputes about landed property, and as frequently about village rank, is mentioned as the commonest crime among the Mahrattas. Arson and cattle-stealing, as a means of revenging wrongs, or extorting justice, is common in the Karnatik. Gang robberies and highway robbery are common, but are almost always committed by Bhils and other predatory tribes, who scarcely form part of the society; and they have never, since I have been in the country, reached to such a pitch as to bear a moment's comparison with the state of Bengal described in the papers laid before Parliament.

It is of vast importance to ascertain the causes that counteracted the corruption and relaxation of the police, and which kept this country in a state superior to our oldest possessions, amidst all the abuses and oppressions of a Native Government. The principal causes to which the disorders in Bengal have been attributed are: the over-population, and the consequent degradation and pusillanimity of the people; the general revolutions of property, in consequence of our revenue arrangements, which drove the upper classes to disaffection, and the lower to desperation; the want of employment to the numerous classes, whether military or otherwise, who were maintained by the Native Government; the abolition of the ancient system of police, in which, besides the usual bad effects of a general change, were included the removal of responsibility from the Zamindars; the loss of their natural influence as an instrument of police; the loss of the services of the village watchmen; the loss of a hold over that class which is naturally disposed to plunder, and, in some cases, the necessity to which individuals of it were driven to turn robbers, from the resumption of their allowances; the separation of the revenue, magisterial, judicial, and military powers, by which all were weakened; the further weakness of each from the checks imposed on it; the delays of trials, the difficulties of conviction, the inadequacy of punishment, the trouble and expense of prosecuting and giving evidence; the restraints imposed by our maxims on the assumption of power by individuals, which, combined by the dread of the Adalat, discouraged all from exertion in support of the police; the want of an upper class among the natives, which could take the lead on such occasions; and, to conclude, the small number of European magistrates (who supply the place of the class last mentioned), their want of connection and communication

Attempt to account for their rarity.

with the natives, and of knowledge of their language and character.

The Mahratta country presents, in many respects, a complete contrast to the above picture. The people are few compared to the quantity of arable land. They are hardy, warlike, and always armed till of late years. The situation of the lower orders was very comfortable, and that of the upper prosperous. There was abundance of employment in the domestic establishments and foreign conquests of the nation. The ancient system of police was maintained. All the powers of the State were united in the same hands, and their rigour was not checked by any suspicions on the part of the Government, or any scruples of their own. In cases that threatened the peace of society, apprehension was sudden and arbitrary, trial summary, and punishment prompt and severe. The innocent might sometimes suffer, but the guilty could scarcely ever escape. As the magistrates were natives, they readily understood the real state of a case submitted to them, and were little retarded by scruples of conscience, so that prosecutors and witnesses had not long to wait. In their lax system, men knew that if they were right in substance, they would not be questioned about the form; and perhaps they likewise knew that if they did not protect themselves, they could not always expect protection from the magistrate, whose business was rather to keep down great disorder than to afford assistance in cases that might be settled without his aid. The Mamlutdars were themselves considerable persons, and there were men of property and consideration in every neighbourhood; Inamdars, Jahagirdars, or old Zamindars. These men associated with the ranks above and below them, and kept up the chain of society to the Prince. By this means the higher orders were kept informed of the situation of the lower; and as there was scarcely any man without a patron, men might be exposed to oppression, but could scarcely suffer from neglect.

Means for preserving an efficient Police.

Many of the evils from which this country has hitherto been exempt are inseparable from the introduction of a foreign Government; but perhaps the greater may be avoided by proper precautions. Many of the upper classes must sink into comparative poverty, and many of those who were employed in the court and army must absolutely lose their bread. Both of these misfortunes happened to a certain extent in the commencement of Baji Ráv's reign; but as the frame of Government was entire, the bad effect of these partial evils was surmounted. Whether we can equally maintain the frame of Government is a question that is yet to be examined. The present system of police, as far as relates to the villages, may be easily kept up; but I doubt whether it is enough that the village establishment be maintained, and the whole put under a Mamlatdar. The Patil's respectability and influence in his village must be kept up, by allowing him some latitude, both in the expenditure of the village expenses, and in restraining petty disorders in his village. So far from wishing that it were possible for the European officers to hear all complaints on such subjects, I think it fortunate that they have not time to investigate them, and think it desirable that the Mamlutdars also should leave them to the Patils, and thus preserve a power on the aid of which we must, in all branches of the Government, greatly depend. Zealous co-operation of the Patils is as essential to the collector of the revenue, and to the administration of civil justice, as to the police; and it ought, therefore, by all means to be secured. Too much care cannot be taken to prevent their duty becoming irksome, and their influence impaired by bringing their conduct too often under the correction of their superiors. I would lend a ready ear to all complaints against them for oppression, but I would not disturb them for inattention to forms; and I would leave them at liberty to settle petty complaints their own way, provided no serious punishment were inflicted on either party. We may weaken the Patils afterwards if we find it necessary, and retrench their emoluments; but our steps should be cautious, for if we once destroyed our influence over the Patils, or theirs over the people, we can never recover either. Care ought also to be taken of the condition of the village watchmen, whose allowance, if not sufficient to support him, and to keep him out of temptation to thieve, ought to be increased; but it ought not to be so high as to make him independent of the community, and it ought always to be in part derived from contributions which may compel him to go his rounds among the villagers, as at present.

If the village police be preserved, the next step is to preserve the efficiency of the Mamlatdar; at present all powers are invested in that officer, and as long as the auxiliary horse and Sebandis are kept up he has ample means of preserving order. The only thing requisite at present is that the Mamlatdar should have higher pay to render him more respectable and more above temptation, and to induce the better sort of natives to accept the office. When the Sebandis are reduced in numbers and the horse discharged, our means of preserving the police will be greatly weakened, at the same time that the number of enemies to the public tranquillity will be increased; the number of Sebandis now in our pay, by giving employment to the idle and needy, contributes, I have no doubt, more than anything else to the remarkable good order which this part of our new conquests has hitherto enjoyed. The Mamlatdar will also feel the want of many of the Jahagirdars and others of the upper class who used to aid his predecessors with their influence, and even with their troops. The want of that class will be still more felt as a channel through which Government could receive the accounts of the state of the districts, and of the conduct of the Mamlutdars themselves. The cessation of all prospects of rise will of itself in a great measure destroy the connection between them and their rulers, and the natural distance which I am afraid must always remain between natives and English gentlemen will tend to complete the separation. Something may be done by keeping up the simplicity and equality of Mahratta manners, and by imitating the facility of access which was conspicuous among their Chiefs. On this also the continuance of the spirit of the people and of our own popularity will probably in a great measure depend. Sir Henry Strachey, in his report laid before Parliament, attributes many of the defects in our administration in Bengal to the unmeasurable distance between us and the natives, and afterwards adds that there is scarcely a native in his district who would think of sitting down in the presence of an English gentleman. Here, every man above the rank of a Hárkára sits down before us, and did before the Peshwa; even a common Rayat, if he had to stay any time, would sit down on the ground. This contributes, as far as the mechanical parts of the society can, to keep up the intercourse that ought to subsist between the governors and the governed: there is, however, a great chance that it will be allowed to die away. The greater means of keeping it up, is for gentlemen to receive the natives often, when not on business. It must be owned there is a great difficulty in this. The society of the natives can never be in itself agreeable; no man can long converse with the generality of them without being provoked with their constant selfishness and design, wearied with their importunities, and disgusted with their flattery. Their own prejudices also exclude them from our society in the hours given up to recreation, and at other times want of leisure is enough to prevent gentlemen receiving them; but it ought to be remembered that this intercourse with the natives is much a point of duty, and contributes as much towards good government as the details in which we are generally occupied.

Much might likewise be done by raising our Mamlatdars to a rank which might render it creditable for native gentlemen to associate with them. It must be owned our Government labours under natural disadvantages in this respect both as to the means of rendering our instruments conspicuous, and of attaching them to our cause. All places of trust and honour must be filled by Europeans. We have no irregular army to afford honourable employment to persons incapable of being admitted to a share of the Government, and no court to make up by honours an empty favour for the absence of the other more solid objects of ambition. As there are no great men in our service, we cannot bestow the higher honours; and the lower, on which also the natives set a high value—as the privilege of using a particular kind of umbrella, or of riding in a palanquin—cease to be honours under us, from their being thrown open to the world. What honours we do confer are lost from our own want of respect for them, and from our want of sufficient discrimination to enable us to suit them exactly to the person and the occasion, on which circumstances the value of these fanciful distinctions entirely depends.

To supply the place of these advantages, we have nothing left but good pay, personal attentions, and occasional commendations and rewards. The first object may be attained without much additional expense by enlarging the districts, diminishing the number of officers, and increasing their pay. The pay might also be augmented for length of service, or in reward of particular activity. It might be from 200 to 250 rupees at first, and increase one-sixth for every five years' service; Khillats might also be given as occasional rewards for service; and above all, lands for life, or even on rare occasions for two or three lives, or in perpetuity, ought to be given to old or to meritorious servants. Besides the immediate effect of improving the conduct of the Mamlatdars by these liberalities, the political advantage would be considerable by spreading over the country a number of respectable persons attached to the Government, and capable of explaining its proceedings. If these grants could often be made hereditary we should also have a source from which hereafter to draw well-educated and respectable men to fill our public offices, and should found an order of families exactly of the rank in life which would render them useful to a Government circumstanced like ours. The Jahagir lands as they fall in might be applied to this purpose; and I think it would be good policy to make the rules regarding the resumption at the death of the present incumbents much stricter, if they were to be applied to this purpose, since we should gain more of useful popularity by grants of this kind than we should lose by dispossessing the heirs of many of the present Jahagirdars. It would be a further stimulus to the Mamlatdars, at the same time that it contributed to the efficiency of the system, to put the office of Daftardar with the collector on such a footing as to render it a sufficient object of emulation. For this purpose I would allow it 1,000 rupees a month, which, considered as the very highest salary to which a native could attain is surely not too much. I have fixed these allowances below what I at first thought it expedient; and in judging of their amount, the great difference in expense between this territory and the old provinces must be borne in mind. The pay of the common servants here is more than double what it is in Bengal. But if the proposed allowances should still seem more than the finances can bear, it ought to be recollected that economy, no less than policy, requires liberal pay where there is considerable trust, a maxim long since confirmed in its application to the natives by the experience and sagacity of General Munro.

Having thus formed a chain from the Patil to the collector, and having provided them with such rewards as circumstances will admit, it is of at least equal importance to take care that they should be punished for neglect. The proposed improvement in the situation of a Mamlatdar provides some means of punishing him by affording him allowances which it would be a serious misfortune to lose, and which would admit of his paying fines, by giving him a character that should make reproof a punishment and prospects which he would be unwilling to forfeit. Imprisonment or other punishment may be added if his offence were more than neglect. A still stronger responsibility must be imposed on the Patil, village watchmen; and in villages where the Kulkarni manages, on him also. The practice of levying the value of the property lost on the village ought not, I think, to be entirely abandoned. I am aware that it has been objected to by the highest authorities, and that it is in reality harsh and often unjust; but I think it better to regulate than abandon it. It is a coarse but effectual remedy against the indifference of the neighbourhood to the sufferings of individuals, and if the great secret of police be to engage many people in the prevention and punishment of crimes, it will not perhaps be easy to find a measure more advisable. It was adopted by our own early law-givers, and is not less suited to the state of society in India than it was in England under Alfred. When it is plain that a village could not prevent a robbery, the exaction of the money could of course be omitted; but where there is either negligence or connivance, it ought to be levied either whole or in part. A fine would at all events be expedient in such a case, and this is a popular and established method of levying it: it keeps a heavy punishment hanging over every village where a robbery is committed, and throws the burden of proving its innocence upon it; whereas a fine would require proof of actual connivance, and would after all be complained of as a hardship; while a levy of the same sum in lieu of the property lost would, if less than the value of the property, be felt as an indulgence.

It appears an objection to this plan, that it affords the Mamlatdar an opportunity of collecting more than he brings to account, but in such a case the villagers will of course complain, as they always did when the money was taken from them unreasonably; and this abuse, like many others, must depend for a remedy on the vigilance of the collector.

On this, indeed, it will have been long since observed, the whole system must depend, its object being to provide sufficient powers, and leave it to the principal officer to guard against the abuse of them. That he will always succeed, is more than I would promise; but perfection is not to be looked for, and we have only the choice of taking away from our agents the power to do good, or leaving them in some degree the power to do harm. Against this even a system of check and limitation will not always guard; for a man may be careful not openly to commit irregularities, while he is secretly guilty of every sort of oppression. As long as the chief power in the district is in able hands, the good done by the inferiors on this system will far preponderate over the evil; and if the collector be deficient, I am afraid that no distribution of powers would make up for his want of capacity, or do more than palliate or conceal the evils to which such a want would give rise.

The highest rank in the chain under Government should be a Court, or an individual vested with a general control of all departments, who should be frequently in motion, and whose business should rather be to superintend the whole system than to administer any part of it, and to see that essentials were attended to rather than rules were not violated. I would vest the fullest power over the officers under them in the collector, and in like manner it would be proper for Government to pay the utmost attention to the principal officer's recommendations, originating in the good or ill conduct of the collectors. So general a charge, of course, requires great industry and abilities: it is to be hoped such may be obtained; and if they are not, I despair of supplying their place by any machinery that can possibly be invented.

I have introduced those remarks under the police where they first occurred to me; but it is evident they apply equally to any other branch of the Government. I now return to the police.

The spirit of the people has been mentioned as of the first importance; and although that may be expected to flag under a foreign rule, and still more under a strong Government which protects all its subjects, and leaves no call for the exertion of their courage and energy in their own defence, yet there are instances in some parts of our old territories of our subjects retaining their military spirit after they have lost their habits of turbulence, and we may hope to accomplish the same object here. The first step towards its attainment is to remove all obstructions to the use of arms. On our first conquest some restriction was necessary on persons travelling with arms; but that has since been relaxed, and ought to be done away. Besides the advantage of arming the people for purposes of police, it would be useful even in cases of war and insurrection, as the bulk of the people, even if disaffected, would be led, for the sake of their property, to employ their arms against our predatory enemies rather than against us. On the same principles villages should be encouraged to keep up their walls, and perhaps allowed some remission to enable them to repair them.

It is important to the police that sudden discharges of Sibandies should for a long time be avoided, and the greatest encouragement given to the plan which I have mentioned elsewhere of settling that class on waste or other lands as a sort of local militia. It is to be considered that the Mahrattas, besides losing what service they had under Baji Ráv, are now in a great measure shut up from those colonies in Hindustan that afforded such a vent for the superfluous military population; Holkar's and the Bhonsle's armies are now nearly annihilated, and it is much to be feared that Scindia's will diminish.

Some rules are required regarding the receipts and sale of stolen or plundered property, regarding which the native practice was weak and irregular.

I insert in this place some remarks on the management of the hill-tribes, which, though at present it belongs to police, might easily be raised by a wrong system to importance in a political view. The plan which has been found most effectual in the old province, especially in the Bhaugalpore hills and in the Jungle Mahals of Midnapore, is to govern this people through their native chiefs, whose assistance is rewarded by the support of Government, and in some cases by pecuniary allowances. This plan has been kept up here, as it had been by the Peshwa, after an unavailing attempt to manage the Bhils by force alone. It is the only one practicable until the gradual effects of civilization shall have undermined the power of the chiefs, at the same time that it removes the necessity for their control over the people. The principal chiefs are at present allowed pensions, and a certain number of Bhils, of their selection, are also paid by the Government. These measures at once fix them in the interest of Government, and secure their influence in their tribe. It is, however, necessary to guard against the abuses of this system, which are the chiefs harbouring thieves, or conniving at robbers, and their acquiring such an influence, as may tempt them to oppose the measures of Government. The first evil will be provided against by exacting strict responsibility from the chief, and fining or otherwise punishing him if frequent offences take place within his jurisdiction; whether the punishment should be imprisonment or removal of the same family must depend on the notions of the Bhils, which ought to be investigated, not only for this purpose, but to prepare us for questions of disputed succession to chiefships, that we may not destroy the power of this engine of government by running counter to the opinion of the people whom it is to sway. For the other object, it is necessary to grant no increase, either in extent of land

Management of the Bhils and other predatory tribes.

or in authority to any chief, without its being clearly necessary for repressing disorder, which necessity is not likely to be felt. The Bhils may also be gradually encouraged to settle in the plains, either as cultivators or as watchmen to villages, a change which would weaken the power of the chiefs by lessening the number of their retainers. In the meantime it will be requisite to ascertain, with as much precision as the case admits of, the powers which the Bhil chiefs are in the habit of exercising under the old Government. This inquiry is indeed necessary, to prevent an inexperienced magistrate from interfering unintentionally with the privileges of those chiefs.

Present system of Police.

The only innovations yet introduced by us into the form of the Mahratta police are our closer superintendence, and the prohibition of the indefinite confinement of suspected persons by the Patils and Mamlatdars; but there must be a great difference in the spirit of our administration, and perhaps bad effects may be felt from it when the great awe with which we are now regarded is worn off, and when our principles come to be better understood. Though the natives put up with petty disorders, they checked great ones with a rough hand, and gave themselves no concern about the attendant evils. If robberies were committed, they seized all the suspicious characters in the neighbourhood; and if they succeeded in restoring quiet, they did not care though a hundred Rámoshis suffered imprisonment and torture without a fault. Such a course would not be thought of under our Government; but we must consider how much our abstaining from such tyranny must weaken us, and must provide a remedy in some more tolerable shape.

I am afraid that remedy is not to be found in our administration of Criminal Justice, which is next to be examined. This differs greatly from the Mahratta practice; the power of punishing is taken from the Patail, and that which is left to the Mamlatdar is limited to a fine of two rupees and confinement for twenty-four hours. The powers of the collector are not less than those of a Sarsubhedár, except in the article of inflicting capital punishment; but his manner of exercising his power is altogether different. According to our practice, a prisoner is formally and publicly brought to trial. He is asked whether he is guily. If he admits it, pains are taken to ascertain that his confession is voluntary; if he denies it, witnesses are called on without further inquiry. They are examined in the presence of the prisoner, who is allowed to cross-examine them, and to call witnesses in his own defence. If there is any doubt when the trial is concluded, he is acquitted; if he is clearly guilty, the Shastri is called on to declare the Hindu law. It often happens that this law is unreasonable; and when the error is on the side of severity, it is modified; when on the side of lenity, it is acquiesced in. The law officers are always present at those trials. In Khandesh a regular jury is generally assembled, who question the witnesses, and pronounce on the guilt of the accused. In Satara the political agent calls in several respectable persons, besides the law officers, and benefits by their opinion, both in the conduct of the trial and in determining the verdict. When the trial is concluded and the sentence passed, in cases of magnitude, it is reported for confirmation by the commissioner, where the same leaning to the side of lenity is shown as in the Court itself.

Present system of Criminal Justice.

The punishments awarded by the Shastris are as ollows: Death, which is executed in cases of murder, and sometimes robbery accompanied with attempts to murder; mutilation, which is commuted into imprisonment with hard labour; and simple imprisonment, which is carried into effect. Women are never put to death, nor Brahmins, except in cases of treason, where, from the nature of our conquest, it was thought necessary to hold out the severest punishment, even to Brahmins.

When the guilt of the accused is not proved, very great caution has been enjoined in imprisoning him on suspicion; it has, indeed, been recommended that no person should be so imprisoned unless notorious leaders of banditti; and when any person does happen to be imprisoned for want of security, the period at which he is to be released is directed to be fixed. These rules are suggested by the injustice of subjecting a man to a greater punishment when his guilt is not proved than would be inflicted if it were, and by the apprehension that the magistrate would be apt to order perpetual imprisonment in this form without much reflection, because it appears to be only temporary and conditional restraint.

Its defects.

The whole of this system is evidently better calculated for protecting the innocent from punishment, and the guilty from undue severity, than for securing the community by deterring from crimes. In the certainty and efficacy of punishment it has the same inferiority to the native system that the police has in detecting and seizing offenders. The natives seized men on slight suspicions, gave way to presumptions of guilt, forced confessions by torture, and inflicted punishments which, although they were inhuman (or rather, because they were inhuman), were effectual in striking terror. Our Government demurs about proofs, discourages and almost rejects confessions, and never punishes while there is a possibility of the innocence of the accused. When it does punish, in its anxiety to prevent its inflictions from being revolting to humanity it prevents their being terrible to offenders. Even death is divested as much as possible of its horrors. No torments, no lengthened exposure, no effusion of blood, or laceration of members, even after life is extinguished. Some of these are properly rejected as detestable in themselves; others that would strike the imagination of the people are set aside, because they also strike the imagination of the legislator. Imprisonment with hard labour is our great resource next to death, and this is by no means one calculated to over-awe offenders. Our imprisonment is so carefully divested of all circumstances of terror, that there is nothing except the fetters that is likely to make the least impression on a native. To a European confinement is irksome, solitary confinement intolerable. Bread and water, or bad fare, bad lodging, public exposure, all are real evils to him; but a native neither loses in point of food nor lodging; and shame, I should think, had less effect on him. In fact, by several of the reports from the districts (specially by Mr. Chaplin's answers to my queries), it appears that the imprisonment ordered by our officers is far from being looked on with dread, and that they think that, with the regular subsistence and comfortable blanket they get in gaol, they are better off than they would be in their own villages. There are even instances—one at Sattara, and one in Puna—of people committing petty offences to procure the maintenance allowed to prisoners. Imprisonment, especially when accompanied with labour, must, however, be a state of suffering to any man; separation from family and friends must also be an aggravation; and, on the whole, it would be absurd to contend that imprisonment is no real hardship to a native. The worst of it is, that it is a hardship to the sufferer without seeming one to the spectators; and if, as I fancy is the case, on the present footing it is at least as ineffectual for reformation; as, for example, it unites all the bad qualities that can be combined in a punishment. If to make up for our defects in convicting offenders, and in punishing them when convicted, we have recourse to imprisonment also, explaining that in this case it is not meant as a punishment, we complete the destruction of its use for example. In short, it may be questioned whether our system does not occasion as much suffering as the native one; but it is spread over a greater surface, and therefore makes less show, and neither shocks the legislator nor alarms the criminal.

These evils have often been remarked before; it is easier to point them out than to suggest a remedy, and greater experience might perhaps only show more clearly the difficulties to be overcome. It is possible that every civilized Government may not be suited to a society on a less advanced stage, and that coarse expedients, at which our minds revolt, may be the only ones likely to check those evils which originate in the barbarism of the people. I shall, however, notice a few points, from the consideration of which some profit may be gained.

Improvements suggested.

Too much care cannot be taken to prevent forced confessions—that is, confessions extorted by fear or torture; but there ought to be no scruple in getting at the truth by cross-examinations of the accused. An innocent man cannot criminate himself, and it is well that a guilty man should do so.

The magistrate ought to have the assistance of some intelligent natives of his own chosing at the trial. Their knowledge of the people would often lead to discoveries of the truth that might escape a European; but it is better that the conduct of the trial and the decision should rest with the magistrate. The Panchayats in Khandesh have answered better than might have been expected; but Captain Briggs has pointed out many inconveniences in that mode of trial, and it is obvious that where a Brahmin on one hand, or a Bhil on the other, was to be tried, it would be too much to expect unprejudiced decision. The Shastri ought still to attend, and to be consulted; but we ought not to be guided by the Hindu law, which is a new introduction of our own. The customary punishments for the most usual offences might easily be ascertained and modified; thus highway robbery and gang robbery (which the natives always punished with death) might be changed into perpetual imprisonment, unless attended with wounding or attempt to murder. The Hindu punishments might also be exchanged for such as we can execute, and thus when we did succeed in convicting an offender, there would be no longer a chance of his escaping by the absurdity of the sentence. Some of the Hindu punishments are too dreadful to be inflicted, others are too trifling to be of any use in deterring. The Hindu law officer at Ahmednagar sentenced one man to be thrown from a height upon a spike, and another to be fined six fanams for the same offence, because in one case the stolen property had been accidentally recovered, and in the other it had not. Caste also had great weight in determining the punishment; and this ought, to a certain extent, to be attended to still, because an opposite conduct shocks the prejudices of the people, which, unless we conciliate, all our justest sentences will be looked on as tyranny. Our punishments, I should think, might be made more intense, but shorter ; severe flogging, solitary confinement in dungeons for short periods, bad fare, severe labour, and similar punishments, always so guarded as to prevent their endangering life or health. Transportation seems a good punishment, provided it be for life ; but the return of a convict destroys the mysterious horror which would otherwise be excited by the sentence. Hanging in chains will probably make a great impression, if not too shocking to the prejudices of the natives, which I apprehend it is not. As much form as possible should be thrown into all punishments, especially capital ones ; and great care should be taken to suit the forms to the native ideas. They have themselves an excellent practice of exposing persons about to suffer death on a camel, stripped of some of their clothes, with their hair loose and covered with red powder, and with flowers, as is usual with a corpse when carried to the funeral pyre. Some of the most terrible modes of capital punishment might be retained when they do not add to the sufferings of the criminal ; beheading and blowing away from a gun are of this nature, but they ought to be reserved for great crimes. The opinions of natives ought, however, to be taken, and may be reckoned conclusive on subjects depending on feeling and on associations. In cases where the judge, though not satisfied of the guilt of the prisoner, is still less satisfied of his innocence, it seems imprudent to turn him loose to prey on society, and yet it is difficult to say on what grounds to detain him. Are we to award a less severe and more remediable punishment ? or are we to declare the prisoner innocent, but imprison him if he cannot give security ? The former seems to strike at the foundations of justice, and the latter destroys the force of example. Means might perhaps be found to manage the imprisonment of suspected persons in such a manner as to preserve the distinction between their treatment and that of convicts. Their place of confinement might be more like a workhouse than a prison. They might be taught trades, and allowed the fruit of their own industry, either in clothes and food at the time, or in a sum of money to be given at their release. Mr. Bruce, the judge of Bellary, has long since introduced the manufacture of blankets and some other articles into his gaol, and all the paper used in the neighbouring Katcheries is the work of his convicts. A place might be constructed for their residence which might combine the plan so much recommended by Mr. Bentham, with the economical arrangement suggested in Bengal. A circular or octagon wall, with an open arcade or tiled veranda to run all round inside, deep enough to afford shelter, and deep enough for concealment; this veranda to be partitioned off into cells with walls, and to be shut in with an iron grating or a deep ditch in front to prevent the prisoners meeting in the open space in the middle. Each cell might contain from two to eight prisoners, who would thus be cut off from the corruption that is always found in crowded prisons; and a wall across the middle of the court might make a still more complete division, so as to admit the convicts, if necessary, into the same enclosure. In the centre should be a circular building for the gaoler, from which he might see into every cell in both courts, while he himself was concealed by blinds. Frequent visits from the European authorities would be sufficient to complete the supervision. Persons less suspected might be consigned to the care and responsibility of the Patils of their villages, on the plan practised by Mr. Bayley at Burdwan; and there are cases where wandering and thievish tribes might be seized and compelled, on pain of imprisonment, to reside in particular villages, according to the plan recommended by General Munro in his letter on the police of the ceded districts.

It is to be observed, in respect to the confinement of suspected persons, that the practice is much less objectionable towards particular castes than others. Some avow that they were born and bred robbers, and that it was the intention of Providence that they should remain so. Surely society is entitled to take measures against men who set out with so open a declaration.

These are all the suggestions that occur to me, except that the powers of the Mamlatdar should be augmented to allow his punishing petty affrays, which ought never to go beyond the Paragna, and that the Patil should be permitted to exercise a similar authority to the very limited extent that is requisite to keep up his influence in his village.

Moral character of the people.

I may here say something of the moral character of the people. Falsehood in all shapes pervades all ranks; and adultery and prostitution are common in the upper classes, but in them alone. Drunkenness, the peculiar vice of the lower orders, is almost unknown in the Mahratta country, which has thence a decided superiority in morals over the old provinces. It arises from the discouragement to the sale of spirituous liquors, and as the revenue from that source is insignificant, we should probably do well to prohibit it altogether. Public opinion, and above all the opinion of the caste, and the dread of expulsion, are the restraint on vices. These powers are, in the Mahratta country, in the hands of the whole caste. In the Karnatik there are regular censors to each caste, called Ganacharies, besides religious Gurus invested with great power. But these institutions are converted into the means of gain, and the morals of the people are there decidedly worse than in the Mahratta country. The other vices are not more rare, and drunkenness is common in addition.

I do not perceive anything that we can do to improve the morals of the people except by improving their education. There are already schools in all towns, and in many villages; but reading is confined to Brahmins, Banyans, and such of the agricultural classes as have to do with accounts. I am not sure that our establishing free schools would alter this state of things, and it might create a suspicion of some concealed design on our part. It would be more practicable and more useful to give a direction to the reading of those who do learn, of which the press affords so easily the means.

Improvements recommended in Education.

Books are scarce, and the common ones probably ill chosen; but there exist in the Hindu languages many tales and fables that would be generally read, and that would circulate sound morals. There must be religious books tending more directly to the same end. If many of these were printed and distributed cheaply or gratuitously, the effect would, without doubt, be great and beneficial. It would, however, be indispensable that they should be purely Hindu. We might silently omit all precepts of questionable morality, but the slightest infusion of religious controversy would secure the failure of the design.

It would be better to call the prejudices of the Hindus to our aid in reforming them, and to control their vices by the ties of religion, which are stronger than those of law. By maintaining and purifying their present tenets at the same time that we enlighten their understandings, we shall bring them nearer to that standard of perfection at which all concur in desiring that they should arrive; while any attack on their faith, if successful, might be expected in theory, as is found in practice, to shake their reverence for all religion, and to set them free from those useful restraints which even a superstitious doctrine imposes on the passions.

In my letter No. 78, I proposed that 200,000 rupees should be set aside for religious expenses, including two colleges. The large religious expenses that fall on the net revenue in the districts induces me to alter this suggestion, and to propose modifying an expenditure which is already directed to an object of this nature in such a manner as to render it more useful. There was in the Peshwa's time an annual distribution of charity, called the Dakshná, which used to cost five lacs of rupees. The plan was originally to give prizes to learned Brahmins; but as a handsome sum was given to every claimant, however ignorant, to pay his expenses, the institution degenerated into a mere giving of alms. The abolition of this practice was extremely unpopular, but the sum was too enormous to waste; I therefore did it away all but the original distribution of prizes, which cost last year 50,000 rupees. This expenditure must still be kept up, but most of the prizes, instead of being conferred on proficients in Hindu divinity, might be allotted to those most skilled in more useful branches of learning—law, mathematics, etc.; and a certain number of professors might be appointed to teach those sciences. These means, with the circulation of a few well-chosen books, such as I believe are now printed at Calcutta, would have a better and more extensive effect than a regular college, and would cost much less to the Government. I shall therefore avail myself of the permission formerly given to me, and put such an establishment in train.

CIVIL JUSTICE.

It is necessary to examine the native system of Civil Justice with attention, and ascertain its success in affording protection to men's rights. If this should prove even moderate, it will scarcely be thought advisable to attempt any alterations; but if the plan be found inadequate to the end required, it will be necessary to see whether any alterations can be introduced to render it more efficient without changing its fundamental principles, or whether it is necessary to set it aside altogether, and to introduce a new system in its room.

Mahratta system of Civil Justice.

The authorities by whom Civil Justice was administered were the following: in the country the Patail, over him the Mamlatdar and Sarsubhedárs; and above all the Peshwa, or his Minister. Jahagirdárs administered justice in their own lands; the great ones with little or no interference on the part of the Government. In some towns there was a judicial officer, called the Nyáyádhish, who tried causes under the Peshwa's authority, and any person whom the Peshwa pleased to authorize might conduct an investigation subject to his Highness's confirmation.

By whom administered.

If a complaint was made to a Patil, he would send for the person complained of; and if he admitted the debt, would interfere partly as a friend to settle the mode and time of payment. If the debt were disputed, and he and his Kulkarni could not by their own influence or sagacity effect a settlement to the satisfaction of both parties, the Patil assembled a Panchayat of inhabitants of the village, who inquired into the matter with very little form, and decided as they thought best; but this decision could not take place without the previous consent of the parties.

If the complainant were refused a Panchayat or disapproved of the decision, or if he thought proper not to apply to the Patil, he went to the Mamlatdár, who proceeded nearly in the same manner as the Patil; with this addition, that he could compel the party complained of to submit to a Panchayat, or else make satisfaction to the complainant. When there was a Sarsubhedár, the same process might be repeated with him or at Court. But in all this there was no regular appeal: the superior authority would not revise the decision of the inferior unless there had been some gross injustice or reason to suspect corruption. In cases of less purity—that is, in almost all cases—the superior was influenced in receiving the appeal by the consideration of the profit promised as a compensation for the trouble.

Though the Government officer endeavoured himself to settle the dispute, and though it rested with him to decide whether or not the case required a Panchayat, yet it was reckoned gross injustice to refuse one on a question at all doubtful, and it was always reckoned a sufficient ground for ordering a new investigation when there had been no Panchayat.

The Panchayat may therefore be considered as the great instrument in the administration of justice, and it is of consequence to determine how the assembly was constituted, what were its powers, and what its method of proceeding and enforcing or procuring the enforcement of its decrees. Panchayat.

The members of a Panchayat were generally selected by the officers of Government, by whom it was granted with the approbation of the parties, and often at their suggestion; sometimes the parties chose an equal number each, and the officer named an umpire. A person on the part of Government not unfrequently presided at Panchayats, especially at Puna, and directed their operations; this officer must, however, be objectionable to the parties. In affairs where Government was concerned, it ordered some of its own officers to investigate the matter; but they were expected to be people not objected to by the other party. The members were people of the same situation in life as the parties, or people likely to understand the subject in discussion; as bankers in a matter of account: Deshmukhs and Deshpandes when the suit was about land. Their number was never less than five, but it has been known to be as great as fifty. The number was required to be odd. It generally met at the house of the officer who summoned it.

In villages the Patil got some of the most intelligent and impartial Rayats to sit under a tree, or in the Temple, or Choultri. Nobody attended on the part of the Government; and as the submission of the parties was voluntary, their wishes were of course more attended to than elsewhere. The consent of the members, however, was everywhere reckoned essential to a Panchayat; and the first act of the meeting was to take a Rájinámá, or acknowledgment, of such a consent. Security was also not unfrequently taken for the parties complying with the award of the Panchayat. In petty disputes in villages, the parties gave two straws in token of submission, instead of a written Rájinámá.

It might be expected that so burdensome a duty would not be willingly undertaken, especially as there was no authorized fee to be gained by it; but besides the compliment of being selected by the parties, there was the hope of presents from one or both, which it was not disgraceful to take, unless to promote injustice. The parties likewise entreated the persons they wished to accept the office, and the officer to Government added his authority. It was, moreover, reckoned disgracefully selfish to refuse to serve on a Panchayat; and as the man who was asked to be a member to-day might be a suitor to-morrow, he was obliged to afford the assistance which he was likely to require. It was rare, therefore, for people to refuse to serve, unless they had a good excuse.

It was more difficult to procure their regular attendance when appointed, and this was generally effected by the entreaties of the party interested. The magistrate also sent peons and injunctions to compel the presence of a person who had once agreed to become a member; and although he would receive a reasonable excuse, yet if he were really anxious for the speedy decision of the cause, he seldom failed in procuring attendance. Besides, there was no precision about the number of members required to attend; so long as the parties were satisfied, all was thought to be regular enough. When an absent member returned, the past proceedings could be explained to him, and any further inquiry he desired carried on.

When the Panchayat was assembled, if the defendant failed to attend, the Panchayat applied to the officer under whose authority it sat to summon him, unless a Kárkun or a Peon had already been attached to it, to perform such duties on the part of the Government; or the plaintiff, by constant demands and other modes of importunity, wearied him into submission. When the officer of Government had to compel his attendance, he sent a summons; or, if that failed, placed a Peon over him, whom he was obliged to maintain, and imposed a fine of a certain sum a day till he appeared. The plaintiff's complaint was then read, and the defendant's answer received; a replication and a rejoinder were sometimes added, and the parties were cross-questioned by the Panchayat as long as they thought it necessary. At that time the parties were kept at a distance from their friends, but afterwards they might assist them as much as they chose. A man might, if it were inconvenient for him to attend, send Kárkun in his service, or a relation; but the trade of a Vakil is not known: accounts and other written evidence were called for after the examination of the parties, and likewise oral evidence when written failed; but a great preference was given to the evidence of written documents. The witnesses seemed to have been examined and cross-examined with great care, but the substance only of their evidence was taken down briefly without the questions, and generally in their own hand if they could write. The natives have not the same deference for testimony that we have; they allow a witness no more credit than his situation and character and connection with the case entitle him to; they also lay great stress on his manner and appearance while giving his testimony. Oaths were seldom imposed, unless there were reason to suspect the veracity of the witness, and then great pains were taken to make them solemn.

When this examination was concluded, the Panchayat, after debating on the case, drew up an award (which was termed Sáràunsh or summary) in which they gave the substance of the complaint, and answer; an abstract of each of the documents presented on either side; a summary of the oral evidence on either side, with their own decision on the whole. A copy of the award was given to the successful party; and to the loser, if he required it; another copy was deposited with the officer of Government. In villages where was much less form, the Panchayat was often conducted in the way of conversation, and nothing was written but the decision, and sometimes not even that. In important cases, however, all the usual writing was performed by the Kulkarni.

Throughout the whole proceedings, the Panchayats appear to have been guided by their own notions of justice, founded no doubt on the Hindu law, and modified by the custom of the country. They consulted no books, and it was only on particular points immediately connected with the Hindu law, such as marriage, or succession, that they referred to a Shastri for his opinion.

On the report of the Panchayat, the officer of Government proceeded to confirm and enforce its decree: the Panchayaṭ having no executive powers of its own. From this cause frequent references to the magistrate were required, and he was given a considerable influence on the progress of the trial.

If either party objected at this stage, and showed good reasons why the award should be set aside, the officer under whose authority it sat might require it to revise its sentence, or even grant a new Panchayat; but this was not reckoned proper, unless corruption were strongly suspected.

No other notice was taken of corruption, unless in such cases the decision of a Panchayat was always respected, as the proverbial expression of Panch Parmeshwar ('A Panchayat is God Almighty') fully testifies.

Even after an award was confirmed, an appeal lay to a higher authority, and a new Panchayat might be granted; even a new Mamlatdár might revise the proceedings under his predecessor. This was probably a stretch of power; but everything under the Mahrattas was so irregular and arbitrary, that the limits of just authority can with difficulty be traced.

In enforcing the decision, much of course depended on the power of the magistrate. If a Patil found the party who gained the cause could not recover his due by the modes of private compulsion, hereafter described, he applied to the Mamlatdár to interpose his authority, and in cases where that was insufficient the Mamlatdár applied to the Government.

It was in this manner that ordinary disputes were settled. Those about boundaries, which are extremely frequent (except in Khandesh), were settled by a Panchayat, composed of Deshmukhs, Deshpandes, Patils, and Kulkarnis, assisted by the Mahars of the disputing villages, who are the established guardians of landmarks and boundaries. They are also very frequently adjusted by ordeal, one mode of which is for the Patil to walk along the disputed boundary, bearing on his head a clod composed of the soil of both villages, kneaded up with various strange ingredients, and consecrated by many superstitious ceremonies: if it hold together, the justice of his claims is established; and if it break, he loses his cause. Many other sorts of ordeal are also performed with boiling oil, or by taking an oath and imprecating certain curses if it should be false. If no evil occur within a fixed time, the gods are conceived to have decided in the swearer's favour.

These ordeals were not uncommon in all cases, as well as in boundary disputes, but chiefly when other means of ascertaining the truth had failed.

Disputes about caste were settled by the caste, unless when a complaint of unjust expulsion took place, when the Government ordered a Panchayat of respectable persons of the caste from an unprejudiced part of the country.

Panchayats, how assembled; and their decisions, how enforced.

As it has been shown that Panchayats had no powers of their own, and were moreover somewhat inert, it is necessary to examine the machinery by which they were kept in motion, and their resolutions carried into effect. It has been observed, that in the country the Mamlatdárs, and the Patils under their authority, performed that duty. In some few towns there also were officers of Justice, called Nyáyádhish. The proceedings of all these officers were of course very irregular, but the model may be learned by observing the proceedings of the Nyáyádhish at Puna, during the long period when Rám Shástri was at the head of that Court, and when Nana Fadnavis was Minister and Regent. This was confessedly the period when the Mahratta Government was in the highest perfection, and Rám Shástri is to this day celebrated for his talents and integrity. A full account of that Court is given by Mr. Lumsden in his report of January 24th, from which much of what follows is extracted. Rám Shástri had several deputies, two of whom were almost as famous as himself, and it was by their assistance chiefly that his business was conducted.

Exemplified in the Nyáyádhish at Puna.

On receiving a complaint, a Peon or a Kárkun, from Rám Shástri or from Nana Fadnavis, according to the consequence of the person, was sent to summon or to invite him to attend at Rám Shástri's. If this were refused, positive orders were repeated by Nana Fadnavis; and in the event of obstinate non-attendance, the house or lands of the defendant would be sequestrated till he appeared.

In case of non-appearance from absence, trial, after many indulgent delays, went on, and the absence of the party was recorded, that he might have a new trial on his return if he accounted for his absence; in cases of land, no decision was final in a man's absence. Evidence was summoned in the same form as the defendant; and if the witness were poor, the person who summoned him paid his expenses. If the witness lived at a distance, or if attendance were inconvenient, a deputation from the Court, with some person from the parties, was sent to take his evidence, and the Mamlatdár gave his aid to the process; or if the witness lived very far off, a letter was written, requesting him to state the facts required. When the witness was a man of rank, a deputation would be sent to him from the Government, accompanied by parties who went as supplicants for his aid rather than as checks on his mis-statement, and he was solicited to relate what he knew, which was repeated in the Court. Even if the witness were not of such rank as to prevent his coming to the Court, still if he were a man of any consequence, he was received as a visitor, and the questions were put to him in the way of conversation, and with all the usual forms of civility.

When persons of this character were the defendants, instead of summoning them to the Nyáyádhish, a letter was written by Nana Fadnavis, desiring them to settle the complaint. If this did not succeed, the Vakil was spoken to; and ultimately they experienced the displeasure of Government, or part of their land was made over to the creditor. Generally, however, great favour was shown to men of rank. If the plaintiff was also a man of rank, a Panchayat of men of the same condition would be appointed if all other means failed. One of the enclosed translations (No. 19) is an award in a case where the ancestors of Juan Rav Nimbálkar, a Jahágirdár of the highest rank, were the parties.

The proceedings were much the same as those I have already mentioned to have been practised in the districts, but more was done in writing than elsewhere. To give a clear idea of the manner in which Panchayats proceeded, I have the honour to enclose the award of one conducted under the superintendence of Rám Shástri

(No. 20); and decision in a simple case of the present day (No. 21).

The Panchayats were more frequently named by the parties than the judge; but Rám Shástri and his deputies seem frequently to have presided at the trial, the Panchayat performing nearly the same functions as a jury in England. A good deal of the investigation seems to have been entrusted to Rám Shástri's Kárkuns, who reported to him and the Panchayat; and in the decree the names of the members of the Panchayat are not mentioned, even when it is merely a repetition of their award. The decision was always in the Peshwa's name, and in all cases of magnitude required his signature; all cases relating to land were of this description, and the same holds all over the country, where claims to land are considered more immediately under the superintendence of Government. It was not unusual, in the country as well as in Puna, for a Government officer to receive the complaint and answer with the documents, and the written evidence of witnesses, and lay the whole in this shape before the Panchayat, who could call for more evidence if they required it. Much time must have been saved by this arrangement, but it gave the officer of Government considerable opportunities of imposing on the Panchayat. The members of the Panchayat received no fee, but when they had much trouble the winner of the suit made them openly a present for their pains.

A sum of money was likewise levied for the Government from the winner, under the name of Hárki, which I believe means congratulatory offering; and from the loser, under the name of Gunhegári, or fine. These Gunhegáries varied with the means of litigants, but in revenue accounts I observe that one-fourth of the property is always put down as the price paid for justice by the plaintiff when he wins his cause.

The plaintiff losing his cause was obliged to pay the expenses of the defendant, if the latter were poor.

No regular monthly or other returns of causes decided were made out.

When a cause was decided against the defendant, the Court settled the mode of payment with reference to his circumstances, either ordering immediate payment, or directing payment by instalments, or granting the debtor, if entirely destitute of the means of payment, an exemption from the demands of his creditor for a certain number of years.

When a matter had once come to a trial, it was always expected that Government should enforce the decision; but with the irregularity so characteristic of the Mahrattas, the plaintiff was often permitted to enforce them himself; and this was effected by means of the system called Takkaza, which, though it strictly means only dunning, is here employed for everything, from simple importunity up to placing a guard over a man, preventing his eating, tying him neck and heels, or making him stand on one leg, with a heavy stone on his head, under a vertical sun.

It is remarkable that in all claims (except for land) when the plaintiff has the power, this Tukkaza is the first step in the suit; and it is not until the person who suffers by it complains of excessive or unjust Tukkaza, that the Government takes any concern in the cause. This in some measure accounts for the ready acquiescence to defendants in the nomination of Panchayats, etc., and it is indeed employed intentionally as a means of accomplishing that end. When Government enforced the debt, it used nearly the same severities as individuals; it also seized and sold the property of the debtor, but generally spared his house, and took care not to reduce him entirely to ruin. It likewise often fixed instalments, by which his debt was gradually to be liquidated.

People were never put in any public prison for private debt, though sometimes confined or tormented by the creditor at his house or in that of his patron, and in rare cases when agreed on in the bond made to serve him till the amount of their nominal wages equalled that of the debt.

Fair bankrupts seem to have been let off pretty nearly as with us. Fraudulent ones were made to pay when discovered, notwithstanding previous release.

The great objects of litigation are stated in the replies of the local officers to my queries to be: Boundary disputes; division of property on the separation of families; inheritance to land, which is perhaps the greatest source of litigation throughout the whole country, even in Khandesh, where waste land is so abundant. Debts to bankers are also frequently subjects for suits.

Defects and abuses of the system.

The judicial system, which has just been described, is evidently liable to great objections, and accordingly in the best of times its success seems to have been very imperfect. There was no regular administration of justice: no certain means of filing a suit, and no fixed rules of proceeding after it had been filed. It rested with the officer of Government applied to, to receive a complaint or to neglect it altogether. The reception of an appeal from his injustice equally depended on the arbitrary will of his superior. The other occupations of these officers rendered it difficult for them to attend to judicial affairs even if well disposed, and these occupations increasing with the rank of the officer, the Peshwa (or the Minister) who was the mainspring of the whole machine, must have been nearly inaccessible to all men, and entirely so to the poor. The power of the local officer must also have had a tendency to check appeals, and even to restrain the demand for Panchayats in cases where he was desirous of deciding in person; and this desire would chiefly be felt in cases where he had an inclination to be the friend of one party, or where he hoped to make something by selling his favour to both. In short, there can be little doubt of the difficulty of getting justice, unless by means of bribery or of powerful friends.

The Panchayats themselves were open to corruption and to partiality, and when free from those stains they were still slow and feeble in their motions and uncertain in their resolutions. When the Panchayat was assembled, which from its interference with the pursuits and interests of the members must have been a matter of difficult and rare occurrence, it had not sufficient powers to seize the defendant, to summon the witnesses, or to compel the production of documents; in the event of any opposition it must apply to the officer of Government, and thus, besides unavoidable delay, it was exposed to constant obstruction from his indolence and want of leisure, and even from his corruption. If a deputy of the Government officer sat with it to execute those duties, it was still liable to be obstructed from corruption, and was besides exposed to the influence of the Kárkun, who presided. When it had got possession of the evidence, the members were not calculated to decide on nice or intricate causes; and if they were perplexed they met without coming to a decision, or allowed the matter to lie over until some circumstance prevented the necessity of meeting any more. Very great delay took place from these causes, and trials were often left entirely unfinished. When members were chosen by the parties and interested in their cause, they were rather advocates than judges, and their disputes produced as much delay as the neglect of the others. When they were impartial they were indifferent and irresolute, unless some member, and very likely one who was stimulated into activity by a bribe, took the trouble of deciding off the hands of his colleagues, and procured their consent to a decision of his own. When their award was signed the Panchayat dissolved, and their decree remained with the local officer to enforce or neglect, as he chose. Where so much was left arbitrary, there was of course much corruption; and it is very frequent now to have a complaint from a man who has a decision of old standing (even from the Nyáyádhish at Puna) which he has not been able to get enforced. Even when the decree of a Panchayat was passed and executed, one would think it must, from the way in which the assembly was constituted, have had little good effect beyond the case it had tried; for as there was no written law, and as Panchayats were composed of men of different habits and conditions, their awards must be supposed to have varied, so as to afford no great certainty beforehand as to the decision to which any Panchayat would come, and this uncertainty must have led unceasingly to new litigation. All accounts, it must be owned, agree in representing the knowledge of the common people in the customary law of their country, and consequently the uniformity of their decisions when formed into Panchayats, is far beyond what could be expected; but the inconvenience alluded to must still, to a certain extent, have existed. The want of principle in the rulers was another cause of uncertainty and litigation. No decision was final; a new Mamlatdár or a new Minister might take up a cause his predecessor had decided; the same man might revise his own decisions from corrupt motives; and there was as much difficulty in being exempt from an unjust revision, as it has already been shown there was in obtaining a just one.

If this were the state of things under Nana Fadnavis, it was doubtless worse under Baji Ráv. The farming system made over each district to the highest bidder, who was generally the most unprincipled man about the Court; and as full support was requisite to enable him to pay his revenue, it consigned the people to his oppression without a remedy. The farmer's whole time and thoughts were occupied in realizing his revenue. Justice was openly sold, and except as a marketable commodity, it was never thought of. The party in the wrong could always, by a bribe, prevent his cause going to a Panchayat, or overturn the decision of one. An appeal lay from the under-farmer to the upper, whose income depended on the exactions of the authorities below him; and from him to the Minister, who never received a complaint without a present; or to the Peshwa, who never received one at all. In consequence the Government afforded little justice to the rich, and none to the poor.

Correctives of these defects and abuses.

But with all these defects, the Mahratta country flourished, and the people seem to have been exempt from some of the evils which exist under our more perfect Government. There must, therefore, have been some advantages in the system to counterbalance its obvious defects, and most of them appear to me to have originated in one fact, that the Government, although it did little to obtain justice for the people, left them the means of procuring it for themselves. The advantage of this was particularly felt among the lower orders, who are most out of reach of their rulers, and most apt to be neglected under all

Governments. By means of the Panchayat, they were enabled to effect a tolerable dispensation of justice among themselves; and it happens, that most of the objections above stated to that institution do not apply in their case.

A Patil was restrained from exercising oppression both by the fear of the Mamlatdár and by the inconvenience of offending the society in which he lived; and when both parties were disposed to a Panchayat, he had no interest in refusing his assistance to assemble one. A Panchayat can scarcely be perplexed in the simple causes that arise under its own eyes, nor can it easily give a corrupt decision when all the neighbours know the merits of the case. Defendants, witnesses, and members are all within the narrow compass of a village; and where all are kept from earning their daily bread during the discussion, there is not likely to be much needless complaint or affected delay.

This branch of the native system, therefore, is excellent for the settlement of the disputes of the Rayats among themselves; but it is of no use in protecting them from the oppression of their superiors, and it is evident that the plan of leaving the people to themselves could never have been sufficient for that purpose. But here another principle comes into operation. The whole of the Government revenue being derived from the Rayat, it was the obvious interest of Government and its agents to protect him, and prevent his being exposed to any exactions but their own. The exactions of Government were limited in good times by the conviction that the best way to enrich itself was to spare the Rayats; and those of its agents, by the common interest of Government, and the Rayats in restraining their depredations. By these principles, while the native Government was good, its Rayats were tolerably protected both from the injustice of their neighbours and tyranny of their superiors, and that class is the most numerous, most important, and most deserving portion of the community.

It was in the class above this that the defects of the judicial system were most felt, and even there they had some advantages. As the great fault of Government was its inertness, people were at least secure from its over-activity. A Government officer might be induced by a bribe to harass an individual, under colour of justice; but he could not be compelled, by the mere filing a petition, to involve those under his jurisdiction in all the vexations of a lawsuit. Even when bribed, he could not do much more than harass the individual; for the right to demand a Panchayat was a bar to arbitrary decrees, and although he might reject or evade the demand, yet the frequent occurrence of a course so contrary to public opinion could not escape his superiors, if at all inclined to do justice.

The inertness of Government was counteracted by various expedients which, though objectionable in themselves, supplied the place of better principles. These were private redress, patronage, and presents. The first occupies the same place in civil justice that private revenge does in criminal among still ruder nations. It is this which is called Tukkaza by the Mahrattas, and which has already been mentioned as so important in bringing on a trial. If a man have a demand from his inferior, or his equal, he places him under restraint, prevents his leaving his house, or eating, and even compels him to sit in the sun until he comes to some accommodation. If the debtor were a superior, the creditors had first recourse to supplications and appeals to the honour and sense of shame of the other party: he laid himself on his threshold, threw himself on his road, clamoured before his door, or he employed others to do all this for him: he would even sit down and fast before the debtor's door, during which time the other was compelled to fast also, or he would appeal to the gods and invoke their curses upon the person by whom he was injured. It was a point of honour with the natives not to disturb the authors of these importunities, so long as they were just, and some satisfaction was generally procured by means of them. If they were unjust, the party thus harassed naturally concurred with the plaintiff in the wish for a Panchayat, and thus an object was obtained which might not have been gained from the indolence of the magistrate. Similar means were employed to extort justice from the ruling power. Standing before the residence of the great man, assailing him with clamour, holding up a torch before him by daylight, pouring water, without ceasing, on the statues of the gods. These extreme measures, when resorted to, seldom failed to obtain a hearing, even under Baji Rav, and there was the still more powerful expedient, both for recovering a debt or for obtaining justice, to get the whole caste, village, or trade, to join in performing the above ceremonies until the demand of one of its members were satisfied.

The next means of obtaining justice was by patronage. If a poor man had a master, a landlord, a great neighbour, or any great connection, or if he had a relation who had a similar claim on a great man, he could interest him in his favour and procure his friendly intercession with the debtor; his application to the friends of the latter, or finally his interest with the public authority, to obtain justice for his client. This principle was not so oppressive as it seems at first sight, or as it must have been if it had been partial, for it was so extended that scarcely any man was without some guardian of his interests. Both sides in a cause were thus brought nearly equal, and the effect of the interference of their patrons was to stimulate the system, which might otherwise have stood still.

If this resource failed, a present or the promise of a present to the public authority or those who had weight with him would be efficacious. The fee of one-fourth of all property gained in lawsuits was, in fact, a standing bribe to invite the assistance of the magistrate.

The number of persons who could grant Panchayats also expedited business. Besides the Nyáyádhish and the numerous Mamlatdárs and Jahagirdars, many people of consequence could hold Panchayats under the express or implied authority of the Peshwa, and every chief settled the disputes of his own retainers, whether among themselves or with others of the lower and middle classes. A great number of disputes were also settled by private arbitration, and their proceedings, in the event of an appeal, were treated by the Government with the same considerations as those of Panchayat held under its own authority.

Thus some sort of justice was obtained, and it was less impure than might be expected, from the sources by which it was supplied, because public opinion and the authority of the magistrate set bounds to Tukkaza, and the institution of Panchayats was a restraint on patronage and bribery.

The Panchayat itself, although in all but village causes it had the defects before ascribed to it, possessed many advantages. Though each might be slow, the number that could sit at a time, even under the superintendence of one person, must have enabled them to decide many causes. The intimate acquaintance of the members with the subject in dispute, and in many cases with the characters of the parties, must have made their decisions frequently correct; and it was an advantage of incalculable value in that mode of trial that the judges, being drawn from the body of the people, could act on no principles that were not generally understood, a circumstance which, by preventing uncertainty and obscurity in the law, struck at the very root of litigation. The liability of Panchayats to corruption was checked by the circumstance that it did not so frequently happen to one man to be a member as to make venality very profitable, while the parties and the members being of his own class he was much exposed to detection and loss of character. Accordingly, the Panchayat appear, even after the corrupt reign of Baji Rav, to have retained in a great degree the confidence of the people, and they do not appear to have been unworthy of their good opinion. All the answers to my queries (except those of the collector of Ahmednagar) give them a very favourable character; and Mr. Chaplin, in particular, is of opinion that in most instances their statement of the evidence is succinct and clear, their reasoning on it solid and perspicuous, and their decision, in a plurality of cases, just and impartial.

Their grand defect was procrastination, and to counteract it the suitors had recourse to the same remedies as with people in power—importunity, intercession of patrons, and sometimes, no doubt, to promises, fees, and bribes.

General result.

It is impossible to form very clear notions on the general result of this administration, either as to its despatch of causes, the degree of justice actually administered by it, or its effect on the character of the people; but I should conjecture that simple causes were speedily decided, and complicated ones very slowly. The Nyáyádhish principally tried the latter description, and in twenty years it filed less than 1,400 causes, of which it is believed that one-half were never decided. Panchayats appear generally to have given just decisions, but men in power could obstruct a reference to those assemblies, and could prevent the execution of their decrees. That justice was often denied, or injustice committed, appears from the frequency of Thullee, which is a term for robbery, arson, and even murder, committed to oblige a village or Government officer to satisfy the claims of the perpetrator. This crime is commonest to the southward of the Krishna, but murders on account of disputes about landed property are everywhere frequent. With regard to its effect on the character of the people, the Rayats seem in most respects simple and honest, but there is no regard for truth or respect for an oath throughout the whole community; and forgery, intrigue, and deceit are carried to the highest pitch among the Patils, Kulkarnis, and all who have much opportunity of practising those iniquities. There is no punishment for perjury or forgery. In the annexed award of a Panchayat (No. 2), it appears that thirty-three persons entered into an engagement to swear to anything that one of the parties might dictate, and for this complicated offence they were mildly reprimanded by the Nyáyádhish. Litigiousness does not seem to have been at all prevalent, unless the obstinacy with which people adhered to any claims to landed property can be brought under that head.

Comparison of the advantages of the native plan with those of the Adalat.

Such are the advantages and disadvantages of the native administration of justice which are to be weighed against those of the plan adopted in our provinces. If we were obliged to take them as they stood under the Native Government, the scale would probably soon be turned; but as it is possible to invigorate the system and to remove its worst abuses, the question is not so easily decided. The most striking advantages in our plan appear to be—that the laws are fixed, and that as means are taken to promulgate them they may be known to everyone; that the decisions of the Adalat, being always on fixed principles, may always be foreseen; that there is a regular and certain mode of obtaining redress; that the decision on each separate case is more speedy than in any native court, and that it is more certain of being enforced; that justice may be obtained by means of the Adalat, even from officers of Government, or from Government itself; that the judges are pure, and their purity and correctness are guarded by appeals; and that the whole system is steady and uniform, and is not liable to be biassed in its notions by fear or affection, policy or respect.

On the other hand, it appears that although the regulations are promulgated, yet, as they are entirely new to the people of India, a long time must pass before they can be generally known, and as both they and the decisions of the Court are founded on European notions, a still longer period must elapse before their principles can be at all understood; that this obscurity of itself throws all questions relating to property into doubt, and produces litigation, which is further promoted by the existence of a class of men rendered necessary by the numerous technical difficulties of our law, whose subsistence depends on the abundance of lawsuits; that by these means an accumulation of suits takes place, which renders the speedy decision of the Adalat of no avail; that the facility given to appeals takes away from the advantage of its vigour in enforcing decrees, and renders it on the whole, in many cases, more feeble and dilatory than even the Panchayat, while in others it acts with a sternness and indifference to rank and circumstances very grating to the feelings of the natives; that its control over the public officers lessens their power without removing the principle of despotism in the Government, or the habits engendered by that principle in the people, and that by weakening one part of the machine without altering the rest, it produced derangement and confusion throughout the whole; that the remoteness of the Adalat prevents the access of the common people, and that if Munsiffs with fees, Vakils, etc., be adopted to remedy this evil, they are not exempt from the corruption of the native system, while they occasion in a remarkable degree the litigious spirit peculiar to ours.

This view of the Adalat is taken from the reports drawn up in Bengal, and it is possible that many of the defects described may originate in the revenue system, in the voluminousness of the regulations, or in other extrinsic circumstances; a supposition which appears to be supported by the state of the Courts under Bombay, where most of the evils alluded to are said to be still unfelt. But enough will remain to satisfy us that the chance of attaining cr approaching to perfection is as small under our own plan as under that of the natives; that on either plan we must submit to many inconveniences and many abuses; and that no very sudden improvement is to be looked for in the actual state of things. If this be the case, it becomes of the first consequence to cherish whatever there is good in the existing system, and to attempt no innovation that can injure the principles now in force, since it is so uncertain whether we can introduce better in their room.

I propose, therefore, that the native system should

still be preserved, and means taken to remove its abuses and revive its energy. Such a course will be more welcome to the natives than any entire change, and, if it should fail entirely, it is never too late to introduce the Adalat.

It is now, however, practicable for us to keep up the native plan entirely unchanged. In removing abuses we destroy the moving powers of Takkaza, patronage and presents, and we must look out for others to supply their place. For this purpose we may hope to have more purity, more steadiness, and more energy, than the Native Government; and I think we can scarcely fail to place the people in a better situation, with respect to justice, than that in which we found them. Such a change in the mere administration of the law will probably in time improve the character of our subjects, and admit of a gradual improvement in their radical principles; but it seems desirable that such improvement should be so slow as to allow the amelioration of the society to keep pace with that of the laws, and thus escape the evil of having a code unsuitable to the circumstances of the people, and beyond the reach of their understanding.

Improvement suggested in the Mahratta system.

Our principal instrument must continue to be the Panchayat, and that must continue to be exempt from all new forms, interference, and regulation, on our part. Such forms would throw over this well-known institution, that mystery which enables litigious people to employ courts of justice as engines of intimidation against their neighbours, and which renders necessary a class of lawyers who among the natives are the great fomenters of disputes.

Another objection to forms is, that they would deter the most respectable people from serving on Panchayats. The indolence of the natives, the aversion to form and restraint, their hatred of novelties, and their dread of getting into difficulties in an unknown course of proceeding, and thus exposing themselves to our supposed strictness, would be sufficient to prevent any honest Patil from calling a Panchayat, or any disinterested inhabitant from serving as a member; but it is only the honest who would be thus deterred: those who looked to profit through fraud would run a little risk in pursuit of their selfish designs, and would study our new laws so as to qualify themselves to evade them.

The Patil should be encouraged, as at present, to settle disputes amicably, if he can, and otherwise to refer them to Panchayats, on the old model.

No papers should be required from those bodies but a Rájiánamá (or consent) by the parties to the arbitration of the members, and a Saraunsh (or decision) as concise as they choose to make it. When these two papers can be produced, the decision should be final, unless in case of corruption or gross injustice. When those papers are wanting, the cause must be considered as still liable to investigation, but no censure is to be passed on the Panchayat for failing to produce them. When a Patil refuses to grant a Panchayat, the Mamlatdár may, on complaint, direct him to afford one; and if either party object to a Panchayat in his own village, the Mamlatdár shall be at liberty to order one at his own residence, or at any other village, as I believe was practised by the Mahratta Government. But unless both parties give their free consent to the arrangement proposed by the Mamlatdár, that officer must report the case to the collector, and await his orders.

Appeals from village Panchayats should be made to the collector, who, if he thinks the Panchayat has not been freely chosen, or that it has not fully decided; or if on a summary inquiry he discovers any gross error or injustice, or sees good ground to suspect corruption, may order a new Panchayat, either at the original village, or elsewhere. In this inquiry the collector can of course direct the Mamlatdár to make any local investigation that may be necessary, and he can employ his assistant, or an Amin, either in conducting the summary inquiry, or in superintending the second Panchayat: but he ought on no account to go into an inquiry in any ordinary case merely because the Panchayat appear to him to have decided erroneously; the object of this appeal being rather to watch over the purity of the courts, than to amend their decisions. The appeal ought to be to the collector, rather than to the Mamlatdár, to prevent that officer either quashing complaints, or needlessly drawing up causes from the village tribunals to his own.

These rules will provide for the adjustment of disputes among villagers, but there are many mercantile and other persons who reside in towns, and are not subject to the authority of any Patil. For these persons another plan must be adopted. When they belong to trades, the Sheti, or head of the trade, may perform the functions performed by the Patel, in summoning a Panchayat, with the consent of the parties, and when these means are insufficient a complaint may be made to the Mamlatdár, who, if he cannot accommodate the matter, either by his own interposition or a Panchayat agreed to by both parties, must report it to the controller, who will authorize a Panchayat of persons of the same order. When the parties leave the nomination of these Panchayats to the Mamlatdár, or other officer of Government, he cannot be too careful to select the members, so as to make attendance as little onerous as possible. Persons unemployed ought to be preferred to men in business, and the whole to be managed as much on the principle of rotation as the disposition of the parties may admit. The objection of the parties to any member ought, however, to be always attended to, and if they show a disinclination to the persons proposed by the Government agent, they ought to be allowed to name four respectable people themselves, who ought to chose a fifth as an umpire. If the members cannot agree, the umpire must be named by the Government officer.

In very large towns the superintendence of these Panchayats may be too much for the Mamlatdárs to undertake, and it will therefore be found necessary to nominate officers (to be called Amins, or whatever name has hitherto been in use among the Mahrattas) expressly for the administration of justice. There might be one to every Mamlatdár's district, or one to every two; but it ought first to be tried whether the Mamlatdárs are sufficient to keep down the business, as the institution of so many dispensers of justice, besides the revenue officers, will certainly be new, and it's effects on the Panchayats and on the people cannot be clearly foreseen; some means, must, however be found out to make up, in Puna especially, for the numerous chiefs and ministers who formerly used to assemble Panchayats. For this purpose, I think, there ought to be three native judges at Puna with salaries amounting to 200 rupees each, and three of inferior rank with inferior salaries, who should receive complaints referred to them by the collector, and submit them to Panchayats, or decide them themselves, when both parties consented to that mode of adjustment.

In such cases as the collector should expressly prescribe, causes to be tried by Panchayats might be shaped by the Amin in such a manner that the pleadings, documents, and evidence might all be brought at once before the Panchayat, and the cause decided at one sitting, unless the Panchayat should call for more information.

In causes decided by the Amin alone, an appeal should lie to the collector, who might always, or on all reasonable grounds, order a Panchayat to try the case anew.

The higher class of Amins might try causes to any amount, but the second class should be limited to 200 rupees. The collector might in all cases call up such causes as he thought of great importance to be tried before him or his assistants. The Shástri to each collector might be an Amin, and might receive an addition to his salary on that account.

In each of the large towns, perhaps two in each district, besides Puna, there might be an Amin, with powers only to grant Panchayats when agreed to by both parties, and to settle such causes as the parties might agree in writing to refer to his decision; but wherever there was a dispute about the mode of trial, he ought to take the orders of the collector.

The Amins in the towns might have 150 rupees a month, and all the Amins might have a certain addition to their salary for every twenty causes decided by them, or by Panchayats under their direction. The expenses might be defrayed from fines, hereafter to be mentioned; but the connection between their allowances and the fund from which they are drawn ought not to be made apparent to the Amin.

To complete the administration of justice references might be made on all doubtful questions of Hindu law to the principal Shâstris, who receive pensions, or Warsháshans. The selection in each reference might be left to the commissioner, as was the practice with the natives, or a small addition might be made to the salary of a certain number, who might be constituted regular authorities, to decide on points of law.

Appeals ought to be received from the Amins on the principle above mentioned, and in the same manner the commissioner should receive special appeals from the collectors, not with a view to revise their decisions on each case, but to give him an opportunity of ascertaining that his instructions are acted up to, and that the custom of the country is not departed from.

It is chiefly by this superintendence that we can hope to purify and invigorate the native system, so as to convert it from a mere engine of oppression into an instrument for a more extensive dispensation of justice than exists even in our own old provinces.

It is indispensable on this principle that the collector should give audience, for at least two hours every day, to all ranks, receive complaints *vivâ voce*, and grant decisions and orders on Mamlatdárs, as the cases require. If he confine himself to receiving petitions in writing, it is impossible that he should have time to become acquainted with the state of things in his district. This practice, combined with the collector's tours round his district, ought to be a great check on the Mamlatdárs, and those officers ought likewise to be obliged to answer speedily and fully every complaint made against them or reference sent to them. The great indulgence and forbearance recommended towards Panchayats and Patils should have no place towards Mamlatdárs, on whose purity and efficiency so much depends, and with whom those qualities can only be preserved by strict discipline.

The amount to be decided on by a Panchayat, under a Patil, might be limited to 150 rupees, and by a Mamlatdár or Amin, without reference, to 1,000 rupees;

when the amount exceeds this, the Mamlatdár ought not to call a Panchayat, even with the consent of the parties, until he has taken the Collector's orders. Any sum might be referred by the collector, but great causes, where delay and distance are of least consequence, would be best done under his own superintendence.

Causes, in which great Sardars are parties, should be reported to the commissioner, who should take measures himself, or send special instructions in each case. No claim for a debt incurred during the Mahratta Government ought to be enforced against this class with more strictness than that Government would have evinced, and all intercourse relating to causes of those persons should be conducted according to the practice of the former Government, as above described.

Rules ought to be made limiting the period at which a suit can be entertained. Twelve years from the commencement of the dispute would be sufficient in cases of personal property, but a very long period must be allowed in disputes about land, provided always that no prior decision by a competent authority has taken place.

These rules must be observed by the Mamlatdárs and Amins, but they must not extend to Patils, who must be guided by custom alone.

A period ought also to be fixed, after which appeals on complaints of gross error, bribery, etc., will not be received: these ought to be short when the cause was tried by a Panchayat, and long when by a single judge.

Mamlatdárs and Amins should send registrars of the causes they try to the collectors, and the collectors to the commissioner, but nothing of the sort should be required from the Patil.

So far, indeed, am I from wishing to clog the proceedings of the lower orders with forms, that I think a decision ought to be received and enforced by the public authorities, by whomsoever it has been passed, in every case where there is a written consent to the arbitration on the behalf of the parties, and a written award on that of the arbitrators.

Too much pains cannot be taken to encourage private arbitrations, and this is the more necessary from an opinion, which appears to be industriously propagated, that our Government resents and punishes any interference of individuals in affairs which are within its jurisdiction.

The employment of professional Vakils ought to be strictly forbidden, both in the Mamlatdárs, Amins, and collectors' Kacheries; with the Patils, they are not likely to exist.

Similar pains must be taken to guard against professional arbitrators, a description of persons who were not unknown under the Mahratta Government, and who appear, from Mr. Lumsden's report, to be becoming common under ours. This class, to all the bad qualities of hired Vakils, adds that of corruption in the decision of the cause. Perhaps some rule should be fixed to compel the Mamlatdárs and Amins to attend to this caution, but this is the only regulation I would venture to propose regarding Panchayats.

The difficulty of assembling the members, and of getting them to come to a decision, suggests, at first view, some rules to promote those ends; but none can, I think, be ventured on without the risk of making attendance first entirely compulsory, and then very odious. The magistrate may exercise his influence, and even an indefinite authority as hitherto, to procure attendance and decision; but he ought to use no absolute force, and, above all, to impose no fines nor other punishments. The utmost would be, to call the Panchayat to his court, and seat them with an Amin from morning to night, until they should decide.

The collector might be empowered to bestow on members of Panchayats, on whom attendance should appear to fall particularly hard, a sum of money at his discretion, to defray their expenses, and he ought to withhold all assistance of the kind where the attendance of the members has been particularly remiss.

Panchayats ought to be furnished with a Peon, to summon witnesses and parties; and in the event of the non-attendance of one of the parties, after due notice, the cause might be decided against him, though liable to revision, on good ground being shown for his absence.

Some check is required to prevent frivolous and litigious complaints, especially in appeals from the decision of Panchayats. Fees have been suggested for this purpose, but it is very doubtful whether they are a check on litigation any further than they are a check upon justice.

It appears a better remedy to allow the Panchayats, or the person who tries the cause, to fine a party whose complaint or whose defence is palpably frivolous; and if this is thought to be too great a latitude to entrust to a Panchayat, the fine might be limited to the extent of the fourth, formerly taken by the Mahratta Government, or even to the amount which would on our own system be levied (even where there was no fault) in the shape of cost and fees, stamped paper, etc. A portion of the money so levied might be given to the injured party when poor, and the rest would go to pay the commission allotted to the Amins and the expense of members of Panchayats. If the fund proved inadequate to this purpose, a further sum might be raised by the sale of stamped paper for all deeds and contracts, which would be a security against forgery, as well as the means of raising a revenue.

In cases of appeals, I would oblige the appellant to enter into a bond to pay a particular fine if the complaint proved vexatious; and this, as well as the fine imposed on the loser, would only be a mitigation of the Mahratta practice in both cases. Decrees should be enforced in the mildest forms in use with the Mahrattas: a Harkárá, or, in a case of a respectable man, a Kárkûn, should be sent to insist on the payment of the sum decreed, and to prevent the debtor eating from sunrise to sunset, unless it were paid. The property of the debtor ought also to be sold, but not his house, nor the implements of his profession. If all this should be insufficient, he should be imprisoned for a period, to be fixed, on the report of the Panchayat, according to the amount of his debt, and the fraudulent or litigious spirit he had displayed.

A question arises regarding the native practice of Takkaza. If left as it was among the natives, it leads to every sort of oppression, and the more as the sufferer is often prevented coming to complain. If done away entirely, the great principle which drives men to Panchayats, private arbitrations, and voluntary compositions, is put an end to, and every creditor is compelled to come to court. It is absolutely necessary to prohibit the use of force, but perhaps all restraints and inconveniences that depend on the point of honour ought to be allowed to remain.

Advantages and disadvantages of the proposed plan.

The plan I have proposed has many obvious and palpable defects, and many more will no doubt appear when its operations are fully observed. It has this advantage, that it leaves unimpaired the institutions, the opinions, and the feelings, that have hitherto kept the community together; and that, as its fault is meddling too little, it may be gradually remedied by interfering when urgently required. An opposite plan, if it fail, fails entirely; it has destroyed everything that could supply its place; and when it sinks, the whole frame of the society sinks with it. This plan has another advantage likewise, that if it does not provide complete instruments for the decision of suits, it keeps clear of the causes that produce litigation. It makes no great changes, either real or apparent, in the laws; and it leads to no revolution in the state of property. The established practice also, though it be worse than another proposed in its room, will be less grievous to the people, who have accommodated themselves to the present defects, and are scarcely aware of their existence; while every fault in a new system, and perhaps many things that are not faults, would be severely felt for want of this adaptation. I do not, however, mean to say that our interference with the native plan is odious at present. On the contrary, several of the collectors are of opinion that a summary decision by a European judge is more agreeable to the natives than any other mode of trial. This may be the case at first; but if the decisions of Europeans should ever be so popular as to occasion the disuse of the native modes of settlement, there would soon be a run on the courts, and justice, however pure when obtained, would never be got without years of delay.

There must, however, in the system now proposed, be a considerable sacrifice of form, and even some sacrifice of essential justice; and it is to be expected that the abuses which will be observed under it will give particular disgust to most of our officers, because they are repugnant to our ways of thinking, and we are apt to forget that there are equal blemishes in every other system, and that those which are the least offensive in our eyes are often most disgusting to the natives. This unsuitableness of the native system to European ideas is, however, a very serious objection to its adoption, and renders it doubtful if we shall be able to maintain it after the officers to whom it is to be entrusted shall have ceased to be selected merely for their fitness.

If our own system be unintelligible to the natives, it is at least intelligible to us, and as its characteristic is strict rules and checks to departure from them, it is not easy to go wrong. Moreover, as it possesses no very nice adaptation to the native way of thinking, a little derangement is of no great consequence. But the native plan can seldom be thoroughly understood by any of us: we may act against its plainest rules from mere ignorance, and we must all be liable to strike at its vital principles when we think we are only removing its defects. Nor is it necessary that the legislator should fall into this error to produce the most fatal effects. The error of an inferior executive officer is sufficient to overthrow the system. The commissioner perceives the numerous irregularities, abuses, and corruptions in village Panchayats, which may be avoided by a few simple rules, and the complete insight and effectual superintendence that would be gained by a mere report of the Patil's proceedings; he makes his regulations, directs a register to be drawn up, punishes the neglect of his orders regarding it, and from that moment there is an end of village Panchayats, until Patils shall be found who will undertake those troublesome and unknown forms from mere public spirit, with the chance of punishment and censure for unintentional failure. Not less effectual would be the decisions of an inexperienced assistant acting with that confidence which inexperience alone confers: he fines some Panchayats for exceeding their power, and imprisons some Patils for confounding their judicial with their fiscal functions, and the effect of his decision is as complete within his district as if a law had been enacted prohibiting all interference in settling disputes, except by the officers of the Government.

To avert these dangers, the best plan is to keep this territory for a considerable time under a separate commissioner, on whose vigilance we must depend for correcting mistakes such as have been described.

Alterations already introduced.

Wishing to give a complete picture of the shape in which I recommended the native system to be preserved, I have not distinguished between the arrangements already adopted and those only proposed. In general the Mahratta system has been kept unchanged. There are, however, some slight differences in the modes of proceeding of the different collectors. Mr. Chaplin receives all complaints that cannot be settled with the consent of the parties, and directs the Mamlatdár to inquire into them, and when necessary to grant Panchayats. Captain Grant adopts the same course, but also has many causes decided by himself and his assistants at Satara. Captain Pottinger's proceedings are similar to Captain Grant's, and in the present state of Khandesh there appears to be scarcely any judicial business. At Puna it has long since been found necessary to appoint three native Amins to assist in the administration of justice. These persons regulate Panchayats and try causes which both parties agree to submit to them, and latterly causes also where the parties neglect to name the members of the Panchayat. There have been

3,428 causes filed at Puna, of which there have been settled without a trial 1,323.

By Panchayats	376
By injunction from the collector	539
Dismissed on the non-attendance of the plaintiff	408
And there have been decided	1,015
By the collector and his assistants	234
By Panchayats, chosen by the parties ...	44
By Amins	248

Ultimate improvements if those now suggested should fail.

In the end of March 1,052 causes were undecided; on the whole, I should think that the means we have hitherto possessed have not been sufficient to meet the demand in Puna, and perhaps, owing to the constant occupation of Mamlatdárs in revenue business, the same may be true in the country. I hope the plan now proposed will be more effectual. Should it fail, it will be necessary to have numerous Amins for holding Panchayats, and to adopt by degrees stricter rules to compel the attendance and hasten the decisions of those bodies. If that should be insufficient, Mansifs must be empowered to try causes by themselves, in which case there must be a European judge to hear appeals from them all; but these improvements must not be introduced until they are wanted, and we must be careful not to induce the natives to give up their present modes of settling disputes, by holding out a prospect of pure and abundant justice which we may not ultimately be able to realize.

Summary of our Civil arrangements.

To sum up the effects of our revenue, police, and judicial systems, we have, in revenue, lighter, more equal and more certain assessment, less peculation, and consequently less profit to the agents of Government. In police, more attention and more vigour, but less violence, and so far less efficiency. In civil justice, the great change is that Government has taken on itself the whole responsibility of protecting people's rights, but there is more form, more purity, more delay in some cases and less in others. In criminal justice, more system, more scruples, more trials, more acquittals, more certain punishment for all crimes except robbery, and for that both less certain and less severe.

APPENDIX.

TRANSLATIONS of a deed of purchase executed in the year Shak 1726 *Raktakshi, on Paush Vadya Prati Pada, between Jánoji Bin Datoji, Patil, Kaddam of the village of Gaivi, in the Pargana of Phaltan, and Bhimaji Bin Assaji, Patil Yadoay, the Mukadam (or Chief Patil) of the village of Jiregaum, in the Patas Taraf of the Prant of Puna, sur* 1214 *Hejri.*

The reason of this deed of purchase being executed is, that the Mukadam (or chiefship) of the above-mentioned village, Jiregaum, being exclusively mine, and that as there has been a severe famine in the land the whole of this year, and many have died for want of food, and as I also find myself reduced to the last extremity, from an absolute want of every kind of sustenance, or means of procuring it, excepting by disposing of my Wattan (hereditary office, and lands perhaps) and Service ; if I were not to dispose of some of it I should die, and the whole world would be lost to me, I have resolved to save my life by dividing my Wattan Vriti, and admitting partner to its engagement.

With this fixed design I have come to you, and fallen

on your neck, begging that you will preserve my life during the continuance of the famine, and that, in consideration of your doing so, you will accept a half of the rights of my Mukadami, while I retain the other half.

Thus petitioning and speaking to you, in the strongest manner you have consented, and I now execute this agreement, to testify my voluntary relinquishment in your favour of half my rights or sole Mukadami of the above-mentioned village, and that in consideration thereof, I have before witnesses accepted and received seven hundred and one rupees. You have thus preserved the lives of my family, and we shall henceforward jointly enjoy all rights (Thag), dignity (Mánpán), etc., according to the undermentioned detail.

First. HAKDARI, OR RIGHTS AND PERQUISITES.

1st. GHUGARI. Two Maunds, at the rate of sixteen Páilis per Maund on each cultivated Chahur of land. Half this grain or half its value shall be yours, and half mine.

2nd. BHÁI. Jamá on the annual present from the Sarkár, on settling the Jamá, amounting to 25 rupees, shall be one half yours and one half mine.

3rd. FALBHÁRÁ. For every Chahur of cultivated land I am entitled (at the reaping season) to an hundred bundles of the grain produced; half of this shall be yours, and half mine.

4th. HURDÁ NIMBOR. The half of what I receive from each field on these accounts shall be yours, and half mine.

Remark. Hurdá is unripe Járvi, which it is considered pleasant to eat roasted: the quantity received by the Patil from each field is from one to two Páilis. Nimbor is unripe Bajari, taken for the same purpose.

5th. MALITUN. For products of the earth from irrigation, you shall receive half of these products, and of all new similar products which come to my share.

Remark. This Thag is very uncertain: it relates chiefly to vegetables and garden products.

6th. RAHADÁRICHA VASÛL. Half shall be yours and half mine.

Remark. This is a small exaction of from one to two annas, taken from travellers who stop at the village. It is distinct from Jáglyá, or what is paid to the Rámoshis of the village for keeping watch at night over travellers' property.

7th. SÁNDHÁR TELACHI (rights from the oilman); half shall be yours, and half mine.

Remark. There is a considerable quantity of oil produced in the Deccan from plants sown annually, and cultivated in fields, either singly or mixed with grain; the most common plants of this kind are the Til, the Javas, the Kaharale, Ambádya, Kardai, and Bhuimûg. The Patils, in some places, send round every evening for oil, when each oilman puts alike in the dish. Others receive their quota monthly, and others annually.

8th. KOSHTIJACHE MÁG (weavers' looms). We shall each have half.

Remark. Each loom pays, at the end of the year, one cloth of the description of cloths woven on it. A Koshti is a weaver of Bands of a cloth which answers the purpose of a Sádis, of Pásodes, and sometimes of Sádis. Besides Koshtis, there are other kinds of village weavers, Jains, Sális, Dhangars (who are also shepherds), and Momins. The last are Mohammedans.

9th. Dhangaráche Mág (woollen weavers' looms). Half shall be yours, and half mine.

10th. Moh Tarafa. What is received on market-days, or fairs, from shopkeepers, Banians, etc.; such as tobacco, Supári, Nágvel Pán, Gûl, etc.

11th. Báproti Jamin (Mirás land). Nineteen Rukás of this land, you shall have half; that is, eight Rukás in one place, and a Ruká and a half in another place which contains a well, the whole of which I give up to you. I retain the other half of the land.

12. I have a well in one Ruká of ground appropriated for the growth of vegetables; half shall be yours, and half shall remain mine.

13th. You shall have half my tenement to reside in.

14th. Attached to the Mukadami, or Patilship, there are Inám lands to the extent or half a Cháhur, or six Rukás. You shall enjoy half of this, while I retain the other half.

15th. The village Máhárs who perform service for me, shall also do yours.

16th. Close to the village I have three Rukás of land; one and a half Ruká shall be yours, and the rest continue to be mine. But besides this, there is a quantity of land without tenants or labourers, and which belongs to the village. You shall take half of this land, while I retain the other half.

Remark. The meaning of the latter sentence is, perhaps, that they should enjoy an equal title to the disposal, or, if it may be termed, to the patronage of the land, because there is always a small fee received by the Patils who let out or sell the occupied fields of the village. This passage, however, argues strongly the right of the Patils to the disposal of all lands not possessed by the Government, as 'Sheri and Kuran' lands.

Second. MÁNPÁN, DIGINTY AND PRECEDENCE.

1st. Tasri. (The annual Government present on the full payment of the revenues.) We shall receive Tasri year and year about.

2nd. On the festival of the Holi, it will be customary for both to bake bread. The musical instrument players shall come to my house first, and go playing before me till I arrive at your house, when we shall both set out; my bread being carried on the right of your bread, and on arriving at the place of worship (a tree) I shall tie up yours under it. We shall then together equally go through the worship and the rest of the ceremony conjointly and at the same time.

3rd. On the occasion of Shirálshet (a ceremony which occurs on the Shasti, or 6th, the day after Nagpanchami), we shall both make an image of Shirálshet (a Rajah who reigned two Ghatkás), and together carry the images, after our women have danced round each, to the well or tank, and throw them into it at the same instant. Your Shirálshet shall go in procession on the left of mine.

4th. On the Pole Amavashyá, the bullocks of both shall set out at the same time—yours on the left, and mine on the right—and in this way, the one equal with the other, they shall be walked in procession round Hanumán; but the music shall precede my bullocks home, while yours remain until it returns, when you shall bring your bullocks home with music also.

5th. On marriages and Páts I shall first receive Vida, Tilak (Pán Supári, and a mark on the forehead), and then you; on like occasion the Khándwa (a large, round sweet cake) shall be equally shared by us.

6th. We shall worship not all the old gods, but all the new ones that may be set up together, and not before or after each other.

7th. The heads of all goats sacrificed to any of the gods which before were wholly mine, shall now be half of each head yours.

Remark. Hanumán is never offered the sacrifice of an animal; to Bhawáni, Khandoba, and Báhairoba, such sacrifices are acceptable; the carcase of the goat is eaten by the owner of the goat and his friends.

8th. On the full moon (of Mágh) I shall receive a goat, and then you shall receive one.

9th. We shall be entitled to a pair of shoes from the Chámbhár once a year.

10th. The village Dherds, on festivals and great occasions, shall give us both a piece of firewood, but mine shall be given first.

11th. On Kaul Patras my name shall be written uppermost, then yours, and below only one Plough (plough is the signature of a cultivator).

12th. We shall each have a goat on the Dasará, and their value will be put in the village expenses.

13th. On the Diváli, etc., the pipers shall play at my door first, and then at yours.

14th. We shall make the Dasará Puja together.

15th. Invitations to marriages, etc., shall be first given to me.

16th. The Shelá given on Páts (marriages of widows, or rather contracts answering the chief end of marriages) is to be shared between us.

17th. The present of the Dhangars from their flocks shall be equally shared by us.

18th. Half the Gûl and Til given on the Sankrànt shall be yours, and half mine. In this manner you and I, etc. (confirming the rights transferred to all futurity).

Then the witnesses' names.

Remark. A confirmation of this deed was granted by former Governments, and the copy of the deed, above translated, was found among the records.

(Signed) H. D. ROBERTSON.

Extract of a Letter, dated the 9th March 1818, *from Captain Robertson, Provisional Collector at Puna, to the Honourable M. Elphinstone.*

On the nature of the tenures by which the land is held by the Deccan Kunbis, my inquiries have been more successful. The general divisions of husbandmen are two—Thalkaris, or men who cultivate their own fields; and Kulwáris or Upris, men who labour on lands not their own. The Thalkaris tenure is uniform; the occupancy of the Kulwári is of different kinds.

The Thalkari is also called a Mirásdár. Thal signifies a field, and perhaps the literal meaning of Thalkari is a man belonging to, or who labours in, a field. The term Mirásdár is more expressive of the actual condition of the Thalkari; Mirás signifying patrimony, heritage, succession. But whatever arguments could be adduced against the word Thalkari or Mirásdár, as definitive of the condition of the person known by these appellations, there can be no doubt entertained of what that condition really is, for he is considered, and acknowledged by the Government, to have the property of the lands he cultivates. I am yet uninformed, and perhaps it may never be clearly established, at what period the Deccan landords acquired their rights to the property of the soil, by purchasing it from the Government, or the village, or whether it has always been inherent to them, and that the Government has either usurped their rights in some instances, or broken through a custom of allowing lands lying waste from a deficiency of population afterwards to become the inheritance of the multiplying descendants of the original number of land proprietors.

The Deccan landlord is proud of his situation, and is envied among his brethren, who are the cultivators of lands not their own: their feeling of attachment to their fields is remarkably keen, and no consideration but the utmost pecuniary distress will induce them to abandon their rights of proprietorship. These rights are either inherited or purchased, and it is a remarkable circumstance, that in the body of the deed of sale it is invariably usual to record that he who sells his lands has begged of him who buys them to become the purchaser. It would seem that this information is deemed requisite as a safeguard to the buyer, in consequence of the known reluctance of all landlords to part with their lands, to show that no subterfuge was used to force or trick them from the original proprietor. I have the honour to enclose the translation of two deeds of sale of land. The first has been executed and acted on without any reference to the Government. The second has been secured to a confirmation, first on the part of the ruler during whose reign it was executed, and afterwards by his successor. When a Thulkurree dies without heirs, or leaves his native country to reside in another, his lands become the property of the village, unless the proprietor returns before thirty years.

The lands of the Deccan villages are all measured, or supposed to be so. The village accounts are made up by accounting for the disposition of its lands. Every field has a name. The lands are appraised according to their quality of Utam, first rate, Madhyam, middling, and Kanist, or poor land. The Thalkari pays land-rent to Government according to the extent and quality of his lands. This land-rent is supposed to admit of no increase.

The Kulwári ought probably to be pronounced Kaulwári, which would signify a person holding a Kaul or permission. The Kulwári, whatever be the origin of his name, is, in fact, a farmer. He cultivated lands not his own under different names, according to the nature of his agreement.

Translation of a Kharedi Patra, or Deed of Purchase, dated 1739 *Shak Ishwar Nám Samwatchar Chaitra Shuddya Tritiá.*

To Pándurang Rav Ramchandar Binge, of the village of Underi Taraf Haveli Kriyat Mawal, Pargana Puna, from Bheyji, the son of Mahadaji, and Madoji, the son of Jagoji Kássid, of the same village. Sur San Saba Áshar Maya Tain va Álaf, 1226 Fasali.

A deed of purchase is executed to this effect for this reason, that inasmuch as we formerly received from you 917 rupees on account of six Rukás of the Thal field, called Gana, transferred to you along with the well in mortgage for 27 years, and that at the end of the abovementioned period you, having received from the enjoyment of the land the value of your money, were to restore it to us; and that as at this time 6½ years of the period of the mortgage having expired, 20½ years still remain, and we are reduced to distress and to the chance of dying from want of food, we have now come to you, to fall on your neck and to petition you, that as you have a right to our land for 20½ years, and we are reduced to want, you will in consequence of our joint desire accept for ever of half—namely, three Rukás of the land mortgaged to you, with half the well—on condition that you will immediately yield your title to the other half to us, making the price of the half we give you up, on a calculation of what we should have to pay, to redeem the whole six Rukás mortgaged for 20½ years, 675 rupees.

We, therefore, hereby give to you the land above-mentioned for 675 rupees, the sum we may be said to owe you for the whole land mortgaged, and with its half the well attached to it, and the western half of the tenement we possess, Thalkaris in the village, with whatever walls there may be thereon, namely, by — Haths in length from north to south, and twelve Haths in breadth from west to east. You are bound to preserve all the customs of the village, and to conform to particular customs heretofore established in respect to the land and rights now made yours; such as the payment of the Sarkár's revenue, Purelapan, etc., the rights of the Kulkarni, and the Balut of the Baluties; and you will enjoy, you and your sons, and your sons' sons, to future generations, the land above-mentioned; and on the ground in the village given to you, you will build a place, what you please, and be undisturbed; and we engage to be answerable for any molestation given you by any of our friends or relations so that you will sustain no injury. This deed of purchase which we have written is valid (Sahi), dated the 16th of the month Jamádilákhar.

Written out in the handwriting of Gopál Sidheshwar of the above-mentioned village.

WITNESSES.

The Mukadams of the said village Kusoji Bin Sakoji Patil Kanwa, and Khandoji Bin Villoji Golay.

Bheyie Bin Krishnoji Pankur, of the same village, etc., etc., etc.

PLOUGHS.

(That is, signature shaped so) Trimbakji Bin Essáji, the Carpenter. Janoji Bin Ramjuellorary, the Barber. Willoji Bin Bherjuthi, Gurav Ramaji Bin Punja, the Currier, etc., etc., etc.

(Signed) H. D. ROBERTSON,
Collector.

Translation of a Government Confirmation of the Deed of Purchase of Land.

To the Deshmukh and Deshpande of the Prant of Puna. Be it known that to you, Mahadaji Bin Najojee and Namaji Bin Ansojee Shejeoul, Rayats of the village of Wadki Taraf Haveli, there is an Inám-patra and Mirás-patra given as follows. (Here is mentioned the year and date.)

You having come to Puna have represented that both your grandfathers Raiji, *alias* Raghoji, and his younger brother Chahuji, lived together in the year 1639, and that the Patils of the above-mentioned village having been reduced to distress, accepted from your said relations a sum of money, and voluntarily gave them a portion of their Inám land, measuring 1½ Rukás and 7½ Rukás of Mirás land, and that having thus sold their lands a deed of purchase was executed in the name of Raiji, *alias* Raghoji, to the following purport :

(Here follows a deed of purchase similar to Enclosure No. 1.)

A deed of purchase of the above tenour having been executed was confirmed in the year Sursan Maya Wa Alaf by the deceased, Baji Ráv Pandit Pradhan to your grandfathers, at which time Sántáji's son Makaji and Tukaji Patil having been brought to the presence and asked what lands they had voluntarily transferred to your grandfathers, stated as follows :

1st.—Part of our Inám lands, to equal to 1½ Rukás, viz., belonging to Makaji Patil - -	Ruká	½
Ditto to Tukaji ditto - - - - - -	„	1
	Rukás	1½
2nd.—Part of Mirás land—		
1. Of the field called Soandur, containing 24 -	Rukás	6
2. Of the do. do. Kole Thal, containing 12 -	„	1⅞
	Rukás	7½

And 3rd.—A part of our premises in the village, 45 Haths long and 40 broad.

Now you having brought a deed of purchase corresponding with the above statement, and having all produced a document executed by the deceased Baji Rav, confirming its validity, and as you are desirous that the present Government should also testify the same, it is hereby decreed that you and your sons and descendants shall enjoy in Inám and in Mirás the lands, etc., according to the tenor of the confirmatory act of the late Baji Rav Pandit Pradhan, and that you shall continue to conform to the practices of the village, in regard to the lands you have acquired.

(Signed) H. D. ROBERTSON.

Extract of a Letter, dated the 22nd December, 1818, *from Captain Briggs, Political Agent in Khandesh, to the Honourable M. Elphinstone.*

The remainder of the province, and that part of Ganthadi under my authority, appears to have undergone a similar survey in the time of Malikambar, the founder of Aurungabad, and the successor to the Government of the last of the Nizam Shái Princes. As far as my inquiries have enabled me to learn, the assessments were pretty much the same as those of Akbar's, but the nature of the landed tenure was essentially different.

This Prince seems thoroughly to have comprehended the use of the soil to Government by identifying the interest of the cultivator with its fertility. While Akbar considered the land the property of Government, Malikambar confirmed the right of cultivating certain fields to the Rayats; he made a considerable portion of the land private property; the lands of the village were considered the joint property of the township, the fallow land was the common for the pasture of the cattle, and the ploughed ground was either the property of individuals or cultivated by tenants, who received a portion of the crops. It appears to have been a principle of his wise administration to encourage the possession of private landed property as a means of attaching their cultivators to their own soil, and making over in perpetuity to them what is only useful to Government as long as they continued to remain on it. The farmer holding private land is called Wattandár, or hereditary proprietor, and the mere cultivator is styled Upri, and is a tenant at will. The whole of the village officers—such as the Patil, the Kulkarni, the barber, the washerman, the watchman, the carpenter, the smith, the goldsmith, the potter, the Joshi, astrologer or schoolmaster, and the carrier—had each his field assigned to him; his office and his land are both hereditary and so far personal that both one and the other are saleable, or transferable by gift; these lands are free of taxes as a remuneration for the performance of their offices, and to ensure in each village, however small, one of these useful members of the community. The Mahars or Dheds, hereditary watchmen of each village, are those to whom boundary disputes are referred for settlement. These boundaries are marked by stones fixed in the ground, and beneath each stone is usually deposited an earthen pot full of charcoal. It is surprising how these landmarks are preserved long after villages are uninhabited, and so tenacious are landholders of their fields that they will often cultivate them at the distance of three or four miles from the place they reside in if their own village is deserted, rather than take up with new ground that may be near or more convenient as mere tenants. The Wattandár, or Mirási Rayat, holds his land of right: it is also hereditary, saleable, or transferable, and on the occasion of its alienation from the family title-deeds are made out and witnessed not only by the military authorities, but the Deshmukh of the district and several of the surrounding Patils are called on to be present at the transaction. The Wattandárs adhere to their lands and village in spite of oppression and cruelty, provided their landed tenure is not interfered with, and where we see half-deserted villages we find on inquiry that the inhabitants who have deserted are for the most part what are termed Upri Rayats, or tenants at will. This class differs only from Wattandárs by having no right to the soil: they come and settle in the village, and are permitted by the Patil to cultivate a certain portion of land. If the soil has lain fallow and requires to be broken up afresh, they only pay portions of the first assessment till the third or fourth year, when they ought to pay the full amount. The exactions on the agricultural classes under the late Government have been so heavy that it was difficult to obtain tenants, but in order to induce them to take farms the assessments were made less than on the Wattandárs, or landed proprietors, although it is quite evident that the assessment from the latter is a land-tax, while that from the former ought to be both a land-tax and ground-rent.

I shall do myself the honour at a future opportunity to transmit the assessment in detail as fixed by the Tanklea or by established custom on the different kinds of land.

The advantages of being an Upri tenant are so great as to induce the Wattandárs frequently to allow their own fields to be fallow and break up new ground, and rent it of the Sarkar on the Upri terms; but this is not allowed when the Mamlatdár or the Government officer discovers it. If, on the contrary, the Upri tenant paid more for the rent of his land, after a certain number of years' residence was allowed to become a Wattandár on a reduced rate of taxation, it would then be an object for each Wattandár to cultivate his own land, and for the Upri tenant to cultivate the same field till by the extra rent he had in fact purchased his right to the soil. A third class of cultivators are those who have neither interest in the soil nor in the crops; those are labourers who receive, according to the price of provisions, four, five, or six rupees monthly. This number is very small, and is merely mentioned to include the whole of the classes composing the husbandmen.

Such are the various modes of cultivating and raising the ground-rents or taxes called Ain Jamá. The assessment appears to have suffered no change within the last two centuries, and I am disposed to think that the system adopted by Malikambar, of making lands over in perpetuity, is of great antiquity among the Hindus, and was probably once uniformly adopted throughout India. Whenever the Ain Jamá appears to have increased, it has been in consequence of additional cultivation, not of an increased rate of assessment, and nothing is more favourable to the extension and improvement of agriculture than a moderate but permanent tax, and an interest in the soil. The portion remaining to the cultivator should be such as to enable him to add indirectly to the wealth of the State; he should not only have the means of improving his field and taking in more ground, but he should have sufficient left to live in such a way as to encourage manufactures and trade, and thus become an indirect promoter of the revenue derived from the customs, as it must be evident when there is no opulence in the people there can be no source from whence revenue can be derived.

Extract of a Letter dated the 15*th January*, 1819, *from Captain Pottinger, Provisional Collector at Ahmednagar, to the Honourable M. Elphinstone.*

When a Patil wished to obtain Istawah for himself or any of the Rayats of his village, he repaired to the Shekdár, or (if near him) to the Kamávisdár, to whom he applied for the usual Kaul. An inquiry was then instituted into the nature of the soil, the number of years it had lain waste, the probable length of time it would require to bring it into complete cultivation, the number of bullocks that would be needed for each plough to till it, the facilities which the situation offered for irrigation, and the means which the cultivators had of availing themselves of this circumstance. As soon as all these points were ascertained the soil was valued, with reference to any contiguous fields or village lands of a similar description, and the Kauls were then drawn out under the Kamávisdár's seal and given to the Patils, who handed them over to the Rayats, with an exhortation to avail themselves of the Sarkár's kindness, and to use their best exertions to profit by the terms he had obtained for them.

When the Kaul had thus been formally executed and delivered, the Rayat became virtually the owner of the field or proportion of ground stated in it, because so long as he fulfilled the terms and paid his rents with regularity he could not be deprived of the right of cultivation; but the moment he failed to do either of these, the Kamávisdár would dispossess him, and entrust his land to another on the same or a different footing as might seem necessary. This, however, was a very harsh measure, and therefore scarcely ever resorted to. If it was found that a Rayat's ground had really been overvalued in the first instance, and that, with every wish to do so, he was unable to pay his rent, the Kamávisdár might on his own responsibility, where they had not been reported, relax in the terms; or, if they had been brought to the notice of the Sarsubha, it was usual to write to that officer and get his leave to alter them.

When the period of an Istawah grant expired, the Rayat might, if he chose, cease to cultivate to the full extent of his ground, but by so doing he forfeited (as I have already stated) his claim to it in future; and the

Patil, in concert with the Shekdár, acting under permission from the Kamávisdár, was bound to find if possible another cultivator whose tenure was exactly that of his predecessor. On the other hand, if the Rayat was pleased with his lands, he had it in his power to secure them in his family as a *Mirási*, or hereditary possession, by simply agreeing to pay the rent of them whether they were cultivated or not. The rent received by it to Government in this case is termed Shahra, and nothing short of utter poverty will prevent its being paid. A man will sell his house and bullocks, or clothes, and even bind himself to serve another, to ensure the payment of his Shahra, because it is honourable and respectable in the eyes of his neighbours to preserve his *Mirási* lands; and when he fails to pay his dues upon them his ruin is considered as decided, and he becomes a bankrupt.

The preceding is a brief view of the practice observed in the just and flourishing periods of sovereignty of the Peshwas, but many of these regulations have been widely deviated from in latter times. *Mirási* lands have been seized from the lawful holders and transferred to relations and dependents of court favourites and partizans of great men. Kauls have been granted by Patils without the sanction of even a Shekdár, and the consequences have been that their friends were favoured whilst other Rayats were overburthened with demands to make up the deficiencies. Every succeeding year increased this evil, by reducing the number of Rayats, some of whom fled, whilst others sold their cattle to pay their last year's rent and become servants of their more fortunate neighbour. The farmers and their agents, having no interest in the general prosperity of the country, did not take the trouble to investigate the motives and fairness of Kauls, and cared not whence the money came, provided they got as much as they expected from a village. The old revenue system ceased even to be thought of, and extortion took the place of a just realization of the revenue.

(Copy.)

Dhulia, 22nd June, 1819.

Sir,

In reply to your circular letter of the —— instant regarding Mirási lands, I have the honour to acquaint you that from all the information I formerly obtained when making out my report on Khandesh, and from more minute investigation lately acquired, it appears that Mirási land is saleable only in the following Parganás, which are said to have formed part of Malikambar's dominions, viz.:

Parganá Jaitápûr.
,, Tilwan.
,, Karolli.
,, Kannassi.
,, Pimpla.
,, Galna.
,, Katghar.

In the remainder of the districts in Khandesh, the Mirási land is not saleable; it is not, however, considered Mirás, or inheritance, if a farmer has cultivated a field for many years, and it is considered as unjust to deprive him of it as long as he pays the Government tax; the only exception to this is in the instance of Ináms, which are everywhere, I believe, saleable.

I have not been able to ascertain whether the land in Khandesh was at any time Mirási. It certainly has not been since the Mohammedan Conquest in 1306, and there are no village records which come within three or four centuries of that period.

The prevalent opinion, which is supported by Hindu laws and by history, is, that unclaimed land cleared by the subject is his inheritance, and that he should pay for the protection he received from the State one-sixth of the produce in ordinary times, and one-fourth in time of war.

The Mohammedans in their conquest considered themselves as masters of the persons and property of all infidels whom they subdued. The conquered possessed therefore nothing of right. It appears to me they were employed to cultivate the land of the conquerors, and received half of the gross produce as wages, and to bear all the expenses of cultivation. As the Mohammedans became identified with the natives, some relaxations occasionally took place; but the hypothesis that the Government is the lord of the soil seems founded on the opinion that the conquered lose everything but what is restored by the victor, and whenever the husbandman alone retains the half of the gross produce, it seems to me that he is rather the labourer than the tenant of Government, much less the proprietor of the soil.

The only Prince, which I know of, who promoted the sale of land, and the privileges of real proprietorship, was Mullic Umber, and I imagine it will be found that these rights were under the last sovereigns of the Nizam Sháhi Dynasty.

I have, etc.,

(Signed) JOHN BRIGGS,

Political Agent in Khandesh.

To the Honourable M. ELPHINSTONE, etc., etc., etc.

Extract of a Letter from Captain Grant, Political Agent at Satara, to the Honourable M. Elphinstone, dated 17th August, 1819.

The hereditary, or those termed such, are the Deshmukh, Deshpánde, Nádgoudá, Desh Chougula, Patil, Kulkarni, and Chougula.

It is not intended to enter on any definition of the duties of these in this report, where I shall merely confine myself by stating generally the claims which they have on the lands and revenues of the district.

Deshmukh and Deshpánde are compound Sanskrit words, and the institution of the offices is accounted very ancient. They have been termed Jamindárs by Mohammedans, a name which the modern Deshmukhs and Deshpándes are ambitious of retaining, but I have seen nothing to prove their having ever been on the footing of Moghul Jamindárs. The only officers, whose situation was nearly approaching the Jamindárs of Bengal, were the Mokásdárs of the Bijapur State; but I have nothing very clear respecting them.

The claims of the hereditary officers, or Hakdárs, in this district, partake of the intricacy and confusion in which the whole accounts are involved.

The Deshmukh's Hak is very variable in Faltan Desh; it is one-fourth of the whole revenue; in Karád it is a twentieth part of the arable land, and 5 per cent. on the land revenue. In Man perhaps nearly the same, but with a claim to one half of all fines levied within the district, which, however, has not been satisfactorily established. In Nirthadi it is the assigned Inám land, and a simple fixed money payment, which is paid wholly or in part. The Deshmukh of Wái was the same as Karád, but the Hak or Wattan, as the right is termed, was for a time attached by Sháhû, the fourth Rajah; the ready-money Hak was then raised to 10 per cent., and when it was restored to the Pisál family, the extra 5 per cent. was not given to them, but it was continued on account of Government, under the head of Panchoutra, literally 5 per cent.

To this exaction, and an extra assessment of 2½ per cent. on the Sardeshmuki of Wái, may be ascribed the permanent extra assessment of 7½ per cent. on Kurve, which has been already noticed.

The Deshpánde Hak is also not uniform; it may be reckoned at one half of that of the Deshmukh; both commonly have claims upon the customs.

The Nádgoudá has also some claims upon the customs; he has his Hak in Inám land, and 2 per cent. on the land revenue.

The Desh Chougla's pay is not general: where it is acknowledged he has Inám land and a money payment from the Sadiwar.

Deshmukhs and Deshpandes style themselves Jamindárs, whilst Patils and Kulkarnis come under the general term of Wattandárs. The Patil has Inám land, Mushárá, a ready-money payment on the Sadelwari, an allowance for Sirpáv and sometimes, though rarely, a share in the customs; he also receives a contribution in kind from the Rayats, termed Ghugari.

The Kulkarni has also Inám lands, an assignment in money on the Sadelwar, besides Sirpáv allowance; the grain payment made to the Kulkarni is termed Mushárá.

The Chougula has a smaller share in a similar manner.

The Balute have land and a Hak in kind from the Rayats.

In the Mahratta country all inheritance goes by the

name of Wattan, and no one would willingly part with his Wattan if much more than its intrinsic value were offered for it. The most serious distress is that of being compelled to sell one's Wattan. The feeling is singularly strong, and is not easily understood or described. The attachment to a house, a field, or garden, we can enter into ; but Wattan is sometimes merely the right to a few blades of Báji from the vegetable-sellers in the Bajár, which I have seen maintained with an eagerness which did not proceed from its value, but from its being Wattan. I have seen two women fight and tear each other in the streets of Satara because the one had removed a loose stone from near the house of the other, which was part (said the aggrieved person) of my Wattan. This feeling will be found universal, but here it is peculiarly observable.

All the hereditary officers can sell their Wattan, but some require to have the sanction of Government. Consent, I am inclined to think, is always requisite to be regular, but in some cases, such as Patils or other executive and important officers, it is indispensably necessary. In the sale of every species of inheritance the next of kin has the first offer, and so down to the nearest neighbour. This is a rule of right, even in the disposal of a house, which may not have been acquired as patrimony. If the house and street are east and west, the neighbour on the east side has the preference. If north and south, the one to the south has the first offer.

The sale of any hereditary office is a very formal procedure ; an attested acknowledgment of the act being voluntary, and proceeding from circumstances which are to be generally stated, is the preliminary adjustment.

I have examined papers of the sale of an hereditary office, and found the amount above fifty years' purchase of all known emolument, but beside the purchase-money there are fees to Government and regular dues to be paid to the other hereditary officers upon admitting another person into the gate. The whole of the hereditary officers bear witness to the deed of sale, which list of signatures is taken in a public assembly and is turned to the gate Muhzar. The share of Hak upon customs shall hereafter form a separate report.

The hereditary officers are amenable to a tax called the Dehak Patti, which is the whole amount of their Hak, exclusive of their Inám lands, and may be levied every tenth year. This has never been regularly levied, and is a very unpopular tax; at first view it seems only reasonable that those officers, when not executive, should be required to contribute something to the exigencies of the State, yet many poor women and families who have small shares of Hak would be greatly distressed by it unless it could be levied on individuals possessing above a certain income derivable from this source; but this would require a minuteness of information which we cannot easily acquire.

As the extent and assignments of all rent-free lands will be shown in the statements which I shall forward next month, I shall at present pass on to the various tenures of the farmers who pay a revenue to Government, leaving the others at rest for the present.

All persons who possess hereditary right to any fields come under the head of Wattandárs of such and such a village, though they may have actually resided all their lives at Gwalior; whereas all others who do not possess this right, though present in the village, and though they and their ancestors may have resided there for a century, are termed, in common with the passing Mahratta traveller who has slept a night in the Dharmsalá, Upri or stranger.

The common farmer holds his land upon a contract or lease from the village authorities, which is called his Kaul; it is generally renewed from year to year, and seldom exceeds three years; he is obliged to conform to the customs of the village, and commonly pays his Sarkár dues in money; he is said to hold his Khand Makta, or Uktá.

A Warrenda Kari is a person who holds lands in a similar manner, but beyond the limits of his own village boundary.

A Share Kari is one who holds lands virtually the property of Government. Shárá is commonly a particular species of property, which may have reverted to Government, either by becoming forfeited, or by some former purchase, for the purpose of planting trees. It may also have been land which, from time immemorial, has not been within the bounds of any village. A Share Kari may be a person holding a few mangoes for the season.

A person renting land under an agreement of paying half the produce in kind is said to hold it in Batái.

The Rayat, however, whose situation merits most particular attention, is the cultivator of lands in which he has an hereditary and proprietary right, and who holds his land in perpetuity on paying a fixed rent to Government. To this tenure you have particularly directed inquiries, and I shall endeavour to state all I have been able to collect respecting these Mirás lands.

The Mirásdár has, without doubt, a perfect property in his field, as long as he continues to pay the amount with which it may be burdened, together with the right of disposing of it, even without the sanction of Government. How he became originally possessed of this right, it is difficult to account for; there is no direct evidence of the whole land having been all Mirási in ancient times, but there is a proof in the Thul Jhora, or record of the fields in villages, that a vast quantity of the land formerly registered Mirás is now Khand Mákta, or held in common lease.

An opinion prevails that all land was originally Mirás, and that in the ancient Hindu Raj the soil became the acknowledged property of the person who first cleared it of stones and jungle.

The usual manner of obtaining this right from Government at a more recent period I have already had the honour of explaining in my letter of the 29th of January, on the subject of the Istawa lease; but since I wrote that letter I have had more opportunity of hearing opinions and judging of Mahratta feeling regarding this tenure, and I now find it as generally considered an overstretch of power on the part of Government to resume any Mirás field, merely because the Mirásdár has failed in paying his rent, or because he has retired to some other part of the country to evade payment.

Simple insolvency on the part of the Mirásdár does not appear to have given Government the power of disposing of field in Mirás to another. When the Mirásdár cannot pay his rent, the amount of the dues falls on the other Mirásdárs should the insolvent Mirásdár remain present in the village; but if he should quit the district, the others are not called upon to pay the rent: during his absence the Government has a right to make the most of the field, and even to let it on lease, but for a period usually not exceeding three years, and till the expiration of which the Mirásdár cannot claim restitution.

That numerous examples of a less forbearing conduct on the part of the late Government can be adduced I am well aware, but there is no species of property in this country that it has so much respected as Mirás land; and though this may have proceeded in a great degree from the insignificancy of its value, and the loss, rather than gain, which its seizure or alienation must have occasioned, and even in cases where immediate advantage would have resulted to the rapacity of Government agents, or revenue contractors, there has always been great consideration shown to the Mirásdár. Instances of declared forfeiture are accordingly very rare; but great crimes, such as treason, robbery, theft, and murder, are always considered as destroying the right to all Mirás, and, indeed, to every species of property whatever: but Mirás land generally goes to the nearest of kin. In all cases it seems to have been considered right that a reasonable provision should be made to relations, even when the ostensible head of a family had committed an unpardonable offence. Had this not been customary, many persons, owing to the divisibility of property amongst heirs, would have been deprived of their only means of livelihood for the commission of crimes in which they had borne no participation. This accounts in some manner for the portions of Hak, etc., which are so frequently credited to Government in the annual village settlement.

Mirásdárs, who are absentees, are termed by the Mahrattas Parganá. It is so well understood that no Mirásdár wilfully quits his land; that it is considered the duty of a good Patil, and of all superior Government agents, to use every endeavour to discover and remove the cause of his leaving his home and the field of his forefathers. If poverty has been the cause, his rent is remitted, and an advance of money granted; and if it has been occasioned by any unsettled dispute, an investigation and adjustment are promised by Government. Should every inducement fail, and the Mirásdár pertinaciously and unreasonably persist in remaining abroad, he can be required to give in a written renunciation of his Mirás right, which, when obtained, allows the Government a full power of disposing of his lands; but without this document there is no authority that can dispose of such land in Mirás to another, until the death of the Mirásdár, and the death or renunciation of his heirs. In case of its being thought an object to ascertain this, the mode of doing so is from the village; should the villagers bear testimony to the certain or supposed death of the Mirásdár and his heirs, Government can then dispose of the land to another person in Mirás; and should any heir afterwards appear, he has no claim whatever, unless he can clearly prove that the evidence of the villagers was given, knowing it to be false, or that he had been in such a situation as had put it entirely out of his power to keep the Patil and Wattandár apprised of his being alive. When such can be proved, he has a right to the field upon the payment of all loss or other equitable charge, either by the Government or the occupant; but under the circumstances just described, and in all others when the field is merely held by an ordinary cultivator, in case of the return of the rightful heir, the Mirás must be restored at the expiration of the lease, which usually is done without requiring arrears of deficiency to be made up, although it is admitted that Government has a right to demand them. As to paying for improvements, the ordinary cultivator had no security until the issue of the late orders for any outlay, and consequently would not incur an expense which was not likely to be returned in crop during the existence of his lease.

Shilledárs about to take the field, or any person in immediate want of money, frequently mortgage their Mirás land, the value of which of course depends entirely on circumstances.

To form a precise estimate of the number of years' purchase of Mirás land is by no means easy, and will require more inquiry and much longer experience than can be obtained in one season. My present notion is, that when the established assessment only is levied, the Rayat has, on a fair average, one-third of the gross produce, the Government has a third, and a third goes for seed, Hakdárs, bullocks, implements, and subsistence to the cattle; the year's purchase would therefore be found by a series of the years of rent, and in an average of thirty deeds of sale from 1780 till 1810 which have been examined, the general rate is ten years' purchase.

Industry and natural advantages may improve a field so much as to yield the Mirásdár upwards of three-fourths of the produce. The year's purchase in these cases can only be ascertained by fair statements from the occupant, which I cannot say I have been able to obtain satisfactorily; either from a want of intelligence, or more probably of candour, the people cannot yet be brought to understand the intention of such inquiries.

Land held at will, I suppose, may have one-fourth of the gross produce in the hands of the Rayats; but for the reason just stated I have no other means of ascertaining the fact than the following observation:

The Kunbis, not Mirásdár, prefer the tenure called Batái—that is, dividing the produce with Government to the ordinary farm. The mode of this division is first to set aside the dues of the Patils, Kulkarnis, and Balute, the quantity required for next year's seed; after which the division is made, and the rest of the Hak dues fall on the Government share. But after the first deductions, the subsequent division, the wear and tear of implements, the purchase of cattle and finding their subsistence, there will remain little more than a fourth of the gross produce.

Mirás hereafter appears to be a very desirable tenure as long as the established fixed assessment, usual in the country, continues to be equitably levied, as the Mirásdár has not only much more personal consideration shown to him by his townsmen, but he has all the advantages which industry can give him in the way of improvement. But when pretences were sought of extorting extra payments it was worse than the ordinary lease, as it placed the proprietor more in the power of the revenue farmer. Thus Mirás land latterly became of no value, and had it been possible for such a system of undefined exaction to have gone on without control for any length of time, it is highly probable that the Mirás tenure would have disappeared.

In estimating what falls to the Rayat of the gross produce, a considerable portion is made up of the daily subsistence he is deriving from his field. If hired labourers are employed, I have with some precision ascertained from Bráhmins who farm in this way that they derive a profit of one-eighth in an ordinary year, but this is calculated on what they save by the produce of the field for family consumption.

With regard to the tenures of land, there does not seem to be any doubt that the Mirás land was considered private property, in as far as it uniformly descended from father to son or to the nearest heir, and only reverted to Government on the failure of kin of the former possessor or its not being claimed by them for a long course of years. The Mirásdár could sell or give it away with the permission of Government, but not otherwise, and as long as he finds his rents the Government had no right to interfere with his lands; but whether the ground was cultivated or not, he was obliged to make good the rent according to the Kamál of the village. The word *Thalkarni* is synonymous with Mirásdár, though it is sometimes confined to a person who himself cultivates his own Mirás land, for a Mirásdár may let his land to any other person, being himself answerable to Government for the rent.

The other lands of the village which belonged to Government are called *Upri* or *Gatkuli*, and of them a portion, called Sherishet, was usually reserved by Government and cultivated on its own account, and was exempted from Grám Kharch, and some other Pattis. The Upri land was entirely at the disposal of the Patil and Kulkarnis, and was cultivated by Kunbis, called Sukwastu (tenants during pleasure); as these were guided entirely by their own inclinations in cultivating the Upri lands or not, the Patils exerted themselves as much as possible to induce them to do so by advancing them seed and money if requisite. The Patils and Kulkarnis had nothing to do with the Mirás lands, except to report the absence of any Mirásdárs from their villages, to recall them, and make them answerable for the full rent; if they would not return, they seized the land for Government, and employed others to cultivate it; or if they resigned it altogether, they took a writing from them to that effect.

If by any misfortune the crops of the Mirás lands are much injured it was usual to allow some remission, but not on account of any part remaining uncultivated; whilst the Upri land paid only for what it produced. A very small proportion of the lands of this country are Upri, nearly the whole being Mirás; and it is said by some that there was formerly no Upri land at all, and that it has gradually fallen into the hands of Government, by the failure of heirs of the

Mirásdárs, or other accidental circumstances, such as quarrels amongst brothers, or relations, about the division of their lands, which they often desired to give up altogether rather than resign to each other any part of what they held to be their rights; or, perhaps, the poverty of the Mirásdárs and declining state of the country may have induced many to give up their lands.

In support of the conjecture that the whole of the land was formerly Mirás, it may be observed that in many villages the whole of the land is still Mirás, and cultivated by Mirásdárs; in others the whole is styled Mirás, and still stands under the name of the Mirásdárs, although part of it has become waste, or has reverted to Government, and is cultivated by Sukwastus in consequence of the absence of the Mirásdárs and their heirs, or other causes; in many villages which have long possessed Upri lands, the fields are still known by the name of the Mirásdár to whom they formerly belonged.

The Patils, Kulkarnis, Deshmukh, Despánde, etc., hold Wattan lands in virtue of their office: but they differ from Mirás lands in that they pay no rent, except in most cases an Inám Tizái; that they are attached to the office, and may be sequestered by Government for any offence, which Mirás land cannot, unless for very great crimes which involve the whole family of the Mirásdár. The Patils and Kulkarnis can, however, sell part or the whole of their Wattans and rights to any person, with the permission of the Deshmukh; and Despándes can do the same. The Patils and Kulkarnis and Jamindárs are often also Mirásdárs as well as the inferior officers of the village. In some districts the Mirás lands pay a triennial tax called Mirás Patti, but this is only in the Puna Subhá and the districts of Junar and Supá. It does not at once appear why the Mirás lands should be so much more valued than the Upri, since if equal in extent and quality they are taxed alike, or rather the Mirásdár pays more than the other, besides the Mirás Patti, as he must pay for the whole of his lands whether cultivated or not; whereas it is only the Upri land actually cultivated which is taxed. There is, however, little doubt that Mirás lands, though rated the same as Upri, are actually more productive, owing either to their having been all at some period Mirás, and the Upri lands being neglected and having become inferior, or to the advantages enjoyed by the Mirásdárs having been sufficient to induce them to bestow labour and expense in improving their lands above Upri; for it appears that the Kamál of Mirás land, once fixed, was not subject to any casual increase in consequence of improvement, as the Upri was; and we may add, the natural attachment of man to a birthright handed down to him from his ancestors, and of which he was sure of enjoying the undisturbed possession, as well as the satisfaction of being able to leave to his family an inheritance, which seems to have been always respected in a country where every other species of property is so extremely uncertain. It is certain that, although the Native Government may have occasionally seized on Mirás lands for its own purposes, it was looked upon as a great act of oppression; that in the time of Náná Fadnavis, when the country was comparatively prosperous and well cultivated and governed, Mirás lands bore a much higher price than during the capricious and arbitrary Government of Báji Ráv; that the Mirás lands are more improved than the rest; and that a very considerable value is set upon the possession of them by all classes of Rayats. If any land, which was wanted for the purposes of Government, happened to be Mirás, some other Upri lands were given in exchange; and, perhaps, in later times nothing at all. But even Báji Ráv always paid for any Mirás lands which he wanted for his own use, and purchased them from the Mirásdárs, generally at their own price, like any private individual. There are instances of Mirásdárs having refused him their lands on any conditions, and his being obliged to submit.

The Government was always willing to grant lands to the Rayats on the Mirás tenure, on payment of a Najar: this power was in many parts of the country delegated to the Deshmukhs and Despándes, and even to the Patils and Kulkarnis. No Sanad was required, the mere registering of the grant in the village papers being usually sufficient. Any Rayat whose ancestors had cultivated a spot of Upri land for a certain period, in some places sixty, in others one hundred years, without interference from former Mirásdárs, became in fact the Mirásdár of that land without any further grant; should, however, the descendants of the former Mirásdár claim and make good their right within sixty or a hundred years, a part of the land was restored to them, and the remainder confirmed to the Mirásdár; after that period all former claims were superseded.

The Government could grant Mirás lands in Inám to other people—that is, the revenues of the lands; but as it possessed no rights over the land itself, it could of course transfer none to the Inámdár. Instances of disputes on this point have occurred, but have always terminated in favour of the Mirásdár.

(Signed) J. MACLEOD,
General.

(A true copy.)
(Signed) J. MACLEOD.

GENERAL ABSTRACT OF TOTAL.

	Puna.	Ahmednagar.	Satara.	Khandesh.	Karnatik.	Patvardhans Jahagirs.	Kittur Taluk.	Total.
	Rs. a. p.	Rs. a. p.	Rs. a. p.	Rs. a. p.	Rs. s. p.	Rs. a. p.	Rs. a. p.	Rs. a. p.
Inâms	89,828 1 0	6,54,491 5 3	1,53,295 5 0	40,543 11 3	2,43,522 15 9	50,070 14 0	8,060 0 0	12,39,812 4 3
Devristhâns . . .	74,058 1 6	49,862 4 9	35,287 14 9	3,926 7 0	26,779 7 6	12,374 7 9	5,595 0 0	2,07,883 11 3
Suriristhâns . . .	30,835 8 0	17,638 14 6	4,705 2 0	401 0 0	—	—	—	53,580 8 3
Warshâsans . . .	2,432 4 0	20,517 0 0	9,724 4 6	2,897 6 0	28,400 7 6	13,269 4 6	2,244 0 0	79,484 10 3
Dewisthâns and Warshâsans (together) .	—	—	—	—	15,474 0 0	—	—	15,474 0 0
Nemnuks . . .	2,359 0 0	19,217 12 0	6,835 4 0	1,075 0 0	1,46,412 8 0	—	—	1,75,899 8 0
Dharmâdays . . .	635 10 6	23,758 0 0	40,705 9 6	25 0 0	23,513 9 6	35,111 11 9	—	1,23,749 9 3
Doubtful Inâms or Dharmâdays . .	—	11,594 2 9	20,162 2 0	—	—	—	—	31,756 4 9
Rozimadârs . . .	360 0 0	27,709 2 0	—	6,626 5 9	3,364 0 0	—	—	38,059 7 9
Pirs	2,018 8 0	2,123 8 6	1,968 7 9	193 8 9	80,543 4 6	—	—	86,847 5 6
Miscellaneous allowances (Ketta) . .	275 0 0	5,526 11 6	63,666 14 3	17,248 4 0	27,112 6 9	28,160 14 6	—	1,41,990 3 0
Khairâts	15 0 0	4,528 11 0	3,394 1 9	13,500 9 6	1,866 11 6	—	102 0 0	23,407 1 9
Allowances to Pirs and Khairât (together) .	—	—	—	—	—	4,619 6 3	—	4,619 6 3
Bâlpururishi . . .	15 0 0	565 0 0	759 0 0	—	398 5 6	—	—	2,037 5 6
Bakshish . . .	614 9 0	—	290 0 0	—	—	—	—	904 9 0
Dehuji	3 10 0	—	1,914 0 0	—	—	—	—	1,917 10 0
Mezuani . . .	—	—	100 0 0	—	—	—	—	100 0 0
Gardens . . .	181 6 0	—	—	—	—	—	—	181 6 0
Exemption (Mâf) . .	—	—	69 0 0	—	—	—	—	69 0 0
Lands and Buildings to Jamindârs, Bhis, etc.	9,518 6 0	5,475 13 0	28,456 0 3	4,376 9 6	1,66,929 4 3	8,879 2 6	—	2,23,635 3 3
Ditto additional (doubtful)	—	—	552 8 0	—	—	—	—	552 8 0
Shet Sannadi . .	190 8 0	—	—	—	—	—	—	190 8 0
Total . . .	2,13,340 8 0	8,43,008 5 0	3,71,885 9 6	90,813 12 0	7,64,317 0 9	1,52,785 13 0	16,001 0 0	24,52,152 2 0

Puna, 31*st August*, 1819.

(Signed) J. MACLEOD.

(True copy)
(Signed) J. MACLEOD.

An Inám is a free grant in perpetuity, without any implied condition, except that in some instances one-third of the rent called Inám Tizái is paid to Government, when it is not otherwise expressed in the Sannad: an Inám is, in fact, private freehold, or not, according to the above condition, but by far most commonly entirely freehold.

Assignments in Saranjam are held on the conditions of military service, and are either as personal pay, Zat Saranjam, or for the support of troops, and the maintenance of forts called Saranjam.

Dewasthán are revenues dedicated to the support of Pagodas; they are granted on all kinds of property, in various ways, and are considered permanent.

Sawasthán is a place where a God is supposed to be actually present, or incarnate; as Ganpati is supposed to animate the Living God at Chinchur. Revenues dedicated to the support of such persons or temples are called Sawasthán, and are grants in perpetuity.

The word Sawasthán is believed to be different from Sarasthán (own place), which is applied to the territories of petty Princes or Rájás, whose districts are considered entirely their own, and governed independently by themselves, without any interference on the part of the Government.

Warshásans are originally religious or charitable pensions, paid either from the Huzur treasury, in which case a Sannad was not required, or by grants on the revenues of the Mahals, or any particular parts of them, which were generally confirmed by Sannad, and were considered as descending from father to son, being usually continued by the Mamlatdárs to the son or immediate heir of the late incumbent, on application to that effect. It would appear, however, that on the death of the present incumbents they may be resumed or disposed of at the pleasure of Government, and accordingly, on the Mamlatdár's reporting such circumstances, should there be no immediate heir, or should he be in any way considered unworthy, the Warshásan is sometimes either reduced, or taken away altogether. In cases, however, where Sannads have been granted, such exercise of power does not seem to have been usual.

Rozinadárs are persons receiving a certain charitable donation, daily or yearly; these, together with allowance to Pirs and Khairáts, were for the most part originally granted by the Mogals, and continued by the Mahráttás. They seem to be considered nearly on the same footing with Warshásans, and to be permitted to go on without much interference.

The same may also be said of Dharmádáws, which are charitable allowances to religious persons, or for religious purposes. And Bálpurwarishis, which are generally pensions to the families of persons killed in the service. Dharmádáws and Bálpurwarishis are usually granted on Sannad, as are sometimes also Dengis.

Miscellaneous pensions or allowances, not coming exactly under any of the above heads, are called Killá; they are in some cases confirmed by Sannad, and considered permanent.

A Nemnuk is a fixed annual payment from any particular specified source, whether in money or kind.

An Itlákh is a payment either in money or kind from a public treasury or store. And a fixed annual payment (Nemnuk), from any public treasury, is peculiarly called an Itlákh Nemnuk.

A Nemnuk, therefore, is a grant conferred on any person as a fixed annuity, either from the Huzur treasury for which Sannads were not issued, or from those of the Mahíls, or out of any specified source of revenue, for which regular Sannads were usually granted. Nemnuks were usually granted, either on account of past or present services, or were fixed in lieu, or in part, of some other allowances formerly enjoyed. Their terms and duration seem to have depended very much on circumstances: such as were confirmed by Sannad were usually held to be permanent, though it would appear that during the late Peshwa's Government they were frequently reduced.

A detached village, which has by any circumstances been separated from the Mahál to which it originally belonged, is called Phulgám, and such villages in one district, or belonging to one person, are generally classed together as a Mahál, under the name of the Dhutgám of such a district, or person.

The allowances to Pagodas (Dewastán), or generally Itlákhs in money or kind, from the treasury of the districts, and the quantities of grain and other articles supplied, are expressed in the regular accounts; they are, however, not accurately fixed, but vary a little from year to year, as the expenses of the Pagoda may require, or other circumstances occasion; they seem, however, to be pretty constant, and very rarely to have been resumed, or even reduced. The articles supplied in kind are many and various: they are usually converted into money, at the average prices of the different years, from whence the particular accounts are taken; and the differences from year to year are so small as not to be worth anything.

(True extract),

(Signed) J. Macleod.

The Huzur Daftar is the records of Government, as registered by the Government officers. In it were kept all accounts of the receipt and expenditure of the revenues of the State, whether the realizations from the provinces or from whatever source, the expenses of troops, establishments, Ináms, and every species of grant, gift and money transaction whatever, excepting only the private affairs of the Prince, or such accounts as it suited not the interest of individuals in power to leave on record.

The Daftar was kept very complete till the time of Báji Ráv, whose arbitrary and capricious Government found little advantage in keeping a correct record of its proceedings ; and besides, in the farming system which he adopted the advantage of registering the acts of the revenue servants of Government was in a great measure lost as it existed under former Peshwas ; it was a very extensive establishment, consisting of about 200 Kárkuns, and divided into several departments for the various branches of business ; the whole was under the Huzur Fadnavis, and was generally distinguished into Chatle Daftar and Ek Berij Daftar, besides the Potnavi's Daftar, treasury, and other departments, not immediately connected with revenue accounts.

The establishment of the Chatle Daftars was always the Fadnavis, for the transaction of current business ; that of the Ek Berij Daftar was always at Puna, it being more particularly for the arrangement, registry, and deposit of accounts.

The business of the Chatle Daftar was distributed amongst the different branches, as the Fad, Beherá, Saranjám, etc.

The Fad was the immediate office of the Fadnavis, from whence were issued all grants, Sannads, and orders, and to which were rendered all accounts required for the information of the Fadnavis from the other departments. Here all accounts were examined and passed by the Fadnavis, and day-books or journals (Rozkirds) were kept of all transactions that occurred, of all sums paid or received, and of all grants or appointments made or resumed.

The Beherá department received the accounts from the districts, which were made up into official forms for the inspection of the Fadnavis, as Tállebands, Azmásh, Beherá, etc. The Tálleband was a complete abstract of the actual receipt and expenditure of the revenues for the past year; from it was framed the Azmásh, or estimate for the next or current year. This was a rough estimate compared with the Beherá, which was a corrected statement of all known receipts and of all fixed authorized expenditure, and formed the basis of collection for the current year.

The Saranjám department was charged with the accounts of all Saranjáms, Inâms, etc.; in short, all Dumállá whatever.

Besides these were the department of accounts generally (Aisál), of military expenses and contributions (Wári), and such like. These arrangements, however, varied with the pleasure of the Fadnavis or the business that might occur.

In the Ek Berij Daftar at Puna were received, arranged and deposited, all accounts from the other departments, and from them were framed abstracts of the total receipts, expenditures, and balances of Government on all accounts, for the year (called Tarjumá) also Khatávnis; which are abstracts of all kinds of expenditure arranged alphabetically under their proper heads, in the manner of a ledger; and, in short, the whole of the revenue and financial transactions of the State were registered and arranged, and their accounts deposited in this office.

The general contents of the Daftar under the

Peshwas may be described as follows, viz., all accounts rendered to the Government of the revenue and expenditure of the districts, with the settlements of them by Government; the accounts of districts rendered by the hereditary district officers, and those of villages by village officers, of farms, of customs, etc.; accounts of all alienations of the public revenue, whether Saranjám, Inám, or otherwise, of the pay, rights, and privileges of the Government and village officers; accounts of the strength and pay of troops, and the expenses of all civil, military, and religious establishments. In the Rozkirds were registers of all revenue transactions generally, together with all grants and payments, and more particularly the accounts of all contributions and exactions levied on foreign states, the whole of which were considered and exhibited in one comprehensive view in the Tarjumás. The records, however, were probably not complete to the extent described. It is said that Náná Fadnavis introduced the greatest improvements into the Daftar, as he did into the transaction of accounts in general, and during his administration, viz., from about 1765, with the exception of a few years up to 1796, it was kept with much regularity. From the accession of Báji Ráv the regular receipts and deposit of accounts in the Daftar was not only much neglected, but its establishment was almost entirely done away, and people were even permitted to carry away the records or do with them what they pleased. The Daftar was in consequence much mutilated, and thrown into great confusion.

After the occupation of Puna, in November, 1817, the records were found in different places, in a state of the utmost disorder; but considering all circumstances, tolerably complete for a period of 88 years—that is, from 1130 (ai) A.D. 1729 inclusive, up to the breaking out of the war, with the exception of a blank of about seven years, viz., from 1157 (1757) A.D. to 1163 (1762) A.D. inclusive, of which most of the records were burnt when Puna was taken by the Mogals; for the 27 years preceding this blank, the Daftar is moderately perfect, and for the 32 succeeding years up to 1179 (1796) A.D. the accession of Báji Ráv, the records are nearly complete, particularly from 1774, when Náná Fadnavis came into full power; but during the reign of Báji Ráv, the last 21 years, they are by no means full.

It is doubtful how far the accounts in the Daftar may be depended upon as true and candid statements; it is probable that they were often manufactured to answer the purpose of individuals; a very remarkable degree, however, of consistency and relative accuracy is to be found in the accounts for many years, such as must have required no small industry to effect, and the more ability if the statements are actually false.

Since the foundation of the Daftar establishments, under the Commission, the Daftar has been completely examined and arranged into separate districts, and mostly also into Parganás, and its arrangement by years also is in considerable progress. Full and complete statements of all allowances, as Saranjám (Fauz and Zát) Tainát and such like, have been made out, and also lists of all Ináms, Dewasthans, and Sáwanstán, Dharmádaws, Kittá, Wárshásan, Nemnuks, Nozinadárs, Khairáts, allowances to Pirs and Fakirs and Mosques, Bálpunwarshi, Máf, Bakshis, Dengi, Mezwáni, Garden and Sanadi lands, Wattan lands of Jamindárs, and for the Deccan, Karnátik, and Khandesh, and the Peshwa's Provinces in the Nizám's country, which have also been translated, and forwarded in Mahráttá and English to the collectors. Similar lists of the Konkan and Gujarát are in progress; the Daftars of the Konkan for the last ten years have been sent to Bombay. Abstracts of the produce, reductions, and net revenue of the whole country during the last year of Báji Ráv have been framed by districts, Parganás, and Mahâls, and in more than half the country by separate villages. For the purpose of authenticating the above lists, each item has been compared with the accounts of the two different periods, viz., the latest in Daftar, from whence it was taken, and another of from fifteen to twenty years preceding, and very often three or four different periods of accounts have been compared; the accurate correspondence which has been observed among them is very remarkable. In many cases the particular dates and circumstances of the original grants have been examined, and with a view to the final and ready adjustment of any disputed title, and to ensure immediate reference, an extract has been made from the Daftar, particularly the Rozkirds, of the date and authority of all grants whatever, and of all forfeitures or restorations of grants from the beginning of the Daftar to the year 1776, and is now in progress towards the present time. It is arranged alphabetically by the names of grantees, like native Khatáwni, containing under each the date, circumstances, and particulars of all Sannads, grants or allowances, that were made, resumed, or restored by Government. This has been a work of much labour, but when finished will form a table of authentic reference, by which any question or doubt, which may at a future time arise, can at once be settled.

Besides the records immediately connected with revenue, from which much matter still remains to be extracted, the Daftar contains many materials of curious general information. Thus the series of accounts of the districts and villages afford a view of the comparative state of cultivation and improvement, and assessment of the country at different times. Those of the armies and establishment, and particularly the Rozkirds, show the progress of the Mahráttá conquests and dominion, and the most important acts and events of their Government; and the Tarjummás furnish complete statements of their general wealth and resources.

(Signed) J. Macleod.
(True Copy.)
(Signed) J. Macleod.

Puna, 15*th September*, 1819.

Translation of a Yád of a Niwádepatra (Award).

Draught of a Niwádepatra to Mudoji Náik Nimbalkar, Deshmukh of Prant Phaltan.

You came to the presence at Purandhar, and stated as follows: 'My great-grandfather, Bijáji Náik, had four sons: the eldest Mahadaji Náik, the second Gokaji Náik, the third Wungaji Náik, and the fourth Modhaji Náik; three of these died without issue. Modhaji Náik had two wives, the elder Siwáw, the younger Jiwáw. First Jiwáw had a child, Janoji Náik, and afterwards Siwáw had a son, named Bijáji Náik. Madaji Náik, the eldest son of the first, Bijáji Náik, possessed the Jahagir of the Parganná of Khattaw, and other Mahals, and resided at the Tháná of Khattaw, which belonged to him. Madaji Náik took (the young) Bijáji Náik for his adopted son, and died at Gwalior. The Wattan and Jahagir were continued to Bijáji Náik, and afterwards the deceased Jhahoo Maharaj gave Rajis Bái in marriage to Modhoji Náik, son of Janoji Náik, and the

Maharáj desired Jánoji Náik's father to give him a village for his subsistence. His father, however, would not comply, but was offended, and went into the Mogal's country after him ; Jánoji Náik and his son Mudhoji Náik enjoyed the Jáhágir. At that time the Wattan was held by my Gumástá. I returned to my Wattan about twenty or twenty-two years after the death of the father of Bijáji Náik, in the Mogal's country, and during the lifetime of Mudhoji Náik, who then gave me in the Pagoda his sword and shield and place, as his elder, and was about to give up the Wattan to me when he died ; on this the deceased Màdho Ráv Pandit Pradhán confirmed to me my Wattan and Jáhágir, which I accordingly enjoyed for six or seven years. But during the troubles which occurred on the death of Náráyan Ráv Pandit Pradhán, Sagunábái, wife of Mudhoji Náik, got the Wattan and Jáhágir for herself, and now enjoys possession of them. But I am the elder in the Deshmukhi. I have never to this day shared my Wattan with any of my younger relations ; I make the main allowance for their support, but do not allow them to interfere. I now pray that orders may be given for my rights, which have existed for many years, being restored, and continued in the same way for the future.'

Mudhoji Náik bin Bijáji, with their seals, etc., addressed to Bijáji Náik bin Mahadaji Náik. Upon this an order was given to Sagunábái to send an agent on this affair to the presence, and Narshinw Ráv Konher was sent by her for this purpose. Narshinw Ráv Konher asserted that Madaji Náik had never adopted Bijáji Náik, that Mudáji Náik is the son, Bijáji Náik the younger brother of Janoji Náik, who was the father-in-law of the Bái, and the eldest son of the first Mudoji Náik, and Mudoji Nálk has therefore no claim to seniority. Having stated this, he produced a Muhuzar, with its seals, etc., naming Bijáji Náik bin Mudhoji Náik, upon which the papers of both parties were examined in the Huzur. Mijálos Mudhoji Náik produced his papers, and in his Rájpatra and Muhuzur appeared the name of Bijáji Náik bin Madaji Náik; and Narshinw Ráv Konher produced his Muhuzur, in which was written Bijáji Náik bin Mudoji Náik. As no decision could be formed from the papers of the two parties, therefore you (Mudoji Náik) were asked what is to be done now. On which you replied: 'Since no decision can be given on this Rájpatra and Muhuzurs, let the Deshpándes, Pátils, and Kulkarnis of the district be sent for and examined, and whatever decision is made on their evidence, that I agree to obey.' Narshinw Ráv Konher, having consulted with the Bái, answered: 'Since Modoji Náik says that Madaji Náik adopted Bijáji at Khattáw, and that he will prove this by the evidence of the inhabitants of Khattáw, this evidence I agree to;' on which an order was sent from Government with some messengers to Khattáw, who brought back some witnesses with them, and some others who happened to be here on their own affairs, were pointed out by you. At length twenty-six witnesses were examined, in the presence of both parties, in the temple of Sopándew. These witnesses deposed that Saguná Bái had given a letter to Bhikáji Mánkeshwar, and sent him to them (the witnesses) desiring them to make inquiry and inform her whether Mahadáji had adopted Bijáji Náik or not; and that Bhikáji Mánkeshwar had told them many matters besides, from which they understood the business. In reply to this, they wrote that they would not interfere in the business; that she would be informed of the whole by Bhikáji Mánkeshwar himself.

After this they (the deponents) came to Sáswad, when they took an Abhaya Patra (writing of security or indemnity) from Rájshri Mudoji Náik, who engaged, that as they had been brought to the presence to give evidence respecting his Wattan, should any trouble ever arise to them regarding the matter, he should be answerable for it; that the deponents had made out a writing amongst themselves (Sunepatra) that whatever Sultánji bin Manáji and Sultánji bin Baihiroji, Parture Deshmukhs, should say, they would all swear to; to this they all agreed. These papers they brought and produced to the Sarkár, upon which they were all closely cross-examined by the Sarkár in the following manner: 'What was the reason that you wrote these letters to Saguná Bái and the Náik, and made such an agreement amongst yourselves? what reliance can we now place on your testimony, without an oath? You must discard this paper of yours, and speak the truth.' They were then taken to the Mandap of three Sopándev at Sáswad, and interrogated in the following order: Roule Kási Deshpánde, Kussu Durgá Deshpánde, Jiwáji Kumbhár, Bahirji Kumbhár, Gangáji Kumbhár, Subhánji Lohár, Shaitu Máhár, Dawya Mahár, Satwá Mahár, Mulgá Mahár, Sukhoji Sutár, Sidhoji Sutár, Bhikáji Gurav, Tukoji Guniá, Chandá Náwri, Janoji Nawri, Anaji Chámbhár, Hiroji Chámbhár; these above eighteen persons gave a writing that they knew not whether Bijáji Náik adopted a son or not. Sultánji bin Bahirji Deshmukh, Tukoji vallad Ránoji Párit, Vyinkáji Ginnaji Palhi, Hussen Shaik Hazrat Kazi, Dongraji Naikwarri, Tazkhan Naikwarri, Bhik Joshi, in all eight persons, gave a writing, that their ancestors had told them that Mahadáji Náik had adopted Bijáji Náik. They were then asked what reason their ancestors had for telling them? On which the Deshmukhs wrote in answer, that a quarrel about their Wattan had formerly been referred to Phlátán, and that they had gone with their fathers to Bijáji Náik, when their fathers had told them. This evidence they subscribed; they were not influenced by the Samapatra which they had before signed. That the son had been adopted was true; upon this Narshinw Ráv Konher named seven witnesses of Khattaw, viz., Surerupji bin Fakirji Bhartare Deshmukh, Khando Jiwáji Deshpande, Gupur Sha wallad Maniksha Kazi, Lingoji wallad Rowloji Naykora, Baboo bin Bhikaji Parit, Sulan wallad Manekhan Moolana, Bhujanga bin Gangaji Shimpi, in all seven. These persons were examined in presence of the parties, in the Pagoda of Nanayndew, near Purandhar, in the following manner:

Surerupji bin Fakirji Bhartare Deshmukh deposed that a paper on this subject from Saguna Bái had been received in his village. That he had inquired of the Ballotis, etc., who replied in writing, that they knew not whether Mahadáji Náik had adopted Bijáji Náik or not. This very paper the witness produced; on which the witnesses were cross-examined, and again desired to speak the truth. The witnesses again gave a written declaration that they knew not, nor had their fathers ever told them, whether a son had been adopted or not. The substance of this evidence and of the Samapatra was mentioned to Narshinw Ráv Konher, and it was remarked that eight persons had given testimony against him, and not one for him; to which he replied: 'Of the twenty-six persons who had agreed to swear anything, eighteen have deposed to nothing, and eight have given evidence for the opposite party; but I will not admit their testimony unless the witnesses are brought to Jejuri, and sworn on the tortoise of the God; if he shall confirm their truth, then will I admit it, and I shall not desire to call any other witnesses from Phâltán.' A Razinama was required by Government to this effect. To this Konher also agreed, but said he was the elder party; that whatever the Sirkar ordered, he would readily obey; but that the Bái had not given any Takrar or Zamin, and therefore he could not now give a Razinama. The Razinama was not further insisted on, but as Narshinw Ráv had desired that the witnesses should be sworn on the tortoise at Jejuri, and promised to admit their evidence, and had requested the Sirkar's consent. Accordingly the twenty-five witnesses, out of the whole thirty-three, who could depose to nothing, were, with the consent of both parties, dismissed. The remaining eight were sent by Government, with Moro Harri, and also the Wattandars of some other Mahals, and one Mahráttá for each of the parties, to Jejuri. On their arrival there, in the presence of Bapuji Mahadew Namzada, and the Karkuns and Pátil and Kulkarni, and Pujaris, and Langis, etc., of Jejuri; and Magoji Taura on the part of the Bái, and on yours Ramsing, on the 15th Kartik, saw the witnesses bathed, and all the marks on their bodies were carefully noted, and the circumstances and marks, the occurrence or appearance of which on their bodies within ten nights was to prove the falsehood of their oath, according to custom, were also written down. Holy water was then placed on their heads, and sandal-wood on their forehead, and a necklace of flowers about their necks, and the witnesses were then separately cross-examined on the tortoise of the God, whether Mahadáji Náik had adopted Bijáji Náik or not, and adjured to speak the truth; on which they declared in writing on the tortoise that Mahadáji Náik had adopted Bijáji Náik; that this their forefathers had told them, and this was true. This writing was confirmed by the eight witnesses, then laid before the shrine of God, and brought back and given to Moro Harri. It was then brought down along with the witnesses to the village, in presence of the Mahráttás, and placed in the Kacheri and watched day and night for ten days; once a day the witnesses were brought before the God, and then carried to the Kacheri, and there in presence of the two Mahráttás examined whether any of the marks should be found on their bodies; on being found pure a certificate was written every day, and the witnesses were dismissed to their houses. In this manner the ten days passed. The witnesses underwent this trial according to their oath, and were proved true; and Moro Harri returned to the presence with the witnesses, and a certificate to the above effect from Bapuji Mahadew Namzada, and the Karkuns and Pátils and Kulkarnis of Jejuri Negoji; the Mahráttá on the part of Sagguná Bái had gone away privately on the seventh night of the trial.

The whole circumstances of the oath were investigated and duly considered in the Huzur Kacheri, in presence of Narshinw Ráv Konher, and it appeared clear that the witnesses from Khattaw had proved the truth of their oath on the tortoise of the God. The right of seniority of Mudhoji Náik to the Deshmukhi was clearly proved, and the claims of the Bái, asserted by Narshinw Ráv Konher, were proved to be false; on which this letter has been written to you that you may obtain possession. You are the chief Deshmukh of Pháltán; the whole of the Wattan of the Deshmukhi, with its rights, benefits, and privileges and Inam lands, and usufruct, etc., as they belonged to your ancestors, and have descended to you, are hereby confirmed to you and your heirs and descendants for ever; may you enjoy them, and live in peace and comfort. Saggunâ Bâi and your other cousins in the Deshmukhi must remain in subjection to your authority according to custom; they have no claim to superiority.

For this purpose this letter is written to the Náik.

In this manner also are written three other letters containing a brief extract of the above, viz., one to the Deshádhikári and Likhek Wartaman Bhawi, one to the Deshpánde, and one to the Mokaddams of the village: of these, copies only to be left with the above persons; the original to be delivered to Mudhoji Náik for his security.

The above four letters to be written dated 24th Julkhad Márgshirsh Shud San 1178, A.D. 1777-78. Puna, 10th September, 1819.

True translation. (Signed) J. MACLEOD.

(True copy.)

(Signed) J. MACLEOD.

TRANSLATION OF A SARAUNSH.

Jiwáji Bhandári *versus* Tátoji and Salwaji and Appaji Bhandári, in the matter of the right to the Chougulki and certain lands of the villages of Wadhu and Apte, in the Sarkár Junar. This dispute having been referred to the presence, and the *Takrár, Zamin and Pursish* of both parties having been taken in writing, and each having produced his papers in support of his case, the following is the Saraunsh Sur San 1169, A. D. 1768-69.

Declaration, security, and examination.

The substance of the Takrár, Pursish, of Tatoji, etc., Bhandáries :

Our original ancestor was Tanoji, whose son was Tátoji, whose son was Máwji, whose son was Tukoji, who had seven sons, four of whom left no issue; of the three others, the eldest was Máwji, the second Santoji, and the third Makáji. The descendants of Máwji are still in the country, and their history shall be inquired into and communicated. Of the second son, Santoji, are descended one son, Tátoji, whose son, Gomáji, had two sons, the elder of whom, Bhikáji, had three sons, Tátoji, Sambáji, and Máhadáji; of these Sambáji left no issue, the other two are still alive. Gomáji's second son, Makáji, had two sons, Firangoji and Gonji, who are still alive. Of Makáji, the third son of Tukoji, are descended a son, Dássoji, whose son, Rukoji, had two sons, the elder of whom, Makáji, had two sons, Satwáji and Subhánji, who are now alive.

This is our genealogy; we know of no common ancestor of Jiwáji's and ours. Our ancestor is Tánoji, and he had enjoyed from early times the Chougulki of Wadhu. The mother of Tánoji left her village and went to Nergursar. At this time Tánoji and his brother Mayáji were children; on their growing up, they began to inquire of their mother where their Wattan was. She replied, 'Our Wattan is the Chougulki and three Sajgannis of land of Wadhu.' On hearing this information, Tánoji went to Wadhu; but the villagers would not admit him; and Tánoji began to vent his revenge in acts of injury towards them. At this time Maske, Pátil of Apte, and Kále and Sewle, Pátils of Wadhu, joined together and rescued and brought back from Tánoji a herd of cattle which he was driving away; upon which Tánoji began to commit violence upon the people of Apte. After this Maske, Pátil of Apte, gave Tánoji 6 Sajgannis of Thall land, and having taken him over, made him his brother; and Kálle and Sewle, Pátils of Wadhu, gave Tánoji 4 Sajgannis of their own Thall land and a house, and talked him over, and restored to him also 3 Sajgannis of land, which had originally belonged to him. Tánoji and his brother Tátoji enjoyed the whole of these lands, until Tátoji was killed by Bhulláji Gumástá of Maske, Pátil of Apte; upon this Máwji, the son of Tátoji, fled to the country and died there, leaving a son Tukoji, who returned to Apte and obtained his Wattan and land and house from Dhuggeg Pátil. Kánoji Bhandári then complained that he was the descendant of Tánoji; but the whole village and the Kunbis of twelve other villages testified that Tukoji was the true descendant of Tánoji, and that Kánoji was not. A judgment was given, and a Mahajár (testimonial of right) of the Chougulki was given to Tukoji, and 1 Sajganni of land to Kánoji. From thenceforth, the Chougulki of Apte and 5 Sajgannis of land and a house have been enjoyed by the family; before Tukoji, the Chougulki of Apte did not belong to us.

Jewoji Bhandári is no blood-relation of ours. His ancestor, Ráhoji, and ours, Mahoji, had a dispute; since which time Ráhoji has possessed the Chougulki of Wadhu. Whether it belonged to them before Ráhoji, we do not know; nor whether Mahoji, son of Tukoji, enjoyed the Chougulki of Wadhu. But he certainly possessed and lived in the house, between the houses of two Sewles in Wadhu, and had 4 Sajgannis of land, but of which his ancestor had before given 9 Rukhás to Vetál; there remained 15 Rukhás of land, which Mahoji enjoyed. Ráhoji then began to quarrel with Mahoji about the land, saying that he was his brother, and ought to have half the land; both of them were much distressed by this quarrel. At length, Herji, Pátil of Wadhu, reconciled them to each other, and gave 8 Rukhás out of the 15 to Ráhoji, and the remaining 7 Rukhás were enjoyed by Mahoji. The certificate of this partition was lost, and Ráhoji began to complain again, on which Mahoji left the village, and is still in the country. One Sajganni of land of Apte had been given to Kánoji, besides which he had enjoyed for many years, from our grandfather, another Sajganni of Thall land.

During the reign of the Pádshás, the ancestor of Jiwji, his grandfather or great-grandfather, by name Kamloji, was a man of power, and had cultivated the whole of the lands of Wadhu and Apte. At that time Tashnif had been sent by the Pádshá to him for the Chougulki; of which half was given to Sewle Chougulki, and half kept by Kamloji, for this reason, that the daughter-in-law of Dhuggeg, who had been seized and carried off to the Mogal's Tánná of Sikápur, had been recovered and brought back by Kamloji, on which account he (Dhuggeg) had bestowed his Chougulki of Apte by writing on Kamloji, who therefore kept half the Tashnif; besides this, he had other claim of possession. A quarrel between his family and ours has existed in the village, but we have enjoyed possession. The village of Apte was given by the Sarkár to Gopál Ráv Barve. At that time Jiwji and Makáji cultivated our lands, and from that time our quarrel has continued.

Being questioned on the Takrár of Jiwji, Tátoji, etc., reply 'that on the quarrel between Jiwji's ancestors, Ráhoji and Mahoji, Ráhoji went through an ordeal in support of his being the true heir of Tánoji, and not Mahoji.' The circumstances of these are as follows:

Ráhoji and Mahoji, having quarrelled, went to Moheri, when the ordeal was undergone by Ráhoji's having rubbed over his hand the leaves of a Wanaspatti (plant). On this Mahoji went to Jiján at Sátárá, and brought an order from her to the village that the ordeal should be performed again; but Sewle Mokaddam having taken them both over, divided the 15 Rukhás of land of Wadhu equally between Ráhoji (and Mahoji); and of the 3 Sajgannis of land he gave 7½ Rukhás, in 15 Rukhás, to Mahoji, and also a house situated between the Sewles. The sons of these two lived in amity. Ráhoji was told that the papers respecting the Thall of Moheri and the other from Sátárá, and the papers respecting the 15 Rukhás of land, had been thrown into the Bimá; but whether they had been got from Dádji or not was unknown. We know not of any Mahajar respecting a dispute between Jiwji Bhandárri and Gunáji Bhandárri. From the time of ordeal the property of Wadhu only has been enjoyed by Jiwji, but none of Apte. Jiwji has no claims on Apte.

The substance of the Takrár and examination of Jiwji Bhandárri:

My ancestors were Sonáji and Kamloji, who were brothers. Sonáji had two sons, the elder Chahoji, and the second Mahoji. Chahoji had a son, Vittoji, whose son was Kintoji, whose son was Siwji, whose son was Somáji. Somáji had two sons, Ráhoji and Khiwji, who left no issue; but Ráhoji had five sons, Jiwji, Gogáji, Kamloji, Somáji, and Jiwáji. The eldest, Jiwji, had four sons, the eldest Paddoji, the second Yamáji, the third Kánoji, the fourth Bhánji; of them, three had no issue, but Yamáji had four sons, the eldest Udáji, the second Ránoji, the third Jiwji, the fourth Mavji, who had no issue. Gogáji, second son of Ráhoji, had four sons, Háwji, ..., Santáji, and Báwáji; Háwji had two sons, Tánáji and Yessáji; . . . . had two sons, Wálloji and Gunáji, who are both still alive; the third son, Santáji, had also two sons, Mankáji and Rághoji, who are also living; the fourth son, Báwáji, is still living. Kamloji, third son of Ráhoji, had four sons, one of whom died without issue; there remained three, Rámji, Máhadji, and Sambháji; Rámji had a son named Táwji, now living; Máhadji had three sons, one of whom is dead: the remaining two, Jánoji and Náwji, are still living; Sambháji had one son, Khandoji, who is also alive. Somáji, fourth son of Ráhoji, had four sons: 1st, Satwáji; 2nd, Subhánji; 3rd, Kussáji; 4th, Tánáji, all of whom are now alive. Jiwáji, fifth son of Ráhoji, had also four sons, Málji, Dháuji, Shetyáji, and Kauji, who are still living. Mahoji, second son of the original Somáji, had a son named Tátoji, who had a son named Mahoji, whose son was Kánoji, who died without issue.

The original Kamloji, the second brother, had a son named Rámji, who had a son, Mayáji, who had two sons, Kamloji and Báwáji, the former of whom died without issue; and Báwáji had two sons, Rámji and Máhadji, who both left the country. This is my genealogy.

My original ancestors, Somáji and Kamloji, had obtained 2½ Rukhás of land—altogether, 9 Cháhur of the village of Wadhu. Abbáji Pátil had given them this land, and the Chougulki of the village. Bhulle Pátil, of Apte, had given Sajgannis of land in

Wattan to them, in which Tánáji obtained the Chougulki, allowed his lands to fall waste, and brought from the Kallewárri Tukoji Bhandárri (a brother by surname) to assist him in the cultivation of the land, and gave him 7 Rukhás of his land of Wadhu; he also gave 7 Rukhás to Kánoji Bhandárri, and 6 Rukhás to Manáji Bhandárri, and 9 Rukhás to Tánáji Vitab, and 4 Rukhás to Kánaji Khosti. In this manner Kamkoji and Jiwji gave their lands to these five persons, and made them their brothers, but they were not relations by blood. After this there remained to themselves 12½ Sajgannis of land. Of this some more was given to persons of whom no heirs now remain. My great-grandfather, Ráhoji Bhandárri, also shared 6 Sajgannis of land of Apte, for the sake of maintaining its cultivation, in the following manner: To Jiwji, son of Kánoji, he gave 6 Rukhás; to Mawji, son of Tukoji, 9 Rukhas; to Gundji Bhandárri, his blood-relation, 6 Rukhás. After dividing the lands in this manner, Ráhoji kept the remaining 15 Rukhás for his own use. Since the administration of Dhábháre, Tátoji and Shahoji made a complaint, and seized and confined my grandfather and uncle, and commanded them to have no intercourse with Mukaji and Bhikáji. Since then the family have enjoyed possession, but the Tashnif has remained with the Pátil, which used formerly to be given to us. On a former occasion, when the Padsha's Tashnif was sent to Apte, my ancestor, Kamlaji, had a dispute with Sewle, saying that the half Chougulki was his, and he would take half the Tashnif, on which the question was taken up by caste at Tulapur, and the Pátil of Apte brought Sewle and Kamloji with him, as the Chougulkis, into the Pagoda; on which the Tashnif was equally divided between them. Formerly my ancestors left the country, at which time Hiskumi Bháû (nominal or assumed brother) Kánoji was at Apte; and Tukoji, coming from Wadhu, began to quarrel with him, calling himself the true descendant of Tánáji. This quarrel was settled in an assembly of twelve villagers, which decided that Tukoji was the rightful heir of Tánáji, and not Kánoji; and accordingly a Mahajar was given to Tukoji, after which, for five or ten years, I know not whether he enjoyed possession or not. Hearing that the Mahajar had been granted, my great-grandfather, Ráhoji, came to the village, and began to quarrel with Mahoji, the son of Tukoji. The dispute lasted for five or ten years without any benefit. At length he established his right by performing the ordeal at Moheri. The certificate of the ordeal, and of the whole affair, which were granted on the occasion were partly spoiled in a box. Mahoji was expelled from Wadhu, and received 9 Rukhás of land in Apte. Since then another dispute has occurred—the Mahajar of that occasion is in my possession—and from that time until the time of Krisnáji Dhábháre he had not possessed the Chougulki of Apte, but now Dhábháre has unjustly given it to him.

The Sadipatra (document in evidence) of Tátoji Bhandárri:

1st. A Mahajar (award), dated Shak 1558, Dhátri Samwattchare 1st Ashwin Shud, assembled at the village of Apte twelve persons, named by the caste; by whom this Mahajar is written. That Tukoji and Kánoji Bhandárri have a dispute regarding the Chougulki; both their statements have been heard, the Mukaddam and all the Dyheyum (Wattandárs of the same caste) and Babule, of Apte, deposed that Tukoji was the true and lineal descendant of Tánoji. Rupáji Bhandárri deposed that Kánoji was not the true and lineal descendant of Tánoji, and Kánoji himself confessed that he was not the true and lineal descendant of Tánoji. Upon this the Chougulki and land of Apte was given to Tukoji, and to Kánoji 6 Rukhás of the land and a house.

Both parties are to abide by this decision, which was granted 132 years ago.

2nd. A letter dated Shak 1641, Vichári Samwattchare, 17th Kártik Wadya, from the Mukaddams and others of Apte, to Bhikáji and Mákaji Bhandárri: 'You are our rightful brother Wattandar; you have been obliged to leave the village by the persecutions that have been raised against you. We have now discovered that your persecutions have been unjust. If anyone shall again trouble you on this subject, we shall have him punished. Pursue the business of your calling in peace. Your welfare or misfortunes shall be held common with our own. Whoever shall prevent or falsify this, shall be accounted false to his caste, and an offender against the State. We shall secure you from any harm. Whoever shall act contrary to this, may the curse of God fall upon him.'

3rd. Letter from Nágoji Deshmukh, to Tejoji, Pátil of Wadhu Budruk: 'You have written to me about the lands of Mahoji and Ráhoji; when both these persons were at Junar, Ráhoji gave a Katbá, according to which I gave a writing to Mahoji, why is Rávji disputing now? His complaint must be without cause; let Mahoji sow the land which he has begun to cultivate, and then send them both to Junar. I will settle their business.'

4th. Samápatra (declaration of the proceedings of an assembly) Shak 1605 Raktákshi, Samwattchare

9 Jeshta Wuddha, at Apte, San 1093, in an assembly of eight persons (named) where is a quarrel about a house and land between Ráhoji and Jatuji Bhandári. Ten persons and others being assembled, declare, 'Our ancestors have never mentioned to us anything about the family or ancestors of Ráhoji Bhandári, nor have we ever in our lives known anything about them. We swear by our forefather and the God to prevent any injustice in this matter.'

Copy of a petition of Sherekár Gomáji Bhandári: 'There is a quarrel between Jiwaji Bhandári and me, respecting our Wattan of Wudhu; on which we both went through ordeal at Moheri, but Matushvar Ai Sáhib sent for us both, and having annulled the former ordeal, ordered us to perform another before the whole of our village; when we returned to our village, the villagers restored to me my lands and house. But now he has taken my house and land from me, and has driven me from the village. I therefore beg that the villagers would assemble, and *inquire into my case.*'

The Sadakpatr of Jiwáji Bhandári.

1st. Letter from the Mukaddams and Shaite Mahájans of Moheri village, Taraf Gunjun Máwál, to some Pátils, Mukaddams, and Shaite Mahájans of the village of Kesnand, in the Puna District: 'You have sent to our village Rávji Bin Somáji Bhandára, complainant; and Mahuji Bin Tukoji Bhandára, defendant, both Wudrook Turuf Pabul, with a letter, requesting us to settle the quarrel which these two people have about some land. We have, therefore, assembled ten persons of the caste to inquire into the affair, to whom Rávji has given him a Tukrar, saying that he had brought Mahuji from Majri, given him seven Rukhás of land, and made him his brother, and that Mahuji is not the descendant of Tánaji.'

'On the other side, Mahuji stated in writing that he was the descendant of Tánáji, being the fourth generation from him.'

On hearing these statements all of us endeavoured to persuade them both to submit to the decision of the caste, to which Ráhoji agreed; but Mahuji would not consent, but appealed to the ordeal. Mahuji was then desired to perform the ordeal, that he was the descendant of Tánáji; but he replied that the complainant Ráhoji ought to do it, to which Ráhoji consented; and on Friday, the 28th of the month Jamádilával, his nails were pared close and his hands fastened up in bags. On Sunday he took out the Ruwa (a small piece of metal at the bottom of a vessel of hot oil) declaring that Mahuji was not the true descendant of Tánáji. On Tuesday, the 25th of Margshirsh Shudha, his hands were examined, and Ráhoji proved to be true. The whole of the Wattan land and possession of Tánáji whatever must be given to Ráhoji; Mahuji has no right to them. Dated 1607.

2nd. Muhuzur Shak 1607, Krodhan Sawantsar, assembled at that village of Wudhu Budruk T. Pábál, San 1095. Rayats of the caste (named) the Patil and other villagers, in all twenty-four persons. These persons being assembled to investigate the case, Gomáji bin Mahoji Bhandári brought a paper from the Deshmukh, desiring that the villagers of the caste should be assembled and do justice to both the persons concerned, and settle the dispute, and a Parvángi from Ali Shaw Fazil Khán Daroghá to the same effect, Jiwáji bin Ráhoji Bhandári brought a Parvángi from Khojá Sanpak, Foujdár of Tháná Kougam, directing the lands to be confirmed according to the ordeal which had been performed at Moheri, and not permit Tátoji to interfere, and that the Parvángi which Tátoji had got before was null. The assembly having examined the above papers, sent Visáji Dádu Kulkarni to Yeswant Ráv Sáwant, Sirojdár at Koregám, to tell him that the Deshmukh had called an assembly of the caste to inquire respecting the Wattan and lands of the Bhandáris, but that an order was necessary for them to proceed to a decision; on which he gave orders for the assembly to decide according to justice, and the whole of the villagers, Mukaddams, and Sakal Prabhu Thalwáis and twelve Balotes of Apte, assembled together to investigate the case. Both persons produced their papers as follows :

Gomáji bin Mahuji produced the Muhuzur which had been given at Apte. Jiwáji bin Ráhoji produced the Muhuzur of the ordeal at Moheri, and also the decision of an assembly of three or four villagers at Apte. Having examined all the papers, and taken security from both parties, viz., for Jiwáji Rávji, Chougule of Koregám; and for Gomáji Subáji Siwbá, Chougule of Apte, that each would submit to whatever the assembly directed, both gave in Rájinamas and Tukras in writing. The witnesses were then examined before the whole of the assembly standing in the Murkkund (a circle described on the ground to represent a hill), with a cow's skin on their heads, and gave testimony as follows:

1st. Siwle Mukaddam deposed that the origin of the family is not of this place, but of Apte—Ráhoji had Mirás land in Wudhu. That on account of some injuries committed by Tánáji he had talked them over, and gained his friendship, by giving him his daughter, and nine Rukhás of land, in Mirás, out of his own; that besides this, he had given him nothing. That he knew not what relation this person was to

Tánáji; that he knew of the Muhuzur which had been granted at Apte, and also of the ordeal.

2nd. Tej Patil Argare Mukaddam deposed that there was a quarrel amongst the Bhandáris at Apte, and that a Muhuzur had been given in his name regarding it; that then Kánoji used to call himself Gumáshtá; but this was proved false. Kánoji took the hand of Tukáji in asseveration of Tukoji's being the descendant of Tánáji; at this time Katroji's family were dead and gone; afterwards an ordeal took place, in which Ráhoji was proved true, and Mahuji false.

3rd. Santáji bin Khandoji Dhigge, of Apte, deposed that Siwle had brought Tukoji Bhandári from Kellewádi; that in their village (Apte) Tánáji had a son named Kankoji, who gave Tukoji into his (the deponent's) hand, saying, 'This is my brother.' That Tukoji and Kánoji afterwards quarrelled, and that an assembly of twelve villagers gave a Muhuzur; that all this he knew to be true. That Ráhoji was not there at that time; that the ancestors of Kánoji and Tukoji were not connected, nor settled Mirásdárs; that the Dhigge were masters of the Mirás land, but that Ráhoji enjoyed the benefit since the ordeal at Moheri.

4th. Apáji Patil Dhigge of Apte, deposed that he had committed thefts in Wudhu, which had been traced to his forefather, that people had been sent to seize the thief, and that he had delivered Tátoji to them. That a fine was exacted of Tátoji, which he demanded of his (the deponent's) ancestor, on which he murdered him. That Tátoji had a grandson named Tánáji, whom he had brought to a reconciliation and given him 6 Sazgannis Thall land out of his own, and made him next in rank to Siwle. That after-

28—2

wards Kánoji Bhandáre was going to leave the village; but that he had given him 6 Rukhás of Thall, and kept him. When the whole of the land was in cultivation, he gave Kánoji 6 Sazgannis of land; that then Kánkoji, son of Tánáji, came from Wudhu, and bringing the Patil and Balotes, brought Tukoji from Kellewádi, and gave him into his (the deponent's) ancestor's hand. That Kánoji and Tukoji began to quarrel about the garden lands of Kánkoji, and that time Tukoji was proved to be the true descendant of Tánáji, and Kánoji's pretensions to be false. That the brother of Ráhoji was one of the assembly who gave this decision—that seven generations have seen no ancestors of Ráhoji. He has only enjoyed possession since the ordeal.

5th. * The Thalwáiks and Sáthi Prajá of Wudhu and the Dhigges and Chougules of Apte deposed that they know not who was the descendant of Tánáji. They knew of the Muhuzur which had been given at Apte by the assembly of the Patils of twelve villagers, on the dispute between Kánoji and Tukoji. At that time Ráhoji's ancestor was not in the village: but on Ráhoji's coming to the village, he fixed upon Resnund, for his Pancháyat; and then having taken security, they referred the case to Moheri, where Ráhoji performed the ordeal and was cleared, and Mahuji proved false; that all this they knew.

Having weighed this evidence, it did not appear to agree in any way with Mahuji's Sukar. Ráhoji's ancestor was not in the village when the Muhuzur was given at Apte. When he came to the village and began his dispute, it was settled by ordeal, on which Ráhoji was proved true, and Mahuji false. Of this the evidence is clear. The Muhuzur of the

* The Wattandárs and all the villagers.

assembly of Moheri, which Gomáji has, is annulled; the villagers knew that Mahuji was unjustly accused. Jiwáji bin Ráhoji has enjoyed his Wattan since the ordeal, and Mahuji has no ground of complaint against him. The ancestors of Ráhoji did with their own hands, and out of their own pleasure, give 9 Rukhás of Apte and 7 Rukhás of Wudhu, which they let Mahuji enjoy in comfort; besides this, he has no claim to the house and land and Chougulki of the two villages. Tánáji is the original Wattandár; an ordeal has been undergone for the Chougulki and house and lands of the villages. The whole Wattan and lands and house above mentioned are Ráhoji's, and let Jiwáji enjoy them.

3rd. Jáminkatbá of Resnund Santoji Jádhav of Kesnand, security for Ráhoji; Newji Arguwra of Wudhu Budruk, security for Mahuji.

4th. * Niwádepatra Shak 1623, Ursish Savantchari, 17th October, Wadhya, dated Tulápur. Assembled seven persons of the caste (named) who having deliberated, have decided that Bábji Siwlá and Mahadji Siwlá, Chougulas of Apte, and Kamláji Bhandári, of Apte, have come to us and preferred for decision a dispute between them, respecting the Chougulki of Apte—and have given a Rájinámá and Katbá, that they agree to the true evidence of the Mukaddams of Apte, given in the Pagoda. Upon this Khetji, Patil of Apte, went into the holy Pagoda, and took them both by the hand, in asseveration that they were both his Chougulás by right, an inheritance and descent: any future interference with this decision will be in vain.

Parwáná under seal of Jurjarul Mulk Myrul Mabhi, Nawáb Assutkhán, dated 7th of the Moon of the month Safar el Muzafar San 27, to the Gumástás,

* Award.

and Jahagirdárs, Deshmukhs and Deshpandis, Mukaddams and Muzafars of Pábul, Sarkár Jumar. Be it known that Rávji wallad Somáji Bhandári, of Wudhu, in the above-mentioned district, has come and complained 'that the office of Chougule has belonged to my family for many generations, but now Tátoji, the son of Tukoji Bhandári, of Apte, supplanted me by violence and injustice: therefore it is written that the said Tutoji has by deceit and fraud carried away the Sannads, and is not to be trusted, and according to the Hindu Sannad under the signature of the Mukaddams and Shuityes and Muhuzurs of Moheri, the right of Chougulkar of the above-mentioned village has been confirmed to the said Ráhoji; that whatever rights or privileges belong to that situation are to be restored him. You are therefore desired to restore him to his rights forthwith, and to obey this order without reply or delay.

Having thus weighed and considered the Takrár, and Pursish, and papers of both parties, it appears by the evidence of both that they are not of the same family, but only brothers by surname. The Wattan land of Wudhu has existed for many years. Tánáji obtained the land of Apte and half the Chougulki. This point is asserted by Jiwáji only. On examining the actual state of possession, it appears by the papers that both have had possession at times in both villages; but the possession of Jiwáji in the village of Wudhu seems to have been more permanent, as it appears that Ravji's descendants have enjoyed uninterrupted possession of the Wattan and lands of Wudhu since the quarrel between Ráhoji and Mahoji Bhandári, and the ordeal which was undergone. In the Shak 1607, Gomáji made an attempt to dispute the point; but this being proved false, no dispute has occurred since. The descendants of Ráhoji, down to the present Jiwáji, have held undisturbed possession of the Wattan of Wudhu, and this Tátoji does not now dispute; but Jiwáji disputes and claims the Chougulki and land of Apte, and therefore it is that Tátoji asserts a right to the Wattan of Wudhu. Both Ravji and Kamláji formerly enjoyed the Wattan of Apte, and the dispute between these two persons has been handed down till now. This dispute happened during the administration of Dhábáre. Tátoji produced the papers, but Dhábáre would not dispense justice, the prayers being only on one side of the question; from that period Tátoji's descendants have enjoyed uninterrupted possession. This appears to be the true state of the case; but Jiwáji says that Dhábáre unjustly confused the lands. It appears, however, that this enjoyment of Wattan of Apte is one confirmation of the rights of Tátoji; another confirmation is the Muhuzur, which was given 132 years ago, by the assembled villagers of Apte and twelve other villagers, in the dispute between Tukoji and Kánoji, deciding that Tukoji was the rightful heir of Tánáji: from this and other papers it appears that this dispute is of many years' standing. The village assembly decided that Kánoji was not the descendant of Tánáji; if Tukoji then had been under similar circumstances with Kánoji, how could they have decided that he was the rightful heir of Tánáji, but by examining and comparing the Muhuzur of the year (Shak 1607). The evidence of the villagers at that period differ from that given in Shak 1558. In the Shak 1607, the villagers of the two villages gave their evidence according to the best of their recollection and belief, but the substance of it is contradictory and inconsistent. The witnesses do not seem to have agreed with each other. In the Muhuzur of Shak 1558, the particulars of the evidence of each village are not given; but Kánoji Bhandári himself confessed the very point in dispute, viz., that Tukoji was the true heir of Tánáji. This being the case, what ground could he have for dispute at all? On minutely examining this Muhuzur, it appears that no cross-questioning or due examination of the witnesses took place. They all said the same at once, and the Muhuzur was made without further inquiry or investigation. But Jiwáji also allows that this Muhuzur was given, but that his ancestor was in another country at the time. When Kánoji began the dispute, Jiwáji and Kamloji, by the desire of the villagers, brought Tukoji from Kellewádi, and the villagers, believing from the circumstance that he was their brother, declared that he was of the family of Tánáji. Looking, therefore, to the matter of ordeal, we have the certificate from Moheri, the place where the ordeal was undergone, by which it appears that the nails of Ráhoji were pared off three days before, and bags put over his hands; that on Sunday he performed the ordeal, that on Tuesday his hands were examined, and his truth proved; but to this Tátoji objects, that he rubbed his hands with the juice of a Wanaspatti (plant), and was thus enabled to undergo the trial. On the other hand, many ordeals have been performed at Moheri, and have been conducted with fairness and justice; how should any trick have been allowed in this instance? Tátoji's assertion of Ráhoji's having rubbed the juice of the Wanaspatti over his hands appears false. That the ordeal was undergone is manifestly established by the papers, as well as the admission of both parties. In short, the ordeal was performed because no just decision had been given upon the evidence of the villagers; falsehood was proved, and the possession on both villages confirmed to Ráhoji. Since then Gomáji, the descendant of Mahoji, again made a complaint which was proved false, and a Muhuzur given to this effect. Tánáji himself made the Wattans of both villages; but Tukoji says that he only reviewed that of Wudhu, and obtained for the first time that of Apte. Ráhoji, however, established by ordeal in the quarrel with Tátoji's ancestor Mahoji, that he, and not Mahoji, was the true descendant of Tánáji, and it was decided that Ráhoji should enjoy Tánáji's Wattan of both villages. Mahoji is not the descendant of Tánáji, and therefore has no claim to the Wattan of either village. This fact has long been decided.

Tátoji now wishes to have the village assembly again called, evidence examined, and a fresh decision passed; but as an ordeal has been undergone, it is not proper that any further investigation should now take place. Since the Gods have signified their decision on the result of the ordeal, what would the words of men avail? We have just seen that the judgments of the village assemblies at two different times had been contrary to each other, and that an ordeal was then resorted to; after this, to send for witnesses and enter into a fresh investigation would be useless. By the Muhuzur of Shak 1558, Jiwáji's ancestor was not proved false in the dispute, nor were they proved false at any time in any subsequent dispute between them and the ancestors of Tátoji; but the ancestors of Tátoji were proved false. The Muhuzur which was granted in favour of Kánoji during the absence of Jiwáji's ancestor, was an irregular intemperate proceeding. However, had no ordeal taken place, this Muhuzur must have been an authority; but it was at once annulled by the result of the ordeal. That Tátoji should have unjustly, and by force, enjoyed the Wattan of Apte after the ordeal is proved by its result to have been improper.

(True translation)

(Signed) J. MACLEOD.

'Puna, 18*th September*.'

(True copy)

(Signed) J. MACLEOD.

TRANSATION OF A SÁRÁUNSH, 1819.

Sakárám Rámchandra Patwardhan *versus* Govind Viswanáth Patwardhan, in a dispute respecting property. These two persons having written and given in their declarations and securities, and produced their documents in evidence, and given in a list of the names of a Pancháyat by which they agreed to abide, this Pancháyat, having investigated the affair, has drawn up the following abstract.

Sakárám Rámchandra complains: 'Shrimant Rájeshri Bábásáheb' (the Peshwa) 'gave me on the occasion of a Shráddh, a Dakshaná of 2,200 rupees, and desired me to go and build a house at Phulgam. This money my uncle Govind Patwardhan lodged for me in the hands of Janobá Ránade, at 10 annas interest. Of this I have received 427-3-0 rupees, and a balance of 1,772-13-0 rupees is due as follows: viz., by Janobá Ránade, 1,192-14½-0 rupees, and Govind Pant Patwardhan, 579-14½-0 rupees. This balance is due by them both, and I now desire an order that the part of it which has been received by Govind Pant may be inquired into and settled.' Dated Phálgun Waddya, 10 Shak 1740. The respondent, Govind Viswanath Patwardhan, answers: 'My nephew Sakárám Rámchandra received this money from the Sarkár to build a house at

Phulgam Apte, and it was lodged in the shop of Janárdhan Ránade. In the month Márgsirsh, Rájeshri Hari Bhán Bhat took me with him to the house of Bálláji Pant Kálle; a Pancháyat was there held, and receipt for the money was taken in name of Sakárám Rámchandra; the receipt, which was in my name, was given back to the person (Janárdhan Ránade). Out of this money I had spent some, on account of which I gave back the receipt which I had received from Rámchandra Viswanath, deceased (father of the complainant), for one-half of my dwelling-house in Puna, valued at 700 rupees, which he had purchased. The Pancháyat further decided that Sakárám Rámchandra should pay me 167-8-0 rupees, which I had advanced to him at Urawri Ambegám, and that I should pay 197-8-0 rupees. This was the decision of the Pancháyat, and the papers to this effect are with Sakárám Rámchandra. I had given up half the house, which he still possesses.' Dated Phálgun Wadhya, 10th Shak 1740.

The Pancháyat deliberated on the declarations of the parties as follows: Under the former Government Báláji Pant Kálle Nisbat Gokhle having named and assembled a Pancháyat, it had decided that Govind Pant should repay whatever money he had taken out of the sum belonging to Sakárám Rámchandra, which he had lodged in the hands of Janárdhan Ránade; and further had, in presence of both parties, decided that Govind Pant should pay 946-1½-0 rupees, of which sum he paid to Rámchandra 698-7-0 rupees; the balance, 647-10½-0 rupees, remains to be paid to Sakárám Pant by Govind Pant. A certificate of this settlement was made out, to which Govind Pant subscribed, and this ought to be complied with; but Govind Pant refuses, and says that he has a written claim of 167-8 rupees against Sakárám Pant from the year (Shak) 1734. On inquiring into the truth of which it appears that Sakárám Pant had owed to Govind Pant 250 rupees, and that an obligation to that effect had been given by Sakárám Pant, dated 10th Shak Márgsirsh Shak 1737; but that the debt had been settled by Sakárám Pant, and his note received back. The above claim of Govind Pant is antecedent to this settlement, and yet no mention of it appears; and the writing itself is incorrect, nor was there any mention of it in the obligation to Sakárám Pant. Four of the Pancháyat accordingly recommended that Bálláji Pant Kálle should be asked about the business, and according to his answer both parties should abide. Upon this Bálláji Pant Kálle was sent for to the Adálat, where, in presence of the parties and Pancháyats, Bálláji Pant Kálle and Bájibhat Kelkar declared in the Huzur Kacheri that a Pancháyat had been assembled by them, and that it had rejected the claim of 167-8-0 rupees. This claim then is false. This being the case, Govind Pant must therefore pay to Sakárám Pant 247-8-0 rupees, besides interest. The members of both parties in the Pancháyat subscribed to the above decision, viz:

Wáman Shástri Sáthe, Bápu Chimnaji Thatte, Balkrishna Gangádhar Joshi, Denkar Annandráv Joshi, in the manner the members of both parties decided that Govind Pant should pay the above balance to Sakárám Pant. Dated 4th of May, 1819.

Confirmed. (Signed) W. J. LUMSDEN.

(True translation)

(Signed) J. MACLEOD.

Puna, 19*th December*, 1819.

(True copy)

(Signed) J. MACLEOD.

MINUTE BY THE PRESIDENT,

EXTRACTED FROM 'EAST INDIA PAPERS,'
VOL. III. pp. 697—701.

MINUTE BY THE PRESIDENT,

EXTRACTED FROM 'EAST INDIA PAPERS,'

VOL. III. pp. 697—701.

1. THE Surat district presents more variety of surface than those hitherto mentioned. The eastern Parganas belong to the hilly and jungly country that extends to the Ghats; those in the south partake of the same character; the rest is flat and in many parts fertile, but a large portion of it is covered with babool-bushes and wild date-trees: nearly one-third of the whole district is waste. The eastern part of the district is inhabited by Dublas otherwise resembling the Bhils, but remarkable for their peaceful and inoffensive disposition. The other inhabitants of the collectorship, excluding the city, are Kanbis and Kolis, Mastans and Bhathelas (or caste of Brahmans), with some Parsis, Bohoras, and Rajputs.

2. There are no Girasias or Mevasis in the district. One or two chiefs of Bhils, nominally dependent on Rajpipla, and some others further south, who seem nearly or entirely independent, have sometimes plundered the district, but are generally restrained by fear. Three Rajput Rajas occupy portions of the jungle to

the east of the Zilla. The first of them, the Raja of Mandvi, has a country about eighteen kos long and ten broad: half of it is open, and his principal town contains about 2,000 houses; the rest is jungle, inhabited by predatory Bhils. His revenue is about 180,000 rupees, 80,000 of which is giras, collected from the British and Gaikwar's territories. He pays a tribute of 60,000 rupees to the British Government.

3. The Raja of Bansda's country is of less extent and more jangli; the inhabitants are Dublas and Dhodias. His revenue is about 60,000 rupees; he pays a tribute of 7,800.

4. The Raja of Dharampor's territory is about thirty kos long and twenty broad: the whole is a thick forest, with scarcely any cultivation. Some of the inhabitants are Dhodias, but by far the greatest proportion are Kokanéas, a tribe resembling the Dhodias, but speaking the language of the Konkan, from whence they originally came. His revenue is about 140,000 rupees. The British Government has Chokis throughout his country, for the purpose of collecting customs.

5. The Navab of Surat is the only chief with any independent authority within the district, and his only extends to his own dependents. He has only 1,600 Bighas of land, about 300 Rayats, 200 armed attendants, and 150 servants and slaves.

6. There is a good deal of Vanta land and pecuniary payments to Girasias. In both cases the payments are fixed, and they are made by the collector to the proprietors, who reside in Rajpipla, and other adjoining districts, and whose outrages and exactions at one time greatly disturbed the district. Most of these pay a Salami, or quit-rent, which is levied direct from the Rayats. The principal other alienations are Vazifa lands, which are managed by the owners, and pay a

Salami or otherwise according to the tenure. The Talpad land is held on different tenures: 1st. That of Khatebandi, here called Japti, is very prevalent. The Japti Rayat has a right to retain his ground, and his rent ought not to be raised; but this last privilege appears to have been little attended to. He pays a higher rent than other Rayats; but except in the neighbourhood of the city, he is entitled to his trees and to a portion of grass-land rent free. 2nd. There is another tenure, called hunda, which resembles that last mentioned; except that the Rayat holds the whole of the lands for a certain sum, and not for a separate rent on each Bigha. In some Parganas it is originally formed by the division of a village in the same manner as is usual among Bhagdars; but there is no mutual responsibility as in Bhagdar villages, and the division once made, the sharers hold exactly on the terms of Khatebandi. To the southward the term Hunda applies to any land paid for in the lump. 3rd. The rest are Ganotias or annual leaseholders, who, though never expelled from their lands, change a good deal from field to field and village to village every year. 4th. Uparvadias, who live in one village and cultivate the lands of another, are particularly common in this district. 5th. Some of the ill-cultivated lands in the east pay an Udhar Fala, or an equal sum on each Bigha; and 6th. Some pay a certain sum on each plough.

7. The system of collection in the Surat district is now almost entirely Rayatwar, but this improvement is very recently introduced. Before we got this district, and for a long time after our acquisition of it, the country was completely in the hands of the Desais, who considered their possession so permanent that each family partitioned its Parganás among its members, like the Patels of a Bhagdar's village. Every Desai

managed the village of his own Bhag as he pleased, and in general they displaced the old Patels, and carried on even the interior management of each village by means of their own agents, who were called Talukdars. The Desai was thus the perfect master of the people, without anyone to check him. The mode of settlement of the revenue was for the Mamlatdar, and in our time for the collector, to send for the Desai and make as good a bargain as he could with him for the year's revenue of his Pargana. The Desai then apportioned the sum to be paid among all the villages of the Pargana, and the Talukdars (or, where there was one, the Patel) divided the assessment among the Rayats. By this plan the collector made his assessment entirely in the dark; and, although it was his intention not to increase the revenue, unless where there was an increase in the cultivation, yet the want of information on his part, as well as the fraud of the Desai, often operated to raise the Bighoti of the old lands. They, indeed, had no protection against the exactions of the Desai, if he chose to complain to the collector, except an appeal to the Talati's accounts, by which his own ignorance of his rights rendered him little able to profit, and which could not be much relied on, in consequence of the dependence of the Talati on the Desai. By the present mode of assessment every Rayat attends at the Kamavisdar's Kacheri. His land and rent for the preceding year are ascertained in his presence from the Talati's books. If he should wish to take up more land, or to throw up part of what he already has, or if it should be necessary to increase or diminish the rent of any portion of his lands, which he may have changed from common lands to garden lands, or *vice versâ*, the requisite alterations are made and agreed to.

If none of these changes are required, he holds the same land on the same rent as the year before. In either case he receives a Pottah under the seal of the Kamavisdar; a paper specifying the lands and rent of each Rayat in the village is also signed by the collector and deposited with the Talati. Each Rayat then becomes security for his neighbour's payment of the revenue; but this ceremony is reckoned nearly nugatory. The Patel also furnishes security (generally that of another Patel) for his not embezzling the collections. There is, then, no more to do till the revenue comes to be paid. Formerly two-thirds of the revenue was paid before the crops were ripe, and the money must have been borrowed at heavy interest by the Rayats; but now no demand is made until the crops are cut. One-half is then paid before the grain can be removed; the rest is paid after the sale of the whole or part of the produce. When any failure has taken place, a remission is made to the individual sufferer after an examination of his field by a Government officer.

8. This system was first introduced in the year 1817-18. There are several Parganas to which it was only extended during the last revenue year, and in some it has not yet been completed. Each man's land was measured, and his rent fixed at the sum which he had paid the preceding year. The great advantage of this plan is the clear view which it gives the collector of the real state of his district, thus enabling him to adapt any increase or remission of the revenue to the actual circumstances of each individual, and also putting it in his power to detect and check any undue exaction which may be practised upon the Rayat. A great objection to it is, that it lessens the power and consequence of the Patel; but this was not felt in the Surat district, where, in consequence of the usurpations

of the Desais, the office of Patel had scarcely an existence. In Bhagdar villages, where the Patidars are numerous, the introduction of the Raaytwar settlement is productive of much hardship and of no advantage; but there were scarcely any villages of this description in the old Surat district. In Olpad, where they were more numerous, more inconvenience must have been felt. The Rayatwar settlement may also prevent the employment of large capitals in improvements and new cultivation; but the opposite system does not appear hitherto to have been attended with that advantage in Surat, as almost all wells and tanks have been made either by Government or the Rayats. The establishment of Patels in the plurality of the villages is one of the advantages of the new system; but the want of experience of those functionaries, and perhaps the smallness of their allowances, have occasioned frequent changes and removals, which are against the respectability of the body. Nothing can be more complete than the state of the Talati's books, which contain every point of information contemplated by the regulations. These remarks relate exclusively to the regular land revenue; there are other taxes, the chief of which are the Abkari and the taxes on trades, which call for no observation.

9. If I were to decide on the present condition of the people in this collectorship, I should pronounce it to be very much depressed. The Rayats seem to be ill-clothed and ill-lodged, and although some parts of the district are highly productive, I should think that in others the cultivation was very imperfect. Land that has been in use for a few years is so exhausted as to be considered unfit for cultivation. From this, or some other cause, the Pargana of Chowrasi, contiguous to the populous city of Surat, is the worst cultivated in the district; and

this is the more remarkable as the Vazifa lands in the same neighbourhood are in a high state of improvement. These evils are by no means to be ascribed to the present system; on the contrary, I am persuaded that the measures now in progress will go far to relieve us from the system which we inherited from our predecessors. The great obstacle will be the extreme heaviness and perhaps the inequality of the assessment. Mr. Morrison has endeavoured to correct this by reducing the revenue in some cases where it appeared to weigh with particular severity; in other places he has promised to lower the assessment if the inhabitants will promise to protect Government from loss by the cultivation of additional lands. I doubt, however, whether these palliations will be sufficient; and if I were not aware of the extreme difficulty of lowering the revenue when it is once raised, I should be induced to recommend some more extensive measure of that nature. I would not, however, wish for a general remission, but for a reduction in the particular cases where there appeared to be a particular pressure. As the cultivation has greatly increased since we got the country, it is probable some parts even now are lightly assessed, while others must be too heavily, as the Bighoti doubles that of Broach, and as the Government share appears by the Talati's books greatly to exceed one-half of the produce. I have applied to the collector for some information regarding the general rates of assessment, on receiving which I may probably resume the subject: in the meantime it is satisfactory to say that no increase has been put upon the district since the introduction of the Rayatwar system, and that in no instance has it been found necessary to send a Rayat to prison, or to sell his house or cattle for arrears of revenue.

10. Scarcely any part of the above remarks apply to

the Pargana of Olpad. That division, like all other possessions of the Vinchur Jahagirdars, was lightly assessed and equitably governed. It is a rich country with few trees, but in the highest state of cultivation. The villages were said to be excellent, and the people easy in their circumstances and independent in their manners. The assessment is said to bear to that of the other Parganas under Surat the proportion of one-third to one-half; but from what I can learn, it does not appear to be more lightly assessed than the Broach district, or near so lightly as that of Kaira. The character of the people is not what one might expect from their favourable circumstances, for they are said to be less honest, as well as less obedient, than the inhabitants of the old Parganas. The generality of the latter are described to be a remarkably quiet, simple, inoffensive, and industrious race of men.

11. It might be expected that the petitions presented in the different districts would give some idea of the grievances suffered in each. Of about three hundred that I received in the districts of Ahmedabad, Kaira, Broach, and Surat, some did not relate to revenue. Of those which did, the stoppage of pensions and old allowances, either from change of system or from particular orders of our Government, and the administration of the allowances of the Pargana officers and Patels, were common to all the districts, though of course most frequent in new acquisitions. Those peculiar to Ahmedabad were the complaints of the Girasias against the introduction of Talatis and the increase in their tribute; nearly similar complaints from the Kasbatis, complaints of assessment on rent-free lands, some few for over-assessment on Government lands.

12. The complaints of Kaira were for over-assessment and for imposing Savadias and assessing rent-free

land, both originating in some partial arrangement of Captain Robertson for equalizing the assessment and for levying on the alienated lands such portions of the nominal rent of Government land as were in reality received from them. In Broach the prevailing grievance was the over-assessment of the present year, which in Anklesvar occasioned much discontent and clamour.

13. In Surat the petitions were not numerous.

14. I am not sure that these facts throw any light on the comparative state of the districts. They show that the smallest addition to the assessment occasions more remonstrance than the heaviest burdens if they are not increasing; and, perhaps, they also show that the silence of the Rayats may be a sign that they are dispirited as often as that they are content.

(Signed) M. ELPHINSTONE.

Vapi, *May* 6*th*, 1821.

MINUTE BY THE GOVERNOR,

EXTRACTED FROM 'EAST INDIA PAPERS,'

VOL. III. pp. 661—664.

MINUTE BY THE GOVERNOR,

EXTRACTED FROM 'EAST INDIA PAPERS,'
VOL. III. pp. 661—664.

THE district of Broach has been so ably reported on, and its general system is so fully known, that I did not think it necessary to give up to it more of the little time I had remaining than six days; my observations on it must therefore be very brief.

There can scarcely be a greater contrast than between the districts beyond the Mahi and the old part of Broach. In the latter there are no Mehvasis and scarcely any Girasias, little variety in the soil and produce, no diversity in the modes of assessment, no unauthorized alienations, no Suadias, no taxes beyond the land-tax but what are merely nominal. The revenue system, though perhaps defective, has been long established and unchanged. The Adalat is exempt even from the few objections that exist to it beyond the Mahi. It is well understood by all classes, and seems both useful and popular.

When I say that there are scarcely any Girasias, I mean such Girasias as are common to the westward, who possess villages and Talukas of their own. Here there are only four or five of this description, and they have no separate jurisdiction, either in theory or in practice. There are other persons who bear the name of Girasias, but they have only portions of land or pecuniary claims in different villages. The land is cultivated on favourable terms by the Sarkar's Rayats. It pays a fixed Salami to Government. The pecuniary claims are paid by the village to the proprietor; the dues of the Pargana officers are also paid in this manner instead of from the Treasury, and I have not heard of any inconvenience resulting from the practice. The other tenures of rent-free land are Vazifa and Pasaitu. The Vechania and Garania lands were resumed by the Revenue Committee, but are still kept separate in the village accounts.

The Talpat villages are all either formed by the Patel, or by an association of Bhagdars, like those called Narva beyond the Mahi. They were farmed by the strangers, and never held Rayatvar.

The assessment is made entirely by villages, without any inquiry into the circumstances of individuals. One of the hereditary revenue officers is sent to inspect the crops of each harvest. He makes a statement of the quantity of land cultivated, with each sort of produce by each Rayat, and calculates the quantity of each sort that will be produced in each field. The sum of these gives the whole amount of each sort of grain produced in the village. The collector compares this with the produce of the last year, and then compares the market price of each article with that of last year; after which he looks at the sum paid by the village for last year, and if he finds that the crops are more abundant or the price higher, he puts a proportionate increase on the revenue. The general principle is to take half of the money produced by the sale of the crops, and leave the rest to the Rayat. The whole of the calculations I have mentioned are in fact only made at the second harvest; a considerable part of the first consists of rice-crops, and in making the estimate for them it is usual to charge the land at twenty rupees a Bigha, whatever may be the state of the crops. This charge is double the rent of the best rice-land, and a deduction to the amount of one-half the sum collected on account of it is made from the Government's claim, on account of the second harvest. The only object of this over-assessment is to secure a large portion of the revenue at an early period of the year. I am not sure that the practice exists in all the Parganas. This first payment is Dhangar Tanji. If the Patel consents to the sum fixed by the collector for the revenue of the village, nothing more is wanting to complete the settlement. Although the names of the Rayats are written down in the estimate for the sake of marking the fields they cultivate, the collector does not interfere in assessing them: that is afterwards done by the Patel, who explains what each Rayat has to pay to the Talati, and it rests with the latter officer to collect it. The collection is made by securing the whole produce of the harvest at the village cornyard, where it remains under Government officers until the revenue is paid. It is not, however, necessary that the whole should be paid before any is removed; on the contrary, a Rayat may remove a portion of his produce as soon as he can pay the price of it; and when his payments are equal to the whole demand against him, he may remove the whole. The Patel is guided in making his assessment by the former payments of the Rayats, among whom he distributes the increase of the year in proportion to the amount of their rents. The same tenures of Khatebandi and Ganot are in use here as in Kaira; but the custom of having a portion of Vehta or highly-assessed land in each Khata, is confined to some villages in this collectorate. Both are liable to increase when the revenue of the village is increased, but not otherwise. A Rayat from whom a Patel required an increase in other circumstances would complain to the collector; but from the dependence of the Talati on the Patel, and from the mode of settlement, in which the collector has so little occasion to watch over the correctness of village accounts, it would probably not be easy for him to ascertain whether the Rayat's complaint was well-founded. The above applies to an undivided village (or Senja, as it is called in Kaira). In Bhagdar villages, Narva in Kaira, the increase is divided into as many portions as there are Bhags, and the Bhagdars apportion them among their Patidars, who levy them on their Rayats. There seems at one time to have been a general Bighoti of four rupees on all the land except the sandy soils near the sea, which paid only three and a half per Bigha, and some rich tracts on rivers, which paid from six to twelve; but it does not seem to be acted on now, the Government revenue being regulated by the state of the crops and of the market, and all the demands being regulated by the Government revenue. Every village account now exhibits a great variety of rates of Bighoti, and each of those is liable to frequent change.

It is always difficult to guess whether the assessment is light or heavy. On the plan here adopted, it is utterly impossible. An increase of four lacs and a half has taken place this year: a circumstance that I cannot contemplate with pleasure, while the sources of the revenue and the principles of increase are so completely in the dark. Until within these three years there is reason to think that the assessment was light; but in appearance the country falls far short of the western districts. Though almost every spot of it is cultivated, yet the total absence of hedges and of trees, except close to villages, makes it seem naked. The villages are entirely built of unburnt bricks, and though good, compared to most in India, have nothing of the comfort and solidity of those beyond the Mahi. The dress of the inhabitants is not so inferior, and they seem a quiet, industrious, and respectable race of men. Considerably more than three-fourths of the villages in this district are managed on the Bhagdar or Narva plan; and in the Broach Pargana, as well as in Jambusar and Amod, the minor Patidars form a great majority of the cultivators. In the Broach Pargana there are ninety-six villages which have not a single cultivator besides the Patidars; but there are some Bhagdar villages in which the heads of the Bhags, five or six in number, are the only persons who hold by that tenure, all the lands being cultivated by common Rayats, either Khatedars or Ganvatias.

The Talati regulation can scarcely be said to be introduced here. The Talati keep their accounts in the old form, and although they are considered as Government officers much more than in the Deccan, and are often removed and appointed by the collector, they seem to be much more closely connected with the Patels than in Ahmedabad and Kaira, and more likely to conceal than to expose any frauds of the village management.

The Parganas of Jambusar and Amod resemble the old possessions almost in all respects but these. Although there has been no settlement, the alienated lands are still unexamined, and the rents of those unalienated are consequently in many cases far above their natural height. In one village the Talpat land pays ninety rupees a Bigha, which can only be defrayed by immense receipts from rent-free land. The character and condition of the people does not seem so different in these Parganas as one would expect from the tyranny of the Peshwa's Government. I may here observe that the Baroda Pargana, though still subject to all the defects of the native system, and although it has for these last ten years notoriously been oppressed, is yet in the appearance of the country, the villages, and the inhabitants, at least equal to the best parts of the Kaira district. This may be supposed to be the effect of former good government; but when the history of the Gaikwar family is recollected, it will be difficult to say when that good government could have existed. It is extremely difficult to account for this circumstance. I can see no advantage the Baroda Pargana has enjoyed, except tranquillity in the neighbourhood of a capital; and yet I have little doubt that, as far as concerns the comfort of the Rayats, it is among the most flourishing spots in all India. The Gaikwar country, south of Broach, though farmed by the same man as Baroda, is in a state of great poverty and oppression. The most striking defects in the mode of assessment in Broach are its uncertainty and its irregularity. It is uncertain, because it depends on the hasty estimate of an Amin, liable to be mistaken, and still more liable to be corrupt. If the collector disregards the estimate and proceeds on his own opinion and on secret information, the uncertainty is increased—he is as much in the dark as before; and the Patels are less acquainted with the principles on which he proceeds, consequently less able to convince him of any mistake. It is unequal, because the Amin may be led by corruption or other motives to favour some villages and throw the burden on the rest; and still more because the assessment is made on the general state of the village, without regard to the circumstances of individuals, and may therefore bear heavy on a man who has a bad crop, while it is light on one who is more fortunate. When the villages are held by Bhágdárs, this evil is in some degree inseparable from the system, but it might be easily amended in the other villages; and even in those of the Bhágdárs the evil is at present unnecessarily aggravated by the practice of making the whole settlement with one, or a very few Bhágdárs, who, by concert with the Taláti, generally contrive to keep the assessment off their own lands and throw it on their neighbours'. That the assessment is subject to increase and decrease as the crops are good or bad, is not perhaps an evil, for though it increases the fluctuations to the Government, it diminishes it to the Rayat, in whose condition a fixed rent with fluctuating crops would occasion more variation than the present plan. If, however, the assessment were light, it would be of advantage to him also to have it fixed, as his chance of gain would be increased without a corresponding risk of loss. The loss to Government by a light Bighoti would in time be made up by the improvement of the land, which would raise the second class to the first; but an immediate indemnification would be procured by transferring the corrupt profits of the Amins to the treasury. I would not, however, venture on the measure of fixing a Bighoti. I would rather propose in the first instance the appointment of an intelligent and experienced revenue officer as collector to inquire into the present state of the assessment, and report cases where it appeared too high, too low or unequal. In any of those cases I would revise the Bighoti by means of a Panchayat of the villages, superintended by a Government officer, and liable to be corrected by another Panchayat in case of error. I would arrange for a vigilant supervision, perhaps by means of European assistants, and would then leave the Bighoti unaltered, unless when there was an evident and considerable improvement in the village, and even then it would be in no way heavy to raise the assessment. In cases where the present assessment seemed tolerably reasonable and equally levied, I would merely record the details of it, and fix it so as to prevent the collectors altering, except in such cases as have been mentioned. The settlement would still be with the Patels, but the rights of every Rayat would be known and fixed, and both the collector and the Adalat could at once afford redress in case of oppression.

The above applies to Senja villages. It would be difficult to introduce the proposed equality of assessment in Bhagdar ones; but as it is usual for flourishing Bhagdars voluntarily to take part of the burden of their poorer brethren, and as there are, I believe, instances of the Government making a new division to equalize the assessment, something might perhaps be done even in them. It would be an improvement in Broach if the Rayats were allowed the option of moving their crops, on giving security of other respectable people of the same class.

The police of the Broach Zilla appears to be very good. The offences are those of a very settled country; no gang robberies or invasions of predatory Kolis. The Kolis, indeed, are among the most respectable cultivators; one out of four of the Amin Patels are of that caste. The Bhils occupy here the place of the Kolis beyond the Mahi, but even they are not turbulent. robbers used sometimes to come in from Rajpipla, and do still from Dehvan. The rule that a village is responsible for stolen goods traced to it by a Pagi, is not in force here.

(Signed) M. ELPHINSTONE.

Camp Velácha, *April 25th*, 1821.

MINUTE BY THE PRESIDENT,

EXTRACTED FROM 'EAST INDIA PAPERS,'

VOL. III. pp. 677—697.

MINUTE BY THE PRESIDENT,*

EXTRACTED FROM 'EAST INDIA PAPERS,'
VOL. III. pp. 677—697.

AHMEDABAD AND KAIRA.

1. EACH of these collectorates contains two sorts of villages, *Khálsa* and *Girásia*. The former are directly under the Government; the latter are held by a Girasia chief, to whom the Government looks for revenue, and formerly looked for maintaining order. The most striking division of the Girasia villages is those held by Rajputs, or Girasias properly so called, and those held by Kolis, generally termed *Mehvás*. The former, though foreigners, were in possession of Gujarat when the Mussalmans invaded it. They retained some Talukas and villages at that time, and they recovered others by encroachment on the final weakness of the Mogals. They are at once a more civilized and a more warlike race than the Kolis; and it is perhaps owing to those circumstances, as well as to their having more recently possessed the government of the province, that their claims appear to be much more respected than those of the Kolis. The latter, though probably the aborigines, seem generally to be considered as rebellious, or at least refractory villagers,

* The original is, in many places, obscure and defective.

who have, from the weakness of former governments, eluded or resisted the just claims of the Sarkar. Both pay a sum to Government, which Government appears to have had the right to increase. It was not usual to interfere with the internal management of their villages, or to examine the state of their receipts. Our Government has asserted the right, without always assuming the exercise of internal interference; but it is only of late that it has begun to inquire into the collections, by establishing Talatis in Girasia and Mehvas villages. The whole of the Pargana of Dhandhuka, Ranpur, and Gogha, except the Kasbas (or chief towns), are in the hands of Girasia Rajputs, as is a considerable part of Dholka. There were a few also in Viramgam, which have been swallowed up during the exactions of the Marathas. The Kasbatis of Dholka, though Mussalmans, and the chief of Patri, though a Kanbi, and though both differ from the others in the nature of their tenure, may yet be reckoned in this class; but by far the greater number are Rajputs. They resemble their neighbours and brethren in Jalawad, but are more intelligent and respectable. The chiefs of Limdi and Bhavnagar are among the number of our subjects in those districts, though they have large possessions elsewhere. They are quiet and obedient. Talatis have been introduced into the villages of those of Dholka, and all their revenue but 20 per cent. of their own share, after deducting that of the Rayats, is now levied by Government. The police, also, has either been committed to Mukhi Patels, in a manner independent of their authority, or left in their own hands, subject to all restrictions of that humble officer of the police. The others are still on their former footing as to revenue; but they are under the Adalat, and are either themselves agents of the magistrate or are superseded by their Patels. The principal Mevasis are the Kolis of Choval and those of Prantej, Harsol, and Modasa districts. The former are quite reduced, have received Talatis, and pay all their revenue but 25 per cent.; but the latter maintain their independence, and in some instances their rebellious and predatory spirit.

2. The land of villages immediately under the Sarkar is divided into Nakaru, Salami, and Talpad. The Nakaru is, or has been, rent-free; the Salami pays a quit-rent, increasing with the prosperity of the field, but no specific share of the produce; the Talpad is that which pays a fixed proportion of the produce to the Sarkar.

3. The principal divisions of Nakaru and Salami are—1st. Vanta; 2nd. Vazifa; 3rd. Pasaitu; 4th. Vechan; 5th. Garaniu; 6th. Haria, Ranvatia, and Palio; 7th. Giras; 8th. Pagia, Baria, and Koliapa; 9th. Koitar, Pasaitu; 10th. Malik Nakru; 11th. Sir Jamin; 12th. Dabania.

1st. Vanta was originally a fourth of the land of each village left or restored by the Mogal Government to the Girasia, who was originally proprietor of the whole. It is now reduced by sale, mortgages, and encroachments of the Patels and of the Government officers, until it has ceased to bear anything like its original proportion to the Talpad. It is sometimes managed by the proprietor, who pays a quit-rent to Government; but it is very often managed by the Patel, who pays a pecuniary amount to the proprietor.

4. 2nd. Vazifa, though strictly an allowance to religious persons of the Mohammedan faith, seems here to be extended to all grants by the kings to individuals, whether from charity, favour, or reward for services.

Many of the lands held by this tenure have been transferred by gift or sale, lost by encroachment, or subjected to assessment, so as to lose their character of rent-free lands.

5. 3rd. Pasaitu includes the lands assigned to district and village officers, and likewise the lands allotted by any besides the kings to Brahmans, Bhats, and other Hindu religionists, as well as to temples, mosques, and fakirs.

6. 4th. Vechan are lands sold; and 5th, Garaniu, lands mortgaged by Patels, to enable them to pay the revenue and other expenses of the villages or of their own. Both Vechan and Garaniu may be Nakaru or Salami, as they are made over entirely free or subject to the payment of a quit-rent, or as they may have been subjected to the last payment by the encroachments of the Sarkar. Garaniu may be, (1) Simple Garaniu, where the property is to be held till the debt be paid; (2) Valaldania Garaniu, where the produce is given up to the mortgagee until the debt be paid with interest; (3) Udara, where the land is only to be held for a fixed period; (4) San Garaniu, where the land is not to be taken possession of until the mortgagor has failed in his stipulated payment.

7. 6th. Haria is land granted to persons whose estates have fallen in defence of the village, Ranvatia to those who have fallen in attacking others, and Pullio to Bhats, or others who have died by traga in its cause.

7th. Giras is a sum paid to a powerful neighbour or turbulent inhabitant of the village, as the price of forbearance, protection, and assistance.

8. 8th. Pagia, Baria, and Koliapa, are lands held by Kolis, similar to the Vanta held by Rajputs; but it is thought that most of them are usurpations on the timidity of the Patels, clothed under the respectable semblance of Vanta.

9th. Koitar is land granted rent-free, or for a Salami, to a person who has dug a well.

10th. Malik Nakru, a favourable tenure of the Maliks of Thasra alone.

11th. Sir Jamin, land granted by an owner of Vanta to his wife, and still held by her descendants, though the rest of the Vanta has escheated to Government.

12th. Dabania, usurpations. Almost all these classes may be Nakru or Salami, according as the grant is full, or with the reservation of a quit-rent.

9. The rest of the lands of every village are Talpad, or the property of Government. This land is cultivated by Rayats, who hold it on different tenures, pay their revenues in different modes, and are under different forms of village government. The commonest tenure here is that which is also commonest throughout India. The Rayat holds his land on a general understanding that he is not to be dispossessed as long as he pays his rent, which though not fixed, is regulated by the custom of the village. He receives a portion of each of the three different classes into which the land is divided, according to its fertility; and he is obliged to cultivate the bad, as the condition of retaining the good land. This is almost the only tenure in Ahmedabad, and it is very common in Kaira likewise; but in many villages in the latter Zilla there is a more complicated tenure, called Khatabandi. Each Rayat receives a perpetual lease of a portion of the best land, which is called his Veheta, and which is assessed much above its value; along with this he receives a portion of inferior land, at a favourable rate. The Veheta varies from one to four Bighas, and the other land bears a proportion to the extent of the Veheta. All cesses fall on this Veheta; and so completely is it the scale for regulating the payments of the Rayats, that he is compelled to

increase it if his circumstances improve, and allowed to diminish it if his means fall off. Should he throw it up entirely, he must sink into a common labourer, and would not, while he remained in the village, be permitted to cultivate on his own account rent-free land, or even land belonging to another village. These tenures greatly resemble that used in the southern Maratha country, when the Veheta is called Chali. Jamin, a third practice, is for a Rayat to take out a written lease (called Ganot), generally engaging the land for a year at a rate specified in the lease. It seldom extends above one year. This is not uncommon in the Kaira Zilla; but in that of Ahmedabad no Rayat takes a writing, unless when he has obtained an increasing lease for the purpose of digging a well or making some similar improvement. These are the differences in tenures; unless it be considered as one that Mussalmans, Rajputs, Kolis, and all the classes who are less skilful in cultivation than their neighbours pay a lighter rent.

10. The modes in which the land revenue is usually paid are two: in kind, by a division of the produce, which is called Bhágbatái; or by a money rent, regulated by the value of the land, and likewise by the nature of the article cultivated: this is called Bighoti. The shares of Government and the Rayats on the Bhágbatái plan vary in different places; but in general it is thought Government is entitled to one-half of the crop cultivated during the rainy season, and from one-third to one-fifth of that cultivated in the dry weather, if raised by irrigation; if not irrigated, a larger portion is taken. The land paying Bighoti is divided into three classes, according to its fertility, and it pays a higher or a lower rent, as it may belong to the first or to an inferior class. But as this classification has not

been found sufficiently minute, the rent further varies in some villages according to the species of produce cultivated on the land. Thus in one district Bájri and Juvar pay on the first sort of ground 4 rupees per Bigha; on the second, 3 rupees; and on the third, 1½ rupee. Sugar-cane pays on the first sort 20 rupees per Bigha; on the second, 17 rupees; and on the third, 10 rupees. Some circumstances raise the Bighoti, such as the use of well-water and manure; and others diminish it, such as the distance of the land from the village: but the proportion between the different kinds of land and of produce is still kept up.

11. The Bighoti also varies in different villages, and this justly; for many circumstances, such as the distance of the market, etc., greatly alter the value of the produce of a Bigha of land of equal fertility. In some villages the three classes of land were subdivided on the same principle, and there the land pays according to its fertility and other advantages, without reference to the produce. This last is the case in almost all the villages of the Kaira district. Even in villages of Kaira, where there is a reference to the produce, it is only in lands watered from wells. In some villages inhabited by Kolis, Mohammedans, and other bad cultivators, every Bigha pays the same rent without reference to its fertility, produce, or situation. This mode of payment is called Fáta Chás. In every poor village uninhabited by Kolis, Rayats sometimes pay a fixed sum for the whole land they cultivated, without reference to the quality or number of Bighas. This is called Udbár Salámi.

12. Besides the land-tax there are many Verás or taxes, some bearing on the land, as those of ploughs, carts, cattle, horses; that called Khot Vera, intended to make up for defalcations; and some on the person

or property, as those on shops, trades, houses, hearths; and that on persons of the military caste, called Dhárála. The former were often imposed by the farmers under the Maráthas to each of the holders of rent-free lands; while to prevent their bearing too hard on the tenant of land paying revenue, he often received an abatement of his revenue exactly equal to the amount levied as a Vera. The others are useful, as drawing a revenue from persons who do not cultivate land at all.

13. There are other more direct ways of making the rent-free land contribute: 1st, by a Salami or quit-rent, which is a certain sum per Bigha, imposed without reference to the produce; 2nd, a Swadea, or tax, on the Sarkar Rayats, who cultivate the lands of rent-free proprietors. This is also fixed without reference to the produce, and it, in fact, differs only in name from the other, since the more the Rayat pays to Government the less he can pay to the proprietor. All Kolis are the Sarkar Rayats, and Kolis and other castes are far inferior husbandmen. The Swadea was not so often employed by the Maratha as the Salami; there is no fixed rate for either.

14. The forms of village government, and consequently the channels through which the revenue is collected, are four.

15. The form which has been most in use in Gujarat, since the introduction at least of the Maratha rule, is for the Patel to engage annually for the payment of a certain sum to Government, which he is to realize according to the established rates and customs of the village. Any profit that may be derived from the goodness of the season or from new cultivation is his, and he is to bear any loss that may accrue from opposite causes. The rights of the owners of alienated land, of all descriptions of Rayats, remain unaffected

by this arrangement, which only transfers to the Patel the rights of the Government.

16. As long as a village remained in this state it was called Senja, or entire; but it sometimes happens that the Patel is incapable of undertaking this responsibility alone, or that all the different branches of the Patel's family are desirous of having their separate shares of the power and profit of the office. In such cases, they proceed exactly as they would partition an estate by the Hindu laws of inheritance: they ascend to their common ancestor, and divide the village into as many portions as he had sons. These portions are called Bhags, and each is made over to the progeny of one of the sons, who divides it into as many shares as there are individuals in that branch of the family. The head of the branch is called Bhagdar: he acts as Patel (as far as Patel is required on this system), and shares with the other Bhagdars the lands and allowances attached to the Patel's office; but he has no larger share than any of the younger members of the same branch, and each has full power to manage as he pleases with his own share. The Rayats fall under the individual to whose share the land belongs, and are called his A'samis; but they retain the same privileges as if the village had been farmed by the Patel. It often happens that the Patel's descendants are so numerous as to cultivate nearly the whole land of the village: in that case, of course, there are few or no Rayats. On the other hand, it sometimes happens that the Patel's family has not had time to branch out, and that there is only a single number for each Bhag, all the lands being cultivated by common Rayats. The minor shares are called Pattis, and the holders Patidars. The whole association is answerable to Government for the revenue; but each Bhag is answerable for the revenue due

by each of its Patidars, and the defalcations occasioned by a few individuals do not fall on the other Bhags unless it is entirely beyond the power of the one to which they belong to make them good. Pattis are saleable, and thus persons not of the Patel's family are sometimes introduced as Patidars into villages. The partition, in many places, did not take in all the land of a village: whatever remained, which was always the moist land, was called Majmu, and was managed by the Bhagdars on account of Government. No stranger can cultivate it, because (even if he were disposed to settle where his presence was so unwelcome) he could not get a house, the whole site of the village being partitioned among the Patidars.

17. A village thus managed is termed Narva. The system is founded on that of leasing the village to the Patel, and is, in fact, nothing more than dividing the lease among his relations. The number of persons interested, and the advantage of their mutual responsibility, has made it more permanent, and it appears to have stood its ground wherever the assessment was at all moderate. It has been swept away by long oppression in the Ahmedabad district, but it still remains in many of the villages under Kaira.

18. Two other modes of village management seem rather to have been occasionally resorted to than uniformly adopted. The first was to farm the village to any stranger who might be willing to agree to higher terms than the Patel; and the other, to keep it in the hands of Government, the Patel, or a person deputed for the purpose by the Government, settling with the Rayats and collecting their revenue, without any avowed profit or any responsibility for the amount. The first of these plans is called Ijara; and in the second a village is said to be held Kacha. Both are applicable either to Senja

or Narva villages. If a Senja village is held Kacha, it is exactly a Rayatwar settlement.

19. In cases of Ijara the farmer steps into the place of Government. If a Narva village be Kaçha, the Government sets aside the Bhagdars, collects from each Patidar, and manages its own Majmun, but leaves the Patidars to settle with the Rayats as formerly. If it be held Ijara, the farmer may either settle with the Bhagdars or hold the village Kacha, and in either case his sole profit must be derived from the Majmun lands, the rest being in effect already farmed to the Patidars. The village establishments seem the same here as in most parts of India. The Patel, however, has no land, and few allowances; and the Talati, till lately, had almost become a cipher.

20. The villages are, as usual, classed into parganas, which have each a Desai or Majmudar, and an Amin Patel. These officers are hereditary; each member of the family is competent to discharge their functions. They are paid by a Dasturi, or fee, on each village, part of which is divided among the family and part given under the name of Sukri, at the discretion of the collector, to the person who does the duty. The business of the Desai was to superintend all the Patels, to furnish every sort of local information which could assist in settling the revenue, and to adjust disputes among villages, especially about land. The Majmudars kept all the accounts of the Pargana, and served both to inform the Kamavisdar of what was usual, and to check him by recording his pecuniary transactions.

21. The Amin was formerly a kind of assistant to the Desai, but he has within these two years nearly superseded his principal, and the Desais are scarcely ever now employed, while all local examinations of the state of produce fall on the Amin.

22. The Desais are still not without their use as checks on the Kamavisdar, whom they always look on as an intruder, and against whom they are always ready to bring forward or to instigate information.

23. The Majmudar has still much employment, as he is at the head of all the Talatis, keeps all their accounts, and frames for them the general accounts of the Pargana.

24. The division into Parganas is in some respects set aside by the distribution of the country into districts under Kamavisdars, which may or may not correspond in extent with the Parganas. The functions of the Kamavisdar need not be explained. It is well known that he is the instrument of the collector, and that it is through him that all the settlements are made and all collections realized; it is from him, also, that the collector should expect most of his information, and on his honesty and intelligence the prosperity of the district must greatly depend.

25. This view of the revenue system will now enable me to explain the steps we have hitherto adopted, both towards the Girasias and our other dependents, and towards the villages immediately under the Government, and to offer some observations on the course to be hereafter pursued.

26. The most striking circumstances in the progress of our government are the extraordinary obstacles that existed to introducing order, and the surprising success with which they have been overcome. The continual intermixture of our territories with those of the Gaikwar, the Peshwa, the Nawab of Cambay, and the unsettled tributaries of Kathiawar and Mahi Kantha, the number of half-subdued Girasias and Mevasis within our own limits, the numerous and ill-defined tenures in almost every village, and the turbulent and predatory character

of a large proportion of the people, combined to make the country beyond the Mahi more difficult to manage than any part of the Company's territories; yet by the caution of Government and the judgment and temper of the local officers, our authority and our system have been established with the utmost tranquillity, without either irritating our subjects or embarrassing ourselves by any sudden or violent changes. Of late years our innovations have been proceeding with accelerated progress; and although the danger of hasty improvement is now diminished, it may still be necessary to retard their advance, or at least to fix the limit beyond which it is not designed they should extend.

27. When we first obtained the Parganas forming the old Kaira collectorship, the whole were put in charge of Colonel Walker, and managed by his assistants. Everything was left entirely on its old footing, and nothing was done but to gain some information regarding the actual condition of things. When regular collectors were appointed, the same system was for a long time pursued.

28. The only change in the revenue department attempted among the Girasias was the increase to their tribute, to which they were at all times liable; but the principle of a tribute was observed as long as they were under Kaira, and with the single and temporary exception of Bapu Miya Kasbati of Dholka, no scrutiny was attempted into their resources or management.

29. The introduction of the judicial regulations was certainly a great innovation, and was very early adopted; but it seems doubtful whether the effect was soon felt. It is not likely that many of the inhabitants of the Girasia villages came to our courts to complain; and where the plaintiff belonged to a Khalsa village, it would be thought natural and proper for Government to interfere in his behalf.

30. The first changes that were much felt were produced by the regulations for the appointment of Mukhi Patels and of Talatis, particularly the latter. The Girasias, who held more villages than one, were compelled to appoint Mukhi Patels, who from the time of their appointment become responsible to the magistrate alone. Those who had one village were themselves appointed Mukhi Patels: in other cases they were obliged to nominate another person for each village, who was responsible to the magistrate and not to the Girasias. Talatis were introduced into all the villages of the Girasias of Dholka, and it was proposed to introduce them into all the Girasia villages in Dhandhuka, Ranpur, and Gogha. A further change has taken place in the alteration of the principle of the Dholka payments, from a tribute paid to Government to a certain proportion of the produce left to the Girasias, and that proportion is only 20 per cent. of the Government share, from which all village expenses, including Talatis' pay, are to be defrayed.

31. The effect of this change on the income of the chiefs is shown by the payments of the three principal Girasias, to which I have added the two chief Kasbatis, though their situation is somewhat different.

	1802.	1817.	1820.
	Rupees.	Rupees.	Rupees.
The Chief of Koth	48,000	57,000	72,000
" " Gáugar	15,500	19,000	23,000
" " Utelia	6,000	6,000	11,000
Bápu Miyá Kasbáti	50,000	73,000	89,000
Latif Khán Kasbáti	11,000	13,000	16,000

Their payments, especially those of the Girasias, have therefore greatly increased; and more within the three last years than in the preceding fifteen.

32. The appointment of a Talati is very disagreeable to the chiefs, and those of Dholka assured me that they felt the presence of that officer more than the increase of their tribute. They said he assumed the character of a representative of Government, received complaints from their Rayats, threw their whole village into confusion, and utterly destroyed their consequence among their people.

33. The Adalat also, as we came into closer contact with the chiefs, has been more felt; and we have reason to regret that some modifications were not made in our code before it was applied to a people in a state of society so different from that which our laws contemplate, and employed to enforce agreements concluded at a time when the strict execution of them was so little foreseen. The Raja of Koth, who, at the time of Colonel Walker's report in 1804, maintained a body of 150 horses and 2,000 Sibandis, was sent to prison for neglecting a summons from a magistrate; and the chief of Patri, who once resisted for two months the attacks of the Gaikwar army, was thrown into goal for his inability to pay debts contracted in consequence of war and contributions during the period of his independence. I cannot more strongly show the change that has taken place than by pointing out that these are the persons whom Colonel Walker, and I believe all the gentlemen employed in the first introduction of our authority, declared to be sovereign princes, with whom we have no right to interfere beyond the collection of a tribute, and that they are now deprived of all power and consequence, and nearly the whole of their revenue. Almost all these changes have, in effect, taken place within these three years. They cannot but feel a change so sudden, and it must be owned that they have suffered hardships, though not perhaps injustice.

34. I could not, however, propose any great change in the present circumstances of the Girasias. With those of Dholka I would be satisfied to remove the Talatis, to fix their payments so as to leave 30 per cent. instead of 20, and would tell them that the sum now settled on that principle would remain without further increase for the next five years, after which it might be revised on the same principle. Their Mukhi Patels might be left as at present, and the only change I should wish in their relation to the Adalat would be, that the judge and the magistrate should not require their personal attendance, except in cases of great necessity; that all claims against them for old debts, even if supported by bonds, should be examined with reference to all circumstances arising from the situation of the parties at the time when they were contracted by which the nature of the debts might be affected; and that instead of seizing and confining the persons of the Girasias, the judges should issue a precept to the collector to sequestrate as large a portion of the lands as might suffice for the gradual payment of the debts, leaving a decent maintenance to the Girasia. The land thus sequestrated might either be managed by the collector, or given over under proper securities to the creditors, but the former would perhaps be the better plan of the two.

35. With the Girasias of Dhandhuka, Ranpur, and Gogha, still less change would be required. They are acknowledged to have a clear proprietary right to their Talukas. Their tribute is still moderate, and although they have Mukhi Patels they have no Talatis. It would be enough to keep them as they are. A small increase might be put on their tribute where their villages had improved, to keep up the right of Govern-

ment, and they might be told that no further increase would be made for five years; or a regular lease for that period might be granted to them as formerly, and likewise to the Girasias and Kasbatis of Dholka. If they are to pay a tribute and not to be brought under a regular assessment, it is of no use to appoint a Talati; and it is hurtful to do so, because even if the Talati does not purposely interfere from love of consequence or corruption, his presence as an agent of Government must weaken the influence of the Girasia, and lead his Rayats to look to Government for redress whenever they are dissatisfied with the Girasia. If such a contest is to be encouraged, we must go further, and see that we secure protection to the weaker party, whom we engage in opposition to the stronger: a point on which we are said to have failed in Bengal, and are surely more likely to fail in Kathiawar.

36. From the motives above stated, I was inclined to make the Mukhi Patels responsible to the chief of the Taluka, and he to the collector; but the opinion of the officers best acquainted with that country induces me to give up the idea. I would, however, recommend that the Girasia should be employed as head of the police wherever he conveniently could, and that he should have no formal appointment of Mukhi Patel, a title which a Rajput chief must look on as a degradation. I would also recommend that the chief of Bhavnagar should be appointed a special commissioner for his own villages in the Gogha Pargana, with powers considerably above those of the Faujdari Amin, and with some title less offensive to his pride than that just mentioned, which he has of late assumed with great reluctance. This change in the Raja's situation should not take place at present, as he labours under

accusations which should be disproved before he receives any marks of favour. All the details connected with this appointment, and with the alterations suggested in the judicial system in relation to the Girasias, might be filled up by the Regulation Committee.

37. On the first formation of the Kaira district the Mevasis were restrained from plundering, but in all other respects they were left entirely on their ancient footing. The Adalat was early introduced without any bad effects, but there are no Talatis or Mukhi Patels till this day, and the tribute is still the same as when we got the country.

38. In Ahmedabad Talatis have been appointed, and in some cases have been resisted by the Mevasis. The Thakor, or persons of their recommendation, have been appointed Mukhi Patels, and attempts are made to make them conform to this regulation for the guidance of those officers. In the district of Choval, the numerous Mevasis have been assessed in a manner that leaves them about 25 per cent. of the Government share of the revenue.

39. In my minute on the Mahi Kantha, the situation of the Mevasis has been fully explained. It appears that there is no trace in history of their ever having been on a footing of greater dependence than they are at present; and it follows that we have derived no claim to reduce them further from our predecessors, and must rest our right to do so on the law of nature, which entitled us to control our neighbours so far as is required by our own security; and this ought, therefore, to be the limit of our interference. Considering the want of military force in the territory, it is surprising how little disturbance the Mevasi have given us since we first came into Gujarat; and it would be

equally inconsistent with justice and policy to risk this tranquillity, for a little addition to the revenue or a fancied improvement in the police. That the improvement would be real, I think more than doubtful, for unless where Kolis have acquired habits of industry and order, they can only be restrained by rendering the communities to which they belong responsible for their conduct; and if we could quietly succeed in bringing each individual under the direct operation of our police, the effect, I doubt not, would be a great increase of robberies. I would, therefore, propose that in Mevasi villages we should hold the Thakor responsible for the tribute and for the maintenance of the public tranquillity. He might be required to give security, if necessary, and should be obliged to restore stolen property and to give up offenders; but he should be under none of the regulations applicable to Mukhi Patels, and it should rest with the magistrate what offences to notice in his village. All serious crimes ought, of course, to be noticed, and the criminal should be demanded of the Thakor. The demand should be enforced by a Mohosal and a daily fine. Obstinate neglect might be punished by apprehending the Thakor; and resistance, by attacking him as a public enemy. Complaints of a serious nature against the Thakor personally should be investigated in a summary way by the collector, before he proceeded to apprehend the accused: when it became necessary to apprehend him, he should be made over to the criminal judge in the usual manner. Thakors habitually guilty of connivance at plunder might be deposed and imprisoned, the office of chief being made over to another member of the family; or their villages might be garrisoned by troops, and deprived of all Mevasi privileges.

40. No Talatis should be appointed, and the tribute

should be kept nearly stationary. A small increase might be put on suitable cases to preserve the right of the Government, but in general the greatest profit should be left to the villages, to encourage their attending to agriculture. Civil justice ought in most cases to be allowed to take its course, but in some villages it would be expedient for complaints to be made, in the first instance, to the magistrate, who might decide whether to send them to the courts or to settle them by the Panchayats, supported by Mohosals. There are many villages to which some only of these exemptions need be granted, and others where the whole would be necessary. Exemption from civil justice, for instance, should be rare; but the removal of Talatis almost universal. The Pargana of Prantej, Modasa, etc., which are situated in the heart of the Mahi Kantha, and some of which we share with the chief of Ahmednagar, are those which should be least interfered with; but the collectors would be best able to discriminate the different classes, and might be called on to send lists of the villages to which they consider each kind of exemption applicable.

41. It would not be expedient to introduce anything into the regulations on the subject of Girasias and Mevasis more than is necessary to legalize the proceedings of the magistrates; and great care ought to be taken to avoid any appearance of restraining any right of Government, as circumstances, especially the conduct of the Mevasis themselves, may compel us to resume the exercise of the control which we are at present relinquishing.

42. The changes in the management of the Khalsa land have been greater, but more beneficial, than those in the Girasia and Mevasi villages.

43. In the Kaira Zilla the Parganas were farmed

out for the first five years to the Desais and Amins, agreeably to the Maratha practice; then this plan was laid aside. That of farming them to the Patel was adopted, but it was soon found that no true account of the resources could be obtained from these persons; and a scheme was therefore partially resorted to of setting up competitors to the Patel, leasing the village to the person who made the highest offer. Many villages in bad order were also let to strangers on increasing leases, for the purpose of their being improved by their capital; but by far the greatest proportion still remained under the Patels, either on ordinary leases, or more frequently on increasing ones. Up to May, 1816, scarcely any were settled Rayatwar; and since then the number has gradually increased till last year, when 370 out of 567, being all those of which the leases were expired, were settled in that manner. The Rayatwar system had, however, since the Talatis became efficient, been more extensively introduced in reality than in appearance. The Patel in many villages continued to go through the forms of farming his village; but as the farm was not given till every Rayat's rent had been settled, the Patel had not avowedly either the chance of gain or the risk of loss, except by discovering abuses, and his influence was greatly impaired by the change in his situation.

44. Many changes were introduced even while the system was ostensibly the same. Our strict administration and readiness to hear complaints checked many abuses in collection and expenditure, and stopped much oppression. The disuse of the custom of requiring security for the revenue saved each Rayat a very large percentage which he used to pay to a banker, who became answerable for him, and the manner of collecting became in other respects much less vexatious. But the greatest change with the least appearance was wrought

by the appointment of new Talatis. These officers are all over India hereditary functionaries of the village, subordinate to the Patels, to whom they serve as a clerk and assistant. When on their best footing they are generally in league with the villagers, and their accounts are often falsified to serve the purpose of the Patel. Even the check afforded by such an officer had been lost in Gujarat, where the Talati's duty had become merely nominal. The new Talati is an officer direct from Government, and looked up to in the village as its agent. He examines every man's condition, and his tenure, and he is now employed to make the collections, and in a great measure to supersede the Patel in all his acts as agent of Government. There can be no doubt of the excellence of this regulation, both as promoting the advantage of Government and of the Rayats; but it must not be overlooked that it has a tendency to extinguish the authority of the Patel, already much weakened by other parts of our management, and care should be taken when the necessary information has been acquired to bring the Talati's power within its natural bounds, and to withdraw it from all interference with the immediate duties of the Patel. The authority of the Desai and other Pargana officers has long since been destroyed. They were first reduced from the masters of the districts to mere ministerial officers, and the extent of their duties, as such, has been greatly limited. There seems nothing to regret in this alteration.

Such has been the progress of the Kaira Zilla in that of Ahmedabad, which was formed after the complete establishment of our power in Gujarat; and after the whole system of our regulations had been completed, the course was much more rapid. All the changes above mentioned were introduced at once, and the plan of letting villages to strangers was carried to a much greater extent. For one year the villages in some Parganas at least were put up to public auction and knocked down to the highest bidder, unless the Patel, to whom a preference was always shown, would agree to nearly the same sum offered by the speculator. This plan, I believe, is by no means unusual in some parts of India, and it is, perhaps, absolutely unavoidable where you have to make hastily the settlement of a new country without accounts or information. As far as regards the Rayats, it appears to be the worst plan possible. It is, however, spoken of by experienced collectors as much less pernicious than it seems. The farmer was bound to respect the tenures of the Rayats and to conform to the customs of the village ; the rates at which each was to pay were well defined and well known ; and above all, the Zilla was of moderate size, and the collector and his assistants were active, zealous, well acquainted with the system, and always ready to redress complaints. It is, indeed, to those circumstances, to the administration rather than to the system, that the prosperity of Gujarat is chiefly to be attributed.

Many villages now nearly waste were also let out at increasing leases on such favourable terms as to bring whole colonies of Rayats from the Gaikwar's district, and to promise the most desirable effects to the revenue. Last year many villages have been settled Rayatwar.

45. It is difficult to ascertain how far the assessment is light or heavy ;*

but they have so obvious an interest in doing so that their testimony is of little value. I should think the assessment was light on most lands, and very light on many, though probably heavy on some. In the Ahmedabad Zilla, the number of villages that have been let

* Blank in original.

to the highest bidder, the consequent detection of all sources of revenue, and in some cases the raising of the Bighotis by Panchaits, granted at the suggestion of the farmer, have a tendency to strain the revenue to the highest pitch. Yet the continual emigrations from the Gaikwar's territory, amounting from Kadi to above 1,300 families, rather prove that the condition of the Rayats cannot be very bad. In the Kaira Zilla one or two Parganas are said to be fully assessed, but none oppressively, except one-half of Petlad, which I understand is much overburdened. The revenue yielded by each village has greatly increased in both Zillas since the country fell into our hands, but little of this is owing to increased assessments. Our steady Government, and the absence of vexation to the Rayats, leave them time to attend to their concerns and draw others from the territories of our neighbours. Our little employment for soldiers and other unproductive labourers has turned them to husbandry, and by all these means the cultivation increased and with it the revenue. Many classes pay with us who were favoured formerly. We have few expenses of collection, few fees, little or no money paid for security, and we check frauds and allow few middlemen to intercept the revenue between the Rayat and the state. It would not therefore be fair to judge of the increase of the assessment by the augmentation of the revenue. On the other hand, a statement sent in by the acting collector of Kaira, makes the average payment on most Parganas in his Zilla only* per Bigha; but this also is in some measure fallacious, since much of the land is alienated, and pays little or nothing, so that the assessment may fall very heavy on some parts, though certainly very light on the whole. It is probably decisive on this

* Blank in original.

question that no distraint is required to collect the revenue, and scarcely any imprisonment; that there are no Rayats quitting the country, or even moving from one village to another; that there is no Takavi and scarcely any remissions.

46. It is not to be supposed that my stay in these Zillas could enable me to form any opinion of the real condition of the people. The facts that present themselves on a hasty view are, that the Girasias are weakened and depressed; that the Desais and all the hereditary officers, including the Patel, are stripped of power and influence, and have security of person and property in exchange; that the bankers are deprived of one large branch of their profit by the change in our system of revenue, and of another by the decline of commerce, occasioned by the downfall of so many native states and the equal diffusion of property; that the Bhats, once so important in Gujarat, are now almost too insignificant to mention; and that the Rayats have gained much in wealth, comfort, and security. Among all the sufferers, those engaged in commerce, and perhaps the Girasias, are the only classes that give rise to regret. There are no hereditary chiefs, no established military leaders, and no body of men that claimed respect from even an apparent devotion to learning or religion. The property of those who have suffered was built on the depression of the people, and their fall has been compensated by the rise of the Rayats, the most numerous, most industrious, and most respectable part of the community. To that order our Government has, beyond all doubt, been a blessing. It has repelled predatory invasion, restrained intestine disorder, administered equal and impartial justice, and has almost extirpated every branch of exaction and oppression. The appearance of the country on this

side of the Sabarmati, which has been long in our possession, is what might be expected in such circumstances. The former affluence of the upper classes is apparent in the excellence of their houses; and the prosperity of the Rayats appears in the comfort of their dwellings, the neatness of their dress, and the high cultivation of their lands.

47. In the fertility and improvements of the fields, there are many parts of the Bengal provinces which cannot be surpassed; but in the abundance of trees and hedges, in handsome and substantial well-built villages, and in the decent and thriving appearance of the people, I have seen nothing in India that can bear a comparison with the eastern Zilla of Gujarat.

48. With regard to the course to be adopted for the future, the first question is, on which of the four plans now in use is it desirable to grant leases for a term of years? Whichever of the plans may be adopted, it is not my intention to enter generally into those questions which have so long divided all those who are best qualified to pronounce on such subjects; but with respect to Gujarat, we must decide which course to adopt, or else come to an equally positive resolution to make over the task to the collectors. No. 8, the plan of Ijara (or farming villages to strangers), especially if they are let to the highest bidder, seems the worst of all. It may be useful in an entirely new country, as the only means of finding out its resources when there is no survey and no true accounts, and it has the advantage of inducing moneyed men to embark their capital in agriculture, and to assist the Rayats with money, the want of which is the great check to their industry; but whether soon or late, it is evidently the interest of the farmer to get as much money from the Rayats before his farm expires as he can; and though

he may be prevented from doing much mischief by clearly defining the rights of the Rayats, and giving a ready ear to their complaints, yet it is bad policy to adopt a system that holds out strong temptations to evil, in the hope of preventing it by checks and punishments.

49. The next plan (that of farming the village to the Patel) is less objectionable, because there are many ties on the Patel to prevent his oppressing the people with whom he has been brought up, and among whom he is to pass the rest of his days. It is not by any means so unpopular among the people. It gives to the person whose business it is to direct and encourage the labours of the Rayats an interest in their success ; it strengthens the influence of the Patel, so much required in revenue police and in settling disputes, and so likely to be undermined by the introduction of the Talati as an officer of Government instead of one of the village, by our restraint of abuses, whether of expenditure or of authority, and by the resumption of alienated lands (should that take place), as a great share of the profits are now in the hands of the Patels. On the other hand, the Patel cannot bring forward a capital so readily as a common farmer, and the plan of farming to him, as well as to the other, is liable to this great objection, that it does not oblige the collector to examine the effects of its operation, and that if the Patel can stifle complaints (which he is more likely to do than another farmer) the greatest abuses may go on for a long series of years, without the least sign that anything is wrong. This applies more particularly where there is a long lease ; but it is true, in a less degree, in all cases.

50. The principal advantage of the Rayatwar plan is that there is no acknowledged sharer in the produce but the Government and the Rayats. If a Kamavisdar bring his whole collections to account, he has no temp-

tation of punishing them beyond justice; and if he do not, the mere complaints of the Rayats convict him without further inquiry. The collector also has more responsibility for the conduct of his own officer, and more control over his actions, than he could have with any farmer, and the Patel (on this plan, as well as on that of farming to a stranger) is sure to come forward with complaints against the abuses of a mode of management that excludes him from his natural consequence and profit. It is objected to the Rayatwar plan, that it involves so much detail that the collector and his assistant cannot perform it all, while it cannot be safely entrusted to natives; but if the farming plans give less trouble to the collector, it is only because some of the most important parts of his duty are relinquished. The system can go on, well or ill, without the interference of the collector; but if that officer be determined to prevent exactions he will have more difficulty in detecting them on this plan than the Rayatwar. It is true that the Rayatwar plan exposes the dues of Government to more hazards than the other; but unless the loss be such as to derange the public finances, it is better the Government should suffer than the Rayat. The evil is felt immediately, and is immediately repaired; but over-exaction, even if it were sure of early detection, leaves the Rayats in a state from which they take a long time to recover. The success of the Rayatwar system in the Madras ceded districts, also, leads me to doubt whether the danger to Government can be so great as is apprehended. It has, however, one serious objection, that when combined with our general revenue and judicial system, it has a great tendency to annihilate the power of the Patel and to dissolve the village government, the value of which has of late been rated so highly.

51. The Narva plan, when the Patidars are numerous, has many of the advantages of the Rayatwar plan, without the risk of loss to Government as long as it is partial, as at present the inferior Rayats can command good treatment by their power of moving to Government villages; and if there be no restraint on one Patidar's receiving another's assurance whenever he chooses to quit his former landlord, the whole of the people must be well protected from oppression. It is an inconvenience in the Narva plan that as long as one Patidar is ill off, the revenue cannot be raised on the others, however their lands may have improved; and, on the other hand, no remission can be granted to one man in distress, because all the rest have a right to participate in whatever is given. This must have been a valuable defence against over-assessment under a rapacious Government; but it is also a bar to the just claims of the state. I understand, however, that these restrictions have often been disregarded in the Kaira Zilla, without any bad consequences resulting.

52. What has been said will enable me to give my opinion regarding leases of a term of years, which have been so earnestly recommended by Mr. Dunlop, and which, indeed, are warmly supported by all gentlemen of experience on the spot.

53. I do not think they ought ever to be given to strangers on the first plan mentioned, unless on Istava leases, because it is not desirable to bind Government to observe for a term of years a plan radically objectionable. The second plan of granting them to the Patels is that generally recommended; and if the terms of the lease were moderate, the payment of each Rayat fixed with precision and simplicity, and at a low rate, if the lease did not exceed five years, and if good security were given for the payment

of a heavy penalty if the village were not in a prosperous condition at the expiration of the lease, I should not think the adoption of it objectionable. But it would, in effect, be a Rayatwar settlement as far as relates to ground already cultivated, and the Patel's whole profit would be derived from the new land he might bring into cultivation, in return for which profit he would be answerable for any Rayats who should be unable to pay their revenue. Unless he had some capital beyond what was invested in the new land, he would be unable to grant any remission to such Rayats as had been unfortunate; because, if they failed to pay him, he could not pay Government, and if Government granted remissions to him it would lose all the benefit of the lease, without having very favourable means of ascertaining whether the remission was necessary, or whether it really went to the benefit of the sufferers. The whole advantage of this plan might therefore, perhaps, be gained by making the settlement with each Rayat for the ground now cultivated, and giving up the waste land for five years to the Patel, or whoever chose to cultivate it, at a quit-rent or on a favourable Istava lease. The third plan of settling with the Rayats is not calculated for long leases. So small a calamity deranges the fortune of a single Rayat, that it is often impossible for him to execute what he engaged to do with every prospect of performance: he must, therefore, be allowed to extend or diminish his cultivation annually, according to his means, and Government can only promise to allow his rent to remain unchanged, without exacting any corresponding engagement from him. To Patidar villages long leases seem particularly adapted. It is the nature of their association to break up as soon as they fail to pay the Government's revenue, and it seems reasonable that the demands of Government should be as fixed towards them as possible. I would, therefore, recommend (in certain circumstances to be explained hereafter) that collectors be allowed to grant leases for five years to Patidars in villages where they are numerous, and to give assurances to the Rayats that the rent of their lands will not be increased for five years. With regard to single Patels and Patidars when very few, I am not prepared to give a decided opinion. The failure of the village leases in the Madras ceded districts, where the payments of the Rayats had been fixed with the utmost precision, is a strong argument against such an experiment; but something of the same kind appears to have succeeded in Gujarat, and if this be the case, the fact is conclusive. I should wish, therefore, that Captain Robertson should be called on to report on the number of leases for terms of years granted by him in the Kaira Zilla, describing the conditions on which they were granted, and the success which attended them. But to whatever persons the leases be granted, I am by no means of opinion that the time is come for the general adoption of such a measure. Before any engagement can be entered into, it is necessary to determine whether there is to be a new survey assessment. Before a whole village can be farmed to a Patel or to Patidars, it is necessary to determine whether the illegally alienated lands are to be assessed or not; and before even a promise can be given to the Rayats that the rent of each man's field is not to be raised, it is necessary that it should first be known that each Bigha is fairly assessed, and that there are none of the abuses by which Government may be defrauded. The two first questions, therefore, being previously disposed of, the collectors should proceed to examine narrowly the state of each village, and to regulate the Bighoti on equitable principles: when satisfied that nothing more remains to be done, they may then grant the leases and assurances above alluded to. By this plan leases will be granted to but a small number of villages at a time, which I consider as a great advantage. It enables the collector to look into each settlement when it is made, and to examine each village when the lease expires, which he could not do if all were to be made and to terminate at the same period; and it also affords an opportunity of observing the success of the measure with the villages first settled, by which Government can be determined to limit or extend its operation.

54. I shall next discuss the questions just alluded to, regarding a survey assessment and the resumption of certain alienations. But I must first observe that none of the objections I have urged extend to leases of every improvable village at an increasing rent, such as are called in the Deccan Istava leases: for as the success of the undertaking depends entirely on getting new Rayats, there is no chance of ill-treatment to that class for the first years; and in the last ones, even if they are not, as is usual, fortified by written agreements obtained before they began to cultivate the new lands, they are not so likely to be oppressed by a person who has for some years fostered them and partaken of their prosperity, as they would be by a farmer who bought them at an auction as an immediate source of profit.

55. I now come to the survey and survey assessment. There can be no doubt of the advantages of a survey: it shows the real state of land, it prevents concealed cultivation or encroachments of rent-free fields on those belonging to Government, it gives

facility and precision to future assessment, and it prevents disputes about boundaries either between villages or individuals.

56. But the question of a new assessment stands on different grounds. It has been pronounced by the highest authorities to be indispensable to any equitable settlement, on the Rayatwar plan at least; but it would make so complete a change in the circumstances of all the cultivators in Gujarat, that I feel disposed to pause before I entertain the proposal. The extraordinary prosperity of the Rayats of Gujarat on their present footing takes away all hope of improving their condition by a change, while it increases the doubt which would be felt in any case, whether they may not be losers by the alteration suggested. The settlement of what each Bigha is to pay hereafter must be confided to numerous natives on low pay, and if they are deficient either in honesty, diligence, or judgment, it will be unjust; even supposing those qualities united, local experience would still be required. The rent of each Bigha I understand to depend on many minute particulars, which it is impossible to appreciate without long knowledge on the spot. The distance of the field from the village, of the village from a market town; the precise degree of fertility of the ground, which cannot be accurately provided for in any classification—all these particulars render an assessment difficult for a stranger; and if a Panchayat of the neighbours is had recourse to, their partiality or envy, obsequiousness or corruption, continually interpose to prevent a just decision. On the other hand, what a field has long paid, we are sure it may continue; and the suitableness of the rent to the land is probably the result of many unsuccessful experiments which, if we commence anew, we must expect to have to repeat. To be sure

of its not bearing hard on the people, it would be necessary to make the new assessment very low; and this, though it would have a good effect in time, would occasion an immediate loss of revenue. Even if the new assessment were fair and accurate, it might still be unadvisable, merely because it was new, as every man's rate of payments, and consequently his circumstances, would be altered; and the inconvenience suffered by him whose income is reduced, is out of all proportion to the advantage gained by him whose profit has been augmented. A new assessment would also require the new modelling, or more probably the breaking up, of all Narva villages; since if each field is to be assessed according to its actual value, it is almost impossible that the proportion of the revenue now due by each Patidar should not be altered. The tenure of the Khata Kaubi would also be destroyed, as the unnaturally high rent in his Khata must be reduced, while that on his other land would perhaps be raised; but whether in the same proportion, or less, or more, would be uncertain. All Veras that fall on land not alienated must also be abolished, for when the land paid all that was deemed equitable in direct rent, it could not be taxed in any other form. I do not know if this would be a loss to Government or to the Rayat, nor will I pronounce that it would be in itself disadvantageous; but it would certainly be a change, and ought, therefore, to be examined on its own merits before a system is adopted to which it is a necessary consequence. For these reasons, I should wish it to be considered whether a general new assessment be actually necessary before it is undertaken. In some Parganas, such as Petlad, where the present assessment is unequal, I have no doubt it will be an improvement, and to such I would at once extend it; in other places, particular villages may require a new Bighoti, which may be fixed without unsettling the whole country. Even for these partial and gradual changes in the assessment, I should wish a plan could be adopted that should secure some supervision to the assessment of the Panchayats, and which should bring the whole of the grounds on which any change in the rent of a field was made more fully under the eye of the collector. The mention of the survey reminds me of the proposed plan for the settlement of boundary disputes between villages by the surveyors during the progress of their work. The advantages of this plan are obvious; but I was before afraid that it would prove a more difficult task than we expected, and might stir up more disputes than we should afterwards be able to settle. I have since conversed with the surveyors and the collectors on the subject, and am satisfied that the arrangement would be as easily accomplished as it would be beneficial. The collector might be associated with the surveyor, but his attendance ought not to be indispensable to the settlement. An appeal might be made to the judge, if preferred within a fixed period, at most three months, though I scarcely see what means of deciding he could obtain to equal those of the surveyor on the spot.

57. I have purposely reserved the question of resuming alienated lands for separate consideration, nor will I now say anything definitive on a subject that is likely still to be fully discussed. I shall, however, note down what occurs to me regarding it. Though there may be alienations under each of the denominations of rent-free land, which may be resumable on account of fraud or defects of title, yet the principal sorts of which the resumption is to be considered are the Vechan and Garania, or lands alienated by the Patels of

their own authority, for the purpose, real or pretended, of meeting demands for revenue which the village could not otherwise discharge. From all that I have heard, there seems little doubt that these alienations were illegal, and that the persons who accepted of them were well aware of their illegality. The question seems, therefore, to be confined to two points: the claims acquired by the possessors from the long forbearance of the Government; and the inexpediency of disturbing actual possession, by whatever title it may have been acquired or retained. To judge of the effect of the long forbearance of the Government, it is necessary to review the conduct both of the Mahratta and British authorities in this respect. It is undisputed that the Mahrattas never admitted sales or mortgages by Patels as a ground for reducing the revenue of a village. Such a reduction, probably, never was proposed to them. They continued to make their old demand, without perhaps being aware of the diminution that had taken place in the revenue of the village. The Patel, whose faith was pledged to the purchaser, endeavoured to screen him and to levy the whole revenue on the Rayats; but when he failed in that, he laid a tax on the purchaser; and if the sum to be raised was very great, he even assessed the alienated land in the same way with the unalienated. In this manner villages have been seen with every Bigha in them alienated, and yet assessed at the same rate as formerly, and paying the amount without demur. Such proceedings must have kept up in the purchasers a constant sense of the weakness of their own title, for as long as the country was under the Mahratta rule. Our Government gave rather more encouragement to the purchasers, but it still took some steps to prevent their feeling secure. It published a proclamation prohibiting and rendering penal future alienations; but the language used (proclamation of*) was such as to promote the belief that past ones would not be disputed. It continued, like the Mahrattas, to keep up the revenue in spite of these alienations; and at first it knew no more than they did from what sources that revenue was derived. When the system of farming was disused, and our collectors began to look into the interior management of villages, they still continued to take from each individual the sum at which he had formerly been assessed, however disproportioned to the value of the land from which it was apparently derived. When circumstances rendered it necessary to alter the rates of assessment, which only occurred within the last two or three years, the collector fixed the new rate with reference to the value of the field on which it was assessed, and as this operation reduced the whole revenue payable by the Rayats, he threw the amount of the deficiency on the alienated land, from which it had in reality been all along derived. He was enabled to do this consistently with the principles of our native predecessors, by imposing a Swadea on the land possessed or cultivated by the owner of the field where the deficiency occurred. The Swadea was a tax payable by Government Rayats who cultivated alienated land; and as almost all the Rayats are Government's, it is a tax from which few lands can escape. It had been resorted to by the Mahrattas as a means of making up deficiencies; but it was rarely required, as they were always content to allow the whole revenue to be assessed on the Talpad land, and never troubled themselves about the regularity of the assessment as long as they got the full revenue. It consequently had, in some measure, the appearance of an innovation when rendered so general by us; and if combined with our long previous forbearance, it might be understood as an

* Blank in original.

acknowledgment of the title of the holders of alienated lands. On the other hand, it certainly had weakened their hopes of much benefit from the tenure; for when they see a sum levied from land nominally rent-free, their former experience leads them to expect that it will continually increase until it reaches the full amount of the revenue. The frequent explanations of the collectors regarding the right to these lands, and the example of the resumptions at Broach, must have warned all who were acquainted with the proceedings of that Zilla of the doubts of Government as to their tenure. These remarks refer to Kaira. In Ahmedabad the collector at once imposed a Swadea of one-third on all rent-free lands cultivated by Government Rayats, which must not only have prevented any belief that the occupant would be allowed entire exemption in that Zilla, but must have added greatly to the distrust in their titles already felt in that of Kaira.

58. The third regulation of 1814 may be thought to have confirmed the claim of the holders of land; but independent of the doubts entertained regarding the meaning of that regulation, it does not appear to have been ever acted on, as few or no proprietors took advantage of the power given them of securing their lands by registering them within a certain time. On the other hand, the proceedings of the collectors, who always prosecute for the recovery of land alienated since the cession, and never question a deed executed prior to that date, must have led to the belief that the law recognised the permanency of such alienations. It may therefore, I conceive, be pronounced that, although the hopes left to the proprietors of alienated lands of our long forbearance to proceed to resumption may not form a perfect claim upon our justice, they at least afford a very strong title to our indulgent consideration.

59. We have now, in the second place, to examine how far it is expedient to disturb the present state of possession, even by the resumption of lands acquired unjustly, and retained under no legal title. The present state of Gujarat, where our revenue has been raised so much above its original amount, and where the condition of the Rayats is nevertheless so flourishing, creates a strong repugnance to any such innovation. This repugnance is increased when we look into particulars. We find the revenue levied on all the Veheta land unnaturally high; we know that part of the excess is paid by alienated land, of which the holder of the Veheta is either cultivator or proprietor; we have reason to think that other land may be in the same predicament, and consequently that any great resumption of alienated land will at once derange the assessment of the most part of the land which remains unalienated. A remedy for this may be suggested in a new and equitable assessment of the land, by which every Bigha will pay exactly according to its own value, so as not to depend on alienated land for making up its revenue; but I have already stated the doubts I entertain of the policy of such an experiment, and that question must be determined before this agreement can be used. A complete revision of the Veras, or taxes, would also be necessary, even if not otherwise required by the new assessment, as many, if not most of them fall on the rent-free land. The resumption would also break up all Narva villages, even if there were no new assessment, for the sharers at present pay a sum in the gross of their Pattis, without distinguishing rent-free land from Talpad; and consequently their profits, both absolute and relative, would be entirely changed by the removal of one of those portions. While it retains the effect on the public revenue, we

must not forget the individual distress that will be produced, if every man is to be stripped of the usurpations of his ancestors; the clamour that will be raised by dispossessing Bhats and Brahmans; and the disturbances which may follow depriving of their subsistence a body of Kolis and other plunderers, who are only kept quiet by the easy means of subsistence now afforded them. Great changes of property are seldom made without disorders, and here they are peculiarly to be apprehended from the turbulent and predatory character of so large a proportion of the population, and from the change being directly injurious to those most useful in maintaining the police. On the other hand, there are strong reasons why the possession of alienated lands should not be hastily confirmed. We must not, in our tenderness for the holder of that description of land, forget the case of our less-favoured subjects. If the public burthen were to be increased, equity would require that the new impost should fall on those who already paid the least; and this would be the case even if their titles were undoubted, and if no opportunity like the present were afforded of levying a tax on them with little odium or appearance of injustice. If, therefore, it should be found practicable to draw a considerable revenue from rent-free lands, without pressing on those who already pay their full share of taxation, without reducing the proprietors to ruin, and without driving kolis or other unsettled people to plunder, the measure, I conceive, should be adopted. At all events, some plans must be adopted to prevent loss to Government, by its Rayats cultivating rent-free land, which is likely to happen whenever the property in that sort of estate shall be fixed; and this object must be adverted to in any plan that may be proposed. It is necessary, therefore, before we proceed further, that we should endeavour to ascertain the amount of the revenue alienated, the classes by whom it is possessed, the probable effects of resuming it on the condition of those classes and on their payments to the public, and the classes by whom it is cultivated when not by the possessors themselves.

60. The amount in the Kaira district appears to be 1,050,000 rupees, of which it is probable that about 150,000 rupees may be Vanta, Vazifa, and descriptions of Pasayta that we should not wish to touch. It is conjectured there may be about 200,000 rupees estimated for land, which is now waste, and that about 200,000 rupees may already pay revenue indirectly. There would, therefore, be only five lacs to tax; and as the highest amount that could well be levied would be one-third of the Government share, the whole gain to Government in Kaira would be only 160,000 rupees; 200,000 rupees would certainly be an ample estimate. The returns from Ahmedabad have not yet been received, but as there are only four Parganas where Government could profit by those resumptions, the whole gain on a similar calculation could not possibly exceed the same amount. We may, therefore, reckon our profit at the very utmost at four lacs of rupees: a sum worth attending to if it can be realized without much danger, but one for which it is not worth while to run any great risk of the evils alluded to.

61. The next questions relating to the classes by whom the unauthorized lands are possessed, the rents they pay through other lands or by Veras, and the other means of subsistence possessed by the proprietors, might be referred to the collectors, with a request that they might be careful to specify both the proprietors and the cultivators, and to distinguish between real and fictitious proprietors. Mr. Dunlop might also be called

on to state the amount produced by the tax he has imposed on alienated lands; and perhaps my inquiries when in Broach, regarding those resumed by the commission, may throw some light on the question. When these questions are ascertained, we may determine whether or not it is expedient to raise a revenue from rent-free lands. If it should be determined in the negative, it will still be necessary to guard against loss, by assessing on each portion of rent-free land the share which it now actually bears of the over-assessment of Talpad land. When this is done, it will be practicable to equalize the assessment on all lands of the latter description, and likewise to allow the Rayats to take and relinquish what land they please unrestrained, neither of which is practicable in the present state of things. It will also, I conceive, be expedient to declare that the land now left rent-free is liable to such imposts as may be rendered necessary by the exigencies of the state; and if this declaration should for a time prevent the owners from feeling confident in their possession, it is better to submit to that evil than to close up for ever a source from which so much revenue may be drawn with so little difficulty or ill consequence. If it be determined to raise a revenue, the first mode that occurs is that proposed by Captain Barnewall and Captain Robertson, of a stamp-duty; but this, unless accompanied by a Swadea, will not prevent the emigration of Sarkar Rayats. It might be an improvement to have a Swadea of greater amount than the stamp-duty (say one-third of the Government share) on land cultivated by Sarkars' Rayats, Patidars, etc., and a stamp-duty of one-fourth on land cultivated by the proprietor. Another middle course would be, to allow all lands cultivated by the proprietors to remain on their present footing, but to assess those held by Government Rayats, Patidars, etc., at the full amount, and then pay to the proprietor the sum which he now receives from the Rayats. This plan has often been adopted towards Vanta, and it is much recommended towards Vechan and Garania, by the consideration that the burden will fall on those by whose fraud the alienations have been occasioned, it being the common trick of Patels to assign land to a Bhat or Brahman, keeping the cultivation and the profit in their own hands, and only paying a trifle to the proprietor for the use of his name ; but it is an objection that the tax falls entirely on the classes who already contribute to the revenue, and whose wealth, however acquired, is sure in the end to add to that of the public.

62. In all plans, whatever is now collected by Government should be kept up, there being no doubt of its right to what it possesses, however doubtful that of the holders of the alienations.

63. It is desirable that the questions regarding alienations and a new assessment should be settled soon, to enable us to remove the doubt and anxiety under which the Rayats now labour.

64. An important point to consider is the degree of interference which Government should exercise with the collector, and I think, on the whole, it is expedient to leave him a great latitude. Government must settle such questions as that of resuming the alienated lands and the policy to be observed towards Girasias and Mevasis: it may interfere to correct any proceeding that is obviously erroneous ; and above all, it should permit no great change to be made without its express permission. Besides the advantage of retarding innovations, it would thus be able to bring to every question its own general views, and occasionally the experience of the other Presidencies ; but all details had better be

left to the collector. This is more expedient than at the other Presidencies, because we have no Board of Revenue, and our collectorships are so different from each other that a complete knowledge of one scarcely enables a member of the Government to decide on a question relating to another. It is, however, a serious evil that there is no check on a collector, and no means of knowing, short of the ultimate failure of the revenue, whether his district is in prosperity and content, or in poverty and wretchedness. To make up for the want of this, it has occurred to me that the judge, or judge of circuit, might be empowered to receive complaints and transmit them to Government, even on questions of high assessment or the like, which are unconnected with his judicial functions. There are, however, strong objections to this plan, as likely to lead to discord between two officers whose good understanding with each other it is of importance to preserve, and perhaps even to excite a litigious spirit in the Rayats themselves.

65. I will insert an observation here, as it relates so immediately to the Rayats, though it properly belongs to the administration of justice: it is the hardship felt by the Rayats from the exaction of the debts contracted by them during the Mahratta Government under the decrees of the Adalat. The root of the grievance seems to lie in the readiness with which a bond is admitted as a sufficient evidence of the justice of a claim. In this case it is by no means so, for a Rayat is easily drawn by occasional advances and partial payments into a complicated account, which it is impossible for him to unravel. This account presents a great balance in the lender's favour; and as the practice is for the Rayat to give up his produce each year in part payment, and to take an advance to enable him to go on with the next, he

is so completely in the lender's power that he would sign anything rather than disoblige him. The remedy, therefore, is to settle that in new provinces a bond shall not be conclusive when originating in an old debt of a Rayat, but that his whole account shall be examined as if no bond had been executed, and only the amount which shall then appear fair decreed to the plaintiff. If the debts could be paid by instalments regulated by the amount of the Rayat's payment to Government, it would complete the removal of the evil; but, at all events, steps should be taken to prohibit the sale of a Rayat's cattle and implements of husbandry in satisfaction of debts.

66. Though it appears from the reports of the judges that this practice is seldom resorted to, it is much dreaded and greatly complained of, and as it is not used it may be safely forbidden; the revision of the code affords an opportunity of doing so. A petition which I have received from the Patels of four Parganas in the Kaira district, complaining loudly of these evils, solicits likewise that the sale of houses belonging to Rayats should be forbidden. Those houses being on Government ground, which is required by the villages, cannot be sold to a stranger; the creditor can, therefore, only destroy the house and sell the materials, which is ruinous to the Rayat without being beneficial to the creditor. It is, however, a question whether the prohibition of such sales would not in the end injure the Rayat by lessening his credit.

67. In all discussions connected with the means of improving the situation of the people, our attention is drawn to the amendment of their education. This seems to be nearly in the same state here as in the Deccan. I should rather think there were more schools, but there are no books.

The same plan I recommend in the Deccan may be adopted here, the circulation of cheap editions of such native books, of those already popular, as might have a tendency to improve the morals of the people without strengthening their religious prejudices. Passages remarkable for bigotry or false maxims of morality might be silently omitted, but not a syllable of attack on the religion of the country should be allowed.

68. I was formerly of opinion that the salaries allowed to assistant collectors, on the plan proposed by Mr. Warden and approved by the Supreme Government, were too high, and I therefore recommended that they should be fixed on their present footing. I now find that I did not at the time sufficiently advert to the fees in the judicial line, which render all the appointments there so much superior to those in the revenue, that it is not to be expected that any young man will stay in the latter when he can leave it, although it is indispensable that everyone should spend some years in it. I therefore recommend that the former proposal be reconsidered, and the salaries fixed on a footing nearer equality with the others, though I would perhaps make it worth the while of the youngest judicial assistant to go into the revenue line, and of the oldest revenue assistant to accept of a registership.

69. I shall here introduce a few observations on the employment of the assistants to the collectors, a point of more consequence to the welfare of the public than it at first appears, as by it is formed the character of those on whose ability and public spirit the success of all future measures of Government is to depend. The collectors, I conceive, should be ordered to employ their assistants in the Parganas the moment they are capable: the assistant's allowances to be kept below the standard fixed for his appointment until he has been so deputed.

Each collector should report every six months how his assistant has been employed, and how he discharges his duties. Copies of the collector's instructions to the assistant should be forwarded to Government, as well as occasional copies of his reports to the collector. One great duty of the assistant should be to ascertain at the villages whether the sum charged in the accounts as the payments of each Rayat, is the whole amount that he has paid. If this inquiry be made of each Rayat, personally, at a few villages taken at random in every Pargana, there would be an effectual check on the native officers, and this important object would be closely connected with the improvement of the assistant.

70. I beg here to recall the attention of the Board to the salaries of the Kamavisdars, which I find in many instances totally inadequate. The Kamavisdar of Dholka collects six lacs of rupees, and his whole allowances are 158 rupees. This disproportion is hardly decent. I think we should push into these Zillas the plan already adopted in the Northern Konkan, with the difference that as the districts here are rich and compact, and the country cheap, a smaller percentage might be given; 1,500 rupees a year for one lac of rupees collections, and an increase of 500 rupees or thereabout on every succeeding lac would be sufficient. The allowance of the collector's head native servant should be raised, and perhaps made equal to that of the best paid Kamavisdar. I would also strongly recommend some plan for increasing the pay of Kamavisdars with their standing, as the strongest tie on their honesty, and still more for furnishing a provision for them after long service; a measure not more required by considerations relative to the particular case, than by the general policy of securing a respectable class of

persons accustomed to our views and attached to our Government.

71. I have not had time to make any inquiries about the customs and town duties, but I may make two observations regarding them. No customs levied by Mevasis, Girasias, or petty chiefs, if established before our acquisition of the country, should be abolished without a compensation; and this compensation should be promptly afforded, since, if it is withheld, the complaints of the sufferers will render others in similar circumstances unwilling to give up a right they possess for a pension, while the regular payment would seem to them doubtful.

72. Another regards the abolition of two duties. The Committee at Kaira in 1811 have reported them to be vexatious and pernicious, and Government determined to do them away. I would, however, recommend that they should not be given up without some equivalent tax which should reach the merchants and bankers, the only description of people in our territory that are not subject to taxation. The losses of that class from the introduction of our Government would render it inexpedient to lay any serious impost on them now; but something might be introduced that would enable Government to draw a revenue from them when their circumstances are more flourishing, or the wants of the state more urgent.

73. All accounts agree in reporting the transfer of the police to the revenue officers as eminently successful; and even before that measure the improvements in the police had been prodigious. There is no open violence, and the people can act against any attempt at it without the fear of revenge. Thefts are much diminished, and murders are comparatively extremely rare. From what I can learn, the people (except the

Kolis) are neither much given to affrays or drinking, nor otherwise debauched. One evil of the present plan is the expense to which Kamavisdars are put by the attendance required of them at the sessions as police officers, and the serious inconvenience to themselves and the public occasioned by their absence during seasons when they are wanted for their revenue duties. The increase I have proposed to salaries, if it should take place, will obviate the first objection ; and I really think that all sorts of forms should be sacrificed to remove the second. The Kamavisdar might be summoned for the occasion when his evidence was essential to a trial, but should be dismissed as soon as it is over; and in all cases of verifying depositions and the like, the oath of the person who wrote them, or of some other bystander, should be sufficient.

74. A point very generally and seriously exclaimed against, both by the people and the gentlemen in authority, is the present mode of recovering stolen property from villages to which it is traced. The responsibility of villages not actually convicted of connivance is, I believe, generally considered as extremely harsh and unjust, and as such, I believe, it has been abolished under the other Presidencies. The natives (from whom we borrowed it, exercise it with many limitations. The property must have been placed in charge of the village watchman, and even then it is only in peculiar cases that the whole or a part of the value is levied on the village. For my own part, although I think it rather a rough remedy, I am decidedly of opinion that it should be kept up, to prevent the indifference to the police which we should otherwise have reason to dread from our native subjects ; but it is only as an engine to be employed in the police that I would preserve it, and as such it must be employed with judgment and by the

hands to which the police is entrusted. The present indiscriminate application of it is not only intolerable from its injustice and severity, but absolutely fatal to the principle of activity in the police which it is meant to uphold. The temptation to the inhabitants to share, to connive, or to neglect, is much increased, when the tracing of footsteps (perhaps imprinted for the purpose) to another village relieves them from all responsibility, and the person robbed, who is generally the best agent of the police, becomes at once an indifferent spectator of a search for property of which he is certain to receive at least the full value. It would be a much more effectual plan for the police, and much more equitable towards the villages, to invest the magistrate with a discretionary power to exact a sum not exceeding the value of the property from any village which he suspects of connivance or neglect. He should be at liberty to apportion it on any number of villages that seemed to partake in the neglect, and to levy it at what period he pleased, so as to allow it time to operate as a stimulus to the researches of the villagers; and he might remit it, if he was satisfied before payment had taken place that no exertion had been wanting. But he ought to be directed to be rather rigid than lax, and to allow no appearance even of negligence to escape without some fine. I can see no objection whatever to entrusting the magistrate with this power, which he always possessed till the passing of Regulation III. of 1818. If it is wished to have a check on his exercise of it, it might be subject to the revision of the criminal judge; but it ought, at all events, to be a branch of the police; and I observe that it was so even in Bengal, where the payment for property by villages in certain circumstances was to be ordered by the Court of Circuit and not by the Divani Adalat. Supposing, however, that our system requires it to be subject to the decision of a civil court, it would be necessary to enact that no suit should be received, unless a certificate could be produced from the magistrate or criminal judge that the case was one in which the village was to blame.

75. I may here introduce the subject of military guards employed on civil duties. I made this an object of my particular attention, with a view to relieve the line from a number of duties requiring none of the qualities of a soldier, and yet breaking up battalions that might be wanted for service, and injuring the discipline of those not likely to be so called on. The result of my inquiries showed the number of Sepoys so employed to be less than I had supposed; but still they amount to upwards of 600 men, without including the Northern and Southern Konkan; altogether they cannot fall short of the strength of a complete battalion. Guards for the gaols, however, would at all events be required, and these would take 50 men for each Zilla; 300 in all; so that the reduction in Gujarat would not exceed 300 men. It might be practicable to make such a distribution of the extra battalions as might render them applicable to this duty, and thus leave all the battalions intended for service disposable for that purpose. But these troops, if employed on the gaol guards, would require to be often relieved, as they would otherwise get intimate with the prisoners and cease to be an effectual check on them. The collector of Ahmedabad has a party of his Peons dressed in a blue uniform, with brown belts and a kind of foraging-cap, and armed with muskets and bayonets, who only receive seven rupees for clothes and all, and yet a month or two's exercising with a regular battalion, and, I believe, the superintendence of a discharged Havaldar, has made them at least as good, I think

better than regular Sepoys, for all these duties except gaol guards. If a company of 100 men of this description to each Zilla could be paid by a reduction in the revenue and police establishments, it would be sufficient for the duty, and would ease the troops of the line. The responsibility of collectors for treasure not under a military guard should be dispensed with, where there is no neglect on his part or his officers'. The absence of a military guard should make no difference.

76. Before I conclude this paper, I must record my obligations to the collectors of these Zillas for the cordial assistance I received from them in my inquiries, and for the valuable information and opinions which they communicated. The zeal, activity, and successful management of Mr. Dunlop have already been noticed in various employments, and I have particular pleasure in noticing the remarkable intelligence and acquaintance with his duty displayed by Mr. More.

77. Though from the nature of the judicial establishment, fixed by regulations and controlled by superior courts, I did not think it necessary to devote any of the short time I had at my disposal to inquiries in that line, I have to acknowledge the readiness of the gentlemen at the head of it to afford me every information; and to Mr. Anderson I am indebted for much information and many judicious suggestions.

(Signed) M. ELPHINSTONE.

Camp Chaklasi, *6th April*, 1821.

FURTHER MINUTE BY THE PRESIDENT.

EXTRACTED FROM 'EAST INDIA PAPERS,'

Vol. III. pp. 706—709.

FURTHER MINUTE BY THE PRESIDENT.

EXTRACTED FROM 'EAST INDIA PAPERS,'
VOL. III. pp. 706—709.

I HAVE perused Mr. Prendergast's observations on my minutes on Ahmedabad and Kaira, and on other districts of Gujarat, with much interest and attention. I now proceed to offer such explanation as those observations appear to call for.

To facilitate reference, I shall take the liberty of putting numbers on the parts of Mr. Prendergast's minute to which I wish to allude.

This observation applies to Bhagdar villages only; and in them I think I have said that all the Bhagdars and Patels, though only the few who are at the heads of great divisions (Mota Bhags in Broach) receive the Patel's allowances and communicate with the Government. But the number of Bhagdar villages in Gujarat is comparatively small: there are more in Surat, few in Ahmedabad, not so much as half the number of villages in Kaira. In Broach only they are numerous; in all other villages there is only one Patel.

In one sense of the word all the Company's subjects

are Rayats; but in the village the word is used (in contradistinction to Patel) for the cultivators who do not share in the village Government. It is in this sense I use it in the places noticed by Mr. Prendergast, and I believe in all others.

Those are called 'Sarkar,' the Rayats that cultivate Talpad land, to distinguish them from those who cultivate exclusively land belonging to Girasias, which last are chiefly found in Girasias villages. What control the Government has over them is another question. The Native Government had a great deal once, and I think ought to have none; at least no power of restraining them from throwing up their lands when they choose.

My opinion regarding leases agrees generally with Mr. Prendergast's; but as I have no experience myself, I am unwilling to decide a question so much disputed; I, therefore, am desirous of the reference I have already recommended to Captain Robertson. I also think it desirable that instructions should be issued to the collector, recommending the gradual and partial system of leases as an experiment, which is explained in the part of my minute immediately following the suggestion of a reference to Captain Robertson. Such instructions will, at all events, be necessary to such collectors as have been applying for leave to grant leases generally. I must also own, that I think leases to Patidars, where very numerous, less doubtful than any others. They are already bound by a sort of lease towards the Government, and it is but fair the Government should be similarly bound towards them.

The opinion that the Rayatwar system involves so much detail as to be impracticable of execution, is not brought forward as my own; it is only quoted to be contested.

The objections to the Rayatwar system, from the difficulty the Rayat must experience in complaining to the collector, applies with additional force to the village lease, a district lease system, because there is another native authority interposed between the collector and the Rayat, and that one much more formidable than the Kamavisdar, because more permanent, more intimately connected with the complaint, and possessing greater means of exacting or oppressing without detection.

I observe that the Rayatwar system has been 'more extensively introduced in reality than in appearance, while the Patel continued to go through the forms of farming his villages.' Now that the appearance is entirely Rayatwar, Mr. Prendergast's observation is probably correct.

Mr. Prendergast probably understands the word 'farming' in some sense different from that which I meant to attach to it. I called a village farmed, when Government transfers its rights in it to another person, or association of persons, for a rent. I should say it was not farmed, when Government retained in its own hands its rights over the Rayats.

The number of Bighas, productive and unproductive, assessable and alienated, are, as Mr. Prendergast observes, more accurately known in Broach than in any other district in India, because none has been so carefully surveyed. I will add, that every object of the survey, and every object of the reports made at the time of the first commission, were as fully known as it was possible for such subjects to be. But many of the facts on which the annual assessment is founded could not be touched on either by the survey or the reports; and many are so fluctuating, that if the state of them, as it then stood, had been recorded, it would be totally inapplicable now. Thus the productive assessable land is recorded; but whether the quantity producing grain is not greatly increased cannot of course be ascertained from the survey. A proof that these points are not actually ascertained, is afforded by the prosecutions carrying on (or formerly carried on) against the Pargana officers of Anklesvar for concealing cultivation to a large amount. But if the quantity of land of each description to be assessed were well known, the next step in Broach appears to me full of uncertainty. It is a conjectural estimate of the quantity of grain of each description produced in the season for which the assessment is making. There is no careful examination of each field, or debate with the proprietor about the improvement or decline of its condition. A general estimate is made from a summary inspection of the state of the fields; and although, from the experience of the Pargana officers, it may frequently be right, yet as it is too vague to admit of a close examination, the collector can never be confident that it is not wrong, either owing to mistake or corruption.

If this conjecture, however, be right, and if the price for which the grain will sell be also accurately ascertained, so that the sum laid on the whole village is just, it by no means follows that the distribution will be equally just by the time it reaches the Rayats. One Rayat may be in declining circumstances, while many of his fellows may be increasing in wealth. One part of the village land might be suffering from flood or blight, while the rest is unusually productive. The Patel may perhaps adjust all these inequalities, but he does it unknown to the collector or his officers, who may therefore be fairly said to be in the dark regarding the sources from which the revenue is derived. I have been speaking of villages under one Patel in Bhagdar villages. This evil cannot be entirely remedied, and all Government can do is to see that the whole sum laid on the village is equitable.

A proof of the uncertainty of the assessment is, that the vast increase laid in Broach this year was founded on the supposition of the unusual abundance of cotton produced; and this was the reason assigned by the acting-collector in the end of April, when I believe the season is nearly closed: yet the commercial resident has since announced a failure, and the acting-collector has stated that the produce of this year is a good deal less than that of the last. The power of resorting to a division of the crop is a safeguard against over-assessment possessed by the cultivators in all districts; but I doubt if it is so effectual as Mr. Prendergast considers it, because nobody resorted to it this year in Broach, although the clamour in the district has been excessive.

What Mr. Prendergast says of the Bhagdar's system, I should generally subscribe to, in cases such as Mr. Prendergast supposes, where almost all the cultivators are Bhagdars. I have, indeed, taken a very similar view in my minute; but this only applies to about half the villages in the Broach Zilla, and to very few in the other collectorship.

This is, indeed, a principal cause of the apparent difference between Mr. Prendergast and me, that his view generally applies to a village, cultivated by Bhagdars, while mine also bears on villages where there are few Bhagdars, or those formed by a single Patel, and on those settled Rayatwar.

With regard to the hereditary officers of Parganas, I confess that the concurring opinions of all the revenue officers, whose opinions I have heard on the subject, make me unfavourable to the employment of them; but this question is here only introduced incidentally in discussing the pay of Kamavisdars. In regard to them, all I contend for is, that their pay should bear some proportion to their trust. I do not think that the allowances in Broach could conveniently be adopted as a standard, because that district has a system entirely peculiar, and not at all resembling those of the other districts, which system leaves all the settlement of the revenue to the Patels and Pargana officers, so that the Kamavisdars have little else to do than to receive the collections.

I beg to explain what I have said about the different limits of Parganas and Kamavisdars' divisions. The latter often include several of the former; but I do not believe the Parganas are ever divided, except by the boundary line of different collectorships.

The account given of Vanta in all the reports of the collectors beyond the Mahi, is that which I have mentioned; it is supported by the Mohammedan histories and documents connected with revenue, and I believe by the traditions of the hereditary Hindu officers. My idea of the history is, that there were several Rajput principalities in Gujarat under different dynasties of Solankis, Sumas, Gohils, Waghelas, etc., each of which, according to the Rajput practice, divided the country among the relations and Tattayets of the Raja, till the whole country was shared out among them, as Cutch, Kathiawar, and other neighbouring countries, not subdued by the Mussulmans, are still. That when the Mussalmans got the country they took three-fourths of the Government share of the revenue to themselves, leaving the Rajputs in possession of the remaining one, precisely as it is now proposed that we should do with the Girasias of Dhandhuka, Gogha,

Ranpur. The Rayats retained their share generally under both Governments, and retain it still.

Mevasi seems to be used for 'refractory,' and as such is no doubt applicable occasionally either to Rajput or Koli; but as all independence in a Koli is reckoned usurpation, and not so in a Rajput, the term has come to be applied to the former in contradistinction to a Girasia.

Each Rajput tribe gives you a separate account of its own settlement in Gujarat; scarcely any at a very remote period. I should suppose they all came originally from Meywar, Marwar, and the other countries which the Mussalmans and we call Rajputana; but some of them seem first to have passed into Scind and returned by Cutch into Gujarat. Those mentioned by Mr. Prendergast (Jhallas and Gohils) are stated by Colonel Walker to have entered their present seats, I think, within these last 500 years.

I do not intend to propose a complete revision of the Veras, but to mention that as one of the consequences attending a new assessment or a resumption of alienated lands, each of which measures I wished to show in all its bearings.

I fully concur in the policy of preserving the Bhagdar villages wherever we find them established, and am of opinion that their increasing in number may be taken as a sign of prosperity in the country.

I meant to have circulated the returns from the collectors, showing the number of villages held by single Patels, the number held by Bhagdars; but this being Sunday, I have not been able to get them. They shall be circulated whenever they arrive.

P.S.—The returns are now sent duly. That from Ahmedabad gives the information required in a distinct form. It appears that there are, out of 700 villages, only 29 Bhagdars, the rest being managed by single Patels. In Kaira I should conjecture that two-thirds were managed by single Patels. In Surat almost all, or all; in Broach very few.

(Signed.) M. ELPHINSTONE.

(Without date.)

MINUTES

BY THE

HON. MOUNTSTUART ELPHINSTONE,

DATED FEBRUARY 21;

AND

CHOBARI, CUTCH, JANUARY 26, 1821.

MINUTE

BY THE

HON. MOUNTSTUART ELPHINSTONE,

DATED FEBRUARY 21, 1821.

WE labour under a great disadvantage in all deliberations regarding this tract of country, as I believe no account of it is before the Government, for Major Ballantyne's report is chiefly confined to the proceedings of the Gaikwar force in 1813. This deficiency cannot be made up by information collected during a passage through the country; but I hope it will soon be removed by the inquiries which I have directed Captain Miles to make, and by those of Major Ballantyne when he shall have taken charge. In the meantime, I owe much to the information I have received from Captain Barnewall, whose long employment in the Kaira district has rendered him particularly well acquainted with the adjoining parts of the Mahi Kantha.

Description of the Mahi Kantha.

It is scarcely necessary to mention that the fiscal and military division known by the name of Mahi Kantha is not, as that name implies, confined to the banks of the Mahi; but extends northward from that river to the Banas, a distance of 120 miles, and includes all the part of Gujarat which requires the presence of a military force to procure the payment of the Gaikwar tribute; that is, all the north or north-eastern portion of the province.

The mountains which bound Gujarat in that direction are steep, craggy, and difficult of access. They send many branches into the nearest parts of Gujarat, and the intervals between them are nearly filled up with jungle. Further south the hills cease, and afterwards the jungles become less extensive; but the rivers are very numerous, and their banks abound in long, deep, and intricate ravines, overgrown with thick jungle. All these obstacles diminish as we go south, the jungle nearly disappears, and the rivers unite in the streams of the Sabarmati and the Mahi; and nearly the whole of the south-west of Gujarat, a tract sixty miles deep, extending for 150 miles along the gulf and Cambay, the frontier of Kathiawar and the Ran, is an open and fertile plain. This description explains the degrees of subjugation in which the province is found. The plain was almost entirely reduced, and the Government of the Marathas, though the jungles of Chuval, west of Ahmedabad, and the banks of the Mahi as far south as the neighbourhood of Baroda, still furnish shelter to independent villages. When the streams begin to be numerous, many independent communities appear among the ravines and jungle on their banks. The rivers increase, the jungle grows thicker and more continued as we advance, and the independent villages become more frequent and in more solid masses until we reach the principalities of Idar and Lunavada, amidst the mountains and the forest of the north-east.

The degree of independence in those communities increases with their numbers. In the plain to the south, and in the open spaces that run up between the rivers, the Maratha Government had the right of administering justice in every village by means of its own officers, and it always took an account of the produce of the village lands, of which it was entitled to a certain share. All the other villages retained their independence on the payment of a tribute. Most of those which lay on the rivers in the midst of subjugated country paid it regularly every year to the nearest revenue officer; but those whose situations were stronger or more remote withheld their tribute until compelled to pay by the presence of an invalid army. The villages which submit to the administration of justice and the inspection of their produce are called *Ryoti;* those which only pay a tribute, *Mehvasi;* but this last term is not extended to princes like those of Idar and Lunavada. The tribute paid annually to the revenue officer is called *Jamabandi*; that collected by an officer at the head of an army is called *Ghasdana.* There are many Mehvasis, who, though they are willing to pay a small sum to the Kamavisdars, will not submit to the exaction of a large one unless supported by force. These pay both Jamabandi and Ghasdana, the former to the collector every year, the latter to the commandant of the force that is occasionally sent to levy it. Both descriptions, however, are equally tribute, and neither is a fixed share of the produce.

Although the whole of the above distinctions took their origin from the different degrees in which the communities which are the subjects of them were subjected to the power of the Maratha Government, yet the distinction has often been preserved when the cause has been removed. Many villages remain Mehvasi, which the Gaikwar could have rendered Ryoti; and in many cases the Ghasdana is still collected by the military commander where the Mehvasi would have been equally ready to pay it to the Kamavisdar, and where his payment to that officer much exceeds his contribution to the army. The amount of the payments continued to fluctuate after the denominations had become fixed; when the Kamavisdar, or the military chief, was strong, he increased the Jamabandi or the Ghasdana; and when weak, he was glad to take a smaller sum than had been paid the year before. On the whole, however, there was a progressive increase in the payment.

It is the Ghasdana alone that is included in the Mahi Kantha collections.

The Mahi Kantha, though so much of it is neglected, shows great fertility wherever it is cultivated. The fields seem well taken care of and covered with fine crops. Mangoes and other planted trees are unusually numerous, and as the surface is undulating, and the woods and mountains soften in sight, no part of India presents a richer or more agreeable prospect.

Inhabitants.

There are in the Mahi Kantha many Kanbis, some Vanias and other peaceable classes; but the castes that bear arms, and those in whom all authority of the country is vested, are the Rajputs, Kolis and Makvanis, of whom the Kolis are by far the most numerous, even in the country belonging to the Rajputs. Of the 121 chiefs settled with by Major Ballantyne, 11 are Rajputs, 79 Kolis, and 31 Makvanis, and other Mussalmans; but this bears no proportion to the number of each caste. The Rajput and Mussalman principalities of Idar and Palanpur are nearly as extensive as all the rest put together, but many, perhaps most, of their subjects are Kolis. The Rajputs are of two descriptions—the Marvadis, who accompanied the Raja of Idar in his emigration from Jodhpur, and the Gujaratis, who have long been settled in the province, chiefly in the central parts. The Marvadis resemble the people of Jodhpur in their dress and manners, but with additional rudeness contracted in their sequestered situation. They are said to be very brave, but stupid, slothful, unprincipled, and devoted to the use of opium and intoxicating liquors. Those of Gujarat are said to resemble more the inhabitants of that province, to be more civilized than the Marvadis, more honest, more submissive, and more inactive and unwarlike. All the Rajputs use swords and spears, matchlocks and shields. They often use defensive armour of leather, both for themselves and their horses, and sometimes, but rarely, carry bows. Their plan of war is to defend their villages. They seldom take to the woods like Kolis, and are quite incapable of the desultory warfare so congenial to the habits of the latter tribe. The Kolis or Bhils (for they are called indiscriminately by both names) are by much the most numerous and most important of the inhabitants of the Mahi Kantha. Though there is not perhaps a very marked difference in feature between them and the other inhabitants, yet they are generally to be distinguished without difficulty; they seem more diminutive, and have an expression both of liveliness and cunning in their eyes. They wear small turbans and few clothes, and are seldom seen without a quiver of arrows and a long bamboo bow, which is instantly bent on any alarm, or on the sudden approach of a stranger. If they have less appearance of strength and activity than the generality of their neighbours, the defect is confined to their appearance.

The natives describe them as wonderfully swift, active and hardy; incredibly patient of hunger, thirst, fatigue, and want of sleep; vigilant, enterprising, secret, fertile in expedients, and admirably calculated for night attacks, surprises and ambuscades. These qualities are probably exaggerated; but they certainly are active, hardy, and as remarkable for sagacity as for secrecy and celerity in their predatory operations. Their arms and habits render them unfit to stand in the field, and they must be admitted to be timid where attacked; but they have on several occasions shown extraordinary boldness in assaults even on English stations. They are of an independent spirit, and although they are all professed robbers, they are said to be remarkably faithful when they are trusted, and they are certainly never sanguinary. They are averse to regular industry, exceedingly addicted to drunkenness, and very quarrelsome when intoxicated. Their delight is plunder, and nothing is so welcome to them as a general disturbance in the country.

The numbers of this tribe can scarcely be guessed at. The whole of the country between Gujarat and Milwa at the mountainous tracts on the Narbada and in Khandesh and Berar, together with the range of Ghats and its neighbourhood as far south as Puna, are filled with Bhils and Kolis; but it is those only to the west of the Mahi that are connected with the Mahi Kantha. It has been calculated on tolerable grounds that there are 6,600 in the Kaira district; and as there are fewer there than in any division in Gujarat, the whole amount must be very considerable. Their numbers would certainly be formidable if they were at all united; but though the Kolis have a strong fellow-feeling for each other, they never think of themselves as a nation, and never make a common cause to oppose an external enemy.

The Mussalmans of Gujarat are generally indolent and effeminate, but those in Mehvasi villages, especially the Malaiks, have almost as much activity as the Kolis, with much courage.

The Makvanis are Kolis nominally converted to Mohammedanism, but scarcely altered in the religion, manner, or character. They are chiefly settled towards the south-east of the Mahi Kantha.

Chiefs.

The chiefs by whom the Gaikwar tribute is paid, and the transactions which have taken place regarding it as far as they affect our interposition, and the measures to be adopted for realizing it in future, and for securing the quiet of the country and of our own districts in the neighbourhood, are as follows :

Beginning from the north, the first chief to notice would be the Diwan of Palanpur. But as his country is of a different character from the rest of the Mahi Kantha, and is now separated from it by our own political arrangements, it will be convenient to pass him over for the present.

The Raja of Idar.

The Raja of Idar is the fifth in descent from Ajitsing, who reigned at Jodhpur about a hundred years ago. His ancestor obtained possession of Idar about eighty years ago. It was at that time a part of the Jodhpur territory, Ajitsing having driven out another Rathod prince who was called the Rao, and still retains that title, though his territory is confined to the small but strong district of Pol in the hills between Idar and Udepur. He still continues his claims to Idar, and often harasses the Raja, who some years ago had a temporary possession of Pol.

The revenue of the state of Idar amounts to about 400,000 rupees (£40,000), without including its dependencies of Ahmednagar and Modasa. But the Raja's share is not more than from 100,000 to 150,000 rupees. The rest is allotted to chiefs who hold of him under the Rajput designation of Patavat, on condition of military service and of a small pecuniary payment. Besides these eight chiefs, who are all Rathods like the Raja, and whose ancestors accompanied him from Jodhpur, there are between twenty or thirty Patavats of the Rao's, who held lands of the Prince for military service, but who now pay an annual tribute instead of it to the Raja. These persons are Rajputs and Kolis. They owe no service to the Raja; they settle their Ghasdana separately with the Gaikwar, and appear to look up to him as their superior rather than to the Raja. The Raja of Idar's tribute, as fixed by Major Ballantyne, amounts to 24,000 rupees (£2,400), though much more has been exacted by the Gaikwar's officer. Only one-fourth of the amount falls on the Raja. The remaining three-fourths are paid by his Patavats, from whom, since the decline of the Raja's power, it has been levied separately by the Gaikwar. The whole ultimately falls on the Rayats, on whom an extra cess is imposed to meet it. The troops in the Raja of Idar's own pay amount at present to 250 horse and 1,000 foot, but these are raised for a particular occasion; his usual force is 50 horse and 150 foot. His Patavats should furnish 500 horses and as many foot, but very few ever attend. He has, however, about 600 men who hold lands direct of the Raja on condition of service, which they never fail to afford.

Besides the Raja's and the Rao's Patavats, there are three other chiefs, whose territory is included in the principality of Idar, though in reality they are almost entirely independent of that government.

The names of these petty chiefships are Ahmednagar, Modasa, and Baur. Each of the former yields a revenue of about 30,000 rupees (£3,000) a year, and their payments to the Gaikwar are 10,000 rupees (£1,000) for Ahmednagar, and 7,305 rupees (£730) for Modasa. Both together maintain about 100 horse and 200 foot. Baur yields only 5,000 rupees (£500) a year. The Chief of Ahmednagar is the mortal enemy of his cousin, the Raja of Idar; and their enmity is at present raised to the highest pitch by a dispute regarding Modasa, which the Raja claims as having reverted to him by the death of the last chief without issue, while the chief of Ahmednagar holds it for his son, whom he alleges to have been adopted by the deceased chief.

To complete the list of the Idar chiefs, it may be necessary to mention nine Koli villages on the Sabarmati which used to belong to Idar, and still pay a trifling tribute; but they have been long considered as separate, and are probably entirely beyond the Raja's control.

The territory of Idar, though open towards the west, is generally very strong, abounding in rivers, hills, and forests. The soil is fertile, and from the innumerable mango trees it seems to have been once well cultivated, but at present the greater portion is overrun with jungle. The Raja's government is said to be very oppressive, those of his Patavats less so. The town of Idar is conjectured to contain upwards of 2,500 houses, which would give from 10,000 to 12,000 inhabitants. Modasa is less than Idar. Ahmednagar, situated within the walls of a magnificent fort of the Mohammedan kings, is only a large village.

The whole of the Idar country is now disturbed by the Chief of Titui, who, though a Patavat of the Raja, has latterly settled separately with the Gaikwar. This innovation has led to fresh assertions of independence, and has finally brought about a war between the Chief of Titui and the Raja, the result of which has subjected all the neighbourhood to plunder. The Raja is on bad terms with all his Patavats, and though a plausible man in his behaviour, is generally considered as of a wavering and faithless character, quite incapable of steadily conducting his affairs. His misfortunes, however, are not entirely to be ascribed to his want of liberty. The Chief of Ahmednagar was always rather a rival than a support to the head of his family; and the Modasa chief with most of the Patavats established their present independence during the long minority of the Raja.

The Raja of Lunavada is descended from a family of Salonka Rajputs, who have long possessed the small territory now under his government. His income is stated by Captain MacDonald to be 40,473 rupees (£4,047), and for his chiefs about 40,000 more, making the whole revenue of the territory amount to about 80,000 rupees (£8,000). From this he pays a tribute to Sindia of 12,000 rupees (£1,200), and another to the Gaikwar of 6,501 rupees (£650.) It is not known when the former tribute was first levied, nor indeed can the first payment to the Gaikwar be ascertained with precision, the earliest on Baroda records being stated by Mr. Norris to be in A.D. 1783. This tribute was settled for ten years at 6,501 rupees (£650) per annum by Major Ballantyne in 1813.

The Raja of Lunavada.

The remaining chiefs have sometimes only one village, and sometimes as many as fifty. Their incomes vary from 30,000 rupees (£3,000) a year to 1,000 rupees (£100), but their importance depends on the number of fighting men they can assemble from villages or those of their allies. The annexed Table A, prepared by Captain Barnewall, will give some notion of the income and number of retainers of each chief. The most considerable among them may be divided into four or five clusters, according to their geographical position. The first is composed of the Koli villages of Amballa and Lohar (both of which have several times defeated the Gaikwar armies), the Koli village of Nirmal, and the Makvani ones of Mandva, Punadra, and Koral.

Smaller chiefs.

These all lie within a space of fifteen miles, and mostly on the river Vatrak. Another of nine Koli villages of Aglode Huppa, Taujpuri, etc., lies on the Sabarmati, in the Bijapur sub-division Pargana. Immediately to the south of the above are the Rajput villages of Varsoda, Pelvuni, Maunsa, and Pitapur. The Kolis of Kankrej, near the Banas, and those of Chuval and Chore Barochra, in the north-west of the Ahmedabad district, are very numerous, the former amounting, it is said, to 8,000, and the other to 5,000 bows; but their country is not strong, and they have ceased to be troublesome to their neighbours. Each of the others can produce from 1,500 to 3,000 fighting men, and all are in the neighbourhood of very strong retreats.

In all the Mehvasi communities the Rajputs, Kolis and Mussalmans hold their lands free of rent, on condition of military service; the other classes pay revenue to the chief. The chief's authority varies with his circumstances and personal character, but in general he is able to keep the people of his village in sufficient order to prevent their disturbing their neighbours, and his power in this respect is increased when supported by the fear of the superior Government.

The Kolis and Makvanis are not usually in the practice of dividing their lands among brothers, and from this and their frugal habits they are generally out of debt. The divisions, the carelessness and waste of the Rajputs, leave most of them considerably involved.

From the ruins of the ancient Mohammedan cities of Patan, Ahmednagar, and Ahmedabad, one would be led to infer that these were at one time the capitals of considerable principalities, and consequently that the neighbouring country, some of which is now the most refractory, must have then been quiet and submissive under the Mogals. Things seem to

Former state of Mahi Kantha.

have been in something like their present state. The ruins of numerous and expensive castles, built by those monarchs to check the Mehvasis, are still to be seen in frequented parts of the Mahi Kantha. But these measures were probably not very effectual when in vigour, and in the decline of the Mogal monarchy the garrisons were withdrawn and the country abandoned to its turbulent inhabitants.

The case was altered on the appearance of the Marathas, who, without building forts or assuming direct government, carried on their usual harassing inroads until they extorted a tribute, which they continued to increase as opportunity offered. Their power was at its highest about thirty years ago, when Sivaram Gardi, a Hindustani commandant of regular infantry, was employed in the settlement of the Mahi Kantha. The disorders of the Gaikwar Government subsequent to the death of Fatehsing did away the effects of Sivaram's successes; but after the treaty of Baroda, about the year 1804, order was very effectually restored by Kakaji, the cousin of Raroji A'paji; and although the Gaikwar's troops have met with some reverses since then, yet there has never been any general spirit of resistance. In 1813 Major Ballantyne entered into engagements with all the Mahi Kantha tributaries, and although by some unaccountable mistake those terms were never either conformed to or formally annulled, the chiefs have submitted quietly to the arbitrary proceedings of the Gaikwar's officers. During the ensuing period, the Mahi Kantha was entrusted to Bucha Jamadar, who maintained a considerable force and kept up the Gaikwar's authority with tolerable energy. He greatly increased the pecuniary payments of the chiefs, and he chastised any villages that went into open rebellion; but he was not successful in preventing depredations, and the complaints from our districts of the outrages of the Kolis were loud and frequent. In 1818 the bulk of Bucha's force was called off on foreign service, and the whole was afterwards withdrawn. The alterations made by this measure seem (although I have formerly stated it otherwise) to have been rather unfavourable to the tranquillity of the district. But the attack on Lohaur and the judicious steps afterwards taken for obtaining securities established a degree of order not known since the days of Sivaram. The absence of all troops, and of everything like a representative of Government, have since admitted of a renewal of former disorders; but it is rather surprising that the confusion should not in such circumstances have been universal, than that it should, to a certain extent, have occurred.

Mode of levying the tribute under the Gaikwar.

The Mahi Kantha force used to canton during the rains wherever its presence seemed most required, but for the whole of the remaining eight months of the year it was constantly in motion. When the tribute was not paid on demand, Mohussail (or horseman entitled to levy a fixed sum every day) was despatched to the chief. If that was not effectual, the force moved to his lands; when, if the presence of such undisciplined visitors did not by its own inconvenience bring him into terms, they proceeded to cut down his crop, spoil his trees, and waste his lands. These measures were generally rendered necessary by the imposition of some additions to the tribute, but many villages also made it a point of honour not to pay unless a force came against them. In cases of extreme obstinacy in refusing the tribute, or in committing or encouraging depredations, the Gaikwar officer entered on open hostilities, when he generally endeavoured by a forced march to surprise the Mehvasis in their villages, and seize their Thakor or their women.

If he succeeded, the Mehvasis submitted; but if he failed, he burned the village, and the people (especially if they were Kolis) retired to the jungle and set his attacks at defiance. The strongest Koli villages are open on the side farthest from the river, and their only object seems to be to secure a retreat to the ravines. The facilities afforded by these recesses, whether for flight or concealment, inspire the Kolis with the greatest confidence, while the roads leading along the exposed ridges are by no means equally encouraging to the assailants. In such places the Kolis, with their bows and matchlocks, would often keep the Gaikwar troops for a long time at bay; but if they were dislodged they scattered, and by long and rapid marches united again at a concerted point beyond the reach of their enemies. In the meantime, they sometimes attempted night attacks on the camp, in which the suddenness of their onset often struck a panic into the undisciplined troops opposed to them; but they more frequently avoided the enemy, and annoyed him indirectly by the depredations they committed on the villages in which he was interested. In the meantime, the Gaikwar chief endeavoured to obtain intelligence and to cut up the Kolis or seize their families. He also tried by all means to prevent their receiving provisions, and fined and otherwise punished all who supported them. If this were successful, the Kolis would subsist for a long time on the flowers of the mahuda-tree and on other esculent plants. But in time the bulk of their followers would fall off and return to their villages, while the chief, with the most determined of his adherents, remained in the jungle, and either was neglected, or easily eluded the pursuit of the Marathas until he could, by some compromise or even by submission, be restored to his village. There are many instances in which quarrels with Kolis have terminated still less favourably to the Gaikwar. The village of Amballa, though on one side only defended by a narrow strip of jungle and a hedge of dry thorns, stood a siege of six months against a body of 7,000 men. The village was then carried by assault, but a part of the Kolis rallied, and the besiegers fled with the utmost precipitation, leaving their guns and four of their principal chiefs on the field. On another occasion the inhabitants of Lohaur, about 1,000 strong, enticed a Gaikwar force of 10,000 men through a long defile into the bed of the Vatrak, and while a small party made a show of resistance on the opposite bank, an ambuscade started upon and opened a fire on the rear in the defile. The whole army immediately took to flight, and Babaji, who commanded it, with difficulty escaped by the swiftness of his horse.

When the affair was with Rajputs, they almost always defended their village, and that of Varsoda, situated among strong ravines on the Sabarmati, once beat off several assaults of the Gaikwar troops, and compelled them to raise the siege. The Rajputs sometimes (though rarely) hired foreign mercenaries and often called in Kolis; but the Kolis never had recourse to the assistance of any other tribe.

Whatever was the nature of the adjustment between the Government and a Mehvasi chief, it was of no avail unless securities were given by the latter. The securities were a Bhat and a neighbouring chief. The first enforced the agreement in the last extremity by killing or maiming himself or some of his relations; the other, by private war. These means could not be permitted now, but shame must have great hold in both cases. The influence of the securities must be useful in keeping their principal to his duty, and the chief may be of use in operations by his intelligence and his knowledge of the country. Under the Gaikwar, the security was liable to fine, imprisonment and other hardship, in which, indeed, the essence of the system appears to consist. To prevent the security being nugatory, it is necessary that some penalty should be imposed on the person who undertakes it, and it is equally necessary that Government should be vigilant and trace offences to the village which commits them. The perpetrators may often be few, and may easily escape by the connivance of the chief, or a band of twenty or thirty men of different villages may sometimes assemble in the jungle, and become formidable banditti over whom it is difficult to establish any control. These are the sort of offenders against whom, once a settlement is made, it will be most necessary to guard. As to the chiefs, if care be taken that all give security, it will only be necessary to avoid encroaching on their rights, it being almost unknown for a chief to enter on unprovoked resistance to Government after he has once given security.

Present state of the Mahi Kantha.

In explaining the present state of the Mahi Kantha and the events to which we are now to apply a remedy, it is necessary to advert to two omissions on the part of our own officers: the first is the disregard of Major Ballantyne's engagements; and the second, the long interval that has been allowed to elapse since the transfer of the Gaikwar's authority to the Company, without any assumption on the part of the British Government of the superintendence of the district. I have called on the Resident at Baroda to explain the cause of those omissions, and I have now only to state their effects.

Almost all the chiefs I have met with have complained of the exactions of the Bacha Jamadar, which sometimes amounted to double the amount settled by Major Ballantyne. The addition was levied under some other name, but it was not the less an increase to the tributes. These chiëfs, indeed, were few in number, but I have every reason to think the grievance general. Complaints were also made on all hands of the Gaikwar Government abetting encroachments by one chief on another, or at least of its failing to restrain such encroachments, and neglecting to repress the depredations of the Kolis and other Mehvasis residing both within its immediate districts and in the tributary country.

This last evil has greatly increased during the interregnum that has been allowed to take place since the Gaikwar withdrew from the management of the Mahi Kantha, during which time the chiefs have been left to their own management without any common head to refer to. In consequence, their quarrels have run from verbal discussions to petty wars, and the predatory villages, invited by the unsettled state of the neighbourhood, have commenced depredations on all around. The disputes between the Patavat of Titui and the Raja of Idar is the chief of the quarrels above alluded to. Both parties levied troops, and both were guilty of exactions in the country through which they passed. But on an accommodation between the parties, the Raja withdrew his troops without difficulty, while those of the Titui chief remained in a state of real or pretended insubordination, making incursions into the Dungarpur country, that of the Raja of Ahmednagar, and of various petty chiefs, and threatening the nearest even of the Company's districts. His mercenaries amount to 700, of whom 200 or 300 are Arabs.

The Mehvasi villages now active in plundering are scattered over nearly the whole of the Mahi Kantha.

Gaujun, Bakroli, and some others plunder the north-east of the Modasa sub-division Pargana, as does Amodra in the Bayad Pargana. While Antroli in Harsole and Ruparel in Parantij are both in a state of rebellion against the Company as well as the Gaikwar, Anoria, a village of the Gaikwar's in the Bijapur Pargana, plunders the Company's territory, as those of Kuberpur and Chaublea in Vadnagar do that of the Rajas of Idar and Ahmednagar. Balla Miya, also of Bhujpura, in the south-east, is openly plundering the country; and those disorders, which have increased rapidly within these few months, would soon become universal if prompt measures were not taken to repress them. With this view I have directed Captain Miles to repair to Modasa and endeavour to put a stop to these irregularities, as far as can be done by remonstrance. I have left a party of fifty men from my escort at Modasa, to afford some little protection to that part of the Company's territory, and I have directed a detachment of 700 Native Infantry, with 1 gun, and 200 Gaikwar Horse to assemble at the same place to support Captain Miles. I do not think this detachment sufficient to settle the whole country; and if I had the means, I would send such a detachment as that now in Kathiawar to obtain securities from the chiefs, and to hunt down any who might obstinately persevere in their depredations. But the present detachment, if it can be formed at all, will be formed with great difficulty, and I hope it will check the pressing evils. Captain Miles will be able to judge whether it will enable him to obtain the securities; and if a further force is found necessary, it can be sent after the rains, when the crops are on the ground, which is always the best time for settling with Mehvasis.

The principle of the settlement ought to be to take

security for ten years for the payment of the tribute settled by Major Ballantyne, and for the observance of our engagements. The principal articles of which should be as follows: Plan for the future.

1. To abstain from plundering.

2. To give up plunderers and others guilty of offences in the territory of the Government or of any other chief.

3. The chiefs to employ their whole means to resist and destroy plunderers, to give no succour to any person in opposition to the authority of the British Government or the Gaikwar, and to use every exertion to cut off his supplies, and to apprehend him.

4. To abstain from private war and from maintaining foreign mercenaries.

5. To refer all disputes to the arbitration of the British Government.

6. To protect the passage of merchants, and (if the chief can be persuaded to accede to it) to accept of a compensation for the privilege of levying transit duties.

7. To prevent illicit trade in opium.

Besides these general arrangements, there are many particular ones applicable to each chief.

The relation between the Raja of Idar and his relations and Patavats, the Patavats of the former Raos and the Koli chiefs with his territory, should be fixed with precision. Where it is consistent with established practice, the Raja's authority should be restored to such an extent as to enable him to call out the contingents of his Patavats, and maintain order without the direct interference of the British Government; on the other hand, where the practice does not admit of his exercising such a degree of authority, the British Government must make effectual arrangements on its own part for preventing disorders being committed by the chiefs.

Many of the Mahi Kantha chiefs are entitled to pecuniary collections, Giras, in the Company's and Gaikwar's districts. The amount of these should be fixed, and means taken to provide for the payment in such a manner as to prevent the clashing of authorities without injuring the chief by converting his territorial right into pecuniary pension from a Government. A mode consistent with the practice of the country would be to allow the collection to be made by the Bhat who is security for the chief, assisted, if necessary, by the collector's officers.

Some of those chiefs (especially the Raja of Idar) have similar claims on each other which should be settled with equal precision, and a mode of payment fixed on that may prevent disagreement. In many cases it might be practicable for the British Government to make the collection, and admit the money received in part payment of the Ghasdana. The amount might perhaps, in most cases, be fixed on an average of the last ten or fifteen years' payments.

Including those of the Raja of Idar's dependents, which used to settle with the Gaikwar separately from him, there are 121 chiefs in the Mahi Kantha with whom Major Ballantine made settlement. Of these, 63 pay Jamabandi to the Company, and are included in the eye of our regulations in the districts of Kaira and Ahmedabad, and 24 pay Jamabandi to different Kamavisdars of the Gaikwar.

It would simplify our transactions if the chiefs within our districts were to pay their Ghasdana through the collector. The question also arises regarding the persons, whether it is consistent with justice and sound policy to subject them to the direct interference of our Courts and to the ordinary regulations of our Government, or whether it would be expedient to place them on some other footing, if such can be found, that should secure the quiet of our own districts without diminishing the independence of the tributaries. I shall endeavour to examine this question on my progress through the Company's districts.

With respect to the 24 that pay Jamabandi to the Gaikwar, it is indispensable that the amount of that tribute should be fixed, or our guarantee of the fixed rate of Ghasdana will be nugatory. The Gaikwar may perhaps be persuaded to acquiesce in this, on our engaging to assist his officers in recovering their Jamabandi ; but the negotiation would not be without difficulty, as it is the constant practice of the Gaikwar Government to increase the Jamabandi whenever an opportunity offers. Should the Gaikwar refuse to accede, I see no course but to make over the whole management of those villages to his Highness, without our participation or guarantee.

There are at present a vast number of unsettled disputes between the chiefs, which might be adjusted by the political agent, through the names of Panchayats. I do not think it would be found convenient to make the present state of possession permanent, as was done in Kathiawar. The political agent might, however, endeavour, in all cases where the right of the claimant was at all doubtful, to persuade him to acquiesce in the actual state of possession or to come to some compromise with the occupant.

The particular relation of Lunavada to Sindia will render it necessary for Major Ballantyne to abstain for the present from all interference with that petty state, for the tribute of which he should apply to Captain MacDonald, but should be called on for a full account of Lunavada and the progress of its connection with the Gaikwar state. These are all the points which at present occur to me as requiring notice, but the full accounts we may hereafter expect will doubtless suggest many more.

Until all pending questions are finally settled, it will be necessary for the political agent to move about the country, and it may be necessary for the troops to remain there also; but when affairs are once put into a regular train, the political agent may take up a fixed station, and it should, I conceive, be towards the south, at an equal distance from the eastern and western extremities of the district. It is desirable that the Raja of Idar should be left to the exercise of his own authority; and, on the other hand, the Kolis bordering on our districts require constant vigilance to repress their depredations. Very great attention and judgment will always be necessary to unite that vigilance with an abstinence from the opposite fault of our interference, which often serves only to destroy the established authority, without setting up anything equally efficacious in its place.

The utmost personal attention will also be necessary among so many chiefs, who have all disputes with their neighbours, to prevent native agents from fostering a litigious spirit, and producing irritation by corruption and partiality. For this and other reasons I think it impossible for the same officer to undertake the management of the Mahi Kantha and of Kathiawar. I propose, therefore, that the whole duty of the latter province should be made over to Captain Barnewell, whose allowances may be increased to those of a collector, which, indeed, they ought to be, on the principle on which they were first fixed. Major Ballantyne may then give up his whole attention to Mahi Kantha, and it may be practicable at some future period to unite his office with that of the political agent at Palanpur, unless the duties of the latter should be increased by the management of the Jodhpur tributaries.

The troops ought not, I conceive, to remain in the country after it is once settled; but prompt measures should be adopted from time to time to send detachments from Deesa, Kaira, and Baroda, to make examples like that of Lohaur, which never fail to make a strong and lasting impression, and which are the more effectual because the tributaries never know when they are safe from them. Whereas if a battalion were stationed in the country, any circumstance that called it off to foreign service would be the signal for general depredation and disorder. It is not necessary or expedient to employ regular troops against small parties of banditti on the roads. These would be put down by the irregulars under the revenue officers, and by the people of the country, which will always succeed, if great attention be paid to prevent any relaxation in their exertions. These means will, I think, be very effectual in establishing the tranquillity of the Mahi Kantha, which, from its contiguity to our own districts, is of much greater consequence than that of Kathiawar or any other tributary state.

In the course of events, it may, I think, be expected that the southern parts of the Mahi Kantha will at no distant period be turned into a quiet and submissive country. The long continuance of tranquillity will turn the attention of the Kolis to agriculture, and their predatory habits and their jungles will disappear together. If the progress of civilization be less rapid in the strong country on the frontier, it is a satisfaction to reflect that the nature of those fastnesses and the character of their defenders are a protection to the peaceful inhabitants of the plains, and that they have hitherto afforded an effectual barrier against the hordes of freebooters, who have so long ravaged the neighbouring provinces of Hindustan.

The principality of Palanpur is included in the Mahi Kantha settlement, and pays Ghasdana to the Gaikwar; but it could not be comprised in a general description with the other communities, from which it differs so much in all respects. It has owed its independence more to distance than to natural strength, the country being in most parts open and easy of access. It is naturally not unfertile, and though it has felt the effects of the famine which was so severe in Cutch, Kathiawar, and on the north-western frontier, it has suffered less than its western neighbours. It seems tolerably well governed, and appears to be prosperous. The town of Palanpur is reckoned to contain about 20,000 inhabitants. The Diwan's revenue is somewhat less than three lakhs of rupees, but this is charged with a tribute of 50,000 rupees (£5,000), etc., a subsidy of 81,600 rupees (£8,160) to the Gaikwar. His military force amounts to 300 horse and 500 foot, in which are included 150 horse and 100 foot subsidized from the Gaikwar. His debts amount to 40,000 rupees (£4,000).

The family of the Diwan have had possession of Palanpur for many generations. About twenty-seven years ago, the state fell into the hands of a rebellious soldiery, who expelled the lawful Diwan, set up first his relation, Shamshir Khan, the chief of Deesa, and next Firuz Khan. They afterwards murdered Firuz Khan, and recalled Shamshir Khan from Deesa, to which place he had retired. Shamshir Khan was emancipated from the control of the soldiery, and established as guardian to Fateh Khan, the son of Firuz Khan, by a British force acting on the part of the Gaikwar (in 1809); but having afterwards failed to pay his tribute, he was removed by another in 1817, and the exercise of the Government was entrusted to Fateh Khan under the superintendence of Captain Miles, the British political agent. At this time the Gaikwar's subsidy was imposed. It serves to pay the salary of the political agent, which is 6,000 rupees (£600) a year, and the horse and foot already specified. This arrangement answers well at present. The subsidized troops are entirely at the disposal of the political agent, whose supervision of the Diwan's expenses is certainly beneficial. But without the control of the political agent, the present plan would probably end either in the rebellion of the Diwan, or in his being swallowed up by the Gaikwar. Should his debts not disappear under the expected improvement of his country, it may be questioned whether he will not be relieved from part of his subsidiary arrangements with the Gaikwar, which ought to be proportioned to the means of his principality.

The Diwan has no foreign connections. He corresponds with the neighbouring petty states with whom he formerly kept up mutual incursions. His territory has occasionally and even very lately suffered by the depredations of the Jodhpur armies levying tribute in his neighbourhood; but he has never paid anything to that Government.

The appointment of a separate political agent at Palanpur prevents its being included in the Mahi Kantha settlement, and renders inapplicable to it almost all the plans that have been proposed for the rest of that division.

Gaikwar's claims to Ghasdana in the Peshwa's districts.

Steps have already been taken to ascertain the Gaikwar's right to Ghasdanas within the Peshwa's districts adjoining the Mahi Kantha. I shall make no observations on them here, except that, as the disputed items are all included in the list of tributaries settled with by Major Ballantine, it will be necessary that that officer be expressly directed to forbear making any demand on them until the questions now under discussion shall have been determined.

MINUTE

BY THE

HON. MOUNTSTUART ELPHINSTONE,

DATED JANUARY 26, 1821.

CUTCH.

I HAVE the honour to communicate such considerations on the subject of Cutch as have been suggested by my visit to that country.

Mr. Elphinstone's Minute. 1821.

It is a territory of small extent * and of little fertility. Water is scarce, and often salt; the soil is generally either rocky or sandy, and the proportion that is cultivated, though very superior to that in Kathiawar, is insufficient to support its own scanty population.

The capital, Bhuj, contains only 20,000 souls. Lakhpat Bandar, Anjar, and perhaps Mundra, may have 10,000 inhabitants each. The other towns are generally much smaller. The seaport of Mandvi alone bears the marks of industry and prosperity. It carries on a considerable trade, especially with Arabia and the coast of Africa, and contains from 30,000 to 40,000 inhabitants.

The whole revenue of this territory is under 50 lakhs of koris (about 16 lakhs of rupees); and of this less than

* About 180 miles long and 60 broad.

30 lakhs of koris belong to the Rao; the country which yields the remaining 20 lakhs being assigned to the collateral branches of his Highness's family, each of whom received a certain appanage on the death of the Rao from whom it is immediately descended. The family of these chiefs is derived at a recent period from Tatta in Sind, and they are all sprung from a common ancestor, Hamirji, whose son Rao Khengar acquired the sovereignty of Cutch before the middle of the sixteenth century of our era. The number of these chiefs is at present about 200, and the whole number of their tribe in Cutch is guessed at 10,000 or 12,000 persons. This tribe is called Jadeja; it is a branch of the Rajputs. The other inhabitants of Cutch are computed by the natives at 500,000 souls, of which more than one-third are Mohammedans (mostly converts from the religion of the Brahmans), and the rest Hindus, chiefly of the peaceful castes: the Jadejas are all soldiers, and the Mussalmans supply the rest of the military class.

The Rao's ordinary jurisdiction is confined to his own demesne, each Jadeja chief exercising unlimited authority within his own lands. The Rao can call on the Jadejas to serve him in war, but must furnish them with pay at a fixed rate while they are with his army. He is the guardian of the public peace, and as such chastises all robbers and other general enemies. It would seem that he ought likewise to repress private war, and to decide all disputes between chiefs; but this prerogative, though constantly exerted, is not admitted without disputes. Each chief has a similar body of kinsmen, who possess shares of the original appanage of the family, and stand in the same relation of nominal dependence to him that he bears to the Rao. These kinsmen form what is called the Bhayad or brotherhood of the chiefs, and the chiefs themselves compose the Bhayad of the Rao. The annual income of these chiefs varies from a lakh of koris (upwards of 30,000 rupees) to 400, which is little more than 100 rupees. There are not less than fifty whose income exceeds 5,000 rupees a year, and who can bring 150 men into the field. The greatest are ambitious of serving at the capital, for which they receive a small pension, seldom exceeding 150 rupees a month. Only thirteen chiefs enjoy this advantage. Besides the Jadejas, there are still in Cutch a few chiefs of inferior importance belonging to other Rajput tribes, and a still smaller number of the Mohammedan religion.

The prosperity of this principality appears to have been at its highest about the middle of the last century, when Rao Desal is said to have possessed garrisons in Sind, Parkar, and in Kathiawar. These foreign possessions were lost by Rao Lakha, who succeeded in 1751, and in a reign of nine years dissipated the treasures of his father in expensive luxury. He was succeeded by his son, Rao Godji, whose rebellion against his father, as well as his suspicious character, and his frequent change, and even execution of his ministers, are proofs of the unsettled state of his territory. He was succeeded in 1778 by his son Rao Rayadhan, the father of the late Rao Bhara or Bharmalji. Rao Rayadhan's understanding was deranged, and his madness was of such a nature as to require the strictest personal restraint. His brother Prithiraj (better known by the name of Bhaiji Bava) was too young to assume the direction of affairs, and the Government was conducted by twelve commanders of mercenary troops, who appear to have been all Mohammedans, and who were guided by the authority of Dosal Ven, the principal of their own body. Among these leaders was Fateh Mohammed, a native of Sindh. This person appears to have been endued with capacity and courage. Finding the Government of Dosal Ven at once weak and odious, he successfully intrigued with the troops, with the ministers by whom the civil business of the Government was still conducted, and with some of the leading Jadejas; until, in the year 1792, he was enabled to expel Dosal Ven and his colleagues, and to transfer the reins of Government into his own hands. He conducted the affairs of Cutch with firmness and ability for ten years, until Bhaiji Bava, in whose name, as Regent, Fateh Mohammed appears to have administered the Government, became of an age to feel the hardships of his exclusion from the Regency. Hansraj and other ministers, who were dissatisfied with the predominance of Fateh Mohammed, availed themselves of this feeling, and seizing the opportunity of a casual absence of Fateh Mohammed from the capital, they carried off Bhaiji to Mandvi, of which Hansraj was at that time in charge. The wealth and the respectable character of Hansraj, the junction of the other ministers, and the popular manners of Bhaiji, joined to the goodness of his cause, soon drew the majority to his party, and Fateh Mohammed was glad to abandon Bhuj, and to compromise his claim to the administration for the possession of the fort and dependencies of Anjar. The death of Bhaiji, which happened in 1802 (sixteen months after the revolution), restored the ascendancy of Fateh Mohammed. Hansraj was a merchant, and his wealth and popularity were insufficient to make up for the want of knowledge and confidence in military affairs. He withdrew to Mandvi, leaving Bhuj to be captured by Fateh Mohammed, while Lakhpat Bandar, Mundra, Bitta, and Sisagad, with their districts, remained in the hands of independent chiefs, who, though three of them were Mohammedans, were all close confederates of Hansraj.

All these parties were supported entirely by their mercenary troops, Arabs, Sindhis and Mussalmans of Cutch. The Jadejas appear to have possessed but little weight and to have taken little interest in the struggle. Some remained at their forts entirely neutral, others served the contending parties for pay; and although the Rao's person was in the hands of Fateh Mohammed, and Hansraj had not even the shadow of legitimate authority, the greater part of the Bhayad were entertained in his service or attached to his party. Fateh Mohammed, proceeded with vigour against such of these as came within his reach: he fomented their family quarrels; he besieged their forts and levied contributions on various pretences, as well to fill his treasury as to gratify his revenge. His necessities obliged him to impose numerous and severe taxes and fines on the merchants and Rayats; but although these proceedings created general discontent, there seems to have been no attempt to form any combination against him. He continued to govern the capital and the greater part of the Rao's territories, and to carry on depredations in the possessions of his rivals until his death; and the name of the Jamadar is now as much respected in Cutch as that of any of the Raos his predecessors in authority. The death of Fateh Mohammed took place in 1813; it was preceded by that of Hansraj, and shortly followed by that of Rao Rayadhan. The incapacity of the Jamadar's son Husain Miya, enabled Shivraj (who succeeded his father in the possession of Mandvi) to occupy the capital and to call Rao Bharmal to the head of the Government about a year after the death of Fateh Mohammed. Husain Miya fled to Anjar, where he remained unmolested until that place was taken by the British. Both he and Dosal Ven are now living in poverty and contempt.

Though Rao Bharmal had attained to the age of twenty during his father's lifetime, there appears to have been no thought of setting up his claim to the Regency against those of the different usurpers, nor did he on his own accession recover possession of the portion of the country that he found in their hands. But within his own share he soon assumed the real exercise of the authority he had gained. Shivraj withdrew to Mandvi, and the business of the state was carried on for some time satisfactorily by ministers who had served under Fateh Mohammed.

But Rao Bharmalji had contracted a habit of constant intoxication which disqualified him from business, secluded him from the society of his chiefs and ministers, and ultimately exasperated his temper and impaired his understanding. His misgovernment, if left to its own operation, would probably have ended like that of his father in his imprisonment, and perhaps in the further partition of his dominions; but the invasion of Cutch by the force under Colonel East (which was rendered unavoidable by the depredations of the people of Vagad) led to the further interposition of the British Government, and at last brought things into their present shape.

The district of Vagad, which comprehends all the eastern part of the Cutch territory, either had never been subjected to the Rao, or had long ago thrown off its dependence on him. It paid at one time occasional tribute to the Nawab of Radhanpur; but the chiefs were no further controllable by any superior, and continued to plunder the territories of all their neighbours, including those of the Rao of Cutch. Their independence was first broken by Fateh Mohammed, who reduced some parts of Vagad under the Rao's direct authority, and levied annual contributions from all the chiefs of that country. He did not endeavour to restrain the predatory habits of those chiefs, and Rao Bharmalji's refusal either to punish their inroads into Kathiawar or to allow the Gaikwar to do so, obliged us to commence military operations, which ended in the first treaty.

That agreement was on the whole by no means unfavourable to the Rao. In the reduction of Vagad, the fines he levied on the chiefs and the establishment of a regular tribute, he obtained an ample equivalent for the compensation which he was obliged to afford to those who had been plundered by the inhabitants of that country; and the surrender of Anjar was a moderate price for the restoration of Mandvi and the other dismembered districts, and for the arrears which he was enabled to recover from the usurpers of those possessions. His habits of intoxication prevented his enjoying these advantages. He fell into the hands of low flatterers, and his distempered mind was urged on by their profligate counsels. His offences against the British Government are too well known to require repetition. He alienated the minds of his subjects by the murder of his cousin Ladhubha (the son of Bhaiji Bava, whose claim to the succession had at one time been set up in opposition to his own), alarmed his immediate adherents for their personal safety, and excited the enmity of the Jadejas by attacks on individuals, and even by a rash demand of a tribute from the whole body. Notwithstanding these provocations, such was the superiority of his mercenary force, that the Jadejas offered no opposition. They marched in his train against the forts of their brethren, and they reluctantly subscribed an engagement by which they bound themselves to pay the tax which was imposed on them. But their submission was the effect of fear alone; they secretly applied for the assistance of the British, which in time was granted. Ten of the principal chiefs joined the army on its advance; and the present form of Government, together with the last treaty, were settled in consultation with them. It was determined on all hands that Bharmalji should be imprisoned, but it is said to have been the wish of the Jadejas that the Government should still be administered in his name. When they saw that this was not intended, they seem to have been inclined to elect the son of Ladhubha, but were prevailed on by the arguments of Lakhmidas to choose the present Rao. They likewise entered into a treaty in the name of the whole Jadeja body, and established the Regency which still conducts the Government.

At the head of the Regency must be reckoned the British Resident, who was introduced at the earnest request of the Jadejas, and still more of the other members, who refused to take on themselves the responsibility of the office without his full support and participation. The others were: 1st. Vajerajji or Vazerajji, the Jadeja chief of Roha, who derives consequence from his experience—from his possessions, which exceed those of any other chief—from his military retinues and his fort, which is reckoned, next to Bhujia, the strongest in Cutch; 2nd. Prithiraj, the chief of Nagarecha, who, though young and not distinguished for ability, was chosen on account of his family, which is reckoned the first among the Jadejas; 3rd. Lakhmidas, whose family have long been ministers, and who himself was prime minister to Rao Bharmalji; 4th. Odhavji Rajgar, a rich merchant, who had been employed in charge of districts, and had a high character in the country; and 5th.

Ratansi, the nephew of Sundarji, who, though his family have wealth and weight in Cutch, was probably elected in compliment of the British Government, on the support of which he still entirely depends. Upheld by that Government, he may be considered as the principal member of the Regency; and he appears to conduct himself with good sense and moderation, so as to give perfect satisfaction to the English gentlemen with whom he has acted, at the same time that his conciliating manners exempt him from the unpopularity which his sudden elevation and his connection with the British Government might be expected to raise among the Jadejas.

Lakhmidas possesses an influence in the Regency only inferior to that of Ratansi. He has long been in power, is looked up to by the Jadejas, and partakes in the character and feelings of the people of Cutch: from these qualities, no less than from his ability in business, he is a valuable member of the Regency.

These are the only efficient members. Vajerajji, a selfish old man, accustomed to the solitary independence of his own fort, and only entering into the affairs of Bhuj during the intrigues that preceded a revolution, takes little interest in ordinary business, and seldom interferes, unless to recommend some measure calculated to increase his influence or popularity. The other two were only expected to lend the aid of their names, and they are now both dead, Odhavji within the last week.

The Rao's revenues being farmed out, and each branch of his expenditure being fixed, the ordinary business of the Regency is to see that the farmers perform their contract, and that the charges do not exceed the estimate; to check depredations, and punish offences; and, above all, to attend to the claims, and decide the disputes of the Jadeja chiefs. At the most important of these cases the Resident assists, as he does at all consultations on political questions, foreign or domestic ; but he judiciously leaves the detail of the Government to the other members, and contents himself with obtaining a thorough knowledge of their proceedings, over which he exercises an occasional control.

The Rao's land revenue amounts to 1,515,000 koris, and that derived from customs and other sources unconnected with the land to upwards of 1,400,000—in all, about 2,950,000 koris, of which near 300,000 is alienated to maintain the ladies of the family, 300,000 for charitable purposes, and near 500,000 in Inam. His income, therefore, is only 2,300,000 koris (or 760,000 rupees) ; and his expenses, as shown by the annexed Table A, amount to upwards of 2,400,000 koris (or 8 lakhs of rupees), of which near 700,000 koris is the subsidy of the British brigade. But some of these charges are of a temporary nature, and there seems little reason to doubt that in ordinary years the Rao will be easily able to live within his income.

The debt of the Government is 1,250,000 koris, of which upwards of a lakh is annually paid from a fund allotted to that object.

His troops consist of about 500 horse and 2,000 infantry, besides the contingent of the Jadejas. It is calculated that these chiefs could furnish 20,000 men ; but, admitting this to be the case, they can only be reckoned as a force of which the Rao can have the services whenever he is willing to pay for them. The number of this body that is really efficient probably does not exceed 4,000 or 5,000.

The internal government of the Rao's immediate demesne appears to be good. It is a great defect in the system that the revenue is farmed, and the greater because the principal farmers are nearly related to members of the Regency; but the original tenures of the land are favourable to the cultivator. The superintendence of the Resident prevents their being encroached on. The certainty of retaining the lease for five years is an inducement to the farmer to improve his country, while the neighbourhood of so many chiefs, in whose lands an oppressed Rayat would find a refuge, is a check on his exactions. The competition of Rayats likewise secures those on the lands of the Jadejas from oppression, though they do not possess the favourable tenure which is general in the Rao's country. The tenure is called Buta. It gives a perpetual right of occupancy to the Rayat on his paying a fixed proportion of his produce, which varies in different places from one-half to one-eighth, but is generally one-third. That the ground is the Rao's appears never to be questioned; but the Rayats sell their right in it without any opposition—generally at a very short purchase (about five years).

The neighbourhood of Sindh (on importation from which it at all times depends for a large portion of its subsistence) prevented Cutch from feeling the famine of 1813, so much as Kathiawar. It has never been so much harassed by plunderers; and although the earthquake of 1819 was a severe calamity, it was not one of that sort which seriously affects the population or cultivation; so that Cutch is, on the whole, probably in as flourishing a condition as it ever has been.

The police is good, notwithstanding the number of independent divisions; indeed, the example of this country and Kathiawar makes one question whether, when the chiefs are really well disposed, the number of persons possessing influence does not make up in police for the want of extensive jurisdiction. The only disturbers of the public peace appear to be the outlaws, who find a refuge in the dependencies of Sindh, or in the desert. Justice is administered by the Patels and by Panchayats, and the people do not complain of the want of it.

The last revolution was effected at the request of the Jadejas, and the last treaty affords them a guarantee of their possessions. It might, therefore, be expected that they would be content, and accordingly I have not been able to learn that any dissatisfaction exists among them. Three persons of that class came to me with complaints, but all related to oppressions committed by Bharmalji, or Fateh Mohammed, and not redressed by the present Regency. I had long separate interviews with more than twenty of the principal persons in Cutch, and although it was scarcely to be expected that they would be very unreserved on such an occasion, yet it is satisfactory to know that I gave them many openings in the course of conversation to discover their real sentiments, and likewise put direct questions to them regarding the conduct of the Regency without hearing of anything offensive or inconsistent with former practice. One chief complained that the decisions of the Regency were not always just, but he confined himself to general censure; and I found that he had lately lost a cause by the Regency's confirming the award of a Panchayat, against which he had appealed.

The Jadeja chiefs have been the great losers by the earthquake, which demolished their forts; but they are still in a prosperous condition. Few of them are much in debt; they have few disputes among themselves, and no private wars. Some of them are reduced to poverty by the numerous sub-divisions of their estates, every younger brother being entitled to a share equal to one-third, and often to one-half, of that of the elder ; but, on the whole, the number of estates that have descended to single heirs induces a suspicion that in Cutch infanticide is not confined to females.

The Jadeja chiefs of Cutch are generally accused of treachery. Poisoning is said to be a prevalent crime among them; but in what I have heard of their history, I have found no instance of it, and I perceive more of the unsteadiness that results from indifference than of deliberate treachery in their public conduct. This want of attachment to any sovereign is produced by their own independence of the Rao's authority, and by the want of energy in the chief, and consequent distraction in the administration, which his Government, in common with most of those under Rajputs, has almost always displayed. The appearance and behaviour of the chiefs, though not much polished, is decent, manly, and prepossessing.

The character of the common people appears to be peaceable and inoffensive. The inhabitants of Vagad are said to retain their propensity to plunder, the Mohammedan herdsmen in the Banni (a tract of grass-lands extending along the edge of the northern Ran) are reckoned fierce and unsettled ; and the Mianas (another Mohammedan tribe in the east of the Rao's territories) are notorious for their desperate character, always ready for hire to undertake any enterprise, however dangerous, or however flagitious. These tribes are under hereditary heads of their own.

The external relations of Cutch scarcely deserve to be mentioned. It has escaped the ravages and exactions of the Mahrattas, and it has twice repelled invasions from Sindh. Its offensive operations since the days of Rao Desal have been confined to three invasions of the north of Kathiawar by Fateh Mohammed, and one incursion to Varahi, in the neighbourhood of Radhanpur. The use of a connection with Cutch to us is to curb the plunderers of Vagad, to check the Khosas, to keep Sindh at a distance, and to afford an opening into that country in the unwelcome event of our being engaged in a war with the Amirs. The most desirable situation of Cutch for us is that it should be under a strong and independent government. The first of these conditions was found to be unattainable, and the want of strength has led to the loss of independence. We are now too deeply engaged in the affairs of Cutch ever to retreat, and the option reserved to us of withdrawing from the subsidiary alliance is rendered nugatory by our guarantee of the rights of the Rao and of the Jadejas. Of all our alliances this is probably the most intimate and the most difficult to dissolve, since to free us from its obligations requires the consent, not of one prince, but of 200 nobles.

It is, therefore, of the most importance to consider the manner in which our influence is to be exerted. During the Rao's minority we must continue to superintend and control every branch of the Government; but our Resident's interference should be confined, as at present, to superintendence. While Ratansi is properly supported he will always have a preponderance in the Regency, and will guide it in the direction which is given to it by our Government.

Unless the Resident be supine, Lakhmidas will be an adequate counterpoise to Ratansi's influence; the very knowledge that there exists such a rival ready to communicate any misconduct of his to the Resident will be sufficient to make Ratansi cautious and moderate; and, as it is the policy of the Lakhmidas, and must be the ambition of every Jadeja in the Regency, to maintain the principles most popular among their countrymen, the Resident, if he shows himself disposed to listen to their communications, can never be ignorant of any action adverse to the ancient practice or the public feeling. The chief business of the Resident must be to watch over the conduct of his colleagues in those points where they are likely to be united by a common interest. In the internal management of the Rao's country he ought not to exercise so minute a control as to destroy the spirit or lessen the responsibility of the other members. When any great change of system is proposed, it is, of course, his duty to examine it carefully; but except on such occasions, it is enough if he readily listens to complaints, and calls for explanations when they seem to be well founded. In all measures affecting the Jadejas he ought to take a more active part. Experience has shown that they are ready to submit to a Government of ministers supported by a power unconnected with their own, and it is probable that as long as their personal honour and interest are attended to, they will be, if not friendly, at least indifferent to our proceedings; but it is necessary that they should be treated with attention and civility, and that care should be taken not to encroach on their privileges. The vigilance of the Resident should guard against the negligence, partiality, or corruption which may be evinced by the Regency in deciding on the quarrels of the chiefs. His authority should repress all attempts on their part to renew the practice of plunder or of private war; and his moderation should guard against the temptation of adding to the Rao's possessions by forfeitures, even in cases where the resistance of a chief should have required the employment of a military force. Without this precaution, a slight offence will lead to a fine; delay in payment, to the employment of a detachment; and that to the dispossession of the individual and the discontent and alarm of all the other Jadejas. A fine has been the usual punishment, and ought still to be sufficient; and if it should be absolutely necessary to dispossess a chief, the disinterestedness of the Government should be shown by restoring his lands to his next heir. The three most probable points of difference with the Jadejas are: settling their disputes among themselves; enforcing the prohibition of female infanticide; and compelling them to act against plunderers within their own districts. In the first, all danger may be averted by the prompt and impartial administration of justice; in the second, by caution and delicacy in the means of detecting guilt, and moderation in punishing it. The third is an object of great importance. It is more likely to be attained by vigilance than by severity, by explaining what is expected, censuring neglect, and compelling restitution, with the addition of a fine as the punishment of participation. Great care should be taken to avoid any appearance of arrogance in our treatment of the Jadeja chiefs; but I do not think there is any necessity for referring political questions to the decision of their body to the extent which a superficial view of the correspondence of the Residency would lead us to think usual. It is natural to suppose that the former Raos would consult the principal Jadejas before they entered on any measure that required the cordial co-operation of the Bhayad, and, in the absence of an efficient sovereign, it is still more necessary that the Regency should learn the sentiments of that body; but it does not appear to be usual, or to be expected, or to be practicable, that all should be assembled to give their votes even on the most important questions. The Resident should continue to consult the greatest chiefs separately or together as the skhin best suited to the occasion, and may extend or confine the number according to the importance of the question ; but I should think fifty or sixty the greatest number that need ever be consulted. These are all the general observations that suggest themselves, but there are various subjects of temporary importance which require our immediate attention.

The first is the situation of the late Rao.

The odium of that Prince's measures has been lost in the sight of his misfortunes, and all fear of his power among the Jadejas has been removed by the British guarantee. The consequence is that he is now an object of general compassion, and, under the erroneous impression that our power would afford a sufficient security against a renewal of his misconduct, the greater part of his late subjects would probably be glad to see him restored to the Masnad. An opinion prevails of the indefeasible rights of a prince to the nominal exercise at least of a sovereignty which he has once possessed; and this is shown by the language of the people of Cutch, who, when off their guard, generally call Bharmalji the Rao, and Rao Desal only the Kunvar or Prince. I consulted several of the principal persons in Cutch about the succession to the Masnad in the event of the death of Rao Desal, and all who delivered their sentiments with frankness declared at once for Bharmalji, although all agreed that he ought to be kept in prison, and the Government administered by a Regency.

The wives of Bharmalji, especially the mother of the present Rao, are all naturally anxious to promote his interests, and with them go the wishes and intrigues of all the inhabitants of the palace. Rao Bharmalji must have some adherents, especially among the soldiery who were disbanded at his fall; any unpopularity of the present Government would throw the Jadejas into his seal; the dwelling which he inhabits being built more for commodiousness than security, might easily allow of his escape; and the Mianas and Jats would soon supply him with a desperate band who might protect him until further support could be obtained. For these reasons it seems highly desirable to remove Bharmalji from Cutch, or at least from Bhuj; but this is unfortunately prevented by a stipulation in the treaty. The dangers I have alluded to can therefore only be counteracted by greater attention to the security of his person and by destroying the impression that he is ever to recover his power. To show the resolution of the British Government I declined seeing him (although in the least offensive terms), and I rejected all the applications that were made to me to allow him to return to the palace. My correspondence with the Resident will show my sentiments regarding his restoration to his family, in which I think humanity requires every indulgence that can safely be conceded; but I should think it a most desirable arrangement if he could be removed to some place of strength more completely cut off from the town.

The next step that occurs for destroying the chance of his recovering his influence is to call on the Jadejas to declare an heir to the present Rao, but this on examination appears both unnecessary and impolitic. As Bharmalji has already been pronounced by the treaty to have forfeited the Government as fully as can be done in any public instrument, nothing could be gained by a new declaration to that effect; and as it has never been disputed that the next heir is the chief of Khakhar descended from the Raja Godji, the only effect of a call for a declaration would be to invite a fruitless and probably an angry discussion. It is also not improbable that Rao Bharmalji may yet have children whom it would be both unpopular and unjust to set aside; the insanity or incapacity of their father being certainly no bar to their claim, and there being no distinction between the title which would be possessed by such children, and that which has actually been admitted in the person of Rao Desal. It seems therefore most expedient to treat the question of the succession as already settled, and to admit no further mention of Bharmalji's restoration.

The Regency ought no doubt to be filled up, and as the object is to gain the confidence of the Jadejas as well as to have a natural mode of ascertaining their feelings, I should think it desirable that the choice should fall on two Jadejas. I have requested the Resident to take the opinions of as many chiefs as he conveniently can on this subject, and to be guided by the prevailing sentiment among them. The new Regents should understand that after the expiration of the present lease no member of the Regency will be allowed to be a farmer of the revenue.

The exposed and unconnected situation of Anjar suggested a question whether it might not be politic to restore it to the Rao's Government, taking a money payment instead; and if this payment could be well secured, I do not see a single advantage in keeping the district. As long as our influence at Bhuj continues, it is of no use whatever; and if that influence were to expire, it would require a strong force to defend it: even then, the jealousy it would occasion between us and the Rao would probably soon involve us, as it did before, in hostilities with that Prince. The only questions therefore are, whether we can obtain adequate security for the revenue we give up, and whether it would be satisfactory to the Rayats if Anjar be restored to the Rao. The failure of the Cutch Government in paying the subsidy makes the answer to the first of these questions very doubtful. I have referred both to the Resident for his report.

It would be popular to restore the fort of Bhujia to the Rao, and it would be popularity easily purchased, for the fort is, I believe, incapable of being defended, especially in its present state; but as it commands our cantonments, it would be necessary to move the brigade to some other ground. If a good position could be found near Bhuj (for it ought not, I think, to be at any distance from the Rao's person), it would be desirable to remove the brigade thither, and to construct a redoubt within which a residence might be erected for the late Rao, and where the stores, etc., might be deposited if the force were obliged to move. The expense of such a work would, however, be considerable, and it will be necessary to call for an estimate before it can be determined on. At any rate the cantonment can be moved, and some sort of field-work thrown up for the stores. The present force in Cutch appears to me no more than sufficient. It would be insufficient if we had any reason to distrust the goodwill of the inhabitants. The detachments at Patan and Rajkot could, however, reinforce it within a fortnight.

The wish of the people of Bhuj is strongly in favour of repairing their walls, which I think ought to be done as soon as the finances of the state will admit of it. The same observations apply to Lakhpat Bandar, but I do not think it necessary to incur the expense of repairing Anjar, which we could never spare an adequate force to defend.

THE END.